4/9/24

BRIXMIS
AND
THE SECRET
COLD WAR

To the brave and resourceful personnel of the Allied Military Liaison Missions.

BRIXMIS

AND
THE SECRET
COLD WAR

Intelligence Collection Operations Behind
Enemy Lines in East Germany

ANDREW LONG

PEN & SWORD
HISTORY

AN IMPRINT OF PEN & SWORD BOOKS LTD.
YORKSHIRE – PHILADELPHIA

First published in Great Britain in 2024 by
PEN AND SWORD HISTORY
An imprint of
Pen & Sword Books Ltd
Yorkshire – Philadelphia

ISBN 978 1 39906 784 3

Typeset in Times New Roman 9.5/12 by
SJmagic DESIGN SERVICES, India.
Printed and bound in the UK by CPI Group (UK) Ltd.

Pen & Sword Books Limited incorporates the imprints of Atlas, Archaeology,
Aviation, Discovery, Family History, Fiction, History, Maritime, Military,
After the Battle, Military Classics, Politics, Select, Transport, True Crime,
Air World, Frontline Publishing, Leo Cooper, Remember When,
Seaforth Publishing, The Praetorian Press, Wharncliffe Local History,
Wharncliffe Transport, Wharncliffe True Crime and White Owl.

For a complete list of Pen & Sword titles please contact
PEN & SWORD BOOKS LIMITED
George House, Units 12 & 13, Beevor Street, Off Pontefract Road,
Barnsley, South Yorkshire, S71 1HN, England
E-mail: enquiries@pen-and-sword.co.uk
Website: www.pen-and-sword.co.uk

or
PEN AND SWORD BOOKS
1950 Lawrence Rd, Havertown, PA 19083, USA
E-mail: uspen-and-sword@casematepublishers.com
Website: www.penandswordbooks.com

Contents

Foreword

The news that Andrew Long, an established author with a long-standing interest in the history of Berlin in the Cold War, intended to write the definitive account of the British Commanders'-in-Chief Mission to the Soviet Forces in Germany (BRIXMIS) was warmly welcomed by 'the Mission's' surviving veterans and has received their full support.

Initial accounts about BRIXMIS's modus operandi and the exploits of its three-man 'tour' patrols out on the ground in the former Soviet Occupation Zone were written back in the mid-1990s by Tony Geraghty and Steve Gibson. However, since then a mass of formerly classified British and American records and the surviving reports in the archives of the East German Ministry of State Security (the infamous 'Stasi') have been released.

Andrew Long has exploited these official sources, as well as dipping into the many interviews with and memoirs by Mission veterans that are held in the BRIXMIS Association's archive at King's College London. The result is the most comprehensive and accurate overview to date of a highly successful and largely forgotten British military unit in the Cold War era.

The key to BRIXMIS's success was the bilateral 'Robertson–Malinin Agreement' concluded with the Soviet military authorities in September 1946; it was to endure unamended, until the eve of German reunification in October 1990. Reciprocal in nature, it permitted both the British and Soviet commanders-in-chief to establish military liaison missions, consisting of eleven officers and twenty other ranks and enjoying quasi-diplomatic immunity, on the territory of the other party. Most importantly, the agreement was surprisingly imprecise where the tasking of these missions was concerned: it stated simply that they were 'to maintain liaison', but no attempt was made to define what was meant by 'liaison'. This imprecision allowed BRIXMIS not only to conduct formal military diplomatic liaison duties, but also to carry out increasingly sophisticated intelligence-collection operations, known euphemistically as 'tours', within the majority of the Soviet Occupation Zone, which became the German Democratic Republic in 1949.

These highly classified activities were grudgingly tolerated by the Soviets, who did whatever they could to restrict the loss of their secrets. On several occasions the Soviet commander-in-chief exhorted Chief BRIXMIS to ensure that his 'tourers' behaved in a sensible manner, even though he appreciated that intelligence-collection operations required high levels of professionalism and calculated risk-taking. Accredited exclusively to the Soviet military authorities, BRIXMIS and its fellow

Allied (American and French) military liaison missions were a constant irritant to the East German regime. In the late 1970s and early 1980s the 5,000-strong Stasi main directorate tasked with keeping an eye on the Allied 'tours' was authorised to ambush them if they got too close to sensitive East German military installations.

Having narrowly failed in August 1982 to kill the Chief BRIXMIS in a Stasi-directed truck ramming, in March 1984 the Stasi finally managed to kill a member of the French mission and injured his two comrades in another deliberate 'traffic accident'. Almost exactly a year later a Soviet sentry shot and killed an American major when his 'tour' was collecting intelligence on a training area. This may have been only the second occasion when an Allied mission member was fatally injured, but during the Cold War a number of 'tourers' were injured in shootings and in traffic accidents, often the result of deliberate collisions with 'tour' vehicles.

That more members of BRIXMIS and its fellow Allied missions were not killed or seriously hurt was not because the 'touring' environment was benign – it certainly was not – but because 'tourers' were highly experienced, were skilled at taking calculated risks and were determined to bring home whatever intelligence could be collected by rigorous, close-quarter patrolling.

Backed by a galaxy of senior officers, ambassadors and civil servants who served in the Mission or received its hard-won intelligence, the BRIXMIS Association has waged a long campaign in Whitehall to gain the public recognition that it feels its members deserved. Despite receiving the Association's 210-page, meticulously researched and lavishly illustrated submission document, the Cabinet Office continues to insist that the achievements of 'tourers' did not reach its undefined 'risk and rigour' threshold for the issue of a clasp to the General Service Medal. Readers can reach their own decision as to the merit of the Association's claim.

Andrew Long's book is a fitting tribute to the relentless, but under-rewarded efforts of the members of BRIXMIS, 'Britain's forgotten Cold Warriors', who operated armed only with their wits and cunning against hostile forces in East Germany for more than forty years.

Major General (retd.) Peter Williams CMG, OBE
Chairman of The BRIXMIS Association

Preface

This project began back in May 2020 when I stumbled upon a monograph by Major General (retd.) Peter Williams, CMG, OBE, *BRIXMIS in the 1980s: The Cold War's "Great Game" – Memories of Liaising with the Soviet Army in East Germany*, on a Swiss university's website while I was researching for another book – before then I was completely unaware of this unique military unit's existence.[1] Peter's witty prose captured my imagination, and I quickly became obsessed, reading deeply into the subject. When I contacted Peter for clarification on a few points, he generously provided me with a mass of background information and introduced me to Squadron Leader (retd.) Rod Saar MBE, the archivist of the BRIXMIS Association (of which Peter is chairman), who has been extremely helpful, sharing his extensive knowledge and memoirs with me. They also introduced me to many former members of BRIXMIS, who have kindly advised on their individual areas of expertise. The BRIXMIS Association have placed their archive at the Liddell Hart Centre for Military Archives at King's College London, and I spent an enjoyable week buried in the files back in March 2022. This material, along with the generous contributions from Peter, Rod, and their former colleagues, has formed the backbone of this book, much of which was not in the public domain when Tony Geraghty's *Beyond the Frontline* and Steve Gibson's *BRIXMIS, The Last Cold War Mission* were published in 1996/1997.

A note on ranks - I have deliberately chosen to use the rank of the individual *during* their service with the Mission, and specifically at the time of the episode discussed, rather than the rank they retired with. For example, Major General (retd.) Peter Williams is mentioned as Captain Williams, and later, in his second posting with the Mission, as Major Williams, and he is Major Williams in the index. The contemporaneous rank is very important to the role undertaken at the Mission, so to include future promotions would be very confusing for the reader. However, I have based the many well-deserved decorations and awards as they were at retirement.

In a book with so many facts and dates, there is every chance that some errors have slipped through, despite the best efforts of the team who have worked on the book. If you spot any mistakes, please contact me via my website and I will gladly amend them for future editions.

I hope you find the stories of BRIXMIS intelligence-gathering tours deep behind enemy lines in Cold War East Germany as exciting as I have.

Andrew Long
Cornwall, August 2023
www.andrewlong.info

List of Maps

Maps

Map 1. Occupation Zones of Germany, 1945. (Author)

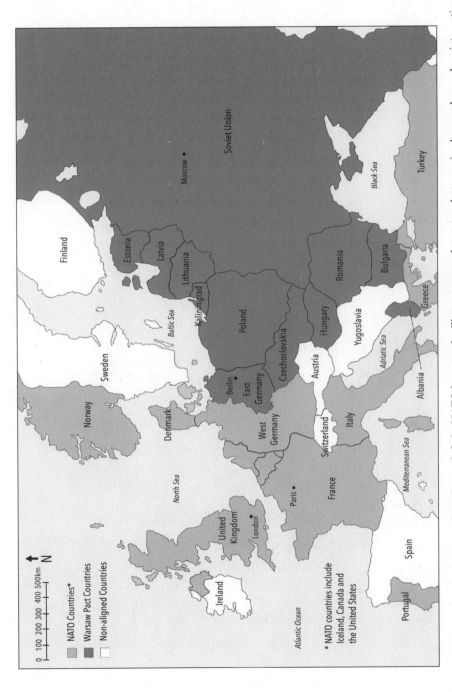

Map 2. NATO *vs.* the Warsaw Pact. Note: France left the NATO integrated military command structure but remained a member, only reintegrating in 2009; Albania was a founder member of the Warsaw Pact but withdrew in 1968. (Author)

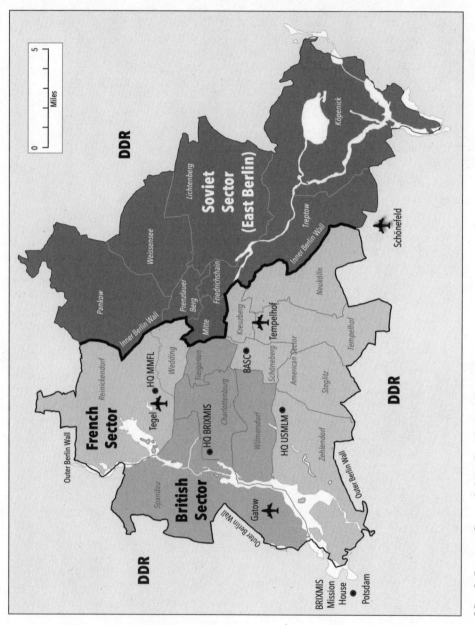

Map 3. Sectors of occupied Berlin, 1945–1990. (Author)

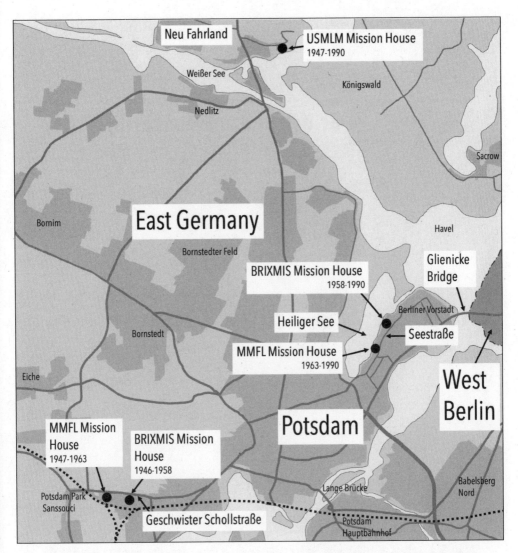

Map 4. Locations of the British, French, and American mission houses in Potsdam, East Germany. (Author)

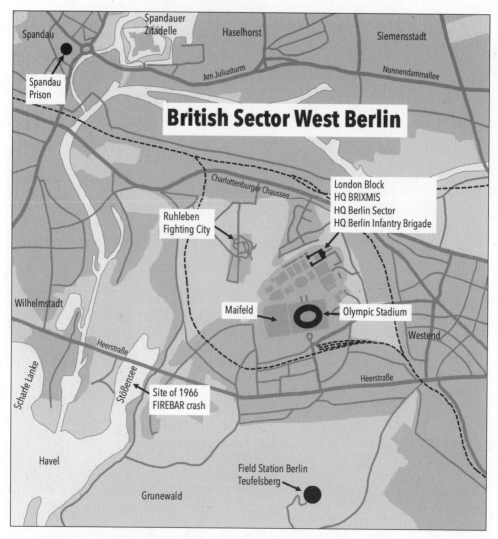

Map 5. Location of HQ Berlin Sector, HQ Berlin Infantry Brigade, and HQ BRIXMIS, Olympic Stadium Complex, West Berlin. (Author)

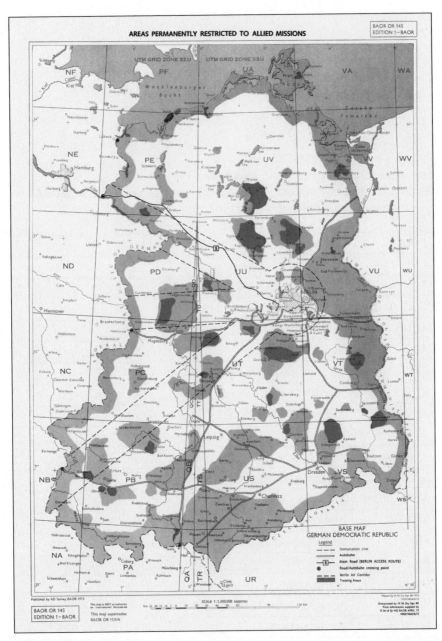

Map 6. Areas Permanently Restricted to Allied Missions, 1:1,350,000 map BAOR OR 145 Edition 1 – BAOR, prepared by 14 Field Survey Squadron Royal Engineers, April 1973. Note the whole of the Baltic coast, the Inner German Border, and the borders with Czechoslovakia and Poland were all *inside* PRAs. The darker shading denotes training areas. Also note the Berlin Control Zone and the three Berlin air corridors are overlaid with dashed lines. (BRIXMIS Association Archives)

Glossary

The military world is full of acronyms, abbreviations, and jargon, which can be daunting for the 'civilian' reader, but hopefully this glossary will help navigate the military vernacular used throughout this book.

2TAF	2nd Tactical Air Force, RAF (UK Mil)
4WD	Four-wheel drive (vehicle)
A	
ACC	Allied Control Council
ACOS	Assistant Chief of Staff (Mil Role)
ACOUSTINT	Acoustic Intelligence
AFC	Air Force Cross (Decoration, UK)
AFN	American Forces Network (US)
AFV	Armoured Fighting Vehicle
Akt	Affidavit-style legal statement (USSR)
AMLM	Allied Military Liaison Mission
APC	Armoured Personnel Carrier
APO	Army Post Office (US)
ASA	Army Security Agency (US)
ASA	Film speed (American Standards Association)
B	
BAOR	British Army of the Rhine (UK Mil)
BASC	Berlin Air Safety Centre
BBV	Box-bodied vehicle
BCZ	Berlin Control Zone
BDU	Battle dress uniform, camouflage (US)
BEM	British Empire Medal (Decoration, UK)
BFBS	British Forces Broadcasting Service (UK Mil)

BFG	British Forces Germany (UK Mil)
BFPO	British Forces Post Office (UK Mil)
BGS	Bundesgrenzschutz, Federal Border Guard (FRG)
BLO	British Liaison Officer (UK Mil)
BMG	British Military Government (UK Mil)
BMP	Tracked infantry fighting vehicle (USSR)
BND	Bundesnachrichtendienst, Federal Intelligence Service (FRG)
Bort	The 'side' number on the front fuselage of a Soviet aircraft (USSR)
BRDM	Wheeled armoured reconnaissance vehicle (USSR)
BRIXMIS	British Commanders'-in-Chief Mission to the Soviet Forces in Germany (BRX)
BRX	Short form of BRIXMIS (BRX)
BSIU(G)	British Services Intelligence Unit (Germany) (UK Mil)
BSSO(G)	British Services Security Organisation (Germany) (UK Mil)
BTR	Wheeled armoured personnel carrier (USSR)
C	
C2	Command and control
C3	Command, control, and communications
CAD(B)	Combined Analysis Detachment, Berlin (US)
CB	Companion of the Most Honourable Order of the Bath (Decoration, UK)
CBE	Commander of the Most Excellent Order of the British Empire (Decoration, UK)
CBRN	Chemical, biological, radiological, and nuclear (see NBC)
CCG(BE)	Control Commission Germany (British Element) (UK)
C-in-C	Commander-in-Chief (Cs-in-C, Commanders-in-Chief) (Mil Role)
CIA	Central Intelligence Agency (US)
CICC(G)	Commander-in-Chiefs Committee (Germany) (UK Mil)
CMG	Companion of the Most Distinguished Order of Saint Michael and Saint George (Decoration, UK)
COMINT	Communications Intelligence
COS	Chief of Staff (Role)
Coy	Company (UK Mil)
D	
DDR	Deutsche Demokratische Republik, German Democratic Republic (East Germany, see GDR)

DFC	Distinguished Flying Cross (Decoration, UK)
DFM	Distinguished Flying Medal (Decoration, UK)
DIS	Defence Intelligence Staff (MoD) (UK Gov)
DPM	Disruptive Pattern Material camouflage (UK Mil)
DSO	Distinguished Service Order (Decoration, UK)
E	
EAC	European Advisory Commission
ECM	Electronic countermeasures
EDA	Emergency Deployment Area
EGAF	East German Air Force (BRX)
ELINT	Electronic Intelligence
ERA	Explosive Reactive Armour
F	
FDJ	Freie Deutsche Jugend (GDR)
FF	Ferguson Formula (4WD system)
FFA	Françaises en Allemagne, French Forces in Germany (FR)
FMLM	French Military Liaison Mission (anglicisation of MMFL) (FR)
FRG	Federal Republic of Germany (Bundesrepublik Deutschland, West Germany)
Flt Sgt	Flight sergeant, RAF (UK Mil Rank)
FO	Foreign Office (UK Gov)
FPN	Field post (office) number
FSB	Field Station Berlin, Teufelsberg listening station
G	
GAZ	Gorkovsky avtomobilny zavod, military vehicle manufacturer (USSR)
GCHQ	Government Communications Headquarters (UK Gov)
GDR	German Democratic Republic (East Germany, see DDR)
Geo	Geographic (mapping) department (BRX)
GOC	General Officer, Commanding (Mil Role)
Gp	Group
Grepo	Grenzpolizei, East German Frontier or border Police, pl. Grepos (GDR)
GRU	Glavnoye Razvedyvatel'noye Upravleniye, Main Intelligence Directorate, Soviet Military Intelligence (USSR, see WGF)

GSO1	General staff officer grade 1, an army lieutenant colonel or RAF wing commander (see SO1) (UK Mil Rank)
GSO2	General staff officer grade 2, an army major or RAF squadron leader (see SO3) (UK Mil Rank)
GSO3	General staff officer grade 3, an army captain or RAF flight lieutenant (see SO3) (UK Mil Rank)
GSOFG	Group of Soviet Occupation Forces in Germany (1945–1954) (USSR)
GSFG	Group of Soviet Forces in Germany (1954–1988) (USSR)
GTD	Guards tank division (USSR)
H	
HA	Hauptabteilung, main department
HMA	Huebner–Malinin Agreement (USMLM, US)
HUMINT	Human Intelligence
HQ	Headquarters
I	
IFF	Identification Friend or Foe
IGB	Inner (Intra) German Border
II	Image Intensifier
IM	Inoffizieller Mitarbeiter, informer (GDR)
Int	Intelligence
IoH	Indicator(s) of Hostility(ies)
J	
JHQ	Joint Headquarters (Rheindahlen, West Germany) (UK Mil)
JIB	Joint Intelligence Bureau (UK Gov)
JIS(B)	Joint Intelligence Staff (Berlin), successor to BRIXMIS (BRX)
JNCO	Junior non-commissioned officer (UK Mil Rank)
K	
KdA	Kampfgruppen der Arbeiterklasse, factory militia (GDR)
KGB	Komitet Gosudarstvennoy Bezopasnosti, the Committee of State Security, the Soviet domestic and foreign security service, 1954–1991 (USSR)
KIT	BRIXMIS slang for an interesting piece of military equipment (BRX)
L	
Lt	Lieutenant: army & Royal Marine officer rank, equivalent to RAF flying officer. Also prefix for colonel or general (Mil Rank)

Lt Col	Lieutenant colonel: army & Royal Marine officer rank, equivalent to RAF wing commander (Mil Rank)
LVO	Member of the Royal Victorian Order (Decoration, UK)
LWB	Long wheel base (vehicle)
M	
MALM	Master air load master, RAF (UK Mil Rank)
Mapper	A mapping tour (BRX)
MBE	Member of the Most Excellent Order of the British Empire (Decoration, UK)
MC	Military Cross (Decoration, UK)
MfS	Ministerium für Staatssicherheit, the East German Ministry for State Security, 1950–1990 (GDR)
MI5	British Security Service (UK Gov)
MI6	An incorrect but much used acronym for the British Secret Intelligence Service, SIS (UK Gov)
MiG	Mikoyan, aircraft manufacturer (USSR)
Mission, The	The Mission, internal name for BRIXMIS (BRX)
MLM	Military Liaison Mission
MMFL	La Mission Militaire Française de Liaison, the French Military Mission to the Soviet Forces in Germany (FR)
MoD	Ministry of Defence (UK Gov)
MRD	Motor rifle division (USSR/GDR)
MRS	Mission Restricted Sign
M/T	Motor Transport (UK Mil)
MTO	Maksutov Tele-Objectiv 1,000-mm Soviet camera lens
N	
NAAFI	Navy, Army, and Air Forces Institutes (UK Mil)
Nark	Stasi agent, BRIXMIS slang (BRX)
NATO	North Atlantic Treaty Organization
NBC	Nuclear, biological, and chemical
NCO	Non-commissioned officer (Mil Rank)
NMA	Noiret–Malinin Agreement (MMFL, FR)
NSA	National Security Agency, 1952–present (US)
NVA	Nationale Volksarmee, National People's Army, East German Armed Forces (GDR)
NVG	Night Vision Goggles

O	
OBE	Officer of the Most Excellent Order of the British Empire (Decoration, UK)
OP	Observation position/point/post
Ops	Operations
OPSEC	Operational security
ORBAT	Order of Battle
P	
Persona non grata	A Latin phrase meaning an unacceptable person, used to mean someone who is not welcome or acceptable. The designation received diplomatic meaning in the 1961 Vienna Convention for Diplomatic Relations. Under Article 9 of the treaty, a country can declare any member of a diplomatic staff *persona non grata* 'at any time and without having to explain its decision', although retaliation may follow.
PI	Photographic interpreter
PNG	persona non grata
PoW	Prisoner of War
PR	Photo reconnaissance
PR	Public relations
PRA	Permanent Restricted Area
Q	
Q	Quartermaster (UK Mil Role)
QGM	Queen's Gallantry Medal (Decoration, UK)
R	
RA	Royal Artillery (UK Mil)
RAF	Royal Air Force (UK Mil)
RAFG	Royal Air Force Germany (UK Mil)
RAOC	Royal Army Ordnance Corps (UK Mil)
RASC	Royal Army Service Corps (UK Mil)
RCT	Royal Corps of Transport (UK Mil)
RE	Royal Engineers (UK Mil)
Recce	Short form of 'reconnoitre' or 'reconnaissance'
Reggie	Soviet army traffic regulator, BRIXMIS slang (BRX)
REME	Royal Electrical and Mechanical Engineers (UK Mil)
retd.	Retired (Rank)

RIAS	Radio in (the) American Sector (US)
RM	Royal Marines (UK Mil)
RMP	Royal Military Police (UK Mil)
RSM	Regimental sergeant major: army and Royal Marines, SNCO (UK Mil Rank)
RMA	Robertson–Malinin Agreement (BRX UK)
RO	Retired officer (Role)
RTR	Royal Tank Regiment (UK Mil)
RV	Rendezvous, meeting, or meeting point
S	
SAM	Surface-to-Air Missile
SAS	Special Air Service (UK Mil)
SD	Special Duties
SED	Sozialistische Einheitspartei Deutschlands, Socialist Unity Party of Germany, East German ruling party 1946–1989 (GDR)
SERB	Soviet External Relations Branch (USSR)
Sgt	Sergeant (Mil Rank)
SHAPE	Supreme Headquarters Allied Powers Europe (NATO)
SIGINT	Signals Intelligence
SIS	Secret Intelligence Service (MI6)
SLO	Soviet Liaison Officer/Officer (UK Mil Role)
SLOps	Squadron Leader Operations (BRX)
SLR	Self-loading rifle (UK Mil)
SLR	Single lens reflex (camera)
SMLM	Soviet Military Liaison Mission (USSR)
SO1	Staff officer grade 1, an army lieutenant colonel or RAF wing commander (UK Mil Rank, see GSO1)
SO2	Staff officer grade 2, an army major or RAF squadron leader (UK Mil Rank, see GSO2)
SO3	Staff officer grade 3, an army captain or RAF flight lieutenant (UK Mil Rank, see GSO3)
SOXMIS	Soviet Military Liaison Mission (British Zone) (USSR)
SNCO	Senior non-commissioned officer (Mil Rank)
Spetsnaz	Russian abbreviation for the term 'special designation' or 'special purpose', but generally used to describe Soviet GRU special forces. (USSR)

SQMS	Squadron quartermaster sergeant (UK Mil Role)
Sqn Ldr	Squadron leader, RAF officer rank equivalent to army major (UK Mil Rank)
SSgt	Staff sergeant, army SNCO rank (Mil Rank)
Stasi	Staatssicherheitsdienst, the East German State Security Service (GDR)
SU	Sukhoi, aircraft manufacturer (USSR)
SWB	Short wheel base (vehicle)
Sy	Security (UK Mil)
T	
TAC	Tactical, as in TAC route
TAREX	Target Exploitation (US)
TASM	Tactical air-to-surface missile
Tatra	Czechoslovakian vehicle manufacturer (CZ)
Tech	Technical
TECHINT	Technical Intelligence
TI	Thermal imaging
TRA	Temporary Restricted Area
Trapo	TransportPolizei, Transport Police pl. Trapos (GDR)
TTL	Through the lens (metering on a camera)
TTW	Transition to War
U	
UAZ	Ulyanovsky Avtomobilny Zavod, military vehicle manufacturer (USSR)
UFO	Unauthorised (unofficial) fly-off (or fly-on)
Ural	Uralskiy Avtomobilnyi Zavod, truck manufacturer (USSR)
URS	Unattended repeater station
USAF	United States Air Force (US)
USAREUR	US Army Europe (US)
USCOB	United States Command Berlin US)
USMLM	United States Military Liaison Mission, the American Military Mission to the Soviet Forces in Germany (US)
V	
Vopo	Volkspolizei, the East German 'People's' Police Force, pl. Vopos (GDR)

VPB	Volkspolizei-Bereitschaften, People's Police 'Alert' or 'Readiness' Units, Public Order/Riot Police (GDR)
VRN	Vehicle registration number
W	
WAAF	Women's Auxiliary Air Force, RAF (UK Mil)
WGF	Western Group of (Soviet) Forces (successor to GSFG, 1988–1994) (USSR, see GSFG)
Wpns	Weapons department (BRX)
WO[†]	Warrant officer: RAF SNCO rank (UK Mil Rank)
WOI	Warrant officer, first class: army, Royal Marines and Royal Navy SNCO rank (UK Mil Rank)
WOII	Warrant officer, second class: army, Royal Marines and Royal Navy SNCO rank (UK Mil Rank)
WRAC	Women's Royal Army Corps, British Army (UK Mil)
WRNS	Women's Royal Naval Service (known as Wrens) (UK Mil)
W/T	Wireless transmission, radio
Y	
Yak	Yakovlev, aircraft manufacturer (USSR)
Z	
ZIL	Zavod imeni Likhachyova, vehicle manufacturer (USSR)
Z-platz	Overnight sleeping location (BRX)
ZSU	Zenitnaya Samokhodnaya Ustanovka, self-propelled anti-aircraft system (USSR)

[†] Warrant officer in the British armed forces is a separate classification of SNCO, receiving the Queen's (or King's) Warrant, which is signed on her/his behalf by the Secretary of State for Defence. They are addressed as 'Sir' or 'Ma'am' by subordinates and 'Mr', 'Mrs', or 'Ms' followed by their last name by commissioned officers.

Introduction

'From Stettin in the Baltic to Trieste in the Adriatic,
an iron curtain has descended across the Continent.'
Winston Churchill[1]

There is much debate in historical circles about when the Cold War began, and when it finished. Because much of the Cold War, the longest global confrontation of the twentieth century, took place in the shadows, behind the rhetoric of politicians, or in faraway third-world proxy conflicts, it is hard to pinpoint specific dates. There were no convenient invasions, formal declarations of war by belligerent governments, no blitzkriegs, area bombing, or formal surrender ceremonies – it was a nebulous war played out through competing ideologies, political manoeuvring, brinkmanship, and rampant technological development, creating weapons of unimaginable power. Some historians will pick VE Day as the start date, 8/9 May 1945, when the Germans surrendered to the allies, ending the long war in Europe and securing Stalin's place in Berlin, at the very heart of Western Europe. Others will choose the Potsdam Conference in July/August 1945, where the allied leaders concluded a series of wartime meetings that planned the new world order – epic power-plays that carved the world up between the victors. Some may suggest the detonation of the world's first atomic bomb over Hiroshima on 6 August 1945, which heralded the dawn of the nuclear age and a world changed forever. A popular choice is Winston Churchill's famous 'Sinews of Peace' speech, which he delivered at Westminster College in Fulton, Missouri on 5 March 1946, in which he declared that 'an iron curtain has descended across the Continent.'[2] Or possibly 29 August 1949, when the Soviet Union detonated *their* atomic bomb, albeit one that was built from plans stolen by Stalin's spies from the Manhattan Project. This author has even suggested that the Cold War can be traced back to the First World War and the twin Russian revolutions of 1917, which launched Bolshevism and Communism to the world.

As for the end of the Cold War, the most quoted date would be 9 November 1989, when a bungled press conference in East Berlin created sufficient chaos for hordes of East Berliners, fired up by the 'people-power' that had been building inside East Germany for some months, to peacefully overwhelm the baffled Grepos (Grenzpolizei, East German border police) at crossing points across the city. The Berlin Wall, which had stood for all that was wrong with the East German communist regime, collapsed without a shot being fired. The grand reopening of the Brandenburg Gate, an iconic symbol of the Cold War, on 22 December 1989 was another important milestone. Two years before this, US President Ronald Reagan joined the growing pressure in June 1987 when he implored Soviet leader Mikhail Gorbachev to 'Tear down this wall' in his famous speech in front of the Brandenburg Gate. When Gorbachev declined to send in troops after the Polish communist government was toppled in June 1989, the world looked on expectedly. The previous summer, Gorbachev had announced the end of the 'international class struggle', which had been the basis of seventy years of Soviet foreign policy, and the lack of intervention in Poland was the first test of his so-called 'Sinatra Doctrine'. Throughout 1989 the dominos continued to topple – that summer thousands of East Germans exploited a loophole to get to the West by driving their Trabants and Wartburgs to Czechoslovakia and Hungary on normal tourist visas and slipping across the increasingly permeable Austro-Hungarian frontier.[3] In September an East German popular movement called 'Neues Forum' or New Forum (New Forum) was created and their 'manifesto' energised mass demonstrations across all the major cities in East Germany.[4] On 7 October, Erich Honecker, the East German leader, proudly hosted General Secretary Gorbachev at lavish celebrations in East Berlin to celebrate the fortieth anniversary of the creation of the Deutsche Demokratische Republik (DDR), the German Democratic Republic (GDR), only to be told by his Soviet 'boss' that 'life punishes those who come too late', an implicit warning that Honecker was running out of friends and time.[5] Eleven days later, with protests growing across the country, Honecker was ousted in a last-ditch attempt to reverse the irreversible, to be succeeded by the hapless Egon Krenz. The Wall came down twenty-two days after his appointment, and Krenz would himself be ousted in early December as the communist regime tried to clean up its act.

The Cold War, however, still had some way to go. German reunification on 3 October 1990 solved the 'German problem' that had been at the top of successive Soviet leaders' agendas since 1945, but the Soviet Union would cling on for another fourteen months before it too was dissolved on 25 December 1991. Even then, tens of thousands of heavily armed front-line Russian troops remained in the former East Germany, and continued to be supplied with updated military hardware right up until their final withdrawal in August 1994, followed the next month with the final withdrawal of the last British, French, and American troops from Berlin.

All these theories are correct in their own contexts, but for the purposes of this book, the assumption will be made that the Cold War began after the Potsdam Conference and ended with the final withdrawal of Soviet (Russian) troops from Germany in 1994, a period of forty-nine years during which the future of the world hung by a thread.

The roots of BRIXMIS and the military liaison missions can be traced back to a conference that was held in Moscow on 30 October 1943. The British, American, and Soviet foreign ministers proposed setting up a European Advisory Commission (EAC) to prepare for a post-war Europe, and the delightfully termed 'Dismemberment of Germany'. The 'Big Three' (Churchill, Roosevelt, and Stalin) agreed to their proposal and the EAC started work in January 1944. The EAC worked quickly and by September they had come up with a plan to roll back Germany's borders to where they had been in December 1937 (before Hitler began his territorial expansion) and divide the country into three occupation zones: British; American; and Soviet, which were to be administered separately – the French were not involved at this stage. It was also decided that Berlin would be split three (and later four) ways and governed by a Kommandatura.[6] A follow-up to the agreement was made in November, confirming that the British would get the north-western zone and the Americans the south-western zone – the Soviets had already 'claimed' the eastern zone. The French were also invited to become observers but were not party to the agreements.[7] At the same meeting, the allies came to an agreement on the 'Control Machinery in Germany', which fleshed out how Germany was going to be administered and laid the foundation for what became the Military Liaison Missions.[8] The agreement stated that:

> Supreme authority in Germany will be exercised, on instructions from their respective Governments, by the Commanders-in-Chief of the armed forces of the United States of America, the United Kingdom and the Union of Soviet Socialist Republics, each in his own zone of occupation, and also jointly, in matters affecting Germany as a whole. ... The three Commanders-in-Chief, acting together as a body, will constitute a supreme organ of control called the [Allied] Control Council. ... An Inter-Allied Governing Authority (Kommandatura) consisting of three Commandants, one from each Power, appointed by their respective Commanders-in-Chief, will be established to direct jointly the administration of the "Greater Berlin" area.

Article 2 of the agreement stated:

> Each Commander-in-Chief in his zone of occupation will have attached to him military, naval and air representatives of the other two Commanders-in-Chief for liaison duties.

However, it did not specify what those 'liaison duties' entailed, and this ambiguity would be critical to the military liaison missions' modi operandi for the next forty-six years.

The 'Big Three' met for the second time in February 1945 at Yalta, where they agreed that the French should have a slice of the pie, although the Soviets insisted that it had to come out of the British and American zones, perhaps the first sign of the Soviet intransigence that became the norm after the war was won.[9] The British were happy to relinquish a triangle of territory in the south-west corner of their zone that bordered France, and the Americans did likewise, the two triangles connected by a narrow isthmus (as shown in map 1). The thorny issue of access rights to jointly controlled Berlin was deferred for later discussion.

With the war (at least in Europe) won, on 5 June 1945 the victorious allies (now including the French) issued a very powerfully worded declaration 'Regarding the Defeat of Germany and the Assumption of Supreme Authority by Allied Powers', which had been hastily prepared by the EAC when it was realised that with Hitler's death and the collapse of his regime, there was no surviving government to work with to run the peace. In addition to very specific instructions for the disarmament, demilitarisation, and denazification of the German people, the declaration collectively assumed 'supreme authority with respect to Germany, including all the powers possessed by the German Government, the High Command and any state, municipal, or local government or authority'.[10] This paved the way for military government in each of the zones of occupation and in the former Reich capital, Berlin, but it would be another month before the Americans and British could get to work.

Meanwhile, over in San Francisco, California, delegates from fifty nations met for the United Nations Conference on International Organization. Its culmination was the signing of the UN Charter and the Statute of the International Court of Justice on 26 June 1945, creating the international body that would have such an important role to play during the Cold War.[11]

Chapter 1

Liaison

'... the Soviet and British Commanders-in- Chief of the
Zones of Occupation in Germany have decided to exchange
Military Liaison Missions to be accredited to their respective
Staffs in the Zone.'

Robertson–Malinin Agreement,
16 September 1946[1]

In April 1945, Stalin began amassing a huge force at the Oder, east of Berlin, ready for the final push into the heart of the Third Reich. Controversially, General Eisenhower, the Supreme Commander of British and American forces, stopped his eastward advance on 12 April 1945. Conventional wisdom has this decision to stop short of Berlin as a political concession made by Roosevelt at the Yalta Conference to give Stalin the 'prize' of Berlin, but it is now understood to have been based on military expediency and the wish to minimise further American casualties. This decision would have serious consequences for the post-war map of Europe.

The city of Berlin, the former capital of Hitler's Third Reich, was deep in the 'Eastern' occupation zone of Germany that Stalin had 'claimed' the previous year. The Red Army began its assault on the heart of the Third Reich on 16 April, backed by more than a million troops more than over 20,000 tanks and artillery pieces, beginning a bloody and brutal attack on the city. On 30 April 1945, after two weeks of absolute carnage, and with the Red Army only a few hundred metres from his bunker in central Berlin, Adolf Hitler committed suicide, the Nazi hierarchy collapsed, and the Germans surrendered, bringing the long war to an end and heralding, although most of the parties would not recognise it yet, the start of a much longer and even more dangerous conflict. The western allies, the British and Americans, had stopped their advance at the River Elbe, near Magdeburg, some fifty miles from Berlin, giving Stalin the prize of Berlin. The allies had agreed to a three-way split of the city back in 1944, but for the moment, Stalin had the city to himself. Using the tried-and-tested model perfected in the other 'liberated' countries, the Soviets went about establishing a communist-led society, taking over local government, utilities, law and order, and the media, all without any input from the other allies – they even worked to Moscow time! They also began stripping the city of much of its industry and infrastructure, which was dismantled, crated up and transported by rail to the Soviet Union. This takeover and officially sanctioned looting was citywide, including the sectors that were to be handed over to the British and Americans. The same process went on all over the Eastern Zone of occupation, and British troops, whose advance had taken them into what was now the Soviet Zone, pulled back to the agreed British lines.

The British and American forces finally made it to Berlin to take possession of their sectors of occupation on 4 July 1945 after a difficult journey across the Soviet Zone in armed convoys. They were greeted by devastation, camping out in the shells of the few remaining buildings that had not been stripped of all fixtures and fittings or left in an appalling state by their temporary Russian lodgers. The Americans chose an old Luftwaffe headquarters in the Dahlem Zehlendorf district of south-west Berlin as their base, while the British established their headquarters in the Charlottenburg-Wilmersdorf district in the west of Berlin, taking over an imposing building overlooking Fehrbelliner Platz that they named Lancaster House (they would not move to the more famous Olympic Stadium Complex until the early 1950s). They also had to accept limited access to the city across the Soviet Zone: two highways, a single railway line, and two air corridors – the number of crossing options ebbed and flowed for the next forty-five years in line with the wider political climate.

The Allied Kommandatura, the three- (and later four-) power body that was supposed to govern the city of Berlin, first met on 11 July 1945, and immediately had to deal with squabbles about sector borders and the eviction of Soviet units who had overstayed their welcome in the British and American sectors. The venue chosen for the Kommandatura was the former administration building for a German insurance company, located at Kaiserswerther Straße 16–18 in Berlin-Dahlem in the American sector. The Kommandatura moved there on 25 July 1945, staying until 1991, although the four-power cooperation would not last the course. At this time, the French were still in limbo.

The third and final meeting of the 'Big Three' took place in Potsdam, a town south-west of Berlin, between 17 July and 2 August 1945, but there was much change around the negotiating table: US President Franklin D. Roosevelt, the grand elder statesman, had died on 14 April 1945 to be succeeded by Harry Truman, who had little foreign policy experience; Winston Churchill, the British wartime leader who could claim much of the credit for their ultimate victory, was unceremoniously replaced as prime minister by Clement Attlee after losing the 1945 general election; but the one constant was Joseph Vissarionovich Stalin, who had held the Soviet Union in his iron grip since the 1920s. The trust, goodwill, and cooperation that drove the allies to victory gave way to inflexibility, recrimination, mistrust, and obfuscation. The orderly work undertaken by the EAC, and the progress made in the various conferences right up to Yalta earlier that year, gave way to a series of faits accomplis and very uncomfortable compromises.

On 26 July 1945, one of the final acts of the EAC was the proposal for France to become the fourth allied power with their own zone of occupation in Germany and their own sector of Berlin that the conference confirmed. The four zones of occupation were confirmed as:

> North-Western Zone (British)
> Eastern Zone (Soviet)
> South-Western Zone (United States)
> Western Zone (French)

As with the occupation zones of Germany, when it came to Berlin the Soviets refused to give the French any of their territory, so the French were allocated the districts of Wedding and Reinickendorf in the north-west of the city, both formerly in the British sector. French forces would not arrive until August 1945, setting up their headquarters in what became known as the Quartier Napoléon. It would take until mid-August to finally eject the Soviets from the western sectors – more indicators of future Soviet intransigence and obstruction. The EAC, which had done an excellent and mostly non-partisan job planning for a post-war Europe, was formally wound up at the Potsdam Conference – it was a shame that the spirit of solidarity and cooperation did not last beyond it.

The Allied Control Council (ACC) met for the first time on 30 July 1945 at the very grand former Prussian Kammergericht (Supreme Court) building in the district of Schöneberg. The marbled corridors of the Kammergericht would soon, however, echo with sounds of discord, rather than the harmony the EAC had originally intended. Unfortunately, when setting up the Allied Control Council, the EAC made the serious mistake of stipulating that all decisions had to be unanimous. Given the souring of relations between the Soviet Union and the other three occupying powers, the ACC was never going to be a very effective organisation, and after the Western Allies had been hoodwinked into accepting the unanimous decision clause, the Soviets effectively had a veto over *every* issue.

Germany continued to be a dangerous place in the months immediately following the end of the Second World War. There were thousands of heavily armed troops milling around, brutalised by war and with little to do – the allies had their occupation responsibilities to fulfil but there was also immense pressure to rotate combat troops (who may have been away for years) back home. The allies had to tackle the complex tasks of administering a conquered nation: demilitarisation, denazification, the processing and repatriation of released allied prisoners of war (PoWs), the grim but important task of graves registration, and the 'acquisition' of German technology by way of reparations. There were also millions of displaced persons (DPs) drifting towards the main population centres, who all needed feeding and housing, and the regulation of a thriving black market ready to exploit them. With the Soviets becoming increasingly difficult, it became clear that some ground rules needed to be laid down to avoid the risk of an incident between roving troops and their opposite numbers escalating into a full-blown confrontation. It was also increasingly important to find out what the neighbouring 'ally' was up to in their zone – this intelligence collection soon became the primary role for the Mission as 'ally' developed into potential 'enemy'. Liaison missions were not a new invention – the allies had 'exchanged' missions in all the main theatres during the Second World War. There were also various 'irregular' units roaming around Europe, such as the Field Information Agency, Technical (FIAT), and T-Force, who were tasked with 'acquiring' German technology and the scientists and engineers who developed it before the Soviets did. There were also small Special Air Service (SAS) teams searching for missing British personnel and tracking down the perpetrators of atrocities and other war crimes.

Using the principles set down in the 1944 London Protocol, Lieutenant General Sir Brian Robertson, Bart., the Deputy Military Governor, Control Commission

Germany (British Element), and Colonel General Mikhail S. Malinin, Deputy Commander-in-Chief and Chief of Staff of the Soviet Group of Forces of Occupation in Germany, put their names to an agreement formalising the 'rules' of liaison between their respective occupying forces. On 16 September 1946, the Robertson–Malinin Agreement (RMA) went into effect – their thirteen-point agreement governing mutual military liaison missions, the full text of which is included in the appendices:*

> the Soviet and British Commanders-in-Chief of the Zones of Occupation in Germany have decided to exchange Military Liaison Missions to be accredited to their respective Staffs in the Zone ...
>
> The Missions will consist of 11 officers assisted by not more than 20 technicians, clerks and other personnel ...
>
> The Mission will be placed under the authority of one member of the Mission who will be nominated and termed the "Chief of the Soviet/ British Military Mission".
>
> The Chief of the Mission will be accredited to the Commander-in-Chief of the Forces of Occupation.
>
> Each Mission will have similar travellers' facilities. Passes of an identical nature in Russian and English will be prepared. Generally speaking there will be freedom of travel and circulation for the members of Missions in each Zone with the exception of restricted areas in which respect each Commander-in-Chief will notify the Mission and act on a reciprocal basis.
>
> The object of the Mission is to maintain Liaison between the Staff of the two Commanders-in-Chief and their Military Governments in the Zones. The Missions can also in each Zone concern themselves and make representation regarding their Nationals and interests in the Zones in which they are operating. They can afford assistance to authorized visitors of their own country visiting the Zone to which the Mission is accredited.[2]

The title of the British Mission was British Commanders'-in-Chief Mission to the Soviet Forces of Occupation in Germany, which was shortened to BRIXMISS (British Exchange Mission) and then to just BRIXMIS.† It is sometimes abbreviated to BRX and known to those involved as simply 'The Mission'.

---

* There is no evidence that Robertson and Malinin actually met, let alone put their signatures on a physical document, and there is no original signed copy of the Robertson–Malinin Agreement (RMA) available in Western archives, only unsigned copies. Conceivably a Soviet copy exists in the Russian archives, but these are not open to historians. When it came to be, no one expected the agreement was going to still be in force for more than forty years, so preserving a copy was probably a low priority.

† The plural 'Commanders' reflects the fact that there were two British Commanders-in Chief: of the British Army of the Rhine (BAOR), and of Royal Air Force Germany (RAFG).

The key tool required for 'liaison' was the 'pass', as issued by the Soviet Liaison Office (SLO, better known by the Americanism of Soviet External Relations Branch, SERB, or to the Soviets, the UVS, the Foreign Relations Branch) on behalf of the Chief of Staff Group of Soviet Forces Germany (GSFG), which gave the bearer permission to leave the four-power-controlled city of Berlin and enter the Soviet Zone, allowing them relatively free movement within. SERB, based in Potsdam, was the main point of interface between BRIXMIS and the GSFG. The terms of the RMA granted BRIXMIS thirty-one full passes (known as 'Touring' passes), split between eleven officers and twenty 'other ranks' (technicians, clerks, and other personnel according to the RMA), with the Soviets granted the same number.* These passes were essential to get through the Soviet checkpoints leading out of the city to reach the proposed location for the British Mission at Potsdam, which would become the British outpost *inside* the Soviet Zone. The equivalent Soviet Military Liaison Mission in the British occupation zone would be based initially at Bad Salzuflen and then at Bünde, close to the British Military Headquarters in Bad Oeynhausen, and right in the heart of the British Army of the Rhine (BAOR) – the British referred to the Soviet Mission as SOXMIS.

In anticipation of the RMA being signed, the initial personnel assigned to the British Liaison Mission formed up at Lancaster House in West Berlin on 17 July 1946 under Major General (later Lieutenant General) Sir Geoffrey Evans, who would become the first Chief BRIXMIS, and his deputy, Colonel (later Brigadier and 'local' Major General) Richard Hilton. The core Mission staff were all in place by mid-August.[3] It is notable that, at the time, the Mission was a fully tri-service organisation, with senior representatives from the Army, the RAF, and the Royal Navy. The naval element became redundant when the Baltic coastline became a restricted area and therefore out of bounds to tourers. There were also civilians – senior civil servants, who concentrated on economic and agricultural regeneration in the Soviet Zone – and representatives from the civilian intelligence agencies. They had equivalent military ranks, commonly used to establish the pecking order when a command structure included civilians.

Evans was keen to get his Mission established at the allocated site on Geschwister-Scholl-Straße in Potsdam. His first stop was at Karlshorst to pay his respects to Lieutenant General Mikhail Dratvin, who was chief of staff and deputy head under Marshal Sokolovsky of the Soviet Military Administration in Germany (Sowjetische Militäradministration in Deutschland or SMAD, Sovyetskaya Voyennaya Administratsiya v Germanii or SVAG), the equivalent to the British CCG(BE) and American OMGUS. The British team had intended to move to their new forward HQ on 2 September 1946, but despite Evans presenting himself to the chief of staff and agreeing the date, they arrived to find the site in a dilapidated state, with none of the promised rectifications having been done. The promised rations (the RMA stipulated that the host occupier would provide rations for the Mission, among other things) were also nowhere to be seen and the all-important passes had not turned up. When the increasingly frustrated British team tried to contact the Soviet Liaison Officer

---

* 'Other ranks' is a term in the British military to describe personnel who do not hold a commission (in other words, not an officer). This includes senior non-commissioned officers such as warrant officers.

(SLO – their primary point of contact), he was mysteriously 'away', and nobody knew where he was or when he would return. Clearly the Soviets were trying to make a very unsubtle point, a harbinger of things to come. The team hoped that the arrival of Major General Lavrentiev, deputy chief of staff under Dratvin, on 6 September would get things moving, but all they got was a series of circular negotiations that went nowhere, even after the RMA came into effect on 16 September. On 24 September Evans was summoned to see Marshal Sokolovsky, who was accompanied by Colonel General Mikhail S. Malinin (the M in the RMA) and the elusive SLO; the equally elusive passes finally arrived on 28 September, allowing BRIXMIS to do their first 'tour' into the Soviet Zone (a 220-mile round trip from Potsdam), beginning an activity that would continue uninterrupted for forty-four years.[4]

The British were somewhat taken back by the cool reception from the Soviets. No effort had been made to entertain or even greet their so-called brothers-in-arms, and the inefficiency and indifference were out of character – political officers could be tricky but combat and even rear echelon officers were generally courteous and often friendly, with encounters normally fuelled with lots of vodka. BRIXMIS officers later learnt that the Soviet high command did not believe that the British would turn up when they said they would, and they were holding back to see how SOXMIS (the Soviet Military Mission in the British zone) was received. Most of the Soviet officers had been fed constant negative propaganda about Westerners, so were pleasantly surprised when they finally met them.

BRIXMIS would have *two* bases in Berlin:

> The 'Mission House' or 'forward' HQ was in Potsdam, and, being *outside* Berlin's city limits, was therefore *inside* the Soviet Zone. The Mission House was the 'public' face of the Mission from which they liaised directly with the General Headquarters of the Soviet Forces in Germany, which was originally based in Potsdam but would later move to Karlshorst and then to Zossen-Wünsdorf. As well as 'liaison' and entertaining, it would be the stepping off point for tours around the Soviet Zone.
>
> The 'Rear' headquarters was established in a suite of offices at Lancaster House, one of several buildings requisitioned around Fehrbelliner Platz in the Berlin district of Wilmersdorf, alongside the headquarters of the British Military Government (BMG), the Control Commission Germany (British Element), and the Berlin Infantry Brigade, the British garrison in the city. The BRIXMIS rear HQ was headed up by an RAF wing commander (equivalent to an army lieutenant colonel), who was supported by a secretariat including interpreters, secretaries, clerks (including some Wrens, WRACs and WAAFs), a quartermaster, and a motor transport (M/T) office.*

---

* WRNS– Women's Royal Naval Service, whose members were called Wrens; WRAC – Women's Royal Army Corps; and WAAF – Women's Auxiliary Air Force.

The first Mission House was a fenced-in compound of seven buildings at Geschwister-Scholl-Straße 51 in Potsdam, close to Wildpark Station, which consisted of an officers' mess, soldiers' mess and quarters buildings, the chief of Mission's house (although he had a second house in West Berlin for entertaining purposes), an office building (with a flat above it), and two further residential buildings, each with two flats (including one for the deputy chief, although he also had a flat in West Berlin), with a pond in the middle of it all. In addition, there were stables for three horses, and an M/T area.[5] The site was overseen by the 'Camp Commandant' (for some, living in the Potsdam Mission House felt like being in prison), a BRIXMIS duty officer who would arrive in the evening from West Berlin, stay overnight and return in the morning (unless he was going on tour), plus a small communications team from the Royal Signals. The compound was not particularly secure – it was fenced off from the neighbouring buildings and had a gate at the entrance, but it was a reasonably common occurrence for Soviet officers, often worse for wear, to stumble into the compound (including one on a horse) only to find, to their astonishment, that they were surrounded by British soldiers. There was, however, a Vopo (Volkspolizei, East German 'People's Police') sentry box positioned opposite the entrance, presumably linked by phone or radio to the East German 'political' or 'secret' police.* At the time, it was not unusual for British Army officers to keep horses for recreation and sport (polo) – Major General Manners-Smith, Chief BRIXMIS 1947–1948 and an accomplished polo player, used to insist on a ride in the former Kaiser's deer forest before breakfast – however, they were also used for patrols, and the Soviets provided a groom to look after them. The horses, Kate and Effendi, had their own passes (*propusk*), and were used regularly for 'local' patrols around the Potsdam area, where their cross-country ability considerably exceeded the cars of the time, and the elevated position of the rider was useful to peer over walls and fences – a much better view than from a Humber Snipe or Opel Kapitän. Incidents with the horses were few, thankfully, although Vopos did on occasion try to unseat the rider by scaring the horses. The last tour officer to use the horses for touring was Lieutenant Colonel J. M. Laing MC RE, senior interpreter, 1951–1952, after which the horses were returned to stables in West Berlin.[6]

Major General Evans, Chief BRIXMIS, was promoted and left the Mission in early 1947, to be replaced by Major General L. C. Manners-Smith; following his retirement in 1948, the position of chief was downgraded to a brigadier, remaining at that level for the rest of the Mission's history, the first in post being Brigadier 'Sammy' Hugh M. Curteis MC. The British Army rank brigadier, shortened in 1917 from brigadier general, was rather confusing for the Soviets because *brigadir* in Russian (бригадир) means foreman, gaffer, or gang leader! Manners-Smith's deputy, Colonel Hilton, also

---

* From 1946, the secret police in the Soviet zone were organised as Department K5 of the DVdI, the Deutsche Verwaltung des Innern or the (East) German Administration of the Interior. With the formation of the GDR on 7 October 1949, they became part of the MdI, the Ministerium des Innern or the Ministry of the Interior. On 8 February 1950, they became a ministry in their own right, the Ministerium für Staatssicherheit or MfS, the Ministry of State Security, which included the Staastssicherheitsdienst, the State Security Service, more commonly known as the Stasi.

left at the same time, taking up the position of military attaché in Moscow, and was replaced by Brigadier J. E. F. Meadmore, who would return in 1953 as chief. Despite this change at the top, the Mission continued to attract high-quality personnel from all arms of the military and civil service, including interpreters, political and civil affairs officers, economics and food/agricultural experts, and a few spies. As military and civilian government in the occupation zones became established and reconstruction began, the civil service personnel returned to their CCG(BE) roles and the Mission became an all-military affair.

French and American Missions

For the first six months or so of operations, BRIXMIS was the only Allied Military Liaison Mission working inside the Soviet Zone, and the intelligence value was only just being realised, but it was only a matter of time before the Americans and French got in on the act. On 3 April 1947, the Noiret–Malinin Agreement (NMA) was signed, creating La Mission Militaire Française de Liaison (MMFL, the French Military Mission to the Soviet Forces in Germany, often abbreviated to FMLM), while the equivalent Soviet Military Liaison mission (SMLM) was created in the French Zone, at Baden Baden, home of the French military HQ. The French Mission House was also on Geschwister-Scholl-Straße 43–45, a few doors down from BRIXMIS.* Similarly, on 5 April 1947, the Huebner–Malinin Agreement (HMA) was signed, which created the United States Military Liaison Mission (USMLM) and the SMLM in the American Zone, which was co-located with US forces at Frankfurt am Main. The Americans opted for a Mission House further away from the town centre, a grand villa with grounds leading down to a lake on Am Lehnitzsee on Neu Fahrland. They had to cross two further bridges to get to it from West Berlin. This grand lakeside villa concept would be adopted by BRIXMIS and MMFL following the 1958 demonstrations (see Chapter 3, 'The Unit'), when both BRIXMIS and MMFL moved to Seestraße in the upmarket suburb of Berliner Vorstadt.

The Huebner–Malinin agreement differed from the RMA and Noiret–Malinin Agreement in several ways – it included the right of access for invited guests to their Mission House (BRIXMIS and MMFL had to apply for every visitor and receive a pink 'chit' from SERB), which ensured their parties were always very well attended, and the right to mutually change the agreement as necessary. There was also, inexplicably, a slightly different interpretation of restricted areas, which would cause the Americans lots of problems almost four decades later. The terms of the agreements were never altered, and all three missions operated under the original 1946/47 agreements for their entire duration.

The biggest difference between the Allied Military Liaison Missions (AMLMs) as they were collectively known, however, was in the number of 'touring' passes issued – BRIXMIS received thirty-one passes, notionally split between eleven officers and twenty other ranks (wives and vehicles also had their own passes), and those

---

* The MMFL also moved to a property on Seestraße between 1963 and 1964.

holding a 'touring pass' were described as 'on-pass'. SOXMIS, the Soviet mission in the British zone, had the same number of passes as BRIXMIS, but they were seldom up to full strength. MMFL, on the other hand, were only issued eighteen passes (six officers and twelve other ranks) and USMLM fourteen (eight officers and six other ranks). The reasons for this disparity are lost to time, but possibly at the time (1947) the Americans were hoping to pull out of Europe so did not see the need for too many passes. By contrast, the British recognised the opportunity for long-term intelligence collection inside the Soviet Zone. BRIXMIS clearly had the advantage of being first to the negotiating table, and by the time the French and Americans joined in, the Soviets would have appreciated the potential intelligence value of having reciprocal SMLMs in all three of the Western zones. However, it is puzzling that the Soviets chose to issue so few to the Americans. They clearly were the biggest threat to the Soviet Union and also had the biggest occupation zone, which bordered two Warsaw Pact countries: East Germany *and* Czechoslovakia, so it would have made sense to have more reciprocal passes to allow *their* intelligence teams to see what the Americans were up to. Even the French had more passes, and their zone was smaller, more distant, and therefore less of a threat to the Soviets. There is no documentary evidence why the Soviets issued different numbers of passes to the AMLMs, so one can only speculate that there were military or political reasons for the allocations. Another quirk regarding touring passes was who signed them from the Soviet side. Despite professing to come from a classless society, AMLM officers' passes were signed by the Chief of Staff GSFG, a three-star general, while other ranks, wives and vehicle passes were signed by Chief SERB, a 'mere colonel' – an early example of crude 'Pass Politics' that would plague the three allied missions for years to come.

The upshot of having more passes meant that BRIXMIS could have more tours out in East Germany at any one time. Touring passes were critical to the success of the Mission so were jealously guarded, with the BRIXMIS operations team always trying to have a full complement of tourers available to send out on tours. That meant that if a pass holder was away on leave, on a course, or experiencing a long period of illness, the Mission would temporarily hand back that person's pass to SERB, and request a temporary pass for a new person, either a fully trained-up part-time or former full-time tourer, working in another role at HQ, or someone borrowed from BAOR Intelligence (who had been through BRIXMIS training), swapping back the original tourer on his return. SERB generally went along with these changes, but in 1960, egged on by the East Germans, tried to curtail the practice, claiming too many pass exchanges were being made and their staff 'could not cope with the administrative burden'. They were baulking at the one hundred-plus exchange requests in a twelve-month period, involving fifty different individuals, and demanded a definitive list of accredited tourers. This was more about controlling BRIXMIS operations than helping overworked Soviet clerks but was one example of how the issuing of touring passes could be weaponised by the Soviets. (More examples are discussed in Chapter 6, 'The Opposition'.)

There were fifteen other military missions in West Berlin, representing the Second World War's victorious nations and accredited directly to the ACC. These were much smaller in scale and did not qualify for touring passes in the Soviet Zone (GDR) but formed a good base for intelligence collection within Berlin, the 'city of spies'.* Formal accreditations of new heads of these minor missions to the allied powers were held at the Allied Kommandatura Building. Representing their respective power, the three *allied* city commandants would arrive first. They would then have a 'protocol pause' for several minutes to allow time for the Soviet representative to arrive (they never did, following the withdrawal of the Soviets from the ACC and Kommandatura in 1948) and then the three allied commandants would accept the credentials of the new head of mission.[7] This pantomime continued right into the 1980s.

Accommodation

In the early years of the Mission, families lived in the Potsdam Mission House compound, effectively encamped in 'enemy' territory. The rear HQ personnel were accommodated in hotels, Control Commission (Germany) messes, or at requisitioned premises in the Grunewald forest. The accommodation in Potsdam was of poor quality, even by British standards of the time, but they had locally employed maids, a mess steward, cook, and groom for the horses. The RMA stipulated that 'Each Mission will be administered by the Zone in which it resides in respect of accommodation, rations, petrol and stationery against repayment in Reichsmarks', so rations were delivered every week by Soviet truck even when relations between the United Kingdom and the Soviet Union were at their worst, continuing right through to 1990. Despite receiving the 'superior' grade of rations, the quality varied enormously, and they were typically worse than the most basic British fare. Arriving wrapped in Soviet Army newspapers (which were carefully saved and read for possible snippets of intelligence), the bread was normally hard and gritty, the cigarettes un-smokeable, and the potatoes, eggs, and ham were unusable; however, the pork, tea, and bottled cherries were surprisingly good, and the vodka and caviar were excellent. Water from the tap was supposedly not safe to drink. As a result, the BRIXMIS wives had to supplement these rations with purchases from local shops and from their weekly trips to the NAAFI supermarket in West Berlin.† The petrol supplied was so low octane that it could not be used in Western vehicles, so fuel was brought from West Berlin in jerry cans.‡

Living in Potsdam was sometimes challenging, especially for dependants – getting to the British schools in West Berlin and to West Berlin on shopping trips involved a

---

* The other missions were Canadian, Belgian, Polish, Brazilian, Luxembourg, Czechoslovak, Yugoslav, Danish, Chinese, Norwegian, Australian, Indian, Greek, South African, and Dutch. Source: Allied Liaison and Protocol Section (Ed.), *The Allied Military Missions in Berlin 1945–1948* (Berlin: Allied Control Authority, 1948).

† NAAFI – Navy, Army and Air Forces Institutes, the British equivalent of the American Post Exchange (PX) or Base Exchange (BX), which sold food and consumer goods to the British garrison.

‡ It was a similar situation when out on tour – petrol stations were few and far between, and the fuel quality was poor, so tours took all they needed with them, initially in jerry cans, and later in custom-made increased-capacity fuel tanks.

long bus journey and border checks by scary Soviet (and later East German) guards. The social scene for those based in Potsdam was limited and self-contained, with endless games of bridge, occasionally enlivened by a drinks party with visitors from West Berlin. Most officers would get back to West Berlin weekly to check in at HQ and relax in the British Officers' Club, while wives enjoyed the change of scenery and better-quality shops. Other ranks were allowed one evening off a week in West Berlin.

As British forces got settled in the city, HQ decreed that families living in Potsdam should pay for their accommodation just like families in West Berlin did. For those maintaining a foothold in both camps, it looked as though they were going to have to pay twice for their lodgings until a bright spark suggested invoking the RMA, which stated that accommodation would be provided for Mission personnel. However, by the end of 1946, with the arrival of more families, the Mission had outgrown the compound, so over the next few years, all BRIXMIS families moved back to West Berlin, and the Potsdam Mission House, as it was called, became just the formal HQ for the Mission and a stopping-off point for tours. By 1951, the only permanent resident was the 'camp commandant', whose role developed into the Mission House warrant officer, plus a daily overnight stay for a duty officer from West Berlin.[8]

Families

To accommodate families relocating from the Potsdam Mission House to married quarters in West Berlin, the British Military Government requisitioned several properties in Grunewald previously owned by high-ranking Nazis and for a while BRIXMIS personnel (families and single soldiers) enjoyed some pre-war luxury, with a staff (cook, maid, nanny, with a shared boilerman and gardener) paid for by reparations. Post-war Berlin was a surreal place to live and the residential neighbourhoods where the occupying powers requisitioned property were a mix of grand villas and bombed-out wrecks, such was the random nature of aerial bombing. In another quirk of being the occupying power, some of the children were driven to school every morning in the former Field Marshal Kesselring's bulletproof car.[9] Corporal Len Holman RASC was a young national serviceman posted to BRIXMIS in 1953 as a driver:

> The luxury of the very large detached villa in Taubertstraße [Grunewald] surrounded by millionaire residences was unbelievable and the food even more so. I had my own furnished room with a large communal bathroom close by, a large restaurant type dining room, a large lounge and an even larger bar room. 20 Player's or Senior Service cigarettes cost only one shilling [5p] and bottled beer sixpence [2½p].

Unfortunately for Holman, his taste of the good life did not last long – as the British headquarters in Berlin began moving from Fehrbelliner Platz to the Olympic Stadium complex. Service families and single personnel living in the CCG(BE) quarters in Grunewald were moved (many reluctantly) to be closer to the Stadium; married personnel to new War Department service quarters on Heerstraße, unmarried officers to the officers' mess, and other ranks to quarters within the complex.

All could also take advantage of excellent leisure facilities: tennis, sailing on the Havel, fishing in Berlin's many lakes, swimming at the Olympic Stadium's pools, and an active social life based around the British military community. Shopping included the NAAFI (at duty-free prices) and cheap food from the Family Ration Issue Section (FRIS), a central store of food held in case of another Berlin Blockade, and as the stock was rotated, the older food was sold to forces personnel at very low prices. For example, in 1974, 2 lb of sirloin steak cost 99p, and 2 lb of best end of neck lamb 73p.[10] British personnel also had access to American facilities, which, of course, were top notch. From a cultural point of view, Mission families could enjoy world-class performances at the Deutsche Oper and Berliner Philharmonie in West Berlin, and by nipping over to East Berlin, they could visit the Staatsoper, the Brecht Berliner Ensemble, and the Komische Oper, taking advantage of the very favourable exchange rate (between 6 and 10 Ostmarks to 1 DM). These forays into the East were made in full mess kit, with wives in evening dresses, although their presence did not go down too well with the communist regime. Learning that BRIXMIS had made a block booking of the best seats at the opera, East German leader Walter Ulbricht changed the programme at the last minute from one of the classics to a jarring modern political piece, set on a collective farm with a real tractor on the stage.[11] Over in Potsdam, which Mission families had access to, there were some impressive cultural sites to visit, which were normally remarkably free of tourists. These included the Neues Palais, Cecilienhof (where the Potsdam Conference was held in 1945), the Sanssouci Palace, and the Marmorpalais, just across the Heiliger See lake from the post-1958 Potsdam Mission House. Families were encouraged to go on 'cultural tours', where small groups would travel in official BRIXMIS vehicles (often a minibus) to cities in the GDR. Mission personnel would wear uniform, but otherwise the tour would be for sightseeing or shopping, although it was another good way of practising German or Russian outside of official encounters and sometimes it yielded unexpected intelligence. Apart from the leisure benefits, these trips were a demonstration to the East Germans that the British military were human after all, although the Stasi still doggedly tailed the minibuses and tourers as they pottered around the shops.

The shopping in East Germany was very patchy, depending on what the buyer was after. Normal consumer goods were often hard to obtain and even then, were poor quality, and some types of food were scarce. On the other hand, certain items could be snapped up at bargain prices: porcelain (such as the world-famous Meissen figures), glassware (such as Lausitzer lead crystal), mechanical toys (such as model railways from Piko or VEB Mechanische Speilwaren Brandenburg), and optical products (such as Praktica cameras and Carl Zeiss Jena binoculars), especially with the positive effect of the exchange rate (and the regime was keen to bring in as much hard foreign currency as it could). The RMA/HMA/NMA gave mission personnel and their families access to their host's NAAFI equivalents. For the Soviet officers of the SMLMs and their families living alongside Western forces in West Germany, this reciprocal arrangement was a real perk of the job, allowing them to enjoy all that Western consumerism could deliver, at tax-free prices. Not so, however, for the AMLMs based in Berlin. Although mission personnel had all moved back to West Berlin by the late 1950s, they still had access to the Soviet Army shops in Potsdam. Honor Baines, the wife of Chief BRIXMIS Brigadier David Baines (1972–1974) made a special visit to the two Soviet NAAFI shops in Potsdam in 1973 and was unimpressed: 'the general tattiness and bleakness of the passageway and outside stairway, which was unswept and dangerously steep and slippery, seemed much shabbier than even Potsdam shops are normally ... There were anoraks of good quality for sale ... bananas and tangerines (in great demand) ... very cheap jewellery (Xmas cracker standard) ... the old rather pathetic doll of the cheaper DDR variety.'[12] She purchased some vodka and some bottled cherries (which were excellent) and all the sums were done on an abacus: 'The general impression was of a mining town store in the years of the Depression – and for someone who has never visited Russia rather horrifying – the shops in Potsdam seemed bright and gay afterwards – West Berlin a world away.'

However, there was also a darker side to living in West Berlin. Touring was an all-consuming occupation with very unsocial hours and a certain amount of physical risk. The thrill of touring could be addictive, and that could lead to excessive risk taking if not nipped in the bud by older and wiser heads. If a tour was detained inside the GDR, SERB would not routinely inform the Mission House, so if a tour was badly overdue, the duty officer or Mission House warrant officer would have to make enquiries with the SERB office in Potsdam of their whereabouts. In the meantime, the wives would have an anxious wait for news. Families also had to endure harassment by the Stasi, with abusive, heavy-breather or silent phone calls at all times of the day and night, particularly unsettling if the husband was on tour. This harassment continued right through until the fall of the Wall. The opposition would also routinely follow tour personnel out on family trips in East Germany, which must have been disconcerting. In addition to the infamous 'honey trap' targeting Mission personnel when on tour inside the GDR, it was possible for mission wives to be targeted. In the mid-1950s, a senior allied officer (name, rank and mission withheld) was invited to the Soviet Komendatura in East Berlin, which was quite unusual in itself. There, he was shown a film of his wife in bed with a Soviet officer who was a regular at mission social functions. The Soviets told the officer that the matter need not go any further if he cooperated – the officer politely declined, returned to his HQ, and reported the incident to his chain of command, and he and his family left Berlin that afternoon. The officer was not compromised, but his career in the city was over (which may, of course, have been the Soviet's intention all along).[13] Family members were taught the basics of German and Russian to prepare them for any encounters with the opposition, and carried a card in German, Russian, and English demanding to be seen by a Soviet officer should they be detained.

Mission families tended to tune out the unusual or negative aspects of their posting and enjoy the many distractions available. For most involved, Berlin was a prize assignment and the overriding threat from the Soviets and East Germans was stoically ignored.

Chapter 2

The Mission

*'The worse the situation, the greater the need to keep
the conduits of dialogue open.'*
Group Captain Richard Bates AFC (2001)
Deputy Chief BRIXMIS 1981–1983[1]

The Oxford Dictionary of Current English defines the word 'liaison', which is at the core of the RMA, as 'communication or cooperation esp. between military forces or units.' It describes a 'liaison officer' as 'an officer acting as a link between allied forces or units of the same force.'[2] The RMA, however, did not define what they meant from the term 'liaison', which resulted in an ambiguity that the AMLMs exploited for the next forty-four (or forty-three in the case of the Americans and French) years. The emphasis this 'liaison' took changed over the years from simply interfacing with the Soviets to gathering intelligence on them, but to the outside world, the Mission appeared to live a charmed life, moving from meeting to meeting, from party to party, in their best uniforms.

Official Liaison

Overt liaison took the form of official meetings, functions, events, and communication (such as exchanges of letters) between the Commanders-in-Chief BAOR/RAFG, through their nominated representative, Chief BRIXMIS, with the Commander-in-Chief GSFG, through his nominated representatives at SERB. Many of the tour officers were qualified Russian interpreters (or the lesser 'linguist' qualification), which allowed them to interpret for senior British officers, but also converse with their counterparts on equal terms – it was a vitally important part of Mission work.

SERB was an offshoot of HQ GSFG and an interesting organisation: Chief SERB was a colonel, and the team included his deputy, English, French, and German interpreters (SERB were notionally responsible for relations with the East Germans, although most of their focus was on the AMLMs), and administrators, plus a few supernumerary officers. These officers often appeared to be too old or too young for their rank and wielded disproportionate influence, suggesting they were GRU (or even KGB officers in army uniform). They also stayed in post longer than normal Soviet officer postings. The location of the SERB office close to the Mission House in

Potsdam became particularly important after GSFG moved its HQ away from Potsdam to Karlshorst in East Berlin (where the Soviet Berlin garrison would remain) in 1951, and then to Zossen-Wünsdorf in 1958.[3] SERB was the primary point of contact for the issue of touring passes (including visitor passes), administration and maintenance requests for the Mission House (including local staff and rations), liaising about Western defectors, lower to mid-level protests such as illegal detentions, invitations for functions, events and social occasions, and the issue of PRA (Permanent Restricted Area) and TRA (Temporary Restricted Area) maps, which are explained in Chapter 4, 'Touring'. A new Chief BRIXMIS would present his credentials to C-in-C GSFG on arrival, and subsequently convey protests, messages or invitations from C-in-C BAOR. Otherwise, the day-to-day liaison was through Chief BRIXMIS, or his deputy, and Chief SERB, and this allowed frank exchanges of views to be made between the respective powers *outside* of diplomatic channels. A hierarchical process developed that was useful to de-escalate potentially serious incidents: minor protests would be made at deputy level (Deputy Chief BRIXMIS, Deputy Chief SERB), which could be escalated (and for more serious incidents) to chief level (Chief BRIXMIS, Chief SERB). Further escalation could go to chief of staff (COS) level (COS BAOR, COS GSFG) and finally to commander-in-chief (C-in-C) level (C-in-C BAOR, C-in-C GSFG). Beyond that, it went to the diplomats and government ministers, where things could get serious very quickly.

Protests were regularly delivered to the Soviets (such as for violent detentions), which rarely received an apology; protests would also come from SERB, with the ultimate sanction of being declared persona non grata (PNG) and banned from entering East Germany. This effectively ended the person's tour with the Mission, putting to waste the extensive training given and experience gained, and caused a lot of disruption to operations – a costly and frustrating situation for all concerned. Personnel PNG'd in the GDR were not usually accepted thereafter as attachés in the Soviet Union. Thankfully PNGs were relatively infrequent.

The first official PNG took place in 1956 when Lieutenant Colonel Mark Askwith was given his marching orders after an altercation with some Soviet officers about the Soviet invasion of Hungary. It was preceded by an 'unofficial' PNG in the early 1950s for Wing Commander G. F. B. Hutchinson, the senior RAF officer (until 1955, the deputy chief was army). He was involved in a serious incident at Rechlin/Larz where he was fired upon and detained by Soviet air force sentries. This was followed by a letter from SERB saying that if Hutchinson continued to tour in the Soviet Zone, his 'safety could not be guaranteed' – tantamount to a PNG. Hutchinson was posted out of BRIXMIS on the order of C-in-C RAFG. Askwith's PNG in 1956 was followed in 1957 by the PNGing of Chief BRIXMIS, Brigadier Wynn-Pope (1955–1957), and another 'safety could not be guaranteed' letter for Brigadier Packard (Chief BRIXMIS 1959–1960). Other PNGs included Major Johnathan Backhouse and Squadron Leader Neil McLean in 1966, Squadron Leader Rod Saar in 1972, and Captain Bob Longhorn in 1984.

It should be noted that there was no liaison or socialising with the East Germans – the AMLMs did not recognise what became the German Democratic Republic in 1949, and refused to deal with them at any level, which irritated them immensely. It should also be remembered that there was no formal mechanism for the British forces in

West Germany to communicate with the Soviet forces in East Germany apart from BRIXMIS, and like the famous 'hotline' between Washington D.C. and Moscow, it was a useful communications bridge in times of crisis.

Another aspect of formal liaison was to support the Royal Military Police (RMP) to ensure the regular Soviet ceremonies at their War Memorial in West Berlin went smoothly. The memorial was in the British sector just to the side of Charlottenburger Chaussee, one of Berlin's grandest avenues that ran between the Brandenburg Gate and the Siegessäule victory column in Tiergarten.* When Stalin chose this location back in summer 1945, he fully expected his other allies to leave the city and this prestigious monument would be under his control. Stalin's hopes were not realised, and elaborate arrangements had to be made for a squad of Soviet troops to be processed through Checkpoint CHARLIE every week to take over guard duties at the monument. They stayed in a guardroom behind the monument and would mount guard in front of the curved colonnaded structure topped off with a giant bronze statue of a Red Army soldier and flanked by Red Army artillery pieces and two T-34 tanks. Behind the memorial are the graves of more than 2,000 Soviet soldiers, killed in the battle for Berlin. Three times a year, the Soviet Army put on a remembrance parade at the memorial and BRIXMIS linguists helped organise the event and liaised with the GSFG protocol team and the Royal Military Police who were tasked with ensuring the ceremony went smoothly.

BRIXMIS also sponsored the Remembrance Day service at the Stahnsdorf war graves cemetery just south of Berlin, which was well attended by the diplomatic corps and invited Soviet guests, with tea afterwards at the Mission House. The Mission also organised wreath-laying visits at three former Nazi concentration camps inside the GDR: Buchenwald outside Weimar, Sachsenhausen near Oranienburg, north of Berlin, and Ravensbrück near Fürstenberg in the north of the country. They would always invite the local *komendant* (like a provost marshal) and would lay wreaths at Soviet memorials too, followed by a lunch and much conviviality fuelled by vodka and wartime solidarity. The British were always careful not to bring up the fact that the camps continued to be used by the Soviets and East Germans after the war had ended. Mission personnel also facilitated visits from the Imperial (now Commonwealth) War Graves Commission to First and Second World War cemeteries located in the Soviet zone.

The Weil affair was a good example of formal liaison. On 7 November 1970 (the fifty-third anniversary of the Russian Revolution), Ekkehard Weil, a 22-year-old neo-Nazi from West Berlin, shot and wounded Private Ivan Shcherbak, a Soviet sentry on guard duty at the Soviet War Memorial in Tiergarten. Colonel Grechishken, Chief SERB, delivered a strongly worded protest from C-in-C GSFG to Chief BRIXMIS. On 11 November Deputy Chief BRIXMIS Group Captain John Lewis informed SERB that an arrest had been made in relation to the shooting and the accused would go on trial in

---

* In 1953, Charlottenburger Chaussee was renamed Straße des 17. Juni by the West Berlin Senat to commemorate the lives lost in the 1953 East German workers' uprising. In a direct challenge to their East German neighbours, the Federal Republic also declared 17 June to be a national holiday in West Germany, which continued through to reunification.

a British Military Government court under a legal procedure set up in 1945 to combat looting that had not been used since 1947. It was vitally important for British/Soviet relations that justice was 'done and seen to be done' in this case, and to send a clear message to the other Western Allies and the citizens of West Berlin that Great Britain respected the four-power agreements.[4] The Soviets produced two .22-calibre bullets that had been removed from Private Shcherbak as evidence, and British investigators confirmed that no evidence of other anti-Soviet activity had been found – it appeared to be an isolated and unpremeditated attack. The trial took place between 27 February and 8 March 1971 with a British judge and prosecutor, German defence lawyers, and mostly Soviet witnesses – the courtroom was packed with representatives from GSFG, SERB, the Soviet Embassy and TASS. A BRIXMIS interpreter, Major David O'Connor RA, translated for the Soviet contingent. Weil received a sentence of six years in a German prison, which seemed to satisfy the Russians – there had been no whitewash or cover-up and it had been shown that British justice had teeth.*

During times of increased tension, often following a serious incident with the AMLMs (for example, a shooting) or on a wider international stage (for example, the Soviet invasion of Afghanistan), orders would come down from on high to curtail socialising with the Soviets, although successive Chiefs BRIXMIS argued that it was more important to *maintain* the dialogue in times of tension than it was in calmer moments. In the case of Afghanistan, the Foreign Office (FO) advice of 'business contact only' was contradictory and unhelpful, so Brigadier Perkins, chief at the time, decided to carry on as normal, believing liaison at all levels (from command to tour officer) was vitally important, be that a face-to-face meeting, or a social event.

Equally, from time to time, SERB was ordered to be uncooperative, and the Mission had to navigate around these official mood swings, which would range from hostile, to frosty, to distant, to tolerant, to open, verging on friendly. These personal relationships, at C-in-C, COS or chief of mission level, were hugely important in keeping the peace – professional bonds that transcended political whims and could resolve issues in the background before they escalated.

Liaison was not just for the Soviets: BRIXMIS were also called on to use their local knowledge to give VIP visitors tours of Potsdam, including the Schloss Cecilienhof, the venue of the 1945 Potsdam Conference, and other fine palaces – visitors would often have these stately homes all to themselves as there were not too many tourists inside East Germany. In the mid-1970s, the United Kingdom established diplomatic relations with the GDR and opened an embassy in East Berlin. Once the embassy and ambassador had established themselves, Mission operations officers (ground and air) held monthly meetings with the ambassador and his staff to brief them on military developments in the GDR, and, in return, received valuable political intelligence from the diplomats. This was the Mission's only official business inside East Berlin itself, as Headquarters Berlin Infantry Brigade (the British garrison in Berlin) were responsible for intelligence collection *inside* East Berlin. Despite the recognition of the East

---

* Weil was a slippery customer – he managed to escape from British custody before his trial but was recaptured soon after, and post-trial he escaped from Tegel prison, thankfully a West Berlin facility, not a British one. He was later arrested in Austria for burning down a synagogue.

German state diplomatically, BRIXMIS tours still refused to engage with Vopos (East German police, Volkspolizei) and NVA (Nationale Volksarmee, the East German armed forces) troops because their presence inside the GDR was a result of an agreement with the Soviets, not the East Germans.

Liaison could also be at a more personal level. On several occasions, SERB officers asked if their BRIXMIS colleagues could get hold of Western medication for family members that was not available behind the Iron Curtain. With the full agreement of Chief BRIXMIS and the Commanding Officer of the British Military Hospital in West Berlin, the required medication was sourced and discreetly passed to the very grateful Soviet officer. This and other gestures created goodwill that could be 'called upon' at some point in the future.

There was little formal contact direct with individual GSFG units unless it was linked to a specific event or when out in the field (often at gunpoint!), and most Soviet soldiers had no idea the AMLMs existed. Tours regularly made informal courtesy visits to the local *komendant* (where bonding took place over bottles of vodka or whisky and Western cigarettes), which would often pay dividends when he was summoned following a detention. The *komendant* had numerous responsibilities: he acted as the military police headquarters for the local garrison; he controlled the local VAI (Voyennaya avtomobil'naya inspektsiya, or ВАИ, in their UAZ-469 jeeps with distinctive red stripes and ВАИ stencilled on the side), the military vehicle inspectorate, which checked Soviet vehicles for roadworthiness and their papers and loads to stop the theft or misuse of official goods; he managed and deployed the traffic regulators ('reggies') who would direct military convoys; he was the main point of contact with the local East German authorities (often with no love lost between them); and was involved in the detention and investigation of allied military liaison mission tours.

GSFG personnel were regularly rotated back to the Soviet Union (conscripts were rotated back after serving their two-year national service), and monitoring these withdrawals and replacements was an ongoing task for the AMLMs. However, in the late 1950s, as part of Khrushchev's arms reduction 'olive branch', BRIXMIS personnel were invited to witness several farewell parades for GSFG units that were being 'permanently' withdrawn to the Soviet Union. These parades (at Weimar, Cottbus, Luckenwalde, and Schwerin) were grand affairs, with the troops lined up in front of senior officers, local dignitaries, and crowds of young FDJ members.* After lengthy speeches, the FDJ contingent were sent across the parade ground to garland their Soviet 'protectors' with flowers, and then the soldiers were marched straight to waiting troop trains (carriages for the officers, cattle trucks for the soldiers) with all their equipment already loaded. BRIXMIS were there so they could report back that Khrushchev was withdrawing his troops, but the truth was somewhat different to the glossy PR –

* FDJ – Freie Deutsche Jugend, the official East German youth organisation for 14- to 25-year-olds.

the numbers returning were considerably exaggerated and at the same time he was deploying fresh units into East Germany armed with the latest KIT.*

One of the more unusual liaison tasks undertaken by the Mission was to supply interpreters to Spandau Prison, located in the British sector. Since 1947, Spandau Prison had been used to incarcerate seven former Nazis who were convicted at the Nuremberg War Crimes Tribunals following the end of the Second World War. Part of the post-war agreement was that each of the Four Powers would take turns guarding the prisoners and for the next forty years, the guard rotated monthly. By October 1966, six of the seven inmates had been released apart from Rudolf Hess, Hitler's deputy, who had been sentenced to life.† The official Foreign Office interpreter, Mr Sanders, had continued working long past his retirement date, but eventually got fed up waiting for Hess to die and left. BRIXMIS was therefore called on to supply an interpreter to take over as duty interpreter. The interpreter would attend the monthly governors' meeting (short meeting, long lunch), accompany them and the four medical officers to visit Prisoner No. 7 in his cell, or accompany Hess and his entourage (four governors, four medical officers, and guard) should he have to visit the British Military Hospital in Charlottenburg, where a whole floor was kept ready for him. This strange duty ended in August 1987 when Hess committed suicide, although BRIXMIS (and SERB) got involved in assisting the RMP's Special Investigation Branch (SIB), which investigated the death. Spandau was demolished soon after his suicide to avoid it becoming a Nazi shrine, and a NAAFI supermarket was built on the site.‡ This was not the last mention of Spandau in the BRIXMIS story – it was used as a codeword to disguise a highly secret operation in the 1970s/80s, Operation TAMARISK, and later Operation TOMAHAWK, which are described in Chapter 4, 'Touring'.

Liaison skills were useful in the later careers of BRIXMIS personnel, many of whom went on to become military attachés, or worked in other quasi-diplomatic or intelligence roles. As the Cold War spluttered to an end in the late 1980s/early 1990s, some went on to work in arms control and inspection roles, where such skills were ideal.

Entertaining

Formal and informal entertaining was an important part of the role, and relations were generally cordial between poacher and gamekeeper – it was one of the paradoxes of mission life that during the day tour personnel would be chased, shot at, beaten up, and detained by Soviets, but could be socialising with them in the evening – a real 'Jekyll and Hyde' experience. Mission entertaining took various forms: occasional reciprocal visits by the respective C-in-Cs to each other's headquarters,

---

* The 6th Motor Rifle Division was also repatriated to the USSR at the end of the 1970s – a rare withdrawal that was done for PR purposes.

† The other inmates in Spandau were Erich Raeder, Karl Dönitz, Konstantin von Neurath, Walther Funk, Baldur von Schirach, and Albert Speer.

‡ The NAAFI supermarket became known as 'Hessco', a play on the British supermarket chain Tesco.

official receptions at the Mission House in Potsdam, the annual Queen's birthday parade, and the Berlin Military Tattoo, both held at the Olympic Stadium in West Berlin. The latter two were classic examples of British 'soft power' in action. There were also many informal social events at the Mission House, the SERB offices, Soviet officers' club, or various restaurants and watering holes in Potsdam, where much alcohol was consumed by all concerned. The regular BRIXMIS film nights were very popular, although choosing a film that would not offend the Soviets' surprisingly delicate sensibilities was often a challenge – slapstick comedies were always a safe bet. Christmas parties were also popular where carols were sung and gifts exchanged. Successive chiefs BRIXMIS saw this entertaining as an essential part of Mission operations and argued for their continuation even during times of international tension. As well as building good relationships, low-level intelligence could also be obtained.

There was also a busy social calendar with the other AMLMs: the Bastille Day reception at the French Mission House was always a grand affair, and the 4th of July picnic/barbecue at the US Mission House was very popular, and considerably less formal than the other functions. It was always a challenge to plan social events involving SERB or GSFG personnel as they would never RSVP to invitations and organisers would never know how many were attending (and therefore how many to be catered for) until they turned up at the Mission House. At these functions, the Soviet party was normally tightly controlled by political or senior officers, and if an officer (or his wife) was becoming overly friendly to their hosts, they would be taken to one side and spoken to. It was not unheard of that a Soviet wife would be hauled off the dance floor if she was 'enjoying herself' too much. Other times, the Soviet guests were hard work, and it took some robust social 'marshalling' and lots of booze to get the party going. However, a nod from the senior officer (or political/GRU/KGB representative) would bring the evening to a swift conclusion, and the Soviet party would all traipse (or stagger) out en masse to their waiting cars. Mission personnel would also be entertained by the Soviets, with formal functions at HQ GSFG in Karlshorst (later Zossen-Wünsdorf) and at SOXMIS in Bünde, West Germany, normally to celebrate important dates in the Soviet calendar, such as the anniversary of the October Revolution and Red Army Day. The Soviets always put on a good performance, with guards of honour parading in perfect time and tours of immaculate barracks and gleaming vehicles, but the normal Soviet soldier was never seen – it was all done for show. Formal functions with the Soviets could be more an ordeal than a pleasure and were carefully choreographed.

These examples of formal liaison could, quite reasonably, lead an outsider to see BRIXMIS as 'champagne soldiering': personnel spending their evenings going from party to party or glad handing or schmoozing with fellow officers, where the greatest risk would be from an excess of alcohol or a dodgy vol-au-vent. The outsider would be very wrong because the form of liaison that took up most of their time and energy was anything but glamorous.

The other side of the Mission work was covert 'liaison' in the form of 'touring', where small teams of specially trained officers and men were despatched into East Germany (effectively 'enemy' territory) to collect intelligence on the Soviet and East

German ground and air forces as a key part of NATO's intelligence and early-warning alert. They would wear uniform and travel in marked, highly modified performance vehicles, theoretically with the same protection as diplomatic couriers, while playing an elaborate and often very dangerous game of cat and mouse with the Soviets, Vopos, NVA and the Stasi. The Stasi would be a constant irritation for the Mission throughout its history.* Out in the field, it was down to the ingenuity of the tourers to observe without being seen, and the vigilance of the observed to spot and chase the observers away. As with a thief, the trick for the observer was not to be caught and, in this case, the treasure was intelligence. This part of the BRIXMIS story operated 365 days a year right up to 2359 hours on 2 December 1990, and is told in Chapter 4, 'Touring'.

---

* The Stasi were named after Staatssicherheitsdienst from the Ministerium für Staatssicherheit, the East German Ministry for State Security, or Secret Police, a.k.a. the narks. Nark is an old Anglo-Australian word, used to describe a snitch, informer, or a generally irritating or unpleasant person. It was used by British PoWs during the Second World War to refer to someone who could not be trusted, someone who could betray possible escape attempts to the German guards. In the early days of the Mission, someone (who may once have been a PoW) began using the word to describe the Soviet and later the Stasi officers who tailed and tried to disrupt tours, and the name stuck, being adopted by USMLM as well. The origins of the word were lost on many of the Americans, who confused it with Narc, slang for a narcotics policeman, but it nicely described the typically unpleasant individuals employed by State Security to counter mission activity.

Chapter 3

The Unit

'This was the world of Bulldog Drummond, rather than that of George Smiley.'
Group Captain Richard Bates AFC (2001)
Deputy Chief BRIXMIS 1981–1983[1]

BRIXMIS was hard to pigeon-hole within the British military – it was a small, unusual, and highly strategic unit, whose actions could have a disproportionately large impact on international relations. It was intelligence based, which often blurs the lines, and although its headquarters was in West Berlin, Chief BRIXMIS did not have a formal relationship with the Commander Berlin Infantry Brigade or even the British GOC/Commandant but kept them fully briefed and relied on their support. There was also the nebulous matter of the accreditation to the Commander-in-Chief of the Soviet forces in Germany. Despite these idiosyncrasies, BRIXMIS managed to thrive for more than four decades.

However, for its first decade the responsibility for BRIXMIS bounced around the British establishment. The RMA accredits BRIXMIS to the Commander-in-Chief Group of Soviet Forces Germany (from 1989, the Western Group of Forces, WGF), and because of the political sensitivities around the Soviet Union, BRIXMIS effectively reported to the British Foreign Office via the Combined Service Division of the CCG(BE), the British Military Government in occupied Germany. Although the Foreign Office also controlled the Secret Intelligence Service (SIS, often wrongly referred to as MI6), there was inevitably a degree of culture clash between the military and diplomatic organisations. Over time, it became clear that BRIXMIS did not fit well with the Foreign Office, and discussions began in November 1951 to move them over to the War Office, specifically under BAOR control. The War Office stressed that 'BRIXMIS should NOT repeat NOT be considered under SHAPE [NATO Supreme Headquarters Allied Powers Europe] control in any way', and nothing should be done to alert the Soviets to these discussions.[2] Unsurprisingly, progress was slow between Whitehall and Germany, but the wider political situation would force a decision.

The RMA had SOXMIS accredited to the Commander- (later Commanders-) in-Chief British Occupation Forces Germany. The British C-in-C at the time of signing was Marshal of the Royal Air Force Sir William Sholto Douglas (as incorrectly named in the RMA), who was the British Military Governor of Germany and responsible for the British Army of the Rhine and the British Air Forces of Occupation (which became the Second Tactical Air Force, 2TAF in 1951, and RAFG in 1959).* Douglas was succeeded in November 1947 by Lieutenant General Sir Brian Robertson, Bart., the 'R' in the RMA. As part of the process to rehabilitate (West) Germany into a sovereign state, in September 1949 the military governors became high commissioners, and the post of C-in-C British Occupation Forces Germany was abolished. SOXMIS continued to be accredited to General Robertson, who was now seconded to the Foreign Office, but the Soviets did not object and the status of the RMA was unaffected. Robertson was succeeded as high commissioner in 1950 by career diplomat Sir Ivone Kirkpatrick, losing the military connection at the top of British interests in Germany, but again the Soviets accepted the change. However, with the signing of the Bonn Conventions in May 1952, which cleared the way for the Federal Republic of Germany's independence, the prospect of SOXMIS being accredited to the British Ambassador (who in turn was accredited to the president of the Federal Republic of Germany) may have been a step too far for the Soviets, potentially jeopardising the status of BRIXMIS as 'a valuable source of information and intelligence on the Soviet Zone of Germany'. Kirkpatrick was concerned they might tear up the RMA or force the Mission to be accredited to the Soviet Ambassador to the 'so-called German Democratic Republic', which would have been problematic as the United Kingdom did not recognise the GDR at the time!

Kirkpatrick therefore proposed that it was time to revert to a more literal interpretation of the RMA and SOXMIS should be accredited to C-in-C *BAOR*.[3] Although there was no obligation to act tripartitely, there was a logic to presenting a uniform approach to the Soviets – the Soviet missions in the American and French zones already reported to their respective Western C-in-Cs. At the same time, Kirkpatrick suggested that BRIXMIS should simultaneously become responsible to C-in-C BAOR, although he stressed that the high commissioner, and subsequently the ambassador, should be consulted on 'all matters having political implications, or bearing generally on our relations with the Russians', with the FO having the final say. This solution may have resolved some organisational difficulties but was felt to be a retrograde step for the RAF, whose involvement in the direction of BRIXMIS was further watered down – it would take several years for this to be resolved.

The change was effective from January 1953, although the Foreign Office continued to try to exert influence over BRIXMIS operations for some years after, especially regarding the Mission contravening PRAs and MRSs for operational reasons and the risk of political fallout. There was much hand-wringing between the FO, the Joint Services Intelligence Group Germany (JSIG), and the High Commission in Bonn about the value of BRIXMIS and if/when the high commissioner and/or the FO should be consulted, and it was clear that the Mission's operation effectiveness was reduced by this control.[4] In August 1954 they assessed that 'BRIXMIS in EAST GERMANY supplied a considerable amount of low grade *de visu* intelligence' (*de visu* means 'with one's own eyes'). It was, somewhat grudgingly, conceded that 'If the British mission

---

* Although the RMA name-checks Air Marshal Sir Sholto Douglas, he was, in fact, promoted to Marshal of the Royal Air Force, a five-star rank, in January 1946 – Marshal of the Royal Air Force Sir William Sholto Douglas (later elevated to 1st Baron Douglas of Kirtleside) GCB, MC, DFC.

were withdrawn these advantages would be totally lost to us, since we could not replace the mission with secret agents [given the extent of the police state] or any other type of source'. This wish for FO control was reflected in the Mission's priorities in their early years following the Second World War and as East Germany attempted to rebuild itself. The Cold War was still in its early days and the progress (or lack) of economic development had major political implications. A 1954 list of target areas demonstrates this bias with the *italicised* economic targets accounting for ten of the nineteen areas:

Main subjects and activities covered by BRIXMIS:

1. *Ports and shipbuilding*
2. *Inland waterways*
3. Order of battle (ORBAT)
4. Training areas
5. Barracks
6. New equipment
7. Manoeuvres
8. Airfields
9. Radar
10. Aircraft and associated equipment
11. *Roads, railway bridges*
12. *Fuel storage*
13. *Fuel distribution by road*
14. Ammunition storage
15. *Power stations*
16. *Factories*
17. *Mining etc.*
18. *Agriculture*
19. *Consumer goods situation*[5]

It took some years for the Mission's emphasis to shift from being predominantly economic (with some military on the side) to being predominantly military and technical (with only the bare minimum of economics). The situation came to a head with the arrival of Brigadier Baines, the hard-charging Chief BRIXMIS 1972–1974, and the FO's apron strings were finally cut, although they did not go down in good grace or without a fight.[6]

As with all organisations, the person at the top has a strong influence on the organisation's culture, if not its output. This was especially so with BRIXMIS because of its unique role in the British military and unusual place in the Berlin command structure, and therefore it enjoyed an unusual degree of autonomy and responsibility (a full list of Chiefs and Deputy Chiefs BRIXMIS is included in the appendices). It was also a tri- and later dual-service unit, which was unusual at the time.

The first few years of the Mission were somewhat chaotic as the dust began to settle after the war and the battle lines of the fledgling Cold War were drawn – Chiefs and Deputy Chiefs BRIXMIS tended to be experienced combat leaders, ideal personality types to navigate around an uncertain enemy and a fluid and dynamic operational environment. There was still a lot of sorting out to be done and the intelligence-collection potential of touring was only being realised. While BRIXMIS will have efficiently been run as a *military* unit, it lacked the infrastructure, resources, and processes to maximise the *intelligence* collection. The arrival of Colonel R. P. Mortimer as deputy chief in 1952 brought a much-needed steadying hand and led to the implementation of operational and administrative procedures that helped streamline the organisation and improve efficiency. This approach was reinforced by Brigadier John E. F. Meadmore OBE as chief in 1953, who had benefitted from a posting as deputy chief between 1948 and 1950. These two laid the foundations for the powerful intelligence-collection operation that was to come.

Despite being nominally a tri-service unit, BRIXMIS was dominated by the army – the RAF had been long arguing for more senior representation at the Mission, so in late 1955 it was decided that from then on the deputy chief would be an RAF group captain (equivalent to an army colonel) who would stand in as chief when the latter was away and also head up the RAF contingent at the Mission. The first person to hold this position was Group Captain F. G. (George) Foot OBE who joined at the end of 1955 and the practice continued until the close of the Mission. Foot introduced new touring tactics and photographic techniques that transformed air touring within the Mission and partially improved interservice relations in Whitehall and at the Mission. That said, the RAF continued to lack back-office support for targeting, research, and exploitation of intelligence. Even into the early 1960s, the Air Ministry maintained a separate tasking/reporting channel with BRIXMIS, under the noses of the army hierarchy there, to ensure air tours were aligned with the wider interests of the RAF (especially targeting information for NATO strategic bombers).

The chief, however, could still have a big influence on operations: in March 1956 Brigadier Charles C. D. T. (Denys) Wynn-Pope OBE was appointed Chief BRIXMIS and introduced a new aggressive, hard-charging approach to touring. Wynn-Pope was a man of action who lived life on the edge, loved being out in the field, and sometimes let his enthusiasm cloud his judgement. He already had a bad reputation with the Soviets following an earlier posting as military attaché in Moscow and was refused the normal official courtesies on his arrival in Berlin. His arrival coincided with a change in the monitoring and interception of AMLM tours, with a marked rise in the intensity and aggression of narking. Up to then, Stasi vehicles would patrol with a Soviet MVD (predecessor to the KGB) officer in the back coordinating activity over the radio; from 1956, the MVD withdrew, and Stasi narks went around in pairs with one manning the radio.* Wynn-Pope's new aggressive style would be short-lived, and he was famously PNG'd following the 'Battle of Rembrandtstraße' in August 1957, which is described in Chapter 6, 'The Opposition'.

---

* It was not until the fall of the Berlin Wall that BRIXMIS discovered the true extent of coordination that went into the anti-mission activity. Multiple cars, as many as six or eight, were often involved along with Vopos, NVA units and Soviet intelligence, all coordinated by two-way radio, with sometimes a control vehicle disguised as a van or an ambulance.

Wynn-Pope was succeeded as Chief BRIXMIS in September 1957 by Brigadier the Hon. M. F. (Miles) Fitzalan-Howard MC, who proved to be a far more stabilising influence than his erratic predecessor. He further streamlined the operation and improved relations and coordination with the Americans and French, setting the tone for future cooperation, creating the modern BRIXMIS.

In November 1958 Khrushchev issued his famous ultimatum, giving the Western Powers six months to agree to withdraw from Berlin and make it a free, demilitarised city or he would hand responsibility for the Soviet sector of the city (East Berlin) to the East Germans. This would include all lines of communication into the city (road, rail, and air), and effectively impose a siege on West Berlin and its two million citizens. Although Khrushchev would eventually back down, this pronouncement had the effect of empowering and energising East German leader Walter Ulbricht who sensed an opportunity to take on the hated AMLMs.

When the Mission was formed, the Royal Navy was represented by a tour officer from the naval service or Royal Marines; however, when the Soviets restricted access to the Baltic coastline in 1958, the raison d'être for a naval representative vanished. The last to hold this post as a part-time tourer was Major Gerry Ritson RM, and his departure left a vacancy. The army declined to fill it, so the RAF jumped at the opportunity and appointed Squadron Leader H. (Harry) Nunwick, who joined as an electronics expert, boosting the RAF capability on the ground and in the air. The Royal Navy would have to wait until 1986 when the PRAs were lifted along the Baltic Coast and intelligence collection could begin again. This was led by US Marine Corps personnel from the USMLM on behalf of the US Navy, and indirectly, the Royal Navy.

'There's a bit of a riot going on ... '[7]

In July 1958, political unrest in the Middle East prompted Western governments to intervene – with American and British troops being deployed to strategic locations. The Soviets reacted badly to this neo-imperialism and began a barrage of propaganda throughout the Soviet Bloc, making totally fictitious claims that the British and Americans were bombing innocent women and children. The state-controlled media in East Germany picked the story up and ran it prominently, and it was discussed at the SED party conference in Berlin, which was attended by Soviet leader Nikita Khrushchev.* Ulbricht desperately sought international recognition for his fledgling communist regime and saw the crisis in the Middle East as an ideal opportunity to make political and propaganda capital. However, the only representatives of the Western imperialists in East Germany were the three Allied Military Missions.

On 18 July, Ulbricht, apparently without involving his Soviet masters, decided to stage his own 'spontaneous' and 'popular' demonstrations at the AMLMs. Early that morning, groups of young factory workers in East Berlin belonging to the

---

* SED – Sozialistische Einheitspartei Deutschlands; the Socialist Unity Party of Germany, East German ruling political party.

Kampfgruppen der Arbeiterklasse (KdA: Combat Groups of the Working Class, the East German factory militia) were told to down tools and assemble for a 'special' job. They assumed they were about to get a morning's 'voluntary rubble clearing', but they were given tins of red paint and told to pick up bricks from a nearby bombsite to 'help' with their 'peaceful' demonstration. A fleet of trucks delivered the workers to the BRIXMIS compound on Geschwister Schollstraße (similar groups were sent to the USMLM and MMFL mission houses), where they rampaged around the site, smashing windows, looting buildings, shouting slogans ('*Laßt Arabien ungeschoren, sonst brecht ihr euch dabei die Ohren*' – 'Leave Arabia unmolested, or you will break your ears in the process', which works much better in German!), daubing 'Hands off the Orient' graffiti on the walls and generally making quite a commotion. The duty officer, Major Chris Hallett MBE MC (17th/21st Lancers), had to face the crowd almost single handed and managed to retrieve a slightly charred Union flag after the mob tore it down and tried to set it on fire. The duty office/guardroom nearest the road (where the signals equipment was) was ransacked and all the communications cables were ripped out, effectively cutting the Mission House off from their West Berlin HQ – the 'mob' knew exactly where to look and the two Royal Signals corporals who manned the office beat a hasty retreat.

The corporals must have found a working phone box because Chief BRIXMIS, Brigadier Miles Fitzalan-Howard, was informed about the 'visitors' to his Mission compound and he immediately contacted SERB to ask for their assistance – the SLO told him that the Soviets 'had no power to control the peace-loving people of the Democratic Republic who were simply protesting at the actions of the Anglo-American imperialists'. Squadron Leader Hans Neubroch had just returned from a tour and was dropping off his films at BRIXMIS HQ only to be summoned by the chief: 'Sorry to put this on you, Hans, when you've been out all night, but it seems there's going to be a bit of a riot in Potsdam. When you've had a shave and some breakfast, would you mind going down and having a look around?' Neubroch, a fluent German speaker, got to the compound at around 0930 hours to find around 200 people milling about. The mob stopped and surrounded his car at the entrance, slashed his tyres, and began banging on the windows, trying to get the doors open. Another BRIXMIS car was leaning at a strange angle next to the pond containing the normally impeccably dressed Chris Hallett, nonchalantly doing *The Times* crossword but looking rather dishevelled and seemingly covered in blood. Closer inspection revealed that the blood was red paint, and Hallett was unharmed after the crowd had tried to turn his vehicle over. The crowd appeared to be good-humoured young factory workers having a bit of a lark on a day out, and while they went along with the chanting and singing of Party songs, it was clear that their hearts were not in it. The ringleaders, on the other hand, were party activists who were running around trying to whip the somewhat apathetic crowd into a frenzy of righteous indignation at the actions of Western imperialists. Neubroch was invited to address the crowd, beginning his speech (in fluent German) by saying, 'How nice it is to see so many of you here in the British Mission compound.' After a few minutes of trying to placate the crowd, he made a tactical retreat into the compound. At 1200 hours on the dot the party men shepherded the crowd back to their waiting trucks and they all headed back to their various factories – the Mission House riot was over.

Soon after, Colonel Sergeyev, the head of SERB, arrived accompanied by Brigadier Fitzalan-Howard, who was quietly but firmly delivering a lecture on the shortcomings of SERB and its failure to protect the Mission personnel and property. Although SERB was no use during the riot, it did provide a working party to help clear up afterwards.

A strong protest from C-in-C BAOR to his opposite number at GSFG was accompanied by a detailed claim for compensation, totalling £1,200.* The Mission did not expect to hear back but just over a year later the full amount was paid in brand-new Bank of England £5 notes – in serial number order but not forgeries. This unexpected payment was another example of Soviet scruples – the incident had embarrassed C-in-C GSFG and paying the bill was a way of saving face.

New Mission House, New HQ

Even before the 1958 riot, some of the buildings in the compound were in a poor state, so Chief BRIXMIS took the opportunity to ask SERB for new premises, preferably a large, single property near a lake like the USMLM mission house, rather than a compound of smaller buildings. Several weeks later, Colonel Sergeyev asked that Chief BRIXMIS meet him at the Glienicke Bridge wearing civilian clothes, not his usual uniform. Fitzalan-Howard and his interpreter met the Colonel and his interpreter, also in civvies, who drove them to a grand villa at Seestraße 34–37, not too far from the bridge and close to the SERB offices. Perhaps embarrassed by the actions of the East Germans, Sergeyev proposed that the grand villa, with extensive grounds reaching the water's edge, overlooking the Heiliger See and the Marmorpalais on the opposite bank, would make an ideal mission house for the British. It transpired that the building was currently being used as a school for East German 'intellectual cadres' (including dormitories with bunk beds) but could be made available in twenty-four hours – the subterfuge was to avoid alerting the occupants. Fitzalan-Howard agreed to Sergeyev's proposal, who unceremoniously evicted the East Germans, and a Soviet working party was detailed to completely refurbish the villa and grounds. The building was completely redecorated and furnished with a mix of Soviet and War Department issue furniture, which took a while, but the Mission were able to have a grand 'housewarming' party just before Christmas 1958. With the Soviets undertaking the building work, the British assumed that the villa would have been extensively bugged, so for the next thirty-two years the British Mission House personnel and tour personnel had to maintain strict communications discipline, only talking shop when in the grounds and out of earshot – it was also likely that the East German were using high-power directional microphones from across the water at the Marmorpalais. The old compound had been converted into married quarters for NVA officers, which may have partly been the motivation to move the British mission. BRIXMIS remained at Seestraße 34–37 until 1990, which proved to be an ideal venue for formal events, social occasions, family weekends, and

---

* Different reports have the bill at £500, £1,000, and £1,200 – the actual figure is lost to time (and the Duty Cashier's cashbook).

entertaining friends and visitors. From 1963 to 1990, MMFL occupied Seestraße 40–44, just along the road to the town.

The new Mission House's permanent staff comprised the Mission House warrant officer and his family, who lived in a flat at the top of the building and managed a team of locally employed East German domestic staff. There were two duty drivers, one army and one RAF, who did a week at a time at the Mission House, and each evening a duty officer would come over from HQ BRIXMIS. There were also two Royal Signals radio technicians based in the roof space, operating a radio link back to London Block – signals traffic had to be encoded as it would have been intercepted by the Stasi.* At weekends, the Mission House warrant officer would return to West Berlin, staying at Edinburgh House (the British 'transit' hotel on Theodor-Heuss-Platz) for a change of scenery and was replaced by a duty officer. The highly variable Soviet-supplied rations were supplemented with deliveries from the Cook Sergeant Major in Berlin – all in all, the British lived quite well in Potsdam, with all the domestic duties (including cooking) handled by the staff, with extensive well-manicured gardens going down to the lake, where there were several boats for use by residents and guests, and excellent swimming. In the early 1980s, Mission House Warrant Officer Harry Alderson (a former Tour NCO) even built a mini-golf course on one of the lawns. Tours would come and go at all hours ensuring the place was always busy, and numbers swelled considerably when there was a function or an event. It was confirmed after the fall of the Wall and closure of the Mission that all the locally employed Potsdam Mission House domestic staff were being run by either the Stasi or the KGB as a precondition for their employment, half working for the Stasi and half for the KGB, often playing both sides with varying degrees of success.† For some reason (better handling, better pay, greater influence on their lives from the East German State?), the Stasi staff were far more productive in terms of usable intelligence than their KGB colleagues, which the Soviets resented; in some instances, this led to the Stasi informers being inexplicably sacked.[8] The married quarters domestic staff were also viewed with some suspicion. One of the cleaners was dismissed when it was discovered that she was removing wastepaper from officers' homes, which was passed to the Stasi and resulted in tours being ambushed. Another cleaner admitted that her son's acceptance into the college of his choice was dependent on the quantity and quality of intelligence she could pick up as she moved around the building. The deputy chief sympathised with her plight and arranged to give her 'chickenfeed' (low-grade, out-of-date or inconsequential intelligence) to keep her Stasi handlers happy, and her son duly got his college place.

---

* By the 1980s, the Mission had stopped using radio communications with HQ as the telephone service became more reliable – conversations were in plain speech as the lines were (correctly) assumed to be bugged but were limited to housekeeping and routine matters – operational conversations only happened inside the secure area at London Block. It is assumed that the Mission House Warrant Officer would have used certain code words to alert the personnel at HQ of anything untoward.

† Local staff were employed through the PCLU, the Pioneer and Civil Labour Unit, which acted as a clearing house for civilian staff to work for the British occupation forces. The PCLU was thoroughly penetrated by the Stasi and KGB.

The presence of bugs (electronic sound recording devices) in the Mission House was never confirmed, and stories have now become part of BRIXMIS folklore. One story is that Mission staff complained loudly that repairs or redecoration to the property were overdue and that they were deeply disappointed in SERB for not fulfilling their obligations. As if by magic, the elusive contractors turned up the very next day. Information from a former SERB officer suggested that one particular room was bug-free and was used if they had to have any private conversations. It also transpired that the Mission House janitor, 'Young Werner', was a Stasi officer and happened to have a degree in electronic engineering, which would have been useful to maintain the recording equipment. The truth will probably never be known. As with the previous location, there was a Vopo sentry box opposite to watch the comings and goings of the Mission personnel (and report everything to the local MfS office). It was confirmed after the fall of the Wall that the Stasi were routinely monitoring all phone calls in and out of the Potsdam Mission House (and the USMLM and MMFL mission houses too) at a small MfS unit on Beyerstraße in Potsdam.[9]

In the early 1970s, there was discussion about moving the SOXMIS Mission House out of Bünde to a new location, which the Soviets were objecting to (Bünde was located at the heart of BAOR). In routine discussions with SERB about maintaining the BRIXMIS Potsdam Mission House, Chief SERB dropped the hint that it would not be necessary because a new Mission House was being prepared for BRIXMIS in Rangsdorf, close to GSFG HQ at Zossen-Wünsdorf. This would have been far less convenient for BRIXMIS operations, so the hint was taken, BAOR dropped the plans to relocate SOXMIS, and the Potsdam Mission House got redecorated – reciprocity in action.

Around the same time as the Mission House move from Geschwister Schollstraße to Seestraße, the British military headquarters in West Berlin moved from Fehrbelliner Platz to the Olympic Stadium complex in the Westend district of Charlottenburg, and BRIXMIS moved with them. The Mission's new West Berlin base was the top floor of the former Reich's sports administration building, which was christened 'London Block'.

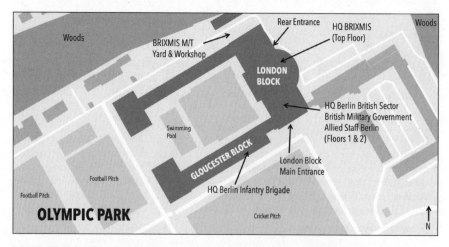

BRIXMIS HQ at London Block, Olympic Stadium Complex, West Berlin. (Author)

The building was shared with Sector HQ (where the general officer commanding, GOC, or commandant was based), the British Military Government, and Allied Staff Berlin. The SIS Berlin Station was one floor down from BRIXMIS. An adjacent wing (Gloucester Block) contained the HQ Berlin Infantry Brigade. The BRIXMIS Motor Transport (M/T) department had its yard and workshop on the opposite side of the building.

Organisation

BRIXMIS was a small organisation, starting at around forty people, and peaking at just under eighty, with an average split of seventy per cent army and thirty per cent RAF. As a result, only around 900 people served with the unit over its history, including the five Canadian officers who served from 1959 to 1972. The tight organisation created a unique esprit de corps among BRIXMIS personnel with less evidence of the inter-service rivalry generally seen in the military. It prepared them well for the rigours and challenges of operating inside the GDR. By 1988, the breakdown of personnel was:

> 21 officers
> 31 senior non-commissioned officers (SNCOs)/warrant officers (WOs)
> 26 other ranks
> **78 in total**

In addition, there were thirteen civilians, including the East German domestic staff, German mechanics, and some British clerical staff.

The core structure was constrained by the number of touring passes agreed in the RMA in 1946 and it therefore stayed relatively constant throughout its history: command, touring, and support. However, as the Mission evolved, the threat intensified, and technology improved, the structure developed with it, including how the thirty-one passes were filled. It should be noted that Mission personnel (especially the touring members) did *not* have a 'war role' (such as admin staff becoming medics or catering staff taking on guard duties) unlike all other British military personnel in Berlin as it was generally assumed they would be involved in covert action inside the GDR, possibly assisting special forces, and that they would be specifically targeted by the Stasi and/or KGB for capture or assassination because of their specialist knowledge. Mission personnel were also exempt from the regular ROCKING HORSE exercises, where all members of the Berlin Infantry Brigade would deploy to their emergency (wartime) deployment positions.

The thirty-one 'on-pass' touring pass holders, split between eleven officers and twenty 'other ranks', were the beating heart of the Mission. Some positions were filled with 'full-time' tourers, while others were 'part-time'. By the mid-1980s, the full-time officers were as follows:

1. Chief[A]
2. Deputy[A]
3. SO1[B]

4. Army tour officer #1[C]
5. Army tour officer #2
6. Army tour officer #3
7. Army tour officer #4
8. RAF tour officer #1[D]
9. RAF tour officer #2
10. RAF tour officer #3
11. 'Floating' pass for use by part-time tour officers[E]

[A] The chief and deputy retained their full-time passes at all times in case they were summoned to GSFG, but they would only tour occasionally.

[B] The SO1 (staff officer, grade 1, a lieutenant colonel) also toured occasionally but would hand in his pass when he went on leave so it could be used by a part-time tourer.*

[C] The four full-time 'army' tour officer positions were filled by three SO3 (captain) tour officers and the SO2 Liaison/Senior Interpreter (major), *five* nominated tourers for *four* passes ensuring that they were always filled.

[D] The three full-time 'RAF' tour officer positions were filled by three flight lieutenant tour officers and the deputy Squadron Leader Operations, *four* nominated tourers for *three* passes ensuring that they were always filled.

[E] The part-time tourers were SO2 Ops (Army), Squadron Leader Operations (RAF), SO2 Weapons, SO3 Ops, SO3 Research, SO3 Spandau, Squadron Leader Project ELECTRIC LIGHT, and the dedicated Chipmunk aircrew.

The full-time tour officers were typically 'on-pass' for about nine months of the year, the remainder spent on leave, on courses, or instructing at Ashford, and during those periods their passes were used by 'part-timers'. In the same way, the twenty other rank pass slots were always kept filled. The full-time 'other ranks' were the army and RAF Tour NCOs, the Tour Drivers, and the Mission House warrant officer (who didn't tour but needed to be able to move freely between Potsdam and West Berlin). The part-timers who filled the OR pass slots were the Weapons WO/SNCO, the Spandau and Research SNCOs, the REME SSgt, and the Geo Section WO/SNCO. The chief clerk, SQMS, the Special Section, the Women's Royal Army Corps (WRAC) clerks, the junior Geo JNCO, and the other members of the ELECTRIC LIGHT team did not tour. The various roles are discussed below.

Command

From 1948 Chief BRIXMIS was an army brigadier (one-star general) and in overall command. He was mostly involved in protocol matters or top-level liaison and was an 'occasional' tourer. His deputy was an RAF group captain (equivalent to a full army colonel), who deputised for the chief when he was away and was in day-to-day command of the RAF element (discipline, postings in and out, annual reports,

---

* Staff officers are graded 1 to 3, where, in army terms, an SO1 is a lieutenant colonel, an SO2 a major, and an SO3 a captain. Before the 1970s, they were known as General Staff Officers, GSO1, GSO2, and GSO3.

citations, etc.). He was an occasional 'full-time' tourer, sometimes as Chipmunk aircrew, normally as pilot. The army contingent was commanded by a lieutenant colonel (SO1) and was responsible for operations and management, including providing an overview of personnel matters for the chief. Inevitably he got involved in protocol and was another 'full-time' occasional tourer. Reporting to him was the adjutant, a non-touring major (SO2) or another lieutenant colonel (SO1) in charge of administration and protocol. The adjutant was also responsible for the Mission House in Potsdam, the M/T department, civilian labour, welfare (family support), security, and liaising with Berlin Infantry Brigade support departments, such as the Royal Electrical and Mechanical Engineers (REME) vehicle workshops and the brigade quartermaster. Until the early 1960s, the post was often filled by an experienced retired officer (RO), who joined the Mission as a contractor, keeping his former rank, security clearance, and pension. It was a good way of managing headcount and retaining valuable experience, which would normally be lost through promotions, postings, or retirement. However, that practice ended in the 1960s and a regular officer was posted into the unit. Normally an adjutant would be a senior captain or major (SO2 level staff officer); however, in BRIXMIS, the adjutant was often a lieutenant colonel (SO1), reflecting the need for experience/seniority when dealing with the Soviets.

Operations

The more integrated approach to touring introduced by Brigadier Fitzalan-Howard increased the workload for the operations officers, especially when the Soviets changed the PRA map or issued TRAs. The chief asked BAOR to provide an additional full-time non-touring officer to assist with the planning burden but they could not spare anyone without impacting on other intelligence work. However, they suggested offering the position to the Canadian Army, who snapped up the opportunity with five Canadian officers serving with the Mission between 1959 and 1972. However, because Canada was not party to the RMA, the Canadian officers were unable to tour so were limited by their unfamiliarity with the touring environment and its peculiar challenges. In 1966, their role was changed to assisting the British SO2 (Ops), which overcame that issue.[10]

Army (ground) and RAF (air) tours were run separately until the early 1970s, when Brigadier Baines created a joint operations office with the two ops officers sitting together in the same room – this successfully integrated army and RAF touring, and by the 1980s tour officers could be sent on a ground or an air tour, irrespective of their service allegiance. A 'coordination officer' was brought in at SO2 level (a major) as part of the command team, but it was found that the two operations officers could coordinate their activity successfully without the extra layer of management and the role was discontinued at the end of his posting.

Army Operations were run by the SO2 (Ops), a major, who was a part-time tourer responsible for directing the army/ground tour programme.* He was assisted by SO3

---

* The BRIXMIS operations officer was described by Brigadier Baines (Chief 1972–1974) as 'the last *real* major in the British Army'.

(Ops), a captain, again a part-time tourer. The four full-time army tour officer positions were filled with SO3 captains and the SO2 Liaison/Senior Interpreter (see below) – *five* nominated people to ensure the *four* passes were always in use. Because of the 'robust' nature of touring, they tended to come from the 'teeth' or combat arms of the army: special forces (SAS), infantry (including the Parachute Regiment), armour, artillery, engineers, signals, and intelligence, who were comfortable with working in the field. Because of their operational experience, they were also capable of commenting sensibly on the quality of what they were observing. Many also had experience of covert 'special duties' operations in Northern Ireland, which brought valuable skills into the Mission. Language skills were also very important for tour officers, less so for tour NCOs. To preserve security, Intelligence Corps or special forces personnel would normally be 'badged' as Royal Corps of Transport, Royal Signals, or Parachute Regiment. In 1974, the post of SO2 Senior Tour Officer/Interpreter was created as a full-time tourer, and was 'tied' to the Intelligence Corps, giving the corps a foothold in the Operations team. The first incumbent (who later returned for two further tours) was Major Peter Johnston MBE, followed by Major Mike Hill. In the mid-1980s, the Mission's touring capacity was supplemented by a reserve SAS officer, Captain (later Major *and* Squadron Leader) Jerry Avery MBE SAS(V), over four summers (1984–1987) by special arrangement with Director Special Forces (DSF).[11] The Mission maintained a good relationship with the SAS and normally had one or two members (SNCOs or officers) on-pass; the DSF at the time of Avery's posting, Brigadier John Foley, would become Chief BRIXMIS in 1987.

The full-time army tour NCOs were 'tactically aware' senior NCOs – sergeants, staff sergeants or warrant officers. If a tour was being led by a senior officer (chief, deputy, or SO1), the 'tour NCO' role (front passenger) was often undertaken by a tour *officer*, rather than an *NCO*. Some senior NCOs would occasionally take the role of 'tour officer', with a more junior NCO as 'tour NCO'. BRIXMIS maintained close links with the SAS, based in Hereford, and a role developed for an 'SAS' SNCO, serving with the Regiment but on secondment to BRIXMIS as a full-time tourer, who would be tactical and touring equipment lead within the Mission. Using their knowledge of small-team operations, training, and covert warfare, they would accompany new tour officers to show them the ropes, and sometimes take the role of 'tour officer', leading the tour. A covert part of their role was to go out on 'SAS' tours, where they would do close recce of targets, establish sites for forward observation hides, and locate suitable landing zones for special forces insertion in the event of war, where troopers of 22 SAS were tasked with attacking specific targets (mostly route chokepoints) in East Germany.[12]

RAF Operations were led by Squadron Leader Operations (SLOps), a part-time tourer responsible for directing the RAF 'air' tour programme and the Chipmunk aerial reconnaissance sorties, both discussed in Chapter 4, 'Touring'. Because of the highly technical aspects of air intelligence (avionics, missilery, radar, etc.), it was important to keep knowledge within the team, so in the late 1950s it was decided to upgrade a flight lieutenant touring position to a squadron leader, and bring him in from the engineering branch, thus adding useful technical skills to the team. Up until the late 1970s, the more senior of the squadron leaders took the role of Squadron Leader Operations, with the more junior acting as his deputy. The split between these roles developed over time, with one of the squadron leaders concentrated on airfield targets, while the other focused on ground targets, or alternating on- and off-pass to allow more time for planning, but the roles eventually developed into a straightforward Squadron Leader Operations and Squadron Leader Operations 'in waiting', as his deputy, with sometimes as much as ten months' overlap with the deputy touring full time. Three flight lieutenants made up the RAF full-time touring team, that is *four* people to ensure the *three* RAF passes were always in use. The Chipmunk pilot also did ground tours on a part-time basis, and the squadron leader in charge of project ELECTRIC LIGHT (see below) also was a part-time tourer. The unit's de Havilland Chipmunk was based at RAF Gatow – it was initially piloted by any qualified pilot at the Mission or at Gatow (including the Station Commander), but by the 1980s, it was recognised that a dedicated pilot could deliver better and more consistent results. By doing some ground tours, the pilot could better understand what could, and could not, be seen on the ground, which helped him when flying the Chipmunk.

The RAF tour NCOs were sergeants, flight sergeants, or warrant officers and were full-time air tourers. As with the army/ground tours, if a tour was being led by a senior officer (chief or deputy chief), the 'tour NCO' role was often taken by a tour officer. RAF tour personnel tended to be aircrew (pilots or navigators), so were familiar with the rigours of operational flying, air weaponry and air combat, but not necessarily working in the field.

Some, however, joined from the technical, engineering or intelligence specialisms, with knowledge of radar, avionics, and air defence. An alternative approach might have been to recruit from the RAF Regiment (who carry out soldiering tasks relating to the delivery of air power), but this did not appear to be a factor in selection decisions – the Ministry of Defence (MoD) RAF Air Secretaries Branch, who handled the postings for RAF personnel, were rarely briefed on BRIXMIS's role because of security considerations – therefore RAF tour personnel often had a steeper learning curve than their army counterparts. There also tended to be fewer linguists among the RAF contingent.

BRIXMIS started out as a tri-service operation, which was unusual at the time; the Royal Navy was represented by captains (equivalent to full army colonels) and majors from the Royal Marines. They had their own cars and drivers. Their job was to monitor East German and Soviet naval operations along the Baltic coast; however, in 1952, while the East Germans were sealing off the Inner German Border, the Soviets put all the Baltic coast into a Permanent Restricted Area, making it out of bounds for tours. The naval team were reassigned to other roles and British naval intelligence collection would not restart until the mid-1980s when the coastal PRAs were lifted.

Before the various specialist departments were set up, specific officers were given briefs to look after a particular aspect of the Mission's work. For example, the 'senior interpreter' was also in charge of the 'Personalities' database, which profiled individual Soviet officers, a 'touring major' became the Soviet order of battle (ORBAT) specialist, one 'touring captain' focused on the NVA ORBAT, and another oversaw nark activity. However, touring could not have taken place without the support teams who prepared the way for them and handled the raw intelligence product they collected inside East Germany.

Weapons

The Weapons team were responsible for technical intelligence and 'first-line' analysis of tour highlights forms (see below), draft tour reports, and Chipmunk imagery. The team was run by an SO2 non-linguist (major) part-time tourer (before 1960 known as GSO2 Tech and after as SO2 Wpns) and while being a linguist was not essential to the role, many had language skills. He was assisted by an Intelligence Corps SNCO (warrant officer or staff sergeant, a non-linguist part-time tourer) and some Intelligence Corps NCOs (corporals) who also toured on a part-time basis. Their first-pass review of the raw intelligence checked for new or significant changes to the disposition of Soviet and NVA forces (especially changes in the Indicators of Hostility, IoH, the measures used by NATO to assess whether war was near), giving the MoD, the British Forces in Germany, and NATO vital early warning of a potential attack. Following this first look, if necessary, another tour could be despatched to obtain further intelligence on specific items, although returning to the 'scene of a crime' was often risky, especially if the opposition had been alerted. The Weapons Office also produced technical reports, which contained intelligence excluded from the main BRIXMIS reports for security reasons, primarily addressed to the technical intelligence desk officers at the MoD in Northumberland House near Trafalgar Square in London and occasionally their American counterparts. Weapons would liaise with a wide variety of partner organisations: Joint Headquarters (JHQ) Rheindahlen, NATO planners at SHAPE, and other intelligence agencies.* They were also responsible for compiling the Mission's knowledge base of enemy equipment, and producing the recognition guides that all personnel would constantly study. The team was supplemented by an Intelligence Corps SNCO in 1974 (the first incumbent being Sergeant Geoff Greaves); the role was subsequently upgraded to WOII and filled by Intelligence Corps photographic interpreters or instructors from Ashford.

The Weapons knowledge base was refined over time, developing into a series of cards held in sixty-two 'boxes' and in a small booklet format. Each card was in two parts: first the 'Recognition Features', detailing all the distinctive characteristics of the item (both army and RAF), accompanied by a series of photos; and the 'Intelligence Requirements', which summarised what BRIXMIS's 'customers' were interested in, be that the MoD, JHQ Rheindahlen, or elsewhere. Because of the visual nature of most of these cards, they did not lend themselves to computerisation (computers at the time could only handle text, not images).

Economics

In the first few years of the Mission, the complement included one or two civilians, senior civil servants from the British Military Government who monitored the economic recovery of the Soviet zone (later the GDR), looking at agriculture, utilities, logistics and infrastructure. They toured in uniform and held local ranks (typically major or

---

* JHQ (Joint Headquarters) Rheindahlen was the home to British Forces in Germany from 1954 to 2013. It combined HQ BAOR and RAFG plus representatives from NATO.

lieutenant colonel). As the GDR matured and the two Germanies took different paths, the need for this type of intelligence diminished, and it was handled by the GSO2 (Econ), a touring major. Over time, the need further diminished so that infrastructure or economics targets were sometimes added to normal tours, and this work continued as a low-priority/time-filler objective, including projects like railway electrification, gas pipelines, and industrial development. Throughout the life of the Mission, however, low-level intelligence on life in the GDR, the availability of goods in the shops, or the general mood of the civilian population was passed up the chain and used by the Foreign Office in their ongoing economic and political assessment of the country.

Research

Another specialist team created in the early 1970s was the 'Intelligence' cell, which became known as the 'Research Cell' or simply 'Research', although it was badged 'Logistics' for security reasons.[13] Its first dedicated staff member was Corporal Alan Clements, Intelligence Corps, who joined in 1971 and was responsible for the collation and processing of all the intelligence material collected from the ground tours (the RAF never had a dedicated back-office intelligence support function). Clements was the first of a growing group of Intelligence Corps personnel within the Mission – he was replaced in 1973 by two Intelligence Corps SNCOs, sergeants Phil Richardson and Ken Kiley, followed by an Intelligence Corps officer, Captain David Duncan (a part-time tourer), all badged Royal Corps of Transport. They were later joined by a JNCO, forming the 'Research' cell that lasted until the end of the Mission. In the later years, an RAF sergeant provided some research support for the RAF side of the operation. The team was responsible for:

a) Identifying and monitoring targets for tours: updating the 'Area Files', maintaining and annotating the main corridor wall map with practically anything of military significance, updated from tour reports, other intelligence reports, and the specific mapping tours.
b) Preparing briefing material and reviewing the tour 'highlights' forms from all three AMLMs (see below) and draft tour reports (including all photography), adding comments as necessary, extracting information to add to the Research files, and producing summary reports.
c) Plotting TAC routes and Emergency Deployment Areas (EDAs).
d) Compiling the ORBAT files (including the many ORBAT charts adorning the walls of the office) with information like Vehicle Registration Numbers (VRNs), Field Post Numbers (FPNs), tactical markings (Unique Vehicle Indentifier, UVIs), and side/turret numbers, hopefully identifying the units described in the highlights forms/draft tour reports.

In addition to their regular work, the team undertook projects, which may not have been as 'sexy' as rushing around the countryside in high-performance cars but were just as valuable to the Mission's work. These included the cracking of the Soviet VRN code system, which allowed tours to match a vehicle to its parent unit and barracks. Another project looked at the box-bodied vehicles used by the Soviets typically for command, control, and communications (C3). They also mapped and classified deployment areas (Emergency Deployment Areas, EDAs) throughout East Germany, which was an important element in Operation TAMARISK/TOMAHAWK.

The Research team's knowledge base was initially a paper-based system, kept mainly in box files, and analysis/cross-referencing had to be done without the benefit of relational databases. In the later 1970s, before computerisation, the solution for target information was to develop 'area files', where all the available material was organised by geographical area. Records were kept on every installation: when it had been visited (to avoid over-touring), sketch maps showing the sentry posts, barriers (and whether they were locked), occupied and empty buildings, garages, armouries, firing ranges, and, of course, rubbish tips. The files would also include directions on the best way of getting close to the perimeter fence, the best OPs, and any known hazards. The Research team also became trainspotters, experts in East German rolling stock and rail logistics – what type of wagon was needed for what sort of load.

The Research team were responsible for the 'Nark List', and by default, the senior Intelligence officer at the Mission was the 'Nark Officer'. These files retained a list of all numberplates known to be used on East German nark cars (narks would occasionally change their numberplates during a surveillance mission) and profiles of the main personalities involved in counter-mission activity. Tours would carry a list of known nark plates with them and add to it as they encountered more inside the GDR.

In the mid-1980s, the area files were computerised under Project ELECTRIC LIGHT, which took away a lot of the legwork involved, but the data still had to be gathered, sorted, and entered in the correct way. By then, Research had become sufficiently integrated into the British military intelligence structure that they began briefing their own tours, rather than taking tasking in from outside the Mission. They would also liaise with a variety of agencies and other units: Intelligence Corps both at JHQ Rheindahlen and Berlin Sector HQ, HQ Berlin Infantry Brigade, RAF targeting specialists, and other classified sources, and along with the ops officers, the Research team would sometimes receive signals intelligence (SIGINT) to add context to their analyses, although the Mission generally received a lot less *external* intelligence material than their American and French colleagues.

At the end of every tour, the crew called in to the USMLM HQ on Föhrenweg 19/21 to complete a 'tour highlights' triplicate form, detailing any main observations such as new KIT, major troop movements or the level of command of the KIT seen, all of which could be an Indicator of Hostility (IoH) – the Mission had nine specific indicators to review each day.[14] The highlights forms were shared with the other AMLMs and the top copy was then handed in as the tour booked back in at London Block, copied to Weapons and to Research, who would both do a first-pass review to see if any immediate action needed to be taken. This could involve sending out a further tour immediately for further investigation or alerting the chain of command of some important development. The research team also produced a daily summary from the highlights forms to be sent to JHQ Rheindahlen, the MoD in London, and the other AMLMs. Relevant information would be also added to the wall map or to the appropriate area file (later entered into the computer system).

Spandau

The Mission attracted linguists from the outset, providing interpreters for the delicate negotiations between the British and Soviet occupation forces, which BRIXMIS facilitated. They would translate for the meetings between C-in-C BAOR and C-in-C GSFG, their chiefs of staff, and SERB. Language skills also proved very valuable when the Mission began intelligence collection inside the GDR, where fluency or even a working knowledge of Russian and German could be useful in extracting themselves from all kinds of dangerous situations. Initially brought in for their language skills (as interpreter, senior interpreter), the role was gradually merged with tour officer when linguistic ability became viewed as a *core* skill, rather than an add-on, and Russian and/ or German became part of the lengthy training programme.

As described above, BRIXMIS linguists also assisted the British governor at the four-power-administered Spandau Prison, which housed Rudolf Hess and other senior Nazi war criminals. Therefore, when a specialist department was set up for Russian linguists to exploit Russian language material collected by the hugely successful but very unsanitary Operation TAMARISK/TOMAHAWK, 'Spandau' was an excellent nom de guerre for the team. Operation TAMARISK/TOMAHAWK is described in Chapter 4, 'Touring'. Before 1982, the exploitation of TAMARISK-type material was undertaken by the Weapons team (typically non-linguists) with translations done on an ad hoc basis by a Russian-speaking tour officer. The Spandau office was set up in 1982 when the first Intelligence Corps linguist officer was posted in (Captain Ian Henderson, 1982–1985, with the title SO3 Liaison and a part-time tourer), and the team quickly expanded to become another Intelligence Corps enclave within BRIXMIS, with less and less involvement of tour officers, although they did not get involved in the actual TAMARISK collection, just its exploitation. Henderson's role as SO3 Liaison was perfect cover as he was also involved with Spandau Prison and protocol events. By the mid-1980s, it was exclusively an Intelligence Corps operation, including three Russian-speaking analysts: Captain Bill Hogg (SO3 Spandau, and after Hess died, SO3 Training/Coordination) and a succession of Intelligence Corps SNCOs 'borrowed' from Research: sergeants Nigel 'Nick' Rowles, Paul Wilson, and Ted Roberts (as SNCO Research); and Staff Sergeant Andy Barbour (SNCO Training/Coordination 1987–1990), plus a JNCO.[15] Linguists were also useful to have around at the many official functions held at the Mission where Soviet officers would attend. Sometimes they attended wearing full mess kit (albeit badged as Royal Corps of Transport, RCT, or Royal Signals) where they would mingle with the guests, engaging in conversation, or sometimes covertly dressed as waiters, listening to conversations between Russians as they served them drinks and canapés.

Geographic

An offshoot of the Intelligence Cell was the Geographic Department, known simply as 'Geo', who ran the map room, a crucial part of the touring operation. Initially, the Mission had to manage with old and out-of-date maps, which could be very dangerous in the field, so the secondment of a Royal Engineer cartographer from

BAOR in the mid-1970s helped turn the function around, sourcing better base maps and creating bespoke overlays for tourers. After every tour, any corrections or additions were passed to the Geo team who would issue updates periodically. Tours were also despatched specifically to gather mapping information. Mapping is covered in more detail in Chapter 4, 'Touring'.

Special Section

Photography was core to the Mission's intelligence collection and developed in line with the latest technology throughout the history of the unit. Known as 'Special' section to disguise the department's true purpose (photography was not mentioned in the RMA so was a sensitive subject for both sides), the laboratory was manned by RAF NCOs and technicians and became a very slick operation. Tour photography is explored in Chapter 5, 'Tools of the Trade'. The section guaranteed to have an incoming tour's black and white (and later colour) prints on the tour NCO's desk by 0830 hours the following morning – the 'wet' prints produced in the lab were often 'claimed' by anxious tour officers and NCOs before they were fully dry, which meant they stuck together, hence the name 'stickies' ('stickies' were also unfixed and so faded in a matter of weeks). In the early days, the Special Section was housed in two rooms on one of the upper floors of the BIS Building, just outside the main entrance to the Olympic Stadium complex. The set-up was basic but fit for purpose, with red light (for black and white) and total darkness (for colour) darkroom facilities. In late 1960, Corporal Francis Bacon BEM RAF designed a new facility within the BRIXMIS offices, and it came on line in 1961, considerably streamlining the operation; the operation was expanded again in the mid-1980s under Project NEW IMAGE.[16] Colour slides, which were introduced later, used a different process that took a little longer, but never more than forty-eight hours. Prints to go in reports and enlargements (including detailed crops) would also be produced to order. In the mid-1980s, the Mission began trialling the emerging video camera technology on tours, and Special Section received video editing equipment to prepare the tapes for onward distribution. The resolution of video back then could not compete with still photography, but it provided a valuable supplementary tool to capture moving images (such as a tank manoeuvring or a train passing), or filming while on the move (such as running a column). By the time the Mission disbanded, the Special Section had developed into a top-class professional photographic laboratory, operating up to fifteen hours a day, seven days a week, 365 days a year. In 1989, it was in the process of expanding to handle processing work for the other AMLMs, but the fall of the Wall curtailed that expansion.

M/T Motor Transport Department

The M/T (Motor Transport) team, led by a Royal Corps of Transport staff sergeant, was core to the BRIXMIS operation, and was responsible for supplying the tour drivers (both Royal Corps of Transport and RAF) and for keeping the vehicle fleet maintained and in running order. There was a self-contained set of garages behind London Block, which included a small 'first-line' workshop that could handle minor repairs and modifications. This was run by an REME staff sergeant, who was also a part-time tourer, and with two or three locally employed mechanics. The REME staff sergeant liaised closely with 14 Field Workshops, REME, in Alexander Barracks, Spandau, for major modifications and repairs. The whole area of BRIXMIS vehicles is explored in Chapter 5, 'Tools of the Trade'.

Support Staff

A small clerical team supported the operation with an SNCO as chief clerk, an orderly room sergeant, some JNCO military clerks, and a civilian secretarial and administrative staff. Warrant Officer Kevin Hawkins, chief clerk in the late 1980s, described his role as a combination of 'RSM (regimental sergeant major), disciplinarian, families officer, club president, service funds accountant, stand-in Mission House warrant officer, entertainment officer, security officer, and general factotum, with very little actual clerical work involved!'[17] One of the chief clerk's jobs was to organise the annual junior and senior ranks summer ball at the Potsdam Mission House, and invitations to these events were much sought after – they were a great opportunity to build bridges and return favours with contacts such as chefs, quartermasters, air movers, engineers, etc. He also organised the annual 'BRIXMIS Review', which was a great team-building event where no one was safe from a caustic sketch or joke.

The squadron quartermaster sergeant (SQMS or 'Q') was a non-touring army staff sergeant or warrant officer responsible for procuring and managing all the touring and non-touring kit for the Mission. With an office in the admin corridor and a store in the basement of London Block, he could normally be relied upon to acquire whatever the tour personnel needed, including personal camping kit (arctic-specification sleeping bags, GORE-TEX tents), specialist clothing (Canadian parka coats and RAF flying boots), and the various bits of specialist equipment used by tours. He also (allegedly) did a roaring trade in East German goods (optics, porcelain, toys, etc.), bought (or traded) at very advantageous exchange rates via (again, allegedly!) his 'partner in crime', the Mission House warrant officer. Tour personnel were issued their personal kit (including camera gear and specialist optical equipment such as the Modulux image intensifier and night-vision goggles) at the start of their posting and were responsible for its upkeep. If a pass holder was going on leave or on a long course (going 'off-pass'), a request would be made to SERB to temporarily transfer the pass to another member of the Mission, and the personal kit would also be temporarily signed over. The unusual circumstances of the post-war occupation of Berlin meant that the West German government, through the West Berlin Senat, funded all occupation costs by way of reparations and in return for the 'protection' offered by the allied forces in the city. This meant that the SQMS and individual officers could bypass the normal laborious military procurement systems and deal directly with manufacturers and local suppliers. Successful examples include the relationship with Nikon, Opel, Mercedes, and local photographic supplies dealers.

Even with the introduction of Project ELECTRIC LIGHT in 1985, the amount of paperwork coming in and out of the Mission was considerable, which included the preparation and distribution of a myriad of reports, illustrated by photos from the Special Section. In the late 1980s, three Women's Royal Army Corps (WRAC) NCOs were posted into BRIXMIS to assist with the administration. They were, however, not allowed to tour as at the time it was deemed inappropriate to include female soldiers in the claustrophobic and intimate environment of a tour car, even though female Intelligence Corps personnel had been working alongside their male colleagues in the field in Northern Ireland for many years.

Project ELECTRIC LIGHT/GARDEN GATE/ NEW IMAGE 1984–1985[18]

By the 1980s, with ever-increasing amounts of information flooding into the Mission, the support staff were getting swamped and there was a good chance that something important could be missed. The solution was to computerise, which was a brave move at the time, with computers still very much in their infancy. The project was in two parts: Project ELECTRIC LIGHT covered the Mission's requirements, while Project GARDEN GATE covered 3 Intelligence and Security Company (3 Int & Sy Coy), the Intelligence Corps unit co-located at the Olympic Stadium. The main objective behind ELECTRIC LIGHT was to create a database for all the VRNs, side numbers from trucks and armoured vehicles, and *Bort* numbers from helicopters and aircraft, across GSFG. With data coming in every day from BRIXMIS ground, air and Chipmunk tours, the idea was that the information would be searchable, giving type, unit, and location, effectively providing a snapshot of the GSFG ORBAT at that time. It also incorporated unit designations, target files, personality (profile) files and Field Post Numbers (FPNs), and also covered the NVA. From a technical point of view, both systems were identical, so should the ELECTRIC LIGHT hardware fail, then the system could run on GARDEN GATE, and vice versa. With more computing power in a modern smartphone than the two systems had together, it may be hard for the reader to visualise the operation at London Block, but it was elaborate and expensive. The two systems were housed in a secure air-conditioned computer suite built on the top floor of London Block within the BRIXMIS corridor, electromagnetically screened from the outside world to stop any electronic emissions from leaving or entering the room. Each Norsk Data Super-Mini system was contained in three six-feet-tall 'standard' nineteen-inch equipment racks, which housed the 'card' frames (the printed circuit boards for CPU, RAM memory, input/ output devices, etc.), two hard disk drives (huge in physical size, requiring a two-man lift, but only megabytes of usable data storage), a system for the nightly data back-ups and teleprinter-style consoles for the operators. Armoured fibre-optic cables connected ELECTRIC LIGHT to the ultra-secure TEMPEST terminals (shielded from emitting an electromagnetic signature) located in the BRIXMIS offices, allowing the users to interrogate the database and run reports. Similar cables linked the GARDEN GATE system to the 3 Int & Sy Coy building, which was 200 metres or so away from London Block, where they had their own terminals and printer in a similarly screened room – the only way of getting information to their customers was via hard-copy printouts, and the printers were kept inside these screened rooms for security reasons. The cables were strung along the corridors and into various offices, none of which were designed for this purpose, so moving people or desks around, for example, was a major operation.

The equipment was all installed by the end of 1985, and the huge job of data entry began – everything contained in the box files collated by the Research and Weapons teams, which all needed to be organised into a logical structure. By 1987, the systems were up and running and working well. Nobody suspected that the Mission would only have another three years to run, and it is ironic that the operation was at its most efficient just as it closed. After BRIXMIS closed, the system was 'passed' to the Joint Intelligence Staff (Berlin), JIS(B), with more data coming in from ground inspection tours monitoring the withdrawal of Soviet forces – it proved useful to be able to track who was moving where and when. When JIS(B) closed in 1993, ahead of the final withdrawal of Soviet Forces from Germany and allied forces from Berlin, the whole computer suite – computers, terminals, screening, cables, etc. – was dismantled and sent to JHQ Rheindahlen, where its fate was unknown. It was an expensive and complex exercise that came to an end just as it was beginning to bear fruit, and as Europe went through massive changes. Upgrades to the Special Section's photographic laboratory went on around the same time under Project NEW IMAGE.

ELECTRIC LIGHT was managed by an RAF squadron leader or flight lieutenant who worked with a civilian systems integrator from Norsk Data and a civilian systems engineer from Serco. They were assisted by two JNCOs (one army, one RAF) and later by a staff sergeant and then a warrant officer as system supervisor. By the time BRIXMIS closed, the operation was working smoothly run by just the warrant officer supervisor and Serco systems engineer.

London Block

The top floor of London Block was home to BRIXMIS from around 1958 until the Mission closed in 1990, and then home to JIS(B) from 1990–1994 (see the conclusion for more details on what happened after BRIXMIS closed their doors). Entry to the BRIXMIS offices was controlled by the duty NCO who monitored the main entrance via CCTV. Visitors would first enter the admin corridor (Keep Area B), which had a lower security level than the rest of the floor. As well as the orderly/chief clerk's office, this corridor included the chief and deputy chief's office, their PA/secretary, the adjutant/SO1 Admin officer, the squadron quartermaster sergeant, the typing pool, and a conference room. This first level of security allowed non-security-cleared personnel (military and civilian) to come and go on BRIXMIS business, albeit under the watchful eye of the duty NCO.

The operational offices were secured by an additional steel-grilled door with a combination entry code. This section was strictly off-limits to non-military personnel;

there was a red flashing light and siren to warn personnel that an uncleared person was in the area such as a high-level visitor or tradesman, who would be escorted at all times and closely watched. The most obvious feature of the long, curved main corridor was the thirty-metre-long wall map of the GDR used for planning tours from the late 1970s onwards. This vital resource was covered by a heavy curtain when not in use. This corridor was the nerve centre of BRIXMIS and would be humming with activity twenty-four hours a day, 365 days a year.

The whole operation was run out of the joint Army and RAF Operations (Ops) Office, which was the focal point of all intelligence coming in and going out of the Mission. The team comprised the army operations officer (SO2 Ops, a major) supported by an assistant operations officer (SO3 Ops, a captain) who handled primarily army 'ground' operations, and squadron leader operations (Squadron Leader Operations) who handled RAF 'air' operations, but over time the service divide was eroded. Between them the ops team held the pulse of the Soviet and East German military in the GDR in their hands. Three of the four office walls were covered with whiteboards and noticeboards, hidden behind curtains, and the remaining wall was filled with three four-drawer locked filing cabinets for classified documents (SECRET and above), piled high on top with less classified (CONFIDENTIAL and below) material. Their key tool was the monthly planner, and the tourer's life revolved around this board. Down the left-hand side were the names of all the tour officers, tour NCOs, and drivers currently on-pass (never more than thirty-one names) and the serviceable tour vehicles. To the right of the names were pinned three laminated strips, each representing a month (planning was done three months ahead), subdivided into days and weeks and aligned with each name. All the scheduling was done using a chinagraph (grease) pencil. It was a very efficient system – it was easy to see at a glance what was going on at the Mission: scheduled tours, stand-by days, Potsdam Mission House duty, personnel on leave, on courses, and the dates of any special functions. At the end of each month, the current month would be taken down, and months two and three would be bumped up to become months one and two. The old month would be wiped clean and placed on the board as month three. This process was repeated every month. There was also a large area to the right of the panel for memos and notes, and the whole planner was hidden behind curtains. Another curtained display contained a current operational overview of the GSFG and NVA in map form (the vertical louvre map described in Chapter 4, 'Touring'), the summation of the combined efforts of the AMLMs, and other sources of intelligence that fed into the Ops Office (SIGINT, ELINT, HUMINT). These boards were seldom left uncovered, being used primarily to brief the chief and his high-ranking visitors (as a key component in JHQ Rheindahlen's IoH), but tourers would check the map before going out on tour to check for the latest intelligence and get an overall picture of the GDR, useful when trying to understand troop movements. Next to the door was a booth containing the STU-II secure phone lines to HQ BAOR (which was normally in constant use) and RMP Helmstedt (for emergencies).* The ops officers' desks would typically be piled

---

* The STU-II Secure Telephone Unit (STU) was developed by the NSA and introduced to the US' NATO partners in the 1980s. The handset looked like a normal telephone, but it was accompanied by a filing cabinet-sized box of complex electronics.

high with files, photos, and scraps of paper, several telephones, in, out, and pending trays, but no PCs or laptops – BRIXMIS operated before such innovations, and the ELECTRIC LIGHT terminal only arrived in 1987. Just outside the ops room door was another red flashing light and no one was allowed to enter when it was on.

There were separate offices for the tour officers and the tour NCOs (the drivers were based in the M/T department), with photos and non-classified files scattered all over their desks. The NCOs' office had a large, green baize-covered map table in the middle, but this was removed in a reorganisation in the 1980s to create more space for desks. They also designed a wall-mounted guide to the many variations of Soviet box-bodied vehicles with overlays accounting for the different permutations, and the whole thing was, of course, hidden behind curtains. There were also offices for the different operational departments: the Geo section, Research (Intelligence), Weapons, and Spandau, the Special Section photo lab, and the ultra-secure ELECTRIC LIGHT computer suite. Spandau had a 'wet' (rubbish) room, for storing/drying out recovered paperwork and a 'dry' room for analysing the material and writing up reports on the recovered material.

Dirty, smelly tourers returning from a tour and their occasionally malodourous luggage would avoid the grand main entrance to London Block and use an unassuming back door, where up three flights of stairs (no lift!) the BRIXMIS offices could be

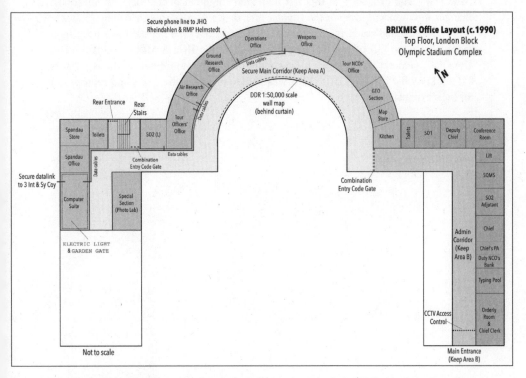

The BRIXMIS office layout on the top floor of London Block (c.1990). (Author via various sources)

found. Given the distinguished guests visiting the GOC Berlin Sector (commandant), the British minister, or the general commanding the Berlin Infantry Brigade, who all shared the same building, this was probably a good idea. The back door was also used by personnel from SIS Berlin Station, which was on the floor below (anonymously labelled as the Protocol Department), and Mission personnel would sometimes meet equally strange-looking characters on the stairs. Reaching the top floor, tourers would get access to the secure operations corridor via a combination code lock and a steel-barred gate. However, if the code had been changed while a tour was out, someone would have to walk the length of the building on a lower floor and enter via the main entrance, getting the new code from the duty NCO.

Most of the furniture on the floor was well worn but functional, a mix between War Department/MoD issue and locally sourced pieces. No cleaners were allowed at this end of the building and BRIXMIS personnel were expected to clean up after themselves. Electronic scans for bugs were regularly undertaken including after any major renovation work. The access security and layout developed over time, and as technology developed. In the early 1980s, the Mission was running out of space to accommodate the extra support staff, the new photographic laboratory, and computer equipment. On the top floor of London Block adjacent to the BRIXMIS offices was a large furnished flat that was reserved and equipped for the GOC/commandant as his 'War Flat'. The existence of this flat had been forgotten over time with successive changes in command, despite the regular attendance of a German cleaning lady who kept it spotless and ready for immediate occupation. Beyond the flat there were more rooms that were full of old newspapers stored by the British Military Government. The GOC, General David Mostyn, was more than happy to relinquish the war flat he did not know he had, and BRIXMIS was able to clear out the space and repurpose it for their expansion.[19]

Chapter 4

Touring

'The reality was that even if the formal liaison tasks might have appealed to those of an alcoholic disposition, the actual business of touring would have found favour with a hardened drug addict! At its best, touring was not unlike gambling, but with a near certainty of winning.'

Major General P. G. Williams CMG OBE,
Tour Officer 1981–1983,
Operations Officer 1987–1989
Chairman of the BRIXMIS Association[1]

Once Stalin's 'Iron Curtain' had descended over Eastern Europe, the West needed to know what he was up to. Most of the Soviet 'satellite' states (Hungary, Czechoslovakia, Poland, and so on) were impenetrable thanks to the police states imposed after the end of the war. There was, however, a chink in Stalin's armour – the Deutsche Demokratische Republik (German Democratic Republic or East Germany). The GDR was the front line in the emerging Cold War and Stalin positioned hundreds of thousands of troops inside the former Soviet zone of occupation ready for a blitzkrieg across Western Europe should World War III break out. Another 'chink' in his armour was Berlin, with its four-power control ensuring the West (Great Britain, United States, and France) maintained a military foothold *inside* the GDR, and the AMLMs, who, thanks to the liaison agreements made in 1946/1947, had roaming rights across the whole country (restricted areas notwithstanding). From the very start of the AMLMs, long patrols, which became known as 'tours', were sent out into the GDR from their bases in Potsdam and West Berlin to observe and report back on what the Soviet forces (and subsequently the East German armed forces, the NVA) were up to. As Stalin reinforced and re-equipped his armies, the AMLMs became a critical part of NATO's defence of Western Europe, monitoring Warsaw Pact activity and looking for any IoHs, signs that an invasion was imminent. These indicators included large-scale troop movements, unusual patterns of behaviour, unexpected training exercises, or the arrival of new equipment. To understand the *unusual*, the West needed to understand the *usual*, such as how the GSFG went about their daily work, their training cycles, or their annual troop rotations. With the establishment of the NVA in the late 1950s, the West also needed to understand their capabilities, and those of other Warsaw Pact forces, which on rare occasions trained inside East Germany.

Touring was 'simply' a matter of sending out suitably qualified military personnel, in highly modified vehicles, into the GDR where they would collect intelligence, seeking out certain objectives or investigating targets of opportunity. Although they had every right to be there (restricted areas notwithstanding), the opposition (Soviet forces, NVA forces, Vopos, and Stasi) would do their best to disrupt the tour, and where possible detain (arrest) the tourers. In turn, the tours would try to evade their pursuers and make their observations covertly. This description, however, over-simplifies what developed into a highly sophisticated intelligence-collection operation involving the latest technology, an efficient support organisation, great skill, ingenuity, and bravery from the participants who faced real danger at every stage of the mission, and for some, serious injury and even death. Touring provided the 'ground truth' inside the GDR, allowing informed threat assessments to be prepared by defence analysts to be passed up the chains of command. The AMLMs could also quickly confirm or deny enemy activity that had been picked up by other sources of intelligence (SIGINT or HUMINT).

Training

Preparation for a posting to BRIXMIS would start a long time before the candidate even set foot in West Berlin, sometimes spending two years working up to a two-year posting – such was the way with the army and RAF HR systems.* For tour officers, language skills were a prerequisite – native Russian, German, or possibly French speakers were always of interest to the intelligence arms, but the various service language schools – such as the Army School of Languages at Beaconsfield or RAF North Luffenham in the East Midlands, later centralised as the Joint Services School for Linguists (JSSL) – were there to teach the rest. The eighteen-month Russian interpreter's course equipped the tour officer with the skills to act as the official interpreter at the formal meetings with SERB and GSFG, at official 'liaison' functions, and to be able to converse with *komendants* or other Soviet soldiers in the field. There are many stories of how tour officers were able to defuse a tense situation or talk themselves out of trouble by engaging with the Soviets in perfect Russian. Learning German was a secondary requirement, so prospective tour officers would also take a six-week colloquial German course – to have survived the eighteen-month Russian course would suggest the candidate had a natural aptitude for languages and living among the Germans would soon increase their vocabulary and understanding anyway.[2] Sometimes the tour NCO was a German speaker, which could be useful.

Touring itself was an unusual if not unique job in the armed services, requiring a special blend of skills, knowledge, common sense and daring. However, it took until the early 1970s before a formalised training plan was put in place. Before that (from 1946 to 1970), tour personnel had some ad hoc training in the UK, or learnt on the job using their wits and experience gained from their previous service, including combat experience or counterinsurgency work. However, as personnel were posted in and

---

* Army postings for pre- and post-Staff College officers tended to be based on two-year tours of regimental duty, alternating with two-years tours on the staff in HQs. The RAF tour rotation was two to three years.

out of the Mission every two to three years or so, their experience was lost to future generations of tourers, and there is only so much knowledge that word of mouth and some scribbled handover notes can impart.

Brigadier Crookenden (Chief BRIXMIS April 1971–October 1972) arranged for some Mission personnel to attend the Service Attaché's course at the Intelligence Corps HQ at Templar Barracks in Ashford, Kent (which prepared military attachés for their postings to British embassies around the world, teaching covert intelligence collection and recognition), which was a step in the right direction, but a dedicated training course to equip candidates for the unusual situation they would face in East Germany was clearly needed. Lieutenant Colonel Angus Southwood MBE, a former BRIXMIS tour officer and linguist, was given the job of setting up a bespoke course that would also be based at Ashford. The resulting course, the 'Intelligence (Special Duties) Course' (Int (SD)) to obscure any connection to BRIXMIS, was trialled between 22 October and 10 November 1972. There were only two students, Sergeant Mike J. Seale MBE BEM (SAS) and Sergeant D. J. G. 'Chip' Wood MBE (Royal Engineers), who had already been posted to the unit, with Brigadier (retd.) Tony Harper and Wing Commander Harry Irving RAF (retd.) as principal instructors. The second course took place between 16 April and 18 May 1973 with nine students: seven from the army and two from the RAF. There were two courses a year in 1973 and 1974, moving to three a year in 1975, which continued to the end of the Mission. The course lasted three weeks until 1982, and then expanded to four weeks. The Int (SD) Course was an all-ranks affair, and officers, tour NCOs, and drivers all participated together, with all personnel destined for BRIXMIS attending, whether they were to be pass-holders (tourers) or not. Course 9 held in 1976 was the first to include an American officer as an 'observer', and Course 29 in 1983 was joined by a French officer, and this tri-mission approach improved interoperability in Berlin. In 1983, the first woman attended, Corporal S. L. 'Cher' Chilard (WRAC), although she was not allowed to tour. In 1986, the first Royal Navy representative since the 1950s attended the course, Warrant Officer D. G. 'Dickie' Dawson.

It was the policy of successive chiefs (or their deputies) to be present at the start of each course, thus demonstrating their commitment to the training. The course was also always attended by experienced tourers to add a sense of realism and was in two parts: classroom and field. The first two weeks of the course would be classroom based with the focus on equipment recognition, photography techniques and touring tactics. Some 400 pieces of Warsaw Pact ground and air equipment were presented on slides in tactical settings (as opposed to the shiny examples that paraded through Red Square), including details of the MoD's current intelligence requirements. For aircraft they used the WEFT system to teach aircraft recognition – wings, engines, fuselage, tail – and all Warsaw Pact aircraft had codenames, which made remembering them easier, with variants denoted by a letter suffix:

F for Fighter:
FISHBED Mikoyan-Gurevich MiG-21 (FISHBED-C, FISHBED-F, etc.)
FLOGGER Mikoyan-Gurevich MiG-23
FITTER Sukhoi Su-7

B for Bomber:
BREWER Yakovlev Yak-28B (BREWER-A, BREWER-B, etc.)
BACKFIRE Tupolev Tu-22M
BLACKJACK Tupolev Tu-160

H for Helicopter:
HIP Mil Mi-8 (HIP-C, HIP-F, etc.)
HIND Mil Mi-24
HALO Mil Mi-26

Unfortunately, ground vehicles were known by their Soviet designators, with complicated names like BTR60P, BTR60PU, T-64R, T-64B1, ZSU-23-4 – the differences between variants could be very subtle, sometimes just an extra lump or bump, or a differently profiled exhaust, and tourers were expected to know them inside out. Each evening, the students would spend hours practising and revising, with a recognition quiz the following morning, building up to the final test covering everything taught on the course – a daunting task.

Photography was a key part of the training. Before the Int (SD) course came along, the photographic training was rudimentary – a summons to the Foreign Office where candidates were shown the basic controls on a camera as part of the military attaché course and then were sent over to Trafalgar Square in central London with a Leica to snap tourist attractions – no training on long lenses or special techniques was given. Photographic training at Ashford started small, but soon developed into a comprehensive course – the instructors started from the very basics as most personnel attending had very limited exposure to professional photographic equipment. Compared to modern cameras (and mobile phones today), the cameras used by the Mission were manually controlled and complicated to use, requiring skills that took time to master. Students were encouraged to practise in their spare time and at weekends, and their results were critiqued in open class on their return. The training introduced the use of long lenses (including the 500 and 1,000-mm mirror lenses), night and video photography, special exposure and processing techniques, and covert photography from vehicles, although later success was often down to a good eye, lots of practice, and knowledge being passed along by more experienced colleagues or by the Special Section NCOs. Aerial photography (from the Chipmunk) required a different set of skills, which were shared between aircrew when in Berlin.

The second half of the course was dedicated to practical touring techniques using the same tour cars that were used by the Mission, and against UK targets that were like those found in East Germany – for example, tours would visit Gatwick Airport so they could photograph aircraft on approach and take-off and analyse the results the following day as a group. Course Directing Staff (DS) would initially accompany students demonstrating security procedures, vehicle recoveries using the winch, finding the best observation positions (OPs), camping in the field, and advanced driving, both defensive and offensive. Squadron Leader Rod Saar MBE, who instructed on the first full course in 1973, describes an exercise where he took two trainees close to the main gates of RAF Wittering at around 0900 hours to demonstrate how it was possible to sneak into the base by tagging onto a line of traffic driving through the gates during rush hour. The course culminated in a three-day exercise where students would be let loose on Salisbury Plain with a set of objectives (mostly army installations), with the DS acting as narks. The tour would always be detained, resulting in an interrogation in Russian by an angry *komendant*, which would be videoed and analysed afterwards. Where possible, the courses were scheduled to coincide with army and RAF large-scale ground and air exercises, allowing the students to covertly observe, photograph and report back on, presenting their findings, photographs, and an intelligence briefing to the group afterwards.[3]

The Int (SD) course was very demanding (although less than the typical Survive, Evade, Resist, and Extract or SERE training given to front-line personnel) and went a long way in preparing the students for the rigours they would experience on tour. The course was also a good opportunity to pass to the next generation the various habits, routines, and rituals that made up Mission folklore. These included:

a) Berets (or other headgear) should be removed on leaving the Mission House and not worn again until the next encounter with the Soviets (but not the East Germans), either when being detained, or at the Glienicke Bridge on the way home.

b) Always turn the numberplate light off on leaving Potsdam and stop at the first suitable puddle to 'muddy-up' the distinctive yellow plates.

c) Stop every two hours for a 'brew' (coffee or tea) or face the wrath of the driver.

d) At all times, day and night, there had to be at least one person in the car with all doors locked.

e) It was expected (certainly from the 1980s) that the tour officer and NCO would sleep *outside* in their carefully selected Z-platz, whatever the weather, and they should be able to set up their tent, bivouac or basha (tent or shelter) *without* the use of lights.

f) Leave no trace of their stay at the Z-platz so it could be used again.

g) Bring along two thermos flasks that the driver would fill with boiling water at the first brew stop. The average life of one of the glass-lined thermos flasks available at the time was about four weeks, and would frequently shatter during violent manoeuvres, soaking the contents of the food bag.

h) Bring some tins of something suitable for the communal curry (often cooked *inside* the car).

i) Bring a selection of cassette tapes that everyone could listen to while doing long rail or road watches (BFBS, AFN, or Radio Free Europe could also be listened to when in range).

j) Do not bring smelly sandwiches.[4]

Course 47 (16 October–10 November 1989) was underway when the Berlin Wall opened in November 1989, heralding the end of BRIXMIS's mission. The last course, Course 49, ran from 18 June–13 July 1990, with the Mission finally closing in December 1990.

Recognition refresher training would be a constant obsession for tour members, especially when tours became more integrated in the 1980s, where an RAF officer could be sent on a ground tour, or an army officer on an air tour. Inevitably there would be some bias to their parent service, but tours were encouraged to be flexible and were trained accordingly. This was important, because they were the only allied personnel on the ground at that time and place, and therefore had to be able to exploit any Soviet/East German activity, whatever the type. Recognition books and reference cards were produced with photos taken by the AMLMs pointing out the various features and listing information that the Mission's customers had asked for, a system that was marginally improved by computerisation, and tests or quizzes would spur on the naturally competitive tour personnel to score better than their colleagues. Occasionally there would be visits from the MoD desk analysts, who received the intelligence gathered by the Mission. This helped reinforce the value of the work the Mission was doing, and helped to point out the sort of intelligence the analysts were after.

Drivers were normally non-linguists, coming to the Mission from the Royal Corps of Transport or from the RAF. RAF drivers normally arrived with limited experience and had to learn on the job, although the Mission established a driver training circuit in Grunewald to put the drivers, and the vehicles, through their paces and they quickly rose to the task. Army drivers, on the other hand, often had experience in close-protection driving (including in Northern Ireland) or had been part of 8 Regiment Royal Corps of Transport based at Nelson Barracks in Münster where their duties involved the transport of tactical nuclear weapons – this meant that they already had high security clearances.

Although the training was very comprehensive, it could not replicate the unique challenges faced by tours when deep inside East Germany, so new personnel would always be paired with experienced hands for their first few forays into the GDR. The training did not stop when the individual arrived in Berlin, with compulsory weekly recognition training and tests (held on a Saturday morning), such was the pace of change within the Soviet and East German military.

PRAs and TRAs

The German Democratic Republic (including East Berlin) was around 108,333 square kilometres (41,828 square miles), which was about the same size as Tennessee or Kentucky, or 83 per cent the size of England (44 per cent of the United Kingdom). Its neighbour, West Germany, was 248,717 square kilometres (96,030 square miles). The GDR's population, however, was small: 16.4 million in 1989, compared to 47.5 million in England (57 million UK). The four-power city of Berlin was located around 100 miles inside East Germany with access to the city via the designated road, air, and waterway corridors. The Robertson–Malinin Agreement states that 'Generally speaking there will be freedom of travel and circulation for the members of Missions in each Zone with the exception of restricted areas in which respect each Commander-in-Chief will notify the Mission and act on a reciprocal basis.' These 'restricted areas' took the form of 'Permanently Restricted Areas' (PRAs) or 'Temporary Restricted

Areas' (TRAs) and were communicated to the AMLMs by hand-drawn maps from SERB, signed by the Chief of Staff GSFG. PRAs were normally around key installations, permanent training areas, or sensitive sites, while TRAs tended to follow exercises or large-scale troop movements, lasting from a few days up to a month. Up to January 1957, there were only three PRAs in the GDR. Following the closure of the Inner German Border (IGB) in 1952, the whole of the border between East and West Germany was put into a PRA, allowing the East Germans to construct fortifications, sow minefields, and prepare the infamous 'death strip'. There was another large PRA in the south that incorporated the Ohrdruf training area and reaching down to the Czech border, and another smaller area south-east of Zerbst incorporating the Rosslau training area by the Elbe River.[5] At the same time, Ulbricht flexed his muscles and imposed restrictions on the movements of the AMLMs in and out of Berlin. As part of the IGB closure, he closed the various crossing points into East Germany, forcing AMLM vehicles to use the Glienicke Bridge between the American sector and Potsdam. This channelled all traffic – the AMLMs and accredited diplomats were the only people allowed to use the bridge – through a single chokepoint where they could be better monitored and controlled. This created a new inconvenience for the AMLMs – until 1951 HQ GSFG was in Potsdam, which was the original rationale for basing the AMLMs there, thus facilitating 'liaison'. However, in 1951 General Chuikov, C-in-C GSFG, decided to move his headquarters to Karlshorst in East Berlin. Because BRIXMIS had no 'official' business in East Berlin, they were unable to cross via one of the many checkpoints between West and East Berlin, so for any official trips (presenting credentials, lodging protests, formal visits), BRIXMIS had to go from their West Berlin HQ at Fehrbelliner Platz in the British sector, across the American sector to the Glienicke Bridge, over into East Germany, and then skirt round south of the city to re-enter it at Schönefeld and head up to Karlshorst – a good hour's journey compared to the 9.4-mile (15-kilometre) direct hop across the city. This was one of Ulbricht's tactics to make life as difficult as possible for the Allied forces in Berlin.[6]

In January 1957, without warning, the Soviets issued a new PRA map to the AMLMs. It now included around ten large individual PRAs, including the whole of East Germany's border with Poland, reducing the tour-able area by 25–30 per cent. It was understood that for every square kilometre of restricted area in East Germany, the Western Allies would make an equivalent area in the Western zones out of bounds for SOXMIS and the other SMLMs, and vice versa (based on the principle of reciprocity). However, in this case, the West was slow to respond with reciprocal PRAs, giving the Soviets the impression that they could act with impunity. The following January, and successive Januarys hereafter, further PRA maps were issued, freeing up some areas, but imposing others, and by 1960 there were about sixteen individual PRAs in place, covering as much as 40 per cent of the whole area of the GDR. The 1974 PRA map included two further PRAs, making an additional 1,700 square kilometres of the GDR out of bounds.

A new PRA map had many implications for the AMLMs. It affected their transit routes across East Germany, so getting from A to B now involved going via C, and C could be via minor roads through small towns and villages or even across country, or deliberately funnelled along narrow corridors, which made it easier for the narks to monitor and/or intercept them. Some high-priority targets, possibly identified as such by previous mission activity, were obscured by the new boundaries, including surface-to-air missiles (SAMs) and radar sites, airfields, training areas, and other military installations, but the Soviets always had to be aware of reciprocity, knowing the allies would (eventually) impose similar restrictions on the SMLMs, which was not in their interest. Use of PRAs therefore became part of the thrust and parry of the ongoing game of cat and mouse and was probably the most effective way of controlling AMLM activity – close observation or surveillance may have informed the narks of AMLM tactics, and detentions would cause short-term aggravation, but officially making an area out of bounds ensured that military activity could carry on unobserved. If there was something temporary to hide, then they always had the option of a TRA.

The imposition of a TRA was an obvious advertisement that something of interest to an AMLM was going on. They were often associated with the GSFG's annual large-scale autumn exercise but could also hide something more sinister. For example, in 1956 a large TRA was imposed close to the Polish border, which was used to stage five GSFG divisions ready to intervene in Poland if the unrest underway in Hungary spread to neighbouring communist bloc countries. This area was later incorporated into a PRA. A TRA at one end of the country could also be used to distract the AMLMs from something happening at the other. The frequency of TRAs increased steadily during the 1960s to between thirty and forty per annum, with some months having four or five new TRA maps to process, a huge burden on operations officers and the Mission's small map section. This increase in TRAs could possibly be explained by the expansion of the NVA or by the East German regime flexing its muscles. The Western powers also made extensive use of TRAs, despite being slower to impose reciprocal PRAs. The perimeters of PRAs/TRAs could yield useful intelligence, however, even if AMLMs stayed outside. Movements in and out of them could reveal what was going on, which could be matched up with intelligence from other sources (SIGINT, aerial reconnaissance). An idiosyncratic interpretation by the Soviets of the RMA (and HMA, NMA) meant that autobahns remained accessible, even when the area they cut through was off limits because of a PRA/TRA. A huge amount could be learnt by parking up next to an autobahn (sometimes even in the middle of the central reservation) and observing who and what drove past.

This geographical anomaly proved very useful in 1980 when reports started to come in about serious unrest in Poland associated with the Solidarity (Solidarność) trade union movement. NATO was understandably concerned about possible Soviet intervention following their previous form (Hungary in 1956, Czechoslovakia in 1968, and Afghanistan in 1979), so tasked all the AMLMs with looking for indications that history was about to repeat itself – large troop movements under radio silence, completely vacating barracks, imposition of TRAs, and so on. Almost immediately a TRA was imposed along the GDR–Polish border, although it only lasted ten days. However, from mid-1980 right through to December 1981 (when martial law was declared in Poland, and the risk of Soviet intervention diminished), AMLMs constantly patrolled the autobahns right up to the Polish border, exploiting (with the tacit permission of the Soviet Army) this geographical anomaly in what became known as Operation SPAHI.

The new PRA maps issued by GSFG in January 1986 showed a dramatic reduction in PRAs across the whole country – while the whole of the IGB remained behind a PRA, the border with Czechoslovakia was suddenly opened, as was much of the border with Poland, and much of the Baltic coast. This created a challenge for the AMLMs because many of the areas had been out of bounds for decades, so no one had any local knowledge or up-to-date maps. Early forays to enjoy this newfound freedom also solicited a more aggressive response from the opposition, who were not used to having AMLM cars in their backyard, but persistent and skilful touring allowed various gaps in the West's knowledge of Soviet and East German activity to be filled, such as East German Air Force base at Peenemünde. Rügen Island, the source of much drama in the early 1950s, was now open, apart from the barracks at Prora. Although BRIXMIS were quick to exploit ground and air targets in this newly available territory, naval intelligence collection was left to US Marine Corps personnel from USMLM, who had up-to-date knowledge of maritime operations. The Royal Navy warrant officer posted to the Mission around this time, Dickie Dawson, was brought in for his special operations experience in Northern Ireland, not his knowledge of ships!

Mission Restricted Signs

There was a further type of restriction for AMLMs – the Mission Restricted Sign or MRS. Up to the mid-1950s, around 450 signs could be seen close to Soviet airfields, training areas, or other military installations warning against low-flying aircraft or roving sentries. These were not covered by the Robertson–/Huebner–/Noiret–Malinin agreements and so were ignored by the allied missions, with signs often toppled or stolen. However, they did act as an 'advertisement' that there was something worth seeing in the neighbourhood. In the late 1950s, with narking increasing, the number of MRSs increased dramatically. On the night of 31 December 1957/1 January 1958 every single one of the old MRSs were replaced with a new standardised sign with black wording in four languages on a white board, nailed or bolted to a red post. 1,000 signs were changed overnight by squads of Soviet and East German soldiers, which was a major logistical feat in itself. None of this changed the AMLMs' attitude to them, and they were still routinely ignored, pushed into ditches, or stolen as souvenirs. In October 1958, the Soviets tried to lay down the law about MRSs, despite their dubious validity. Colonel General Sidelnikov, chief of staff to Marshal M. V. Zakharov, Commander-in-Chief GSFG, wrote to the AMLMs stating that the signs represented the orders of C-in-C GSFG and should be obeyed, and the Chiefs AMLM would be held personally responsible for any breaches. The concept of an MRS was not covered by the conventions controlling MLMs and so had no 'legal' basis, however, this hardening of policy could have serious implications for tourers, resulting in illegal detentions and a lot of wasted time and energy. A crisis meeting between the AMLMs agreed that while not accepting their authority one bit, tours should tread more carefully around MRSs and avoid the provocation of blatantly driving past them – skirting round the signs was the preferred action, thus avoiding confrontation and interruptions, and the locations of all the MRSs were marked on the 1:50,000 'wall' map at London Block (but *not* on the 'strip' maps carried by tours).[7] By the end of 1960 there were more than 2,500 MRSs in the GDR. By 1972, the number had grown to more than 4,000. Under Brigadier Baines (Chief BRIXMIS 1972–1974), the Mission officially adopted a policy of ignoring MRSs: 'We no longer accept the validity of these signs and drive past them when we need to do so, provided we are not under close observation.'[8] By the 1980s, the number had increased to more than 10,000, and all were plotted on the wall maps at HQ. Interestingly, the Western occupying powers and/or the West German federal authorities also used MRSs in West Germany, but the practice died out and the signs were not maintained.

PRAs and TRAs were formally notified exclusion zones and any tours found in them would be instantly detained. Violating restricted areas was a cardinal sin, which could lead to an automatic PNG or worse, and tourers were left in no doubt that if they ignored policy, they could expect little support from senior management. One exception was possibly the 'law of hot pursuit' when a tour could argue that dipping into a PRA was the only way to evade a detention, which was normally an acceptable excuse for BRIXMIS management, but not for the Soviets. The other defence was to exploit the vagueness of the PRA/TRA maps supplied by SERB, which were hand annotated onto large-scale mapping, thus allowing for a degree of interpretation. Genuine map-reading errors were normally forgiven by the Soviets, but less so with the operations officer, who would ensure the officer or NCO concerned invested his days off in private map study until he was satisfied that such an error would not happen again.

It remains a sensitive topic to this day whether tours were ever 'ordered' into PRAs for some high-value prize, something successive chiefs vigorously denied, but it is quite possible that individual tour officers sailed close to the wind citing the eleventh Commandment of 'Thou shall not get caught', and the Soviets certainly believed that PRAs were routinely violated. The final call was left to the tour officer, who could decide to enter a PRA if:

a) The risks were deemed acceptable.
b) The rewards justified the risks.
c) The officer concerned could justify his actions to command after the event.
d) Whether command agreed with a, b, and c.

As with many ventures, the 'end justifies the means,' and of course, fortune favours the brave. For critical situations (such as IoHs), permission could be sought from Chief BRIXMIS, JHQ Rheindahlen or even London to 'risk' a tour officer to obtain high-value intelligence, and during a Transition to War (TTW), all bets would be off anyway. It is also understood that US, French, and Soviet mission chiefs were less fastidious in the search for high-value intelligence. However, most touring objectives could be achieved *without* having to violate PRA boundaries.

One novel excuse, however, was officially sanctioned and enabled by emerging technology. TRAs were imposed by the Soviets with no notice, so tours *already* inside the GDR could not be expected to know about them, given their lack of two-way radio equipment – plausible deniability. Exploiting this loophole became possible with the emergence of reliable radio pager technology in the late 1970s under Operation TALON SNATCH.[9] Tours began carrying anonymous-looking black boxes (about the size of a large Mars Bar) hidden in the roof of the tour car's glove compartment, which if discovered could be explained away as part of the vehicle's electronic systems. The boxes were small paging devices that began bleeping loudly when activated by HQ BRIXMIS. The only way to stop it bleeping was to dismantle it and remove the battery, which would in turn tell London Block that the alert had been received. Inside the device's battery compartment was a coded grid reference for a pre-arranged RV point inside East Germany where they would meet another tour despatched from Berlin, be briefed on the details of the TRA and new targets, resupplied with food and fuel, before heading straight for the restricted area, safe in the knowledge that if they were detained, they could argue that they had no knowledge (and no way of knowing) that a TRA had been imposed. This obviously extended the length of the original tour, which put extra strain on the tourers, but occasionally yielded results. SERB eventually cottoned on to this ruse, so would direct Soviet units to attempt to detain the errant tours, politely inform them about the imposition of the TRA and escort them out of the area 'to safety'. This deception was just one part of the elaborate game of cat and mouse between the Mission and the opposition.

Tasking[10]

Tasking came from a variety of different sources and priorities shifted in line with the overall threat assessment, the intelligence landscape, and the structure of the Ministry of Defence (MoD and its predecessors); for example, in the early 1970s, the Soviets began to give a greater emphasis to training, so BRIXMIS tasking shifted to cover training areas, observing tactics, techniques, standards, and capabilities of GSFG. BRIXMIS formed one piece of an elaborate intelligence jigsaw, and it was ultimately the MoD that was placing the pieces on the board. The organisation within the MoD charged with coordinating the intelligence picture was the Defence Intelligence Staff (DIS) under the direction of a Chief of Defence Intelligence, with different 'desks' manned by analysts (civil servants, serving or 'retired' officers, or exchange officers from the USA or Canada), each desk concentrating on a different area. The army and RAF also maintained their own technical intelligence operations: Tech Int (Army) and Tech Int (Air). The analysts' work involved studying relevant material from unclassified publications (which today would be referred to as 'open source') to highly classified sources (TECHINT, satellite imagery, SIGINT, or even HUMINT), which were sometimes so classified that they were virtually unusable for fear of revealing the source. BRIXMIS's 'product' fell between these two extremes, and was highly valued, so much so that for many years the unit was viewed as the dedicated intelligence collection arm of Tech Int (Army) and Tech Int (Air), with tasking being dominated by these departments.

BRIXMIS provided a unique service that could not be matched by other intelligence sources – the ability to confirm the 'ground truth', to get up close and personal with

Warsaw Pact equipment, photograph it in incredible detail, and occasionally get hands-on – apart from PRAs and TRAs, of course, they had every right to be there. The tasking for BRIXMIS tours was, therefore, varied and far reaching:

> During the mid-1950s, BRIXMIS was tasked by the War Office to take photographs of a range of innocuous and seemingly benign targets in East Germany – bridges across autobahns, churches, and so on. Tourers struggled to understand the point of these targets and put them down to official contrariness. Little did they know that these targets were intended to be used as aiming points for offset bombing – a technique developed during the Second World War that used a rudimentary computer fitted to a bomb sight to deliver a bomb on a target using a different object as an aiming point. BRIXMIS were not told *why* they were taking the pictures – it was on a need-to-know basis, and they did not *need* to know.[11]

For much of the Cold War, satellite imagery could not capture non-linear features less than 4 inches (10 cm) across, but with the 1,000-mm lens used by the Mission and a skilful photographer, photographic interpreters could make out individual rivets on the underside of an aircraft, extraordinary detail that could be very valuable. For example, when the Soviet Mi-24 (NATO reporting name HIND) attack helicopters first deployed in East Germany with the 16th Tactical Air Army in spring 1974, Tech Int (Air) and their CIA colleagues were convinced that these new attack helicopters were fitted with Tactical Air-to-Surface Missiles (TASMs). BRIXMIS and the other AMLMs were briefed to look out for the arrival of the 'TASM equipped HINDs'. BRIXMIS photography subsequently showed that the 'missiles' were covered in rivets and were, in fact, long-range ferry tanks.

Collecting the individual serial numbers of tanks, vehicles, or aircraft allowed the analysts to monitor and map the Soviet military-industrial complex's research and development/procurement cycle. Equipment showcased to the world at the famous Red Square parades in Moscow was often a long way from being ready to deploy, and a sighting in the GDR would often be the first time the West had seen it for real – a genuine scoop. The Soviets kept some equipment back deep inside the impenetrable Soviet Union to avoid being picked up by the AMLMs. For example, the T-64 tank and Mi-24 HIND attack helicopter were held back for several years, and when deployed, the recipient units were under strict orders to not let them be photographed. In practice, this would mean they would be transported into the GDR fully tarped straight into PRAs on rail flatbed trucks. Even after the T-64 was deployed, tank units would strive to hide their new rides, covering them up if they were moved outside a PRA or opened up for maintenance.

Detailed photography of antennas on radar and communications vehicles and installations allowed the boffins to determine what frequencies the equipment was working at, often overturning previous assumptions. This sort of revelation helped explain why ELINT operations had failed to detect these installations and allowed countermeasures to be developed.

Tours could discover crucial fragments of information that were not available from any other source. For example, in the late 1970s, Tech Int (Air) could not explain why the 23-mm cannon on the new Mi-24 HIND attack helicopter had such a high rate of fire. The conundrum was solved when a BRIXMIS tour sneaked onto a firing range and collected a bag full of ammunition links, revealing a new design that permitted faster cycling.

Observations of static targets such as bridges, rail marshalling yards, power stations, airfields, and military bases fed straight into 2nd Tactical Air Force (2TAF, which became RAFG in 1959) targeting. Other infrastructure tasking included oil and gas pipelines, industrial and government installations, which informed both the economic and the military analysts.

Data about individual units discovered from field post office numbers written on abandoned documentation (Operation TAMARISK) or from decoded vehicle registration numbers and UVI markings helped the teams build a comprehensive picture of the Soviet and East German ORBAT. This 'ground truth' information was important to counter 'ORBAT Inflation', where estimates of the number of soldiers/tanks/APCs/helicopters/aircraft in country were artificially inflated by over-enthusiastic analysts or spoofed by deliberate Soviet SIGINT *dezinformatsiya* [disinformation]. Monitoring routine troop roulement in and out of the country, normally in long trains with the hardware on flatbed trucks and the rank-and-file troops in cattle cars, was a dull but important task.

Observing tactics and attack profiles during manoeuvres, training, exercises and at firing ranges helped the analysts determine the capabilities of the Soviet military and their equipment, allowing the development of suitable countermeasures or countertactics. For example, the Mi-8 transport helicopter (NATO reporting name HIP) supposedly could carry twenty-four fully equipped troops, but in practice (with lessons learnt the hard way in Afghanistan) would only carry twelve. Watching columns of tanks moving along a TAC route [TACtical route – a series of unpaved off-road military routes criss-crossing the GDR to aid the rapid movement of tracked armoured vehicles], or their spacing during a practice assault gave valuable data on the vehicle's performance and handling capabilities. The common sight of broken-down or abandoned vehicles on the side of the road would provide information on their reliability and possibly recovery techniques – all useful stuff.

Sometimes tasking was part of a wider project within BRIXMIS or beyond. A good example was the 'Harvest Vehicles' project from the mid-1970s. Tours had reported the mass exodus of Soviet heavy transport trucks each year in the mid- to late summer. These headed eastwards on rail flatbed trucks and returned the same way some months later. The team realised that these trucks were heading home to help with the annual grain harvest (there was insufficient civilian transport capacity in the Soviet Union), but it was unclear how it was organised, how many trucks were involved, and what impact it had on GSFG's logistics capability. The Research team at BRIXMIS embarked on a project to investigate this annual phenomenon, briefing tours to record sightings (ideally with photos), noting the VRNs and the distinctive numerical UVI markings on the roofs and doors of the truck cabs, which seemed to be unique to this harvest role (not the most exciting tour brief, but important, all the same). Similarly, Chipmunk sorties were briefed to look out for similar movements. The project lasted more than a whole year, allowing the full cycle to be observed and recorded. The outcome was that the harvest vehicles and drivers were formed into composite battalions and companies with all GSFG divisions contributing vehicles. The team calculated the number of vehicles involved, which amounted to a third of GSFG heavy transport capacity each year – a major annual weakness in their ORBAT.

A key task for BRIXMIS was to confirm the 'ground truth', which at times contradicted the intelligence picture held at the MoD. In the early 1980s, when international tensions were high, a BRIXMIS tour was lucky to spot a night-time 'crash out' of the whole of the 16th Guards Tank Division from their barracks at Neustrelitz to their Emergency Deployment Areas. Successive tours were able to monitor the division over several days, noting that rather return to their barracks, they deployed further along TAC routes, road, and rail into PRAs to the south and south-west (that is, heading towards West Germany). Tours strategically positioned at known chokepoints (railway sidings, level crossings, bridges) tracked the various sub-units from the temporary UVI markings applied to the vehicles and witnessed the huge formation heading via the Rathenow PRA towards the massive Letzlinger Heide training area. This was a major movement of troops, which should have caught the attention of the MoD and NATO, but because it had taken place in radio silence, controlled by traffic reggies and the Soviet underground landline telephone system, GCHQ had not picked it up – the BRIXMIS reports were therefore met with some scepticism. When the 16th began their training and live-firing exercises at Letzlinger Heide the airwaves went crazy, sending the GCHQ listeners into a panic and turning all the Indicators of Hostility markers red [the IoH board at the MoD was made from coloured discs hanging from hooks on a big noticeboard – not very high-tech!]. Despite the BRIXMIS reports, GCHQ had not picked up that a whole Soviet tank division was on the move and thought the huge spike in radio traffic was the start of World War Three. The MoD official responsible for the IoH board happened to be in Berlin at the time and Chief BRIXMIS used the big louvre blind map in the Ops Office to brief him on what was in fact just a training exercise, using the photos taken by the tours and their reports tracking the division to reassure him that war was not, in fact, imminent.[12]

Overall intelligence objectives were set annually, with time-sensitive tasking being pushed to the front of the queue. Occasionally a desk officer would travel out to Berlin to meet with BRIXMIS personnel to brief or be debriefed on important or urgent matters. One set of pictures would often lead to further tasking to get more, to get closer (or use a longer lens), or shoot the equipment from a different angle, and if an immediate answer was needed, an extra tour (or series of tours to observe changing patterns of activity) would be despatched to investigate, rather than wait for the next scheduled trip, with the results hitting the analysts' desks within days. In such cases, Chief BRIXMIS would override the agreed regional rota if necessary (and may or may not advise his opposite numbers) and even give the tour permission to contravene PRAs or TRAs if the risk/reward calculation supported it. The tour officer, however, had control on the ground and it was his decision to proceed or not to. Elaborate games were sometimes played for security reasons, or for plausible deniability – sometimes a tour crew was not given the background to a particular tasking or were sent innocently to a particular area in the hope/expectation that they would stumble onto a particular target and report it back up the chain – it was sometimes useful to attribute a piece of useful intelligence to BRIXMIS to protect a much more sensitive source, such as satellite or aerial reconnaissance, SIGINT or even HUMINT, thus allowing it to reach a wider audience. Such niceties were not maintained at the USMLM, where tour officers received the full spectrum of background intelligence from various US agencies, which allowed them to obtain relatively more scoops.

Tasking would arrive at the Mission via the Weapons, Research or Operations teams, depending on where it originated from, and the ops officers would allocate it to a specific tour, prepare the brief, and deliver it to the tour crew. From the early days of the Mission, a 'targeting book' was established, which was a 'wish list' of items requested by their customers, and this evolved into the 'Research' cell at HQ BRIXMIS, manned by members of the Intelligence Corps. For years a paper-based system of target folders was maintained, but by the early 1980s, it was being computerised as Project ELECTRIC LIGHT. As GSFG rearmed in the early 1980s, the amount of tasking increased proportionally, and the Mission was in danger of being swamped by conflicting requests. In response to this, Brigadier John Learmont (Chief BRIXMIS 1982–1984) introduced 'The Chief's Directive', which prioritised the tasking based on what he (and his bosses at JHQ Rheindahlen) felt important, and that helped focus the Mission's activities.

Types of Tours

Until touring was integrated in the 1980s, the army and RAF operations (and Royal Navy in the early years) were run independently of each other, even down to having their own vehicles and drivers, but integration aside, tours could generally be classified under five main types, with some inevitable overlap and crossover:

a) The ground tour (army) or army tour concentrated on ground targets: troop movements (often rail based), training, armour, artillery, AFVs, missiles/rocketry, signals, bases, military installations and ORBAT.

b) The ground tour (RAF), or air tour (not to be confused with the Chipmunk airborne reconnaissance) concentrated on airfields, air bases, aircraft, helicopters, air weapons ranges, radar and communications sites, and anti-aircraft weaponry. They also looked at air tactics, including the increasing use of helicopters.

c) A variation of the ground tour was the infrastructure tour, which, as the name suggests, concentrated on less glamourous but equally important Soviet or East German infrastructure targets, such as bridges, factories, or power stations, information that would be fed into RAFG targeting or to the economic analysts. By the 1960s, these became less common. 'Mapper' tours, used to update the maps used by tours, lacked the 'cut and thrust' of normal touring but were also vitally important. Apart from the mapping project in the mid-1970s, mapping (or infrastructure) tasking was used to fill the quiet moments in the Soviet training cycle or tagged on to normal tours, to be undertaken en route to another target.

d) In the early 1970s, 'town' tours were introduced, where a small group of Mission personnel would head off in the Mission minibus to a garrison town somewhere in the GDR. On arrival, they would book into a hotel, pay their compliments to the local *komendant*, and then have a saunter round the town centre, popping into the sort of bars and beer gardens that Soviet officers would frequent. This may sound a bit like a pub crawl on Her Majesty's budget, but these town tours had three important objectives. First, they gave Russian (and German) linguists the chance to practise outside of the stressful environment of a detention. Second, tours could pick up useful bits of low-level intelligence through chatting with officers or locals, and listening to their conversations, picking up on morale or gossip. Lastly, the tour members were on their best behaviour, and this low-impact, or even friendly, interaction would show the Soviets that the British were human after all, a common brotherhood of soldiery and demonstration of British 'soft power'. The bonds developed during these informal interactions could yield surprising results out in the field.

e) The final type of tour was conducted from about 500 feet in the air (often a lot lower) in a de Havilland Chipmunk two-seater training aircraft, giving the Mission a completely different perspective to their targets.

All the types of tours had their own challenges, their differences, but also their similarities, but at the heart of all touring was rigorous planning. The adage 'If you fail to plan, you plan to fail' was core to Mission thinking.

Tri-Mission Coordination

In the early years, the three missions worked independently, and had little contact with each other – Major Jim Symes MC*, tour officer from 1948–1950, admitted to not even knowing where the French mission was, even though it was on the very same street, Geschwister Schollstraße in Potsdam.* They consequently planned their own touring programmes, which inevitably resulted in some areas being 'over-toured' or the embarrassing situation of tours tripping over each other, in full view of the opposition. Tours could also stumble into the carnage left by previous tours, innocently driving into a swarm of angry Stasi/Vopos/NVA/Soviets. Over-touring also meant that other parts of the GDR were neglected.

Group Captain George Foot OBE, deputy chief during Brigadier Wynne-Pope's chaotic tenure (March 1956–September 1957), began discussing some form of coordination with the other two missions, but received little support from his wayward boss. However, under the steadying hand of Brigadier Fitzalan-Howard, who joined as chief in September 1957, Foot started to make some progress. BRIXMIS had always been close to the USMLM, but the elderly *général de brigade* in charge of MMFL refused to cooperate. The British and Americans, therefore, bilaterally adopted new procedures that quickly yielded results:

a) Areas were clearly defined and allocated to the two missions on a week-by-week basis.

b) Tour programmes were jointly planned a week in advance, excluding emergencies or targets of specific interest.

c) All tours would be debriefed at the USMLM rear headquarters at Föhrenweg 19/21, near the Berlin Brigade headquarters complex.

The French *général* retired in 1958 and his successor was happy to cooperate and the tri-mission approach to touring was born. Inevitably there were foul-ups and occasionally poaching on another mission's territory, but the system produced results and lasted right through to the end of the AMLMs.† The coordination took the form of weekly meetings (at various levels within the AMLMs), monthly lunches (good for rapport and team-building), daily phone calls, especially from the operations team, and the shared reporting of the immediate post-tour 'highlights' form and the monthly/annual reports, even though the French were not members of the 'Five Eyes' Intelligence Community.[13] Bonds were also built at the many social functions attended by the AMLMs.

The biggest improvement was the division of the GDR into three regions: the north of the GDR was region A, the east/south-east was C, and west/south-west was B. A ground and an air tour were allocated to each region, each undertaken by a different mission, and these assignments rotated clockwise through the regions (A, C, B, A, C, B, and so on) weekly in a three-weekly pattern. That meant that every region was

---

* Major Symes was awarded two Military Cross medals - MC* after his name denotes this, spoken as 'MC and bar'.

† Some BRIXMIS personnel used the phrase 'French PRA' to describe a colleague who adopted a more laissez-faire approach to the rules of touring.

visited by each mission for a ground tour and an air tour once in the three-week cycle.*
There was a fourth region known as 'Local', which included Potsdam and the target-rich environment out to Brandenburg, approximately 30 kilometres north, west, and south of Potsdam. Local tours were rotated on a twenty-four- or forty-eight-hour basis, one mission at a time. Because much of the 'Local' region fell within the Berlin Control Zone, 'local' tours were coordinated with air reconnaissance, both the light aircraft based in Berlin and the air corridor reconnaissance missions. For example, if an RAF 60 Squadron Percival Pembroke corridor sortie in the morning spotted something interesting as it approached Berlin, a Gatow-based Chipmunk could be sent out to follow up on the sighting in the afternoon. A ground tour could be despatched at the same time to view the target from a different perspective. Patterns are never advisable in the intelligence collection business, but the positives of the tri-region planning outweighed the negatives, with much less chance of tours tripping over each other or areas being over-toured. The vague law of hot pursuit (where all was forgiven if trespassing occurred during a chase – being chased or in pursuit of a scoop) and command prerogative could, of course, override the tri-region pattern.

Table showing an example three-week regional allocation.

Week	Type	A	C	B
1	Ground	MMFL	USMLM	BRIXMIS
	Air	BRIXMIS	MMFL	USMLM
2	Ground	USMLM	BRIXMIS	MMFL
	Air	MMFL	USMLM	BRIXMIS
3	Ground	BRIXMIS	MMFL	USMLM
	Air	USMLM	BRIXMIS	MMFL

Major operations were organised on a tri-mission basis, especially where the AMLMs needed to flood an area to monitor major troop movements, withdrawals, or change-overs, or monitor something out of the ordinary, such as Operation SPAHI in 1980/1981, which looked for any Soviet troop concentrations on the Polish border that could indicate their intention to intervene in Poland during the trade-union-led unrest. Another tri-mission 'special' operation involved monitoring the dispersal of all the KIT seen at the annual parades in East Berlin, where all three AMLMs would follow the various tanks, armoured vehicles, and missiles back to their home bases, thus discovering/confirming who and what was based where.

The relationships between the AMLMs were warm and generally productive, but it would be an exaggeration to say that intelligence was shared equally. The French often worked to their own agenda, and the Americans could be stubborn or even xenophobic such as their unilateral approach to Berlin Control Zone (BCZ) air reconnaissance or

---

* The original plans to leave one region 'fallow' (or rested) each week were abandoned in line with increasing tasking.

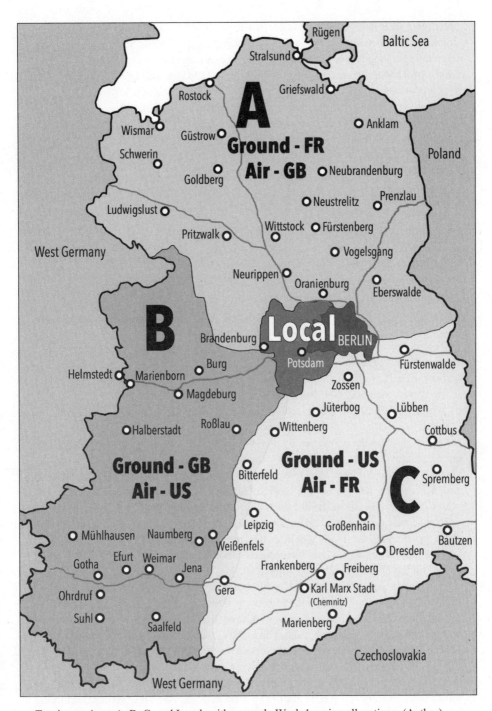

Touring regions, A, B, C, and Local, with example Week 1 region allocations. (Author)

classifying their material as NOFORN (not to be shown to 'foreigners'), but there is no doubt that the three missions were stronger when they worked together. English was the common operating language, but that still led to confusion from time to time. In the mid-1970s, MoD Tech Int sent an urgent request to BRIXMIS to clarify something that had appeared in one of the USMLM's reports. It showed a photo of a MiG-23 FLOGGER, and someone had circled an unidentified protrusion on the aircraft's wing, marking it 'BTFOM' – the MoD analyst wanted to know what a 'BTFOM' was. With much amusement, the USMLM weapons officer replied that 'BTFOM' stood for 'beats the f**k out of me' and left it to the BRIXMIS weapons officer to explain that to London.[14]

Planning

Up until the late 1950s, the pace of touring was relatively relaxed, with tour officers going out for one or two shortish tours per week, normally staying in hotels. As the Cold War intensified and the situation in East Germany became more complicated (formation of the NVA, closure of IGB, building the Berlin Wall, etc.), the workload increased so by the mid-1960s tour officers were expected to do a 'long' thirty-six-hour tour (camping), a 'short' twenty-four-hour tour, and a 'local' per week, quite a packed schedule when all the preparation and debriefing is factored in. Tours were ideally no more than thirty-six hours, because it was realised that with continual stress and little sleep, fatigue and the law of diminishing returns kicked in. However, sometimes they were extended to four or five days to break up the pattern, or where operations called for it. Tired crew members had slower reflexes and made poor decisions, the combination of which could put the whole tour in jeopardy, and the longer they were out, the longer it was before their intelligence could be acted on. There was also the impact on family life to consider. However, by the 1980s the GDR had become a very target-rich environment with both ground and air tours out every day of the week, come rain or shine. Given the different objectives of an air tour vs. an army tour, and the different skill set required, the two services initially maintained separate operations teams, each with their own ops officer. By the mid-1960s, command began to recognise the value of inter-service cooperation and the first joint tours began, which were quite successful, but it was not until the 1980s that tours became properly integrated.

The tour programme would be prepared a month in advance by the ops officers and posted on the ops room noticeboard (see Chapter 6, 'The Opposition', for the alleged intelligence breach in the late 1950s by communist spy George Blake). The touring regions would be allocated from the tri-mission meetings, so the ops officers would know that in a particular week, an air tour was required in one region, while a ground tour was needed in another. For air tours, Squadron Leader Operations also had to factor in known Soviet and East German flying days, and even the long-range weather forecast. The ops officers would then try to bring all the moving parts together into the programme; for example, air tours in the 1980s would normally be sent out on a Sunday evening, returning on Tuesday evening. A second tour would be sent on Thursday evening, returning on Saturday evening. Special arrangements would be made to cover major events such as the May Day and October Revolution parades in East Berlin (where mission vehicles would be strategically placed around the city to watch the parade vehicles move from the city into the barracks), major exercises, closures of autobahns (which were to be used as emergency landing strips for East German and Soviet aircraft), or tri-mission operations. Carefully constructed programmes could be thrown into disarray by emergency targeting, sickness, leave, or when the deputy chief or chief decided they wanted to go out on tour – the areas for the deputy's or chief's tour would need to be carefully chosen to give him something interesting to see but to minimise the chance of a detention. The deputy's tours tended to be a mid-week affair, punching a hole in a carefully crafted schedule. If the nominated tour region changed mid-tour, this would have to be included in the brief to avoid the different missions tripping over each other.

Tour Manning

As has already been discussed, BRIXMIS were able to have three crew per tour because of the larger number of passes allocated by the RMA – USMLM normally toured with two, while MMFL varied between two and three. Up until the mid-1950s, tour crews normally comprised two officers and a JNCO driver. If they were short of an officer, then one of the Intelligence Corps corporals attached to the Mission would stand in. The two corporals were both national servicemen and were not linguists, but they helped with the workload on tour. It was rare for an officer to go out with just a driver unless it was a Potsdam 'local' tour or in an emergency, although the 'civilian' officers (economic, political, agricultural, or SIS) would sometimes go out with just a driver, albeit in uniform with an honorary rank. It was not the 'done thing' for a tour officer to drive himself – his job was to observe and photograph, which could not be done behind the wheel, although Brigadier Wynn-Pope would often take the wheel when he felt his driver was not being aggressive enough. The two Intelligence Corps corporals were not allowed to tour together because they normally lacked the language skills needed during a detention, and at the time touring was still viewed as an *officer's* job. When the supply of national servicemen dried up in the late 1950s (national service was abolished in 1960 with the last serviceman being discharged in 1963) BRIXMIS struggled to fill the vacancies – HQ BAOR could not spare any of its Intelligence Corps corporals, but the 4th Guards Armoured Brigade attached to BAOR provided two corporals on loan, an arrangement that continued for some years. However, by the mid-1960s, the tour manning had settled into a standardised and very effective format:

a) Tour officer – he commanded the tour, and as such was the C-in-C's representative on the ground. The tour officer was responsible for navigation, photography, and was normally a linguist, which was helpful if the tour was detained.

b) Tour NCO – the second navigator, and expert in recognition, who would record what was being photographed (sometimes including film and frame number) in notebooks or dictated into a small Dictaphone. Normally he would be a Senior NCO (sergeant, staff sergeant, or warrant officer) but if the chief or deputy chief was touring, then the 'NCO' would be an officer. In later years the tour 'officer' role was sometimes taken by the SAS warrant officer, making it an all-NCO crew. The SAS NCOs were responsible for tactical training within the Mission and were as, if not more, experienced as many of the commissioned officers.

c) Tour driver – responsible for driving and making use of advanced driving techniques to evade the opposition or travel cross-country. The driver was also responsible for security, to maintain a 360° lookout while the officer and NCO were concentrating on their targets. Drivers underwent special training and were normally from the Royal Corps of Transport or RAF, and apart from the early days, were not service specific, where an RAF driver could drive an 'army' tour or vice versa.

The tour crew was probably one of the tightest teams in the British military because of the unique demands of the job and the practical reality of being cooped up in a car together. Close teamwork and complete trust in each other's abilities were essential, and to a certain extent, everyone had to be able to do each other's job, with some of the traditional barriers of rank broken down. However, the tour officer was still referred to as 'Sir' or perhaps 'Boss', but towards the end of the 1980s as the British Army changed, use of first names may have begun to creep in with junior tour officers. The Mission's secret weapon was the JNCO driver, normally a corporal from the Royal Corps of Transport or RAF (although in the early years they were national servicemen who had learnt to drive in the services, normally on a truck, and had little or no experience of real driving).* Their advanced driving skills, bravery, and common sense got tours out of many a drama. The tour driver was responsible for safely (and covertly) approaching the target, for planning how to exit the area, and ultimately made the decision to stay or go, which most tour officers respected – the driver knew the car and his own limits as a driver, while the officer and/or tour NCO could sometimes let their enthusiasm get the better of them. The driver could also fix most mechanical problems, and normally slept in the car with the doors locked for security. In theory, the tour crew changed for each tour, but it soon became clear that some combinations (officer, NCO, and driver) were more successful than others, so they were often assigned together.[15] The ops officers also tried to balance the skills and experience within each crew: an experienced NCO with a new officer, and vice versa; an experienced driver with a new NCO, and so on. All tour members had a say in key decisions, which had the effect of moderating any excesses of enthusiasm (or risk), and the three-person dynamic meant that the most senior person, or he who shouts loudest, did not necessarily get his own way. Risks were taken, because after all, it was a dangerous environment they were working in, but never casually. Tours were meticulously planned, and the collective decision making and overriding motto of 'there will always be another day' generally prevailed. Their reputation as 'cowboys' or 'hooligans' creating mayhem all over the GDR was a myth spread by the East Germans, who hated having the AMLMs on their supposedly

---

* Corporal Len Holman's sum total of driving experience when he arrived in Berlin (January 1953) as a tour driver was a week on a British Army 3-ton Bedford truck! The first car he ever drove was a BRIXMIS tour car and he suffered from car sickness on his first trip out.

'sovereign' territory. Any high-risk operations, such as deliberately entering a PRA, would have to be approved at command level, where the risk assessment was political as well as physical.

The crew also had to spend days at a time in the forced intimacy of the car's interior: eating, sleeping (in the case of the driver), and working together, with little privacy (apart from possibly a few hours' sleep in their tents). Patience, tolerance, and a keen sense of humour were essential, creating an unusual bond and sense of camaraderie between tourers. That said, there were occasional heated arguments between tour officer and NCO about differing opinions of a target or an incident, especially when all parties were tired, and afterwards it was possible to cut the atmosphere inside the tour car with a knife! Fatigue was sometimes a problem for tour personnel, especially the driver, who had to be alert and fully functioning for most of the tour with the combined role of driving and security, unlike the tour officer, who could 'rest his eyes' from time to time in the back seat.

Mission personnel of differing ranks would also have far more social contact with each other than in other units – this came about because BRIXMIS was a relatively small unit (no more than eighty strong) and personnel worked in close contact with each other, including in the confines of a car. Socialising at formal and informal liaison functions was also part and parcel of Mission life, as was the off-duty socialising at the Potsdam Mission House – the Mission's own 'country club'. Unusually for the British military, there was also the all-ranks BRIXMIS Club – the bar at London Block where Mission personnel could have a few beers after a tour. Successive chiefs and the counterintelligence people encouraged this activity as it allowed tourers to decompress after a stressful outing inside East Germany, safe in the knowledge that they were all security cleared and could talk openly about their experiences and adventures – consequently very few outsiders were ever invited in. The club was also home to all kinds of touring memorabilia and trophies.

The lengthy recruitment and training cycle tended to weed out anybody who would not fit into this unusual set-up, but ultimately if an individual did not perform (too aggressive, too meek, too arrogant, too dangerous), then they would quickly be posted out of the Mission, a waste of a lot of time and money.

The old adage describing military life as '99 per cent boredom, 1 per cent sheer terror' is quite appropriate to touring. It should not be forgotten that all tours were effectively operating in hostile territory, behind 'enemy' lines, and exposed to physical violence and potentially lethal force every time they crossed the Glienicke Bridge into East Germany (especially after Adjudant-Chef Philippe Mariotti's fatal ramming in 1984 and Major Arthur 'Nick' Nicholson's fatal shooting 1985, which are discussed in Chapter 6, 'The Opposition'). The '1 per cent' could be very 'kinetic', with high-speed car chases, violent manoeuvring, and cases of physical violence. Touring was also subject to the stress that comes with covert operations, where tourers had to spend hours or even days in covert OPs under 'hard' routine, sometimes just a few feet away from armed and aggressive 'enemy' soldiers. As well as requiring strong leadership and technical skills plus nerves of steel, touring required a fair amount of personal bravery, with stress levels close to those experiencing combat. The stress would show itself in a variety of ways, depending on the individual's psychological make-up: some internalised it and kept it within his family (which could also lead to problems), while others showed the classic physical symptoms of combat-related stress.

A tour from 1978 illustrates the point: Captain David Duncan BEM (Intelligence Corps, and head of the Research team) was on a tour with Sergeant 'Geordie' Wood and Corporal Colin 'Dinger' Bell (RCT) observing a major assault river crossing exercise on the Elbe near Havelberg.[16] The tour's OP was spotted by a HIND attack helicopter, which began to buzz the tour's position, calling in ground troops and vehicles to intercept. Having stirred up a hornets' nest, Duncan decided it was time to leave, so Corporal Bell made a swift exit, which was going well until he found the path ahead blocked by a BMP tracked AFV. The only way round was across a ploughed field, which the Opel Admiral could just about cope with, but not as well as the tracked Soviet BMP, which began to catch them up. However, Dinger Bell's extraordinary driving skills allowed them to evade their pursuers and they finally got across the field, onto a proper track and away to safety. The acute stress of the escape, unfortunately, took its toll on Corporal Bell, and after they had stopped, he slumped across the wheel, unconscious. Sergeant Wood quickly pulled Dinger from the driver's seat and took his place, and believing Bell was having a heart attack, they sped into Havelberg itself, where they knew a civilian hospital was located. Duncan was the Mission's main German linguist but spoke no Russian, so they were determined to get him to a German civilian hospital, rather than the nearest Soviet military hospital (which was in a PRA, complicating matters further). They arrived at the small hospital unmolested to find the door was locked (it was a weekend) but as the staff did not immediately respond to the frantic ringing of the doorbell, Duncan kicked the door in. Finding the duty doctor ensconced in his office watching television, Duncan explained in perfect German that his services were required, and to his credit, the doctor got straight to work, ignoring the fact that these were uniformed British soldiers (and the minor point of the kicked-in front door). Dinger had begun to come round, and the medical staff did some tests with Duncan translating. Someone must have tipped off the Vopos, who in turn summoned some non-English- (or German-) speaking Soviet officers. Sergeant Wood had also called the Potsdam Mission House and after a while Major Gavin Scott-Forrest MBE arrived, who was a fluent Russian speaker, and he forcefully explained that Corporal Bell was *not* going to go to a Soviet military hospital, but back to the British Military Hospital with them. They all parted on good terms and rushed Bell back, where he was diagnosed as having suffered from a stress-related collapse. Bell had not complained of feeling unduly stressed, nor shown any symptoms of combat-related stress, but after an extremely intense 'kinetic' incident, where he had used all his skills, judgement, resourcefulness and personal bravery, his body simply gave up on him. Thankfully, he made a full recovery, returning to touring after a bit of a rest, but it is interesting to see how even the most rounded individual can be affected by such high-intensity situations. Most tour personnel would privately admit to having the occasional 'wobble' while on-pass, matched with the courage to get back into the car again.

There was no doubt that the adrenaline rush that came with touring could be addictive, so the operations officers and command kept a close eye on any tourers who were getting a bit over-enthusiastic, over-confident and gung-ho, or taking risks that could get somebody killed (the potential sanction of a PNG also tended to moderate such excesses). The role of the great British NCO should also not be overlooked, as they helped moderate any extreme behaviour within the team and could have a 'quiet word' if the edges were beginning to show on a colleague. The close-knit team atmosphere was also a crucial part of keeping body and soul together and made the Mission such a success.

Preparation

Once a crew was assigned to a tour, the preparation began. The day before the tour was due to leave, the tour officer would receive a detailed briefing from the relevant ops officer on the overall objectives of the tour and any specific intelligence they were after, sometimes supplemented by intelligence from other sources, such as SIGINT material from Field Station Berlin (FSB), RAF Gatow, and other listening stations, although the actual source of the information may have been held back for security reasons. Until RAF and army touring became integrated in the 1980s, briefing would be conducted independently. The RAF team, who were mostly aircrew, followed a formal structured briefing format, similar to an operational flying sortie, while army tours adopted their usual 'orders' approach. Tours would be given primary and secondary targets, with additional tasks such as mapping or checking a dispersal airfield or emergency deployment area on the way. The tour officer would then sit down with the tour NCO, discuss the specific objectives, and carefully plan the route using the big 1:50,000 wall map or 1:25,000 sheet maps (see 'Mapping', below), identifying suitable OPs and Z-platzes, including approach and escape routes; because they studied them so closely, tour personnel would often know the roads and tracks around the GDR better than most Soviets and even some East Germans. Referring to the relevant target folders, they would want to know when the site had last been visited (including by the other AMLMs), what previous visits had yielded, how sensitive the target was (Soviet military and nark activity), whether any established OPs had been compromised, and whether there had been any detentions or incidents in the area.

They would then prepare all their travelling maps and kit, checking that the cameras and tape recorders were working, and that there was a good supply of film and plenty of fresh batteries. Any mission-specific kit (see Chapter 5, 'Tools of the Trade') would be booked out and readied. The driver might also be brought in at this stage to get his input on the route, and he would prepare the car and all the car-related equipment.

The Tour

The routine before a tour would be different depending on when the departure time had been set. Army tours tended to leave in the morning, while RAF tours tended to leave early evening. Each tour member was responsible for their own personal and camping kit, plus their preferred food for the trip. The tour began in the M/T office at London Block where the driver signed out the tour car, which he had previously prepared, and would then collect the tour NCO and tour officer (with their personal kit) from their respective quarters. It was the driver's responsibility to stow all the kit where it could be easily accessed and to ensure it would not fly around the interior during violent manoeuvres. In the G-Wagen, the six flasks of hot water for the obligatory brew stops were stowed in a specially built container next to the centrally positioned tour officer's seat, which doubled as a useful tabletop, while in the saloons they would be stashed in a bag. With all the personal kit stowed, they would return to London Block where the tour officer and NCO would head up to the BRIXMIS offices. There, they would check the latest highlights forms for anything worth knowing, check for any updates from the relevant ops officer and pick up any messages for the Potsdam Mission House warrant officer. They would collect their operational briefcases (nav bags), any mission-specific equipment, while the officer would pick up his custom-made camera bag. The final job was to sign out in the tour log. RAF tours, who would be leaving in the evening and driving most of the night, would normally head home to try to snatch a few hours' sleep once everything was squared away.

Normally a tour would head straight to the Glienicke Bridge to cross into the GDR and begin the tour proper, but local tours (Potsdam area) would arrange a rendezvous with the tour just coming off the local, normally one of the other AMLMs, in a specific lay-by just before the bridge, where any specific 'local' information would be shared.

Glienicke Bridge

After the Berlin Wall went up in 1961, the Glienicke Bridge became the designated (and only) crossing point from West Berlin (the bridge was in the south-west corner of the American sector) to Potsdam and the GDR, a single-span, all-metal bridge, the profile of which became one of Cold War Berlin's many icons. Coming from West Berlin, tour cars first stopped at the Berlin police checkpoint, a single-pole cantilever barrier, and then, with berets donned, proceeded across the bridge, over the painted yellow line that separated East and West to a solid-looking red and white (later green) painted fence with an electronically controlled rolling gate, remotely opened from the Soviet guard house. The tour car would drive up to the control point and the ritual of the passes would begin. There was no talking in the car as it was assumed they were subject to electronic surveillance while on the bridge. The driver or tour NCO would get out, with his door being locked after him, and approach the small window, salute smartly, and hand over the three tour passes plus the vehicle pass to the duty officer, before returning to the vehicle. A few minutes later, with the Soviet officer having taken down all the tour's details (name, rank, and service), a sentry would return the passes to the NCO through an open car window. They would then drive through a tight chicane, which was quite a challenge if a coach, truck, or the recovery trailer was being brought over, with many a scrape on the concrete blocks. A sentry would then lift a final cantilever pole barrier while his colleague in a guard hut opened the final rolling gate remotely and the tour entered East Germany proper.

As East/West relations ebbed and flowed, and as technology developed, the design of the checkpoint on the bridge changed: the familiar red and white lifting cantilever poles gave way to electronically operated rolling gates; bollards swelled into massive

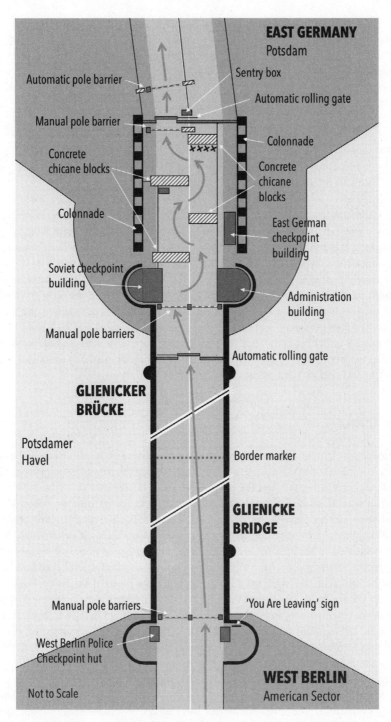

EAST GERMANY
Potsdam

Automatic pole barrier

Sentry box

Automatic rolling gate

Manual pole barrier

Colonnade

Concrete
chicane blocks

Concrete
chicane
blocks

Colonnade

East German
checkpoint
building

Soviet checkpoint
building

Administration
building

Manual pole barriers

Automatic rolling gate

**GLIENICKER
BRÜCKE**

Potsdamer
Havel

Border marker

**GLIENICKE
BRIDGE**

Manual pole barriers

'You Are Leaving' sign

West Berlin Police
Checkpoint hut

Not to Scale

WEST BERLIN
American Sector

Glienicke Bridge border crossing, late 1970s. (Author, based on contemporary descriptions) concrete blocks and then back to just bollards; and towards the end they used electrically operated rising barriers, with presumably some diabolical contraptions built in to the road surface to trap any transgressors; by 1988 there were six barriers to pass through.[17] There was also a change in the appearance and demeanour of the Soviet guards. Lieutenant Colonel John Cormack MBE MC, tour officer 1964–1965, described the Soviets then as:

> distant and surly. There was minimal courtesy. They were slovenly looking. Their uniforms were poor. Their bearing was poor. Most were national service conscripts and they really felt it their business to be as slow as possible about getting you across the bridge.[18]

When Cormack returned in 1986 as part of the BRIXMIS fortieth birthday celebrations, it was very different, with very smart sentries and a much more business-like atmosphere. One thing that did not change, however, was the appalling state of the roads once the tour left the checkpoint. It was assumed that the tour's details were immediately passed to the Vopo/Stasi office on the other side of the bridge, and the relevant departments were informed that a new tour had entered the GDR.[19] The only other use for the Glienicke Bridge was for the exchange of spies, such as the famous Bridge of Spies exchange between KGB Colonel Rudolf Abel and CIA pilot Francis Gary Powers on 10 February 1962. Having cleared the bridge, berets would be stowed, and the tour would stop by the Mission House to pick up/drop off any messages, top up the snack box, before heading into the GDR.

The Target

The shenanigans at the Glienicke Bridge and the challenges of travelling across the GDR were all a precursor to the main event – getting eyes on the target. The objective might be a fixed installation that had the potential to yield intelligence or a specific location where it was believed that something interesting was going to happen. The former could be an airfield, barracks, or radar installation, the latter, a road junction or stretch of railway line. In most cases the tour had to establish a covert or unobtrusive OP (observation post, position, or point) where they could lay up and wait for something to happen. Common places for OPs were where different transport types intersected (road, rail, river, or TAC route) as this increased the likelihood of a sighting. For an 'air' tour, the OP needed to be close to the target airfield and preferably under the flightpath to allow detailed photography of aircraft as they took off or came in to land. In most cases, the OP required vehicular access, and the tour personnel remained in, or close to, the vehicle, but sometimes the officer and/or NCO would move away from the car (known as a 'foot recce') and establish an OP closer to the target using natural cover – clearly the risk increased in proportion to the distance from the relative safety of the tour car. Although the olive drab vehicles and army green uniforms worn were intended to be low visibility, the Mission stopped short of actively camouflaging their cars or themselves. This would have been against the spirit of the RMA and could have led to all sorts of problems down the line. Tours would therefore make use of natural cover by positioning themselves in a wooded area in the shadow of trees, for example, and a tour officer could hide in some bushes, but they would not drape camo nets or branches over the vehicle or don a ghillie suit. The Americans, however, routinely wore camo uniforms and occasionally camouflaged their vehicles, which led to a more aggressive response from the opposition. While the tour officer and NCO were concentrating on photographing and logging the opposition activity, the driver would remain in the vehicle and maintain 360° security around the vehicle, sometimes standing up through the sunroof or roof cupola for a better view. Normally the approach to an OP would have been pre-planned, and possible escape routes in case of discovery reconnoitred in advance; relative rank notwithstanding, it was the driver's decision whether to 'order' his superiors back into the car and beat a hasty retreat.

The ideal OP, therefore, varied according to the objective, but in general terms should allow the target to be observed by the naked eye or through binoculars or telephoto lenses, benefit from natural cover (trees, bushes), and preferably have more than one way to escape (in the opposite direction from the threat).

As well as a static OP, a tour might stumble on a 'target of opportunity' such as a convoy of military vehicles, a unit crashing out of a barracks to go to their emergency deployment area, or a formation of helicopters transiting across the GDR. The tour would therefore need to decide whether to tag along to see what was going on, or to stick with their original objectives. On the basis that 'it is easier to ask for forgiveness than permission', such a diversion would be judged by whether it yielded something of value, and such

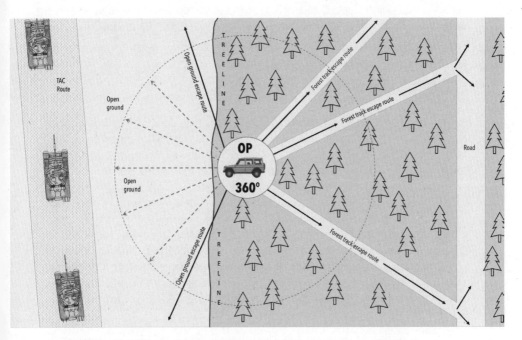

An ideal OP with 360° security observation and multiple escape routes. (Author)

decisions got easier with experience. If out on an 'air tour', for example, a tour would not automatically investigate an 'army' ground target, because a tour from one of the other AMLMs might have already been there – in each of the three regions, there would be a 'ground' tour from one AMLM, and an 'air' tour from another, to avoid them tripping over each other. However, it was standard practice that if a significant KIT train was spotted, the tour would stay in place for another six hours (less for an RAF tour) in case it was the first element of a much larger rail movement. The pre-target routine was developed from years of experience, but the tour would never know quite how things would turn out. First, the doors were locked, and the windows wound up – later cars had the luxury of air conditioning so keeping the windows closed for security was not too unbearable in the heat of summer. All maps were stowed, and cameras made ready, full of fresh film, and with the settings and lens choice anticipating the likely conditions. The target, time, location, and direction of travel had already been murmured into the handheld tape recorder. The driver would try to approach slowly and quietly using low revs (thus in the summer, kicking up less of a dust cloud), knowing that his vehicle had plenty of power to propel them out of trouble, unless something got in the way. The tour officer and NCO would be thinking about the target and the sort of equipment they might see, while the driver would be planning their exit. The call of 'KIT!' would energise the occupants of the vehicle as they sprang into action, each ready to perform his allotted task. The NCO would turn on his recorder and reach for his binoculars to get a good look, with his notepad and pen to hand. The officer would bring his camera up, checking the light conditions, camera settings, and making sure he had the right lens, grabbing an alternative camera body/lens combo if a different sort of shot was required. A rapid exchange of comments, questions, expletives, and orders would follow, with the NCO giving the driver directions while the motor drive of the officer's camera whirred over his shoulder. The driver would also have his eyes peeled for any unwelcome interest from the opposition.

Army/Ground Tour Specifics

'Army' or 'ground' tours had a wider range of targets than their RAF colleagues, and their OPs were more flexible (and therefore easier to conceal). Ground tours also operated every day of the year, while 'Air' tours tended to mostly operate Monday to Friday in line with Soviet or East German Air Force (EGAF) flying patterns. Barracks were heavily guarded and often had high perimeter walls, so the best way of seeing the latest equipment was when it was being moved. Large-scale movements of equipment could be: an indicator of hostility (such as a precursor to an invasion of Western Europe), related to a deployment elsewhere (as seen in the build-up to Soviet intervention in Hungary and Czechoslovakia, in preparation for intervention in Poland, and en route to Afghanistan), a move to an EDA or training area for an exercise, or a unit being relocated to another part of the GDR (or even back to the Soviet Union). In all these cases, it was important that British Forces, Germany and NATO were kept informed, and the AMLMs were best placed to do that.

The Soviets made extensive use of the East German railway network with tracked and large, wheeled, armoured vehicles being transported across the country loaded on flatbed trucks with their crews travelling in cattle truck-style wagons. Therefore, establishing OPs close to rail junctions, loading ramps, marshalling yards, or simply alongside a section of track enabled tours to see what hardware was being moved, and the location and direction hinted as to the ultimate destination. Useful ORBAT intelligence would be obtained, and occasionally tours were rewarded with new bits of KIT and sometimes by an unexpected air display. Soviet helicopters would often navigate at low level using railways and roads rather than maps; one tour observed a swarm of more than seventy Mi-8 HIP and Mi-6 HOOK transport helicopters in an aerial 'convoy'.

Movements of soft-skinned vehicles were normally made by road and the Soviets used traffic regulators ('reggies') to direct the convoys. Reggies could be identified by their white helmets (sometimes with a black or red stripe) and the black and white batons they carried. Often armed, reggies were from the local *komendant's* office, or simply tasked by their own unit to direct traffic. This system meant that the soldiers leading convoys of vehicles did not need to rely on map reading and having to read non-Cyrillic signs to navigate across East Germany (map-reading skills were not universally taught in the Soviet Army and all maps were classified), plus they could operate in complete radio silence. For tours, spotting a reggie was a signpost that something interesting was about to happen, or had just happened – plotting the positions of reggies could reveal the route a convoy was taking. Reggies were often dropped off hours or even days before the convoy was meant to pass (and convoys were often delayed), and it would often take a similar time to pick them up again. Reggie duty was quite miserable work – they would be out in all weathers, and seldom had much to eat or drink, so tours would often stop for a chat, and a bit of company, some cigarettes, sandwiches, and a hot cup of tea could elicit all kinds of useful low-level intelligence. Alternatively, a tour could simply park up next to a likely-looking road junction, wait, and hopefully be rewarded by a convoy of interesting vehicles. A related tactic was called 'running a column', a risky approach where a tour car would drive alongside a convoy, photographing and recording vehicle registrations as they went. Opinions varied whether it was safer to 'run' a column from the rear or head-on. Approaching from behind (that is, overtaking it, on the 'wrong' side of the road) would have the element of surprise, but if the head of the convoy had stopped, there could be soldiers or vehicles blocking the way. It was also possible (likely) to encounter a vehicle approaching at speed head-on. Approaching from the front would alert the convoy commander and drivers of the tour's presence, and vehicles from the column could deliberately pull out into the car's path. It was never advisable to run the column from both ends – a sure way of getting detained.[20] Most convoys were chanced upon as targets of opportunity, but given the risks, it was ultimately the driver's decision to run it or not, having examined (or anticipated) the possible escape routes.

Training for the Soviet Army was conducted at company or battalion level at the small local training areas maintained by a particular garrison (known as 'polygons') or as major exercises (division or above) at the national training areas and ranges around the country (such as Letzlinger Heide, Altengrabow, Jüterbog, Wittstock, and Lieberose). The large training areas were normally *inside* PRAs, but the units involved in the exercises could be observed as they transited from barracks to training area, via routes *outside* the restricted areas. For example, the rail loading ramps (ramps from ground level to load vehicles onto rail flatbed trucks) at Letzlingen, just south of Gardelegen and *outside* the PRA, were used to move tanks and armoured vehicles in and out of the massive Letzlinger Heide training area. Ranges had the benefit (and attendant risk) of being able to observe live firing. For particularly sensitive training (possibly on new equipment), the route *between* barracks and training ground could be put inside a TRA, thus hiding the exercise from start to finish. In September 1970, a TRA was established on two areas north and south of the Eisenach autobahn, an invitation that something interesting was going on. Because of a loophole in the RMA, tours could still use an autobahn even if a TRA was established over it. Captain Nicholas Boggis-Rolfe was sent out to drive up and down the autobahn to see if he could see any action and was treated to a full divisional exercise including BRDM recce vehicles, BTR-60P armoured personnel carriers, T-62 main battle tanks, artillery, mortars, anti-aircraft vehicles, command vehicles and huge numbers of trucks of all shapes and sizes. During the main assault phase, they were joined by ground-attack aircraft and helicopters. Because stretches of the autobahn were higher than the surrounding countryside, it gave the tour panoramic views of the manoeuvring troops, sometimes only 30 metres away from the side of the road. They could follow the structure of the attack (interestingly adhering rigidly to Soviet military doctrine) and identify the different moving parts all coming together, captured in around thirteen rolls of film.[21]

In the mid- to late-1980s, in the spirit of détente, the Stockholm Conference agreed a set of mutual confidence- and security-building measures (CSBMs) designed to increase openness and predictability about military activities in Europe, with the aim of reducing the risk of armed conflict. In practical terms, it meant that the West were notified of all Soviet and East German training exercises (Notified Exercises, NOTEX), and observers were invited (under controlled conditions) to observe them. The AMLMs were not involved in these carefully curated observations but were tasked with tracking the arrival and return to barracks of NOTEX-related units, which had the greater potential for intelligence collection. The major inter-Warsaw Pact (*Waffenbrüderschaft* or Brothers-in-Arms) exercises gave tours the opportunity to see rare or unusual Warsaw Pact KIT in transit to the training areas – the soldiers from outside the Soviet Union and GDR (Hungary, Bulgaria, Czechoslovakia and so on) had no idea who the AMLMs were, so were usually curious but friendly.

Another useful tactic was to monitor the Emergency Deployment Areas (EDAs), where Soviets units would head to on emergency call-out exercises, or for real in case of war. EDAs were often in forest clearings, accessible by roads or forest tracks. They comprised pre-prepared positions, revetted vehicle or gun pits, and bunkers, often with NBC filtration systems, all connected by field and old-fashioned landline telephones, which were impossible to intercept by SIGINT.

A further variant was to monitor TAC routes, which regularly had tanks and tracked AFVs moving along them during training and exercises. They were left badly rutted by the vehicle tracks and were a challenge to cross or drive down even in the Range Rovers or G-Wagens.

The Soviet Army knew there would be numerous river crossings on their march westward towards the English Channel so practised them regularly using specially adapted equipment – snorkel air intakes on tanks, 'swim-able' AFVs, and pontoon

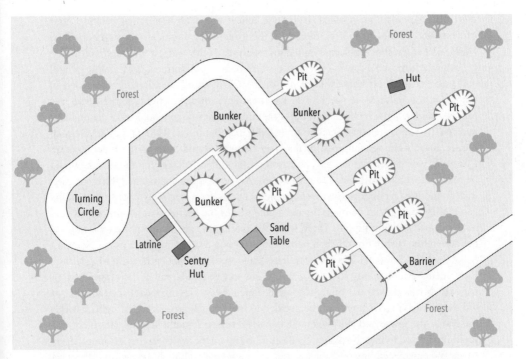

Soviet Emergency Deployment Area (EDA). (Author, based on contemporary sketches)

bridge/raft/ferry systems. The Research team provided advance warning of major tactical river-crossing exercises by scanning the pages of East German newspapers each day, looking for notifications of river closures for shipping, which usually meant a river-crossing exercise was to take place often involving several hundred tracked and wheeled vehicles crossing over a period of several hours.

Getting close during large-scale exercises and deployment practices was dangerous because the Soviets were armed and in 'war' mode, eliciting a more aggressive response than typical garrison soldiers. However, exploring sites that had recently been vacated could be equally fruitful. First, obtaining 'negative' intelligence (that something *was not* there, and was therefore somewhere else) could be useful, and a search of the detritus left after training or a deployment exercise could yield valuable intelligence – see 'Doing a dump – Operation TAMARISK' below. On the other hand, observing the garrison's daily routine could give unique insights into their strengths and weaknesses, their morale, and the reliability of their equipment.

From the earliest days of the Mission, the pretence that tours were only observing activity and not engaging in active intelligence collection was carefully maintained. Tour equipment was kept hidden under blankets or behind curtains, and great lengths were taken not to be seen using cameras or binoculars. This was, of course, a charade practised by both the West and the Soviets, an arrangement that suited both, although the East Germans would constantly try to gather evidence of 'illegal' espionage activity, which the Soviets duly ignored. It did not help if tours left equipment behind – tour officers who carelessly left 'evidence' on the ground were typically posted out of the Mission or if, on the rare occasion, the inviolability of the tour car was *violated*.

Although most KIT was observed on the move *from* barracks *to* training ground and vice versa, or on its way *in* or *out* of the GDR, tours occasionally succeeded in getting *inside* barracks to see KIT in its home environment. This required nerve and bravery bordering on recklessness, but sometimes a tour officer would seize the moment and risk it. Major Jonathan Backhouse RA did just that in late 1965 at an East German border guard training camp east of the Harz mountains and right on the Inner German Border. It was a German holiday, so based on the dubious logic that the guards would be relaxed (drunk), he decided to give it a go. As the tour car approached the main gate, they found it to be open so just went on in. After taking a relatively speedy tour of the camp, they exited back through the main gate just as the barrier was coming down, and as the guard was turning out. There was little intelligence gained, but the tour enjoyed the adrenaline rush.* For others a barracks raid was a more considered move. Sergeant Mike Seale SAS was far less reckless in his stalking of a Soviet barracks in Magdeburg. First, he undertook a long solo recce from a covert OP, a hide, rather than from the tour car, which was parked out of sight some distance away. Having established the guards did three hours on, six hours off, he decided to make his approach at first light, towards the end of the graveyard shift when the conscript sentries would be tired, less alert, and looking forward to their breakfast. Seale climbed up on the wall carrying his long-lensed Leica and began shooting over the top of it. A sentry spotted him, but rather than meet his gaze or duck back behind the wall, Seale deliberately turned away and continued taking photographs. This unexpected reaction confused the sentry sufficiently that Seale could finish taking his shots, climb down and return to the tour car without any fuss or drama – a triumph of coolness under pressure.[22] Seale's photographs revealed the first sighting of the new SAM-6 2K12 'Kub' (NATO reporting name SA-6 GAINFUL) air defence system – a real scoop, although such brazen approaches did not always work out.

The integration of army and RAF tours is normally assumed to have started in the 1980s; however, in the early 1960s, an *army* officer, Captain John Cormack, undertook a task that was 100 per cent *air* related. The difference was that Cormack was 'sponsored' by the tri-service Joint Intelligence Bureau (JIB) and some of his tasking came from them, rather than via the ops team.[23] The JIB was responsible for collecting and collating economic, industrial, scientific, and topographic (study of the forms and features of land surfaces) intelligence, in preparation for war against the Warsaw Pact. His task was to survey all potential obstacles to low-level flying across East Germany by plotting all obstacles above a certain height – factory chimneys, pylons, radio masts – to allow low-flying NATO aircraft to reach their targets without danger of collision. He covered the whole of the country a ten-kilometre square at a time, photographing the offending obstacle, and calculating the height with a bit of trigonometry. The task was too time consuming (and boring) for BRIXMIS RAF air tours, and of no interest to 'normal' army tours, but with JIB's blessing, it was deemed a good use of Captain Cormack's time.

---

* Major Jonathan Backhouse was PNG'd the following year.

RAF/Air Tour Specifics

RAF tours tended to leave West Berlin in the evening, which allowed them to transit East Germany and reach the area of their intended target in the early hours of the morning under cover of darkness, while departure times for army tours were more flexible. Denarking was especially important for air tours to ensure these scarce OPs were not compromised, which involved very high-speed transits (120 mph plus), making sudden manoeuvres into side roads or tracks (including at UFOs – see 'Evasion' below), or suddenly doubling back to see if anything was following; it was much easier to denark at night using the novel lighting controls on the car and night-vision goggles once they were introduced. Arriving in the general area, they would find a Z-platz relatively close to the desired OP to get a few hours' sleep. The day's flying began at first light with the departure of the weather aircraft, which would be sent up several hours before the start of the flight programme to check the conditions (tours would have studied the meteorological forecasts in their planning) and this was often the alarm call to wake up the team, who would pack up camp, have a quick breakfast, and move to their OP, checking for narks all the time. The ideal OP for an air tour would be around two miles from the beginning or end of an operational runway, which would allow them to capture aircraft at about 500 feet off the ground, taking off or landing, and if that location happened to be on a piece of high ground, all the better. Ideally the sun would be *behind* the camera and *on* the aircraft, which gave much better results, but the direction the aircraft was flying would depend on the prevailing winds – aircraft tend to take off and land *into* the wind, which may or may not have been photography friendly. Tour officers would often stand on the roof of the car (reinforced for this purpose) for a better vantage point. Clearly for flightline shots the photographer needed to be a lot closer, although the introduction of compact mirror lenses, such as the 1,000-mm MTO and later the 500- and 1,000-mm Nikons, made this slightly less risky. Monitoring aircraft or helicopter tactics from the ground relied less on split-second timing and more on being well positioned to observe the action from a meaningful angle; viewing aircraft approaching from head-on does not reveal very much. Tours looked for patterns (flying days, length of flying days, sortie profiles, high or low level, intercept or ground attack) that could indicate new capabilities, tactics, or potentially be an indicator of hostilities. Useful ORBAT intelligence could be gained from the *Bort* (or East German *Geschwader*) number on the side of the fuselage, and/or the colour band around the nose. They were particularly interested in technical intelligence: missiles (air-to-air, air-to-ground), guns (what calibre, rate of fire), bombs (conventional, nuclear), ELINT or electronic countermeasure (ECM) pods, cameras (often hidden behind panels), and various lumps, bumps, and antennas (including dielectric patch antennas) that could indicate the aircraft's avionics or role.

Getting to the OP undetected was crucial, and when in position, it would be the driver's responsibility to provide 360° security while the tour officer and NCO scanned the skies through binoculars or camera lenses. This was particularly important when aircraft were overhead, as their noise would drown out the sound of any approaching narks or soldiers. Stasi narks had the bad habit of closing their car doors noisily, so if aircraft were not overhead, tours could hear them from a long way away. Knowing this, tours always took care to close their doors quietly, and that is also the reason electric windows and central locking, both available in the last years of the Mission, were not specified (or removed post-delivery) – the clunk of a solenoid or whirr of a motor could be heard from quite a distance. It was also important to minimise the possibility of reflections from the car windows. Apart from crawling under an aircraft parked on the flightline, which would probably have got the tourer shot, the only way to view and record the underside of an aircraft where most of the interesting bits were located (weapons load, antennas, other external stores) was by taking pictures of the aircraft as it flew over or past the photographer, normally when taking off or landing. This meant that for each aircraft movement, the window for intelligence collection was limited to a few vital seconds, so capturing the shot for later analysis was paramount – Group Captain George Foot's (Deputy Chief 1955–1957) 'golden rule' was 'photography first, visual observation second, and only if time'.

The tour followed a standard routine during a flying programme. As soon as an aircraft was spotted, the NCO would use his binoculars to determine the type, the distinguishing markings (*Bort* number, colour bands, etc.), and alert the tour officer of anything notable worth photographing. The officer would then shoot anywhere between 5 and 36 exposures as the aircraft flew overhead. As soon as the aircraft had gone, the officer would call out the film and frame numbers to the driver, who would note it all down in his log, and the NCO would give him additional details such as *Bort* number/ nose colour. The NCO could also use his Dictaphone to record details or even record the action going on around him – recordings could yield useful information like rate of fire or the delay between weapons release and detonation. As with ground tours, the officer would normally change the film in his camera after an aircraft had gone to ensure a full film was ready for the next aircraft movement.

In 1969, the first MiG-21S FISHBED-Js had been spotted by MMFL and USMLM tours, but it was unclear whether this new variant of interceptor was fitted with a cannon, and if so, what type and calibre. Squadron Leader Frank White MBE went to the Cochstedt deployment airfield, south-west of Magdeburg, where a FISHBED-J squadron was based while their own airfield was being resurfaced. He found an OP in the middle of a large clump of nettles that hid the car completely, and photographed a full flying programme, noting all the aircraft numbers and timing the flying patterns – typically forty-minute sorties with twenty-minute turnarounds with good serviceability (the same aircraft were seen repeatedly). Towards the end of the afternoon, White decided to do a 'smash-and-grab' to get some detailed pictures of the aircraft's underside; based on the timings from the rest of the day, he waited until the aircraft were due to return and then drove to within 200 metres of the end of the runway, where he was treated to four FISHBED-Js coming in to land. He rattled off a few films and the tour made good their escape. The following morning, the prints showed recently fired cannon pods on the underside of the aircraft, plus a hump on their spine, which was probably an additional fuel tank. Some months later, Squadron Leader Rod Saar confirmed the calibre of the cannon by picking up spent cartridge cases and ammunition belt clips from a firing range.[24]

When looking up to the heavens, and especially when following an object through a long-lensed camera, it is easy to get disorientated or become fixated on what is being seen through the viewfinder. Flight Sergeant Colin Birnie MBE BEM relates a story from the early 1980s when his tour officer, Squadron Leader Dave Downes, became so focused on getting photos of a Soviet HIND-E attack helicopter with an unusual cylinder on the side at the Retzow range in the north of the GDR that he did not realise that the helicopter was charging straight at the tour's Range Rover. At the last moment, Birnie pulled Downes back into the vehicle as the HIND skimmed inches from the vehicle's roof. If he had not intervened, they may have got some great images, but the tour officer would have been decapitated in the process. The cylindrical dustbin-shaped object was assessed to be some kind of ELINT pod.[25]

If there were lulls in the flying programme, the tour officer and NCO would sometimes carry out defensive 'clearing' patrols around the OP just to check for nark or Soviet activity, while the driver remained at the car, although flushing out the opposition could sometimes prompt a violent response. With the introduction of four-wheel-drive cars, air tours could also plant themselves right in the middle of a farmer's field with 360° visibility, with pre-reconnoitred exits – they stuck out like a sore thumb but could see any opposition activity from a long way away and rely on their superior off-road performance to escape safely. The Stasi, however, would probably be watching from covert OPs, using long lenses to record all the tour's 'illegal' activity. The experience and 'sixth sense' instincts of tour personnel could also save the day. In the early 1980s, Colin Birnie and Flight Lieutenant Dick Hart were observing MiG-23 (or possibly MiG-27) FLOGGERs at Merseburg, west of Leipzig. They positioned themselves in the middle of an open field and had been watching the flying for about three hours when Birnie began to get the distinct impression they were not alone. The previous night he was sure he heard someone (or something) moving around the nearby Z-platz, and although nothing happened, his senses were on high alert. Deciding to do a foot recce to check, he asked Hart to carry on photographing through the sunroof of the Range Rover. The only cover close by was a bedraggled hawthorn hedge, which Birnie approached slowly, listening for any sounds of life. Rounding the hedge, he spotted a pair of Soviet boots protruding from underneath, at which point all hell broke loose and about fifteen armed Soviet soldiers burst from cover and charged the car, screaming at the top of their voices. The car began to move off while Birnie ran for his life diagonally away from the car. All but one of the soldiers chased the car, which began to do a large loop across the field to intersect with Birnie. One soldier, however, elected to chase the flight sergeant and was right on him by the time the car arrived. The driver slowed to a crawl and Birnie leapt in, kicking away the Russian who had got a loose grip on his leg and who unfortunately fell under the wheels of the car as it made its escape. Birnie's sixth sense, quick reaction, and fast legs got them out of one scrape, but unfortunately, they stumbled straight into another – waiting for them on the road was the ambush team's UAZ-469 jeep, which proceeded to ram the Range Rover and push them down the bank almost into the River Saale. With nowhere to go, the tour accepted a detention, which could have so easily turned nasty if it was not for Hart and Birnie's quick thinking; the fate of the soldier who Birnie booted in the face is not known.[26]

Sometimes, scoops were just a matter of luck and being in the right place at the right time. For example, in the mid-1950s Squadron Leader Hans Neubroch OBE was on a routine visit to an airfield taking stereo pairs of the flightline, which was full of Soviet Yak-25 jet fighters (NATO reporting name FLASHLIGHT). Only when the pictures were analysed back at HQ did they spot that one of the aircraft had its nose cone open revealing its powerful RP-6 'Sokol' radar in some detail, allowing the West to develop electronic countermeasures against this very capable interceptor.[27] On another tour, Neubroch was heading for their normal OP on a patch of high ground next to Werneuchen airfield, north-east of Berlin, only to find that it had been obliterated by the crash of one of the base's Il-28 (NATO reporting name BEAGLE) jet bombers, which had misjudged the terrain on approach. The Soviets had removed the big parts of the wreckage, but never being too concerned with housekeeping, had left small pieces of metal and shattered components scattered all over the hilltop. Neubroch and his crew were able to retrieve aircraft balance weights (demonstrating that Soviet precision engineering left a lot to be desired), documents (including tables of settings for the bomb sight), and maps marked with target coordinates, all of which was of great interest to the Air Ministry boffins. Much later, in 1987, a MiG-29 FULCRUM from Wittstock crashed into a field close to the Wittstock railway line, a popular OP for rail-watches. Tours scavenged the crash site for debris, giving the boffins a valuable insight into the construction of this third-generation fighter.

The Soviet and East German air forces had proper airfields all over the GDR, which were the main targets for air tours, but in the event of war, they also had hundreds of smaller auxiliary or dispersal airstrips (*Agrarflugplätzen*, 'Agricultural' airstrips), normally grassed over, but with concrete hard standing for aircraft servicing). There were about 1,750 of these dotted around the country: about 250 'basic' strips (*Grundflugplätzen*), which were normally unattended, and around 1,500 small working aerodromes (*Arbeitsflugplätzen*), which were also used for light aircraft and gliding.[28] The AMLMs monitored these sites, and if any unusual activity was spotted, they would stop to investigate. In 1970, Squadron Leaders Frank White and Rod Saar were tasked with covertly getting soil samples from five of these *Agrarflugplätzen* to help the MoD determine the maximum all-up weight that these airstrips could handle, and thus determine which Warsaw Pact aircraft could use them, and, if necessary, whether allied aircraft could land on them in a war situation. Although most of the sites were unattended, they approached under cover of darkness using the 'motorcycle' setting on the car's lighting panel and remaining relatively close to the car, did a 360° check for sentries using a Starlight image intensifier that allowed the user to see in the dark if there was some moonlight. Reassured that it was clear, they drove onto the grass runway, using a compass bearing to ensure they were correctly orientated along the take-off and landing axis. The MoD had supplied the specialist tools needed: a penetrometer and augur/bore tool with a hollow screw-on end about an inch and a half in diameter by eight inches long, which collected the soil sample. Working through the night, they were able to get ten samples at the required fifty-yard intervals along the strip. At least twenty-four hours before the operation, they had covertly placed containers on the strip to collect any rainfall, which could be compared to the soil samples to judge the drainage. Having recovered the containers, they headed straight back to Berlin and the samples were flown to the UK on the first available BEA flight, arriving on the scientists' desks within ten hours of them being taken. The outcome was predictable – the strips would have been fine for Harrier VTOL (vertical take-off and landing) operations but not for Lightnings, but the more 'agricultural' Soviet aircraft, designed for rough landing strips, would probably be fine.[29] As well as the *Agrarflugplätzen*, there were hundreds of concrete helicopter landing sites or helipads (*Hubschrauberlandeplätzen*, HLP or *Hubschrauberstart und Landeplätzen*, HSLP) on or near NVA sites, many in the vicinity of the Inner German Border. These were used in peacetime by the border forces (Grenztruppen der GDR) but would have been used as forward operating and staging bases in the event of hostilities. The Soviets/East Germans also used thirteen autobahn landing strips (*Autobahnabschnitten*, ABA) dotted around the country. To operate them, soldiers would close a section of the autobahn, diverting traffic around them, remove any barriers or signage (specially designed for this purpose) and bring up support vehicles (fuel bowsers, servicing vehicles) as needed. The East Germans practised this regularly, the Soviets rarely, and tours would hopefully be there to observe it all. In the late 1970s, Captain (later Squadron Leader) Brook Blackford was lucky to stumble on a very rare full Soviet autobahn airstrip exercise on the autobahn between Wittstock and Neuruppin (Autobahnabschnitt Netzeband).[30] The first hint that something interesting was about to happen was the sight of a rare Antonov An-26 (NATO reporting name CURL), a twin-engine turboprop military transport aircraft that was only used in East Germany for checking ILS (Instrument Landing System) radar equipment. As the car proceeded along the autobahn, they observed and photographed the *parkplätze* and hard shoulder filling up with all sorts of mobile airfield equipment – a very KIT-heavy environment. There were tractors to move aircraft on the ground, and fuel bowsers and associated refuelling equipment. To guide aircraft down onto the motorway strip there were various types of airfield-approach equipment including the HOME TALK PRL-4 precision ground-controlled-approach (GCA) radar, HAY SERIES RSBN-2N navigation beacon, and an assortment of airfield communications vehicles. There was also a BARLOCK P-35 Ground Controlled Intercept (GCI) and area radar, several SIDE NET height-finding radar vehicles, and a 2K11 'Krug' (NATO reporting name SA-4 GANEF) mobile surface-to-air missile battery, complete with its associated radar and comms (including R400/404 mobile radio relay trucks). BTR-60P armoured personnel carriers and various box-bodied vehicles could also be seen, which were busily being camouflaged. The arrival of a Mission vehicle in the middle of all this inevitably attracted some attention, and while the crew would have loved to have waited around to see the aircraft arrive, they decided to make a quick exit and take the precious films of the preparations back to Berlin. The tour returned to an OP overlooking the strip the following morning and were treated to the comings and goings of around thirty aircraft: MiG-23P FLOGGER-Gs from Köthen, SU-17 FITTER-Cs from Templin, MiG-21 FISHBEDs from Wittstock, MiG-23BM FLOGGER-Ds from Finsterwalde, and a MiG-25 FOXBAT and Yak-28 BREWER from Werneuchen – all carefully photographed and logged until the arrival of large numbers of narks suggested that the tour had overstayed their welcome. Altogether, a very successful few days.

East Germany was the Warsaw Pact's front line for air defence, so was packed with surface-to-air missiles (SAMs), either static, protecting specific targets as part of a general air defence picket line, or as mobile systems moving with ground forces. Static SAM sites and their associated radar, standalone radar, and fixed communication sites were often the most difficult to observe as they were fenced off and heavily guarded, requiring good planning, long covert observations to establish patrol or sentry activity, long lenses, a steady nerve (and hand!), and a lot of luck. Tours tried to get detailed photography of the various pieces of hardware: the size and shape of radar scanners, antenna wave guides, cones, feeds, and dishes; the length and angles of aerials, arrays, and cables; and images of any lumps, bumps, fins, pins, and boxes. In the late 1960s, Squadron Leader Frank White was tasked with getting photos of the Soviet LONG TRACK radar, specifically its distinctive horn stack and associated waveguides. The boffins at the MoD suggested that taking a series of shots at twenty-yard intervals would allow the images to be viewed stereoscopically (faux-3D), assuming the antenna was stationary and pointing the right way. White visited a site in Wittstock three times, but each time the antenna was either rotating or pointing away from his vantage point. However, on the fourth visit the conditions were ideal, and he began his photo run, stopping every twenty yards to take another frame. In the first and second frames, there was no one to be seen, but in the third, a sentry could be seen coming round the corner with his rifle slung over his shoulder. In the fourth frame, he could be seen staring at this impertinent photographer, and in the fifth, he is taking his rifle down from his shoulder. As White took the sixth frame a shot was heard, so he beat a hasty retreat – only when the prints came back the following morning did it reveal that the guard was pointing his weapon directly at the camera!

Flexibility with air touring was essential, with every tour having fall-back objectives. From the mid-1950s, under Deputy Chief Group Captain George Foot, it became acceptable for an air tour to abandon their primary objective (and not compromise the all-important OP) if they still had narks in their mirrors. The tour would simply go and do something less sensitive instead, hopefully losing the narks, and returning to the primary objective later in the day. Flying programmes could also be delayed or curtailed because of bad weather, fading light, exercises, or stand-downs around night-flying programmes, so fall-back targets were essential to avoid wasting the trip. Sometimes a tour would park up at a central location from which they could access multiple alternate targets depending on the circumstances. For example, Squadron Leader Andrew Pennington favoured an OP next to the Wittstock–Meyenburg railway line. This OP allowed them to maintain a constant rail-watch for Soviet KIT trains, while listening out for the noise of jet aircraft from nearby Wittstock airfield or the sound of Soviet HIND helicopters operating out of Parchim. From that central location it was also possible to nip down the nearby autobahn to get to the air-to-ground range at Gadow Rossow or make a slightly longer journey in the opposite direction to get to another air-to-ground range at Retzow. USMLM began using radio scanners for air tours in 1986, which picked up radio traffic between the control towers and individual aircraft, directing the tour to where the action was, saving time and mileage, and BRIXMIS adopted them soon after.[31] Other fall-back objectives included mapping, road- or rail-watch, and TAMARISK/TOMAHAWK searches.

The relatively static nature of air touring and finite number of targets created its own set of risks, challenges, and dramas. Most SAM sites (with their associated radar) were in fixed, defended locations – the opposition knew they were targets for the AMLMs, so would mount regular patrols to hopefully catch tours in the act. With airfields, the situation was even worse because OPs were dictated by the direction of the runway and the prevailing wind. The odds were shortened further by the Soviet and East German air forces concentrating their flying programmes into certain days of the week and only in good weather. That meant the Mission had to focus its entire air tour operation to position a tour at a specific place and time that was known to the opposition. To make matters worse, Soviets and East Germans deliberately alternated flying days at different airfields so if an air tour departed Potsdam on a particular day and headed in a particular direction, then there was a good chance they were heading for a particular airfield, where the narks would be waiting for them.

A key difference between air and ground tours was that on most air tours, the tour officer and NCO would be out of the car for extended periods of time, sometimes up to eight hours (the length of a full day's flying programme) in all weather (with temperature down to -25°C, with the observers standing in deep snow). However, these cold clear days were ideal for photography, but not so good for comfort or battery performance – the tour officer had to leave his cameras in the relative warmth of the car (sometimes inside a sleeping bag) to ensure the motor drive battery was ready when the action started.

After the Stasi archives were made available following the fall of the Wall, the intensity of anti-air tour activity became known. Agents were placed in covert 'hides' overlooking known air tour OPs, watching the watchers watch the aircraft. They would also alert the airfield commander that a tour was in the area so he could despatch patrols to intervene, leading to some very violent detentions. It is amazing, and a testament to the skill and bravery of the tour crews, that any air intelligence was gathered given these constraints.

Doing a Dump – Operation TAMARISK and Other Hazardous Operations

Operation TAMARISK (TAMARISK in the 1970s, TOMAHAWK in the 1980s, SANDDUNE to the Americans) was an extremely successful but unpleasant exercise that involved picking through the rubbish left behind by Soviet forces at deployment areas, or in ad hoc rubbish tips at military bases. The success was down to several factors that played straight into the (suitably gloved) hands of the AMLMs. Soviet soldiers appeared to be naturally messy and, unlike their Western counterparts, did not keep their working and living spaces clean and tidy. Rubbish would literally be thrown over the perimeter fence and left to rot, creating an intelligence bonanza for anyone brave enough to pick through it all.

In the Soviet military, maps, manuals, and technical documents were all classified, and only available to officers, who generally maintained good operational security (OPSEC). However, there was a flaw in their logic that the AMLMs exploited with much success. Soldiers would be instructed or briefed on new equipment and tactics in formal lectures (often supported by large visual aids, training boards, posters, and mock-ups) during which the troops would be expected to take copious notes in their notebooks. Even if the lecture was based on classified material, the notes, often including extensive technical information, were *not* considered classified. Western soldiers were issued with toilet paper as part of their daily ration packs, and their barracks toilets were typically scrubbed clean and supplied with toilet paper. Not so for the Soviets – their facilities were typically filthy and not for the faint-hearted, plus they were *not* issued with any toilet paper. Therefore, whether at the barracks or on deployment, when nature called, the Soviet soldier would use whatever came to hand, including pages from their notebooks, from technical manuals, correspondence, official forms, or any paperwork left lying around, and the 'used' paperwork – valuable little 'packets of intelligence' – would be chucked over the fence with the other rubbish or littered around deployment sites, just waiting to be discovered by intrepid tour members. Soviet officers would on occasion, however, have a blind spot when it came to document security, tearing (or cutting) up documents and throwing them in the wastepaper bin or into the fire. The bins and ashes were emptied over the fence with all the other rubbish, and it was possible to reassemble ripped up or slightly charred documents; in the West, classified material was routinely shredded and/or incinerated, making this sort of recovery impossible. Also, the training aids were not always kept under lock and key, allowing tours to photograph and/or steal them.

This casual approach was not limited to paperwork and training aids – personal kit and all types of equipment would also be dumped and when a unit was being rotated back to the Soviet Union, the volume of materiel chucked over the fence was staggering. It was the same on deployment, with various bits of personal kit (including respirators and personal NBC kit including personal decontamination items and detector paper), discarded ration packs, live ammunition, and all manner of rubbish left scattered around.

Searches would normally happen in the dead of night while wearing heavy rubber gloves, and the tourer would attempt to separate as much of the unpleasantness from the material using leaves or twigs before stowing it in a paper or hessian sack, which would then be double wrapped to keep unpleasant odours from filling the tour car. In the heat of summer, the stench must have been indescribable, and in the middle of winter, the only upside of the freezing temperatures was that the unpleasantness was easier to scrape off. Their searches would often be shared with the local rat population, which was also interested in what the dumps had to offer. Mission personnel would save bags and sacks from East German or Soviet food deliveries so if they had to be jettisoned from the car in an emergency, there would be nothing to connect the bag of soiled rubbish with the Mission – anything particularly noxious or remotely connected to CBRN was handled with extra care and double or triple bagged. The most mundane-seeming document (which is why it was probably repurposed as toilet paper) could provide valuable intelligence, although for non-Russian speakers, the significance of the haul could only be discovered once it was reviewed by the Spandau team back at London Block. This malodorous haul yielded a wealth of information. Radio logs, with call signs or various base station nicknames, could be matched with radio intercepts (SIGINT) to give a better understanding of the exercise. Maintenance records could yield valuable information on vehicle reliability and engine lives, while training programmes would give an idea of readiness and capability. The Soviet field post office number (FPN) used to address correspondence (like British BFPO or US APO numbers) could be used to identify the units involved in the deployment – in the Soviet Army, the FPN number was often used as shorthand for a unit's name, so confirming the link between an FPN number and a particular unit allowed the Mission to track it as it moved around the GDR. Newspapers and letters from home (both addressed with FPNs) could also be useful.

In 1979, Captain David Duncan BEM (Intelligence Corps) was following up on the aftermath of a 10 GTD emergency deployment exercise, collecting the usual TAMARISK material. He chanced upon a pile of ashes on a makeshift grate and pulled out pieces of a map that had been roughly cut up with scissors but had survived the fire completely. Although Duncan was not a Russian speaker, he understood enough Cyrillic to decipher 'Minden', a town in West Germany to the west of Hanover. When the map was reassembled, it revealed a 'going map', showing routes *through* the 'Minden Gap' (the less famous sister to the Fulda Gap) where wheeled vehicles could move safely, and where only tracked vehicles could pass – key information for any GSFG advance into Western Europe. Presumably, the area had been surveyed by SOXMIS or other Soviet assets in the West. In the mid-1980s, Sergeant Ted Roberts from the Spandau office identified detailed performance characteristics for the T-80 tank in a Soviet officer's notebook picked up by a TOMAHAWK operation.[32] In 1986/1987, two tours managed to get details of the 2S12 'Sani' 120-mm heavy mortar system, which had just been deployed to GSFG infantry units. The first was by Squadron Leader Andrew Pennington in a TOMAHAWK operation where pages from a Soviet junior officer's notebook confirmed the calibre, specification, and firing procedures of the 2S12.[33] The following year, a tour led by Captain Bill Hogg recovered some more pages of notes on the 2S12, taken from the notebook of a member of a mortar battery from the 244 Guards Motor Rifle Regiment, 27 Guards Motor Rifle Division. These pages gave details of how the mortar was deployed: the mortar tube, base plate, wheeled running gear, and the truck used to carry it all, including a sketch of the preferred trench layout for a firing position.[34]

An even more unpleasant exercise was picking through medical waste from Soviet hospitals, including their main site at Beelitz. Unlike in the West, where used dressings and even body parts were incinerated, GSFG military hospitals dumped medical waste alongside normal waste. During the Afghan War wounded soldiers were sent to East Germany to recover, rather than back to the Soviet Union, where the scale of casualty numbers would have been alarming to the general population. TAMARISK searches obtained samples of bullet fragments and other materials, which were sent back to the UK for gas chromatography analysis, helping to understand the type of munitions being used against the Soviet troops, and discarded documentation (some used as toilet paper, of course) that could identify the wounded soldiers' units. Syringes were, or course, a particular threat. In the mid-1980s, the commanding officer of the British Military Hospital in Berlin told Chief BRIXMIS that the risks associated with handling medical waste (including needles and scalpels) without proper protective suits and masks far exceeded the potential intelligence gain, and the practice was stopped.

Risk of discovery (and blowing the TAMARISK/TOMAHAWK secret) was high, and dump rummagers had to be ready to disappear into the night at the first sign of attention – roaming sentries or patrols, someone about to add something to the pile, or any other nocturnal wanderings from the Soviet soldiers inside the wire. Use of night-vision equipment helped maintain a watch over the scavengers, although any bright lights would cause the goggles to flare out, leaving the user temporarily blinded. There were many close shaves. It should be noted that the East German NVA were scrupulous in tidying up after themselves, with a very different mentality and approach to general hygiene, cleanliness and OPSEC. Although TAMARISK/TOMAHAWK was covered in Tony Geraghty's 1996 and Steve Gibson's 1997 books on BRIXMIS, Ken Connor's 1998 book on the SAS (with a BRIXMIS chapter), Patrick Manificat's 2008 book on MMFL, and Aden Magee's 2021 book on USMLM, the operation was still deemed sensitive as recently as 2012, where similar scavenging operations were known to be yielding results in other parts of the world and under very different circumstances.[35]

Not strictly TAMARISK/TOMAHAWK operations, but tours would often observe and, where possible, break into bunkers (from unmanned semi-underground concrete bunkers, to Nissen-type huts, to more substantial permanently manned bunker complexes), which often contained useful documentation (which should not have been left there) and also allowed the tour to inspect the communications and NBC protection left in place – interesting-looking equipment such as NBC filter cannisters were 'acquired' and sent back to the boffins. Live ammunition (Soviet soldiers did not have to account for *every* round like in the West) such as small-arms rounds, mines, ERA (explosive reactive armour) boxes, tank and artillery shells, or bombs could also be collected, although they were always treated with caution, for obvious reasons. In the late 1980s, Captain Stephen Harrison MBE RTR had been watching Soviet T-64B tanks during a live-firing exercise, noting that some rounds were falling short or missing the target altogether and failing to explode. Returning the following day when the tanks had moved on, he searched for these unexploded rounds, finding a 125-mm HEAT (High-Explosive Anti-Tank) round in what appeared to be good condition. As he was carrying it back to the car, it began to fizz, so he ditched it smartly and scarpered.[36] Squadron Leader Rod Saar relates the story of discovering a four-foot-long bomb on Retzow air-to-ground range in the 1970s and bringing it (with the agreement of the other tour members!) back to Berlin under his feet on the floor of the car. Although Rod was confident that the bomb could not go off – he had handled similar munitions when flying with Coastal Command in Avro Shackletons – his ops room colleagues were not very impressed when he deposited the bomb on the ops room table. Saar summoned the Royal Army Ordnance Corps (RAOC) to remove it, and they duly dismantled, photographed (for Rod's report), and destroyed it. Shortly afterwards, Saar received a note from the chief suggesting he read the RAOC *Annual Report on Ordnance Accidents* and that he should not bring back any unexploded bombs in the future. Staff Sergeant Steve Cole BEM RE spotted some very interesting landmines in the mid-1980s, received some very brief training back in Berlin in how to handle them and returned to collect some examples for analysis – his exploits won him the BEM. Even recovered spent cartridge cases and ammunition belt clips could help determine a gun's calibre, its operation and rate of fire.

Other materials found in deployment or staging areas could also be hazardous. In the late 1980s, a tour spotted a complete NBC field testing laboratory crated up on a Soviet training area. Unsure whether it was safe to move, they returned to HQ where they were reassured that 'of course it's safe' and were sent back out immediately to 'acquire' it. The crate disappeared off to Porton Down and nothing more was heard of it. In 1987, another tour saw something being pumped from a rail tanker into tanks on an ARS-14 decontamination truck. When the coast was clear, they went up to the tanker and decanted off some of the sweet, chloroform-smelling colourless liquid into one of their rinsed-out coffee flasks, which was forwarded to the boffins at Porton Down. The chemical turned out to be trichlorethylene, which is a known carcinogen and now banned from use, so it was revealing that the Soviets used it as part of their decontamination process. In 1989 a tour officer and NCO were contaminated by an unknown substance at a Soviet facility near Leipzig. This contamination led to serious medical issues that ended the NCO's career and compromised both their long-term health. The contamination was later assessed as being consistent with organophosphate poisoning seen with nerve agents such as sarin. The application of common sense and careful risk assessment was vital for this sort of situation but is clear that Operation TAMARISK was a high-risk activity.

Operation TAMARISK/TOMAHAWK was highly classified (SECRET or higher) to ensure the Soviets were not alerted to this productive activity, and the material was processed by a special team of linguists in the Spandau office, a cover name based on the translators provided by the Mission to Spandau prison. Although the prison was demolished in 1987 after its only occupant, Rudolf Hess, committed suicide, the cover name persisted until the Mission closed. Their unsavoury work was undertaken in the 'rubbish' or 'wet' room, with its unmistakable odour, and although the room had a ventilation fan, it was a particularly unpleasant place to be in the heat of summer.[37] They would then move to the relatively more fragrant 'dry' room to do their analysis. Much of the material was literally rubbish, but the occasional 'golden nugget' made the unpleasantness worth it … sort of. The tours on TAMARISK/TOMAHAWK operations were prolific in their scavenging, with a continual backlog of smelly sacks waiting to be processed. Once translated, personnel from Weapons and Research would examine the material and any useful information would be put into a SECRET report and sent to their customers. As with the intelligence that came from Operation OBERON, the Chipmunk recces, TAMARISK/TOMAHAWK intelligence and special operations like the radiation monitoring were not included in the tour highlights, standard tour reports, or Mission annual reporting unless it could be easily attributed to less sensitive operations.

Although TAMARISK and TOMAHAWK were ongoing operations, the Mission was occasionally tasked with special operations, which remained highly classified. For example, in the mid-1980s, BRIXMIS were involved in the placement and subsequent recovery of radiation testing equipment downwind of Soviet nuclear weapons storage facilities and East German nuclear power stations, especially relevant following the Chernobyl disaster in April 1986. By way of camouflage, the sensitive test equipment was transported inside old East German potato sacks. These were risky tasks because nuclear-related sites were heavily guarded, but also because there was a genuine risk of exposure to radiation, given the looser standards employed by the Eastern Bloc. They also used a similar device on specific rail-watches, when it was believed that nuclear material was being transported.[38] The Mission also undertook a systematic investigation and survey of the GSFG Unattended Repeater Station (URS) network in the early 1980s. The Soviets maintained a nationwide secure network of underground communications cables linking their various sites, and being old technology, they were less susceptible to being intercepted by Western SIGINT operations. The signal was boosted by small repeater stations situated under manhole covers or in small metal sheds at 14-kilometre intervals. Squadron Leader Steve Griffiths MBE describes breaking into one, in his case a pipe protruding several feet out of the ground with a padlocked manhole cover. He used a sledgehammer to break the padlock and jumped down inside a small chamber that was packed with cables, junction boxes, and switches, all usefully labelled in Cyrillic. Using his little autofocus flash camera, he photographed everything and stole all the documents left lying around. They assumed the chamber was alarmed, so only stayed a few minutes before moving away to hide in a nearby copse to observe a Soviet truck, a Zil-131 BBV, arriving a few minutes later with a repair crew. Noting the VRN and side number, they could then identify which signals unit was responsible for this stretch of line. Other tours also gained entry to the metal sheds to record similar equipment set-ups, and by mapping the locations of the URSs, it was possible to trace the cables across the GDR. The East Germans had a similar network but disguised their URSs as shepherds' huts or beehive trailers. The West successfully tapped the Soviet phone lines in Berlin in the mid-1950s (Operation GOLD) but there is no evidence to suggest attempts were made to tap the lines served by the URSs.

In the late 1970s, army tours were given the job of covertly placing special sensors next to well-used military routes. These sensors, which were buried just below the surface, would record the vibrations caused by vehicles passing close by. For a set period, the tour would monitor, record (and preferably photograph) all military traffic, noting vehicle type, number of vehicles, and the exact time. The 'Unattended Ground Sensor' (UGS) data would then be analysed in conjunction with the traffic logs so the boffins could compile sound profiles of particular vehicles. Subsequent recordings from other UGSs around the GDR would therefore reveal what traffic had been passing along that particular road, which could be very useful in tracking troop movements operating in radio silence.[39] Other special operations targeted specific areas, often coordinated on a tri-mission basis, such as Operation PINNOCHIO focused on tracking down a new self-propelled artillery vehicle at the Letzlinger Heide training area; Operation SPRING BLOSSOM concentrated on the 9th Guards Tank Division of the Soviet 2nd Guards Tank Army to assess the calibre of the recruits they were receiving; and Operation TROIKA was the annual rail-watch monitoring units of the GSFG as they rotated in and out of the GDR. These taskings were over and above the normal day-to-day tasking and tour activity.

A Walk in the Woods

The safest place to observe the opposition was from the relative comfort of the tour car with all the necessary kit to hand, but in many circumstances, this was not practical. Air tours normally required that the tour officer and NCO were *outside* with their cameras and binoculars pointed to the heavens, sometimes standing on the roof of the car with the driver keeping a lookout. However, it was impossible to get the tour car close to some targets, and others could not be photographed from a distance, perhaps because of surrounding trees. In addition, some tasking required close-up photography to capture specific angles or details. The only solution for these sorts of targets was to leave the car and proceed on foot – a 'foot recce' – and sometimes that meant moving several hundred metres from the security of both the driver and the vehicle. Some officers enjoyed the adrenaline rush associated with crawling through the bushes under the noses of the opposition and the intelligence wins could be considerable, but the risks were high. These sorts of adventures were generally not popular with drivers and NCOs as they could not provide any security for their officer – they were typically briefed to wait for a set period, and if the officer had not returned, they should move the car to a pre-agreed rendezvous point, which the officer would hopefully make for. If the officer still had not returned by an agreed time, he almost certainly had been detained and they were to return to Berlin, report to command, and the Mission would contact SERB to track him down and arrange his release. This scenario does not allow for the officer being injured, incapacitated, or being held incommunicado. Tour officers would normally head off on their own, carrying the minimum amount of equipment necessary for the task; they would proceed slowly, moving from cover to cover, stopping

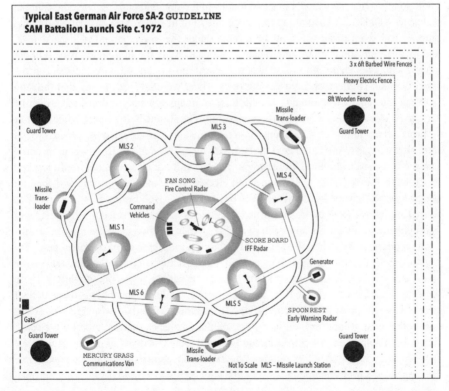

Typical East German Air Force SA-2 GUIDELINE Surface-to-Air missile launch site c.1972. MLS = Missile Launch Station. The site was surrounded by an 8-feet-tall wooden fence, a heavy electric fence, and three layers of 6-feet barbed-wire fences. (Author, based on contemporary reports)

frequently to check for the sound of any unwelcome attention. In these conditions, even the noise of the camera shutter (the motor drive was particularly noisy) could be heard for some distance.*

In 1972, the Mission was tasked to get some photos of the FAN SONG missile guidance radar for the SA-75 'Dvina' SAM system (NATO designation SA-2a GUIDELINE) in East German service. Unlike Soviet SAM batteries, the East Germans situated theirs in forest clearings, and behind several layers of security: two or three six- to seven-foot-tall barbed wire fences (sometimes with attack dogs running freely or on long running wires between them), an electric fence, and finally an eight-foot wooden fence, plus the radar equipment and missiles would be normally shrouded by tarpaulins when not in use.

Squadron Leader Rod Saar thought he would see if the East German Air Force SAM launch site at Groß Döbbern, south of Cottbus, would reveal any secrets. The tour driver, Corporal Ron Hogg, managed to get the car about 300 yards from the outer perimeter fence in the middle of a mature pine forest, and Saar ventured out on foot armed only with his Nikon F2 and 500-mm Nikon mirror lens, leaving Hogg and the tour NCO in the car. Saar knew he needed to penetrate the defences to get the desired photographs – the site was not even visible from the first barbed-wire fence he came to it (barrier #1). He searched along the fence line until he discovered an area where wild animals had worn away some of the ground under the lowest strand of barbed wire, and by wedging some sticks underneath it, he could slide through on his back without getting snagged. There did not appear to be any sensors on the wire (as seen on the Inner German Border), or any roaming dogs. There were no signs to say that the land between the fences was mined, but the East Germans typically did not advertise the fact, so Saar was taking a big risk by proceeding. The second barbed-wire fence (barrier #2) was twenty to thirty yards deeper into the forest, and he repeated the process to get under the wire, arriving at the next barbed-wire fence (barrier #3), from where he could just see the missile site through the trees, but was still not close enough to photograph it. Through the fence he could see about twenty yards of open ground and then an electric fence (barrier #4), and ten feet beyond that, a solid eight-feet-high wooden fence (barrier #5), both of which formed a perimeter around the missile site itself. Saar had deliberately timed his approach at midday, when he thought there may be a shift change, but he had not had the luxury of observing the site over an extended period to log the times of patrols or shift changes, and the maps they used for planning and on the tours themselves gave no clues as to the layout – he had no option but to wing it. There were two guard towers visible from the trees, but they did not appear to be manned. Saar checked that the coast was clear, and slipped under the third barbed-wire fence, crawling across the open ground to hide in a small clump of bushes running along the electric fence. With no guards in sight, Saar stood up, and took a swift set of photos of the FAN SONG radar, which was in the middle of the launch site, and anything else he could see. He dipped back down behind the bushes and slowly turned to head back across the open

---

* During one foot recce to a Soviet radar site, Squadron Leader Saar was so close to a THIN SKIN radar that it took six frames in a pan pattern with a 70-mm lens to capture the whole thing.

94

ground to the woods and the three fences. As he was doing this, he heard loud German voices coming from about 100–200 yards behind him and to his right – an East German Air Force officer armed with a pistol and a sentry armed with a standard MPi-K assault rifle (the East German copy of the AK-47) were walking towards the fence line, making what appeared to be a circuit of the site. Saar froze but having checked they were not heading in his direction, he crawled slowly back across the open ground and retraced his steps through the forest, under the three barbed-wire fences, removing the sticks as he went, and trying to obscure any signs that he had been there.

He finally got back to the tour car, which had not been discovered, and his very relieved colleagues. They carefully withdrew from the forest and made it back to Berlin in one piece. When the prints arrived the following day, they revealed

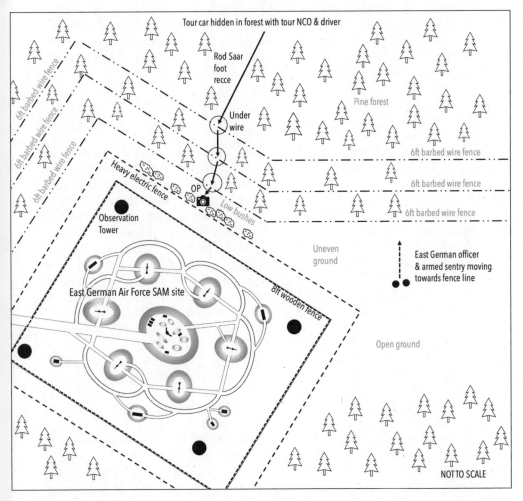

Squadron Leader Saar's foot recce to an EGAF SAM site, 1972. (Author, based on Squadron Leader Saar's descriptions)

the partially camouflaged FAN SONG, with its NRS-12 SCORE BOARD Identification Friend or Foe (IFF) radar next to it. There was an unusual large box mounted on the main sail of the radar and visible through the camouflage netting, which was exactly what the MoD was looking for – some kind of optical device that was fitted to East German FAN SONGs, but not to Soviet models. Unfortunately, the missiles themselves were all under netting. Saar duly filed his report, omitting how he was able to get such good images, and the rest of the crew chose to keep the details between themselves – 'what goes on tour, stays on tour' – in the knowledge that command would not have been impressed with the risks Saar had taken. The tour NCO and driver would have got into trouble too, for letting their intrepid tour officer get carried away with himself. The photos found their way into the 1972 BRIXMIS annual report. It is debatable whether the risks taken with this foot recce were justified – Saar was way out on his own, away from the security of the tour vehicle, and without official sanction to penetrate a heavily guarded East German installation, and while the intelligence he obtained was useful, it was not worth getting shot for. However, using the maxims 'nothing ventured, nothing gained' and the SAS motto 'Who dares, wins', young and enthusiastic tour officers regularly pushed the boundaries of acceptable risk in the quest for the next scoop.

Overnighting

In the relatively benign touring environment of the early years of the Mission, tours often stayed in hotels overnight, rather than sleep rough next to their vehicles. The decision was down to the tour officer and was based on the level of narking and the weather. The hotels were normally those of the 'HO' chain – the Handelsorganisation, a state-owned chain of department stores, restaurants, and hotels, which were of poor standard compared to Western hotels but were clean, and the staff were mostly friendly. On arrival, the hotel manager would call the local Komendatura to obtain permission and then the tour party was directed to their rooms – the rooms were always the same ones, so it was assumed they were bugged, although this was never proven. Favourite hotels included Elefant in Weimar, Chemnitzhof in Karl Mark Stadt (Chemnitz), Eisenacherhof in Eisenach, Regina in Leipzig, and Erfurterhof in Erfurt. It was common to be disturbed in the middle of the night by phone calls or bangs on the door, and the chance of being compromised (including the infamous honey trap) or provoked into a confrontation was always in the background. It was possible that the tour car would be interfered with or searched overnight, despite it theoretically having the same protections as an embassy.

Alerted by the *komendant*, narks would be sitting waiting for the tour party to emerge after breakfast, requiring a high-speed (or cross-country) departure to lose the tail. In the early days, tours would sometimes even stay in Soviet Army hostels (known as transit centres). This bold move relied on good Russian language skills and could often yield low-level intelligence while they queued for food or to use the bathroom. Staff were normally confused by their uniforms (made even more confusing when they wore greatcoats or duffel coats) and when the BRIXMIS officers declined to hand in their pistols on account of them not having any (all Soviet officers routinely carried sidearms). Bemused staff would hand them some blankets and allocate sleeping quarters. The following morning, the tour party would hand back their blankets and head back to their car (with bright Union Jack numberplates), leaving behind some very baffled Soviets.[40]

By the late 1950s, hotel stays were abandoned because of a run of incidents. In 1959, a USMLM tour party was interrupted by a Stasi team, physically assaulted, had their car broken into, and all their equipment stolen. Around the same time a British tour caused an incident at a nearby barracks after their socialising with a group of East German officers in the hotel bar turned nasty.[41] In 1961, Major Doug Thorpe RE, the new BRIXMIS technical officer, stayed overnight in Hotel Elefant in Weimar, prudently hiding his exposed films under his pillow. The following morning Thorpe departed and was well on his way when he realised that he had left the films in the room. A crisis meeting on his return to Berlin decided that it was best not to return cap-in-hand to ask for them back for fear of being accused of spying, which the films would prove. In true British fashion, the Mission decided to carry on as if nothing had happened, although Major Thorpe was quickly posted out of the Mission. Some years later, a tour called into the hotel for a coffee, and was met by the manager who was on duty at the time of the Thorpe incident. He remarked that it had been a long time since British officers had stayed at the hotel and asked if they would they like their films back, handing over Major Thorpe's still undeveloped films that he had kept safe in his office.[42]

After these incidents, tours were banned from staying in hotels and after the practicality of having three people trying to sleep in the car were realised, were issued camping equipment. Over the years tour camping was refined into a fine art, with techniques and experiences becoming part of BRIXMIS folklore. The spot chosen to make camp became known as the Z-platz, from the German word for campsite, *zeltplatz* (or after the zzzz … seen in comic strips when somebody is sleeping). Sites were chosen for ease of escape, being flat and well drained, and having trees to string ropes between. Having de-narked, they would approach the Z-platz very carefully, normally with all lights off using NVGs or just the very dim 'Trabbie' lights, and do a quick recce just in case they had inadvertently selected a spot right in the middle of a Soviet encampment (which did happen!).

At the Z-platz, the driver would always sleep in the car with the doors locked for security; depending on the type of vehicle, some drivers made bespoke bed boards that fitted across the seats and provided at least a flat and level surface to stretch out on. However, the tour officer and NCO would sleep outside, whatever the weather – temperatures could plummet to -25°c in winter. Tour members would have their own tried-and-tested set-up including an all-seasons arctic-spec sleeping bag, plastic foam Karrimats, foil-backed foam DIY insulation sheets, or even a collapsible safari-type bed. Traditionalists would swear by an old-fashioned 'basha', made by stringing a rope between two points and draping over an Australian nylon poncho sheet, but when the one-man hooped GORE-TEX tent (which was pioneered by the SAS and had a built-in groundsheet) came on the market in the late 1970s, this became the chosen solution for most tourers. An experienced tour officer could be snugly zipped up in his sleeping bag under his chosen form of shelter in under two minutes, in total darkness and in all weathers.[43]

It was not just the physical hardship that the sleeping tourers had to cope with. There was always the risk of ambush, although careful de-narking and choice of Z-platz would reduce that risk. They occasionally encountered a *Forstmeister* (forest ranger) in his distinctive green uniform and armed with a shotgun. As with most East German citizens, it was always pot luck whether the particular forester was party-minded, or whether he would turn a blind eye to their presence. They also had to cope with wild animals foraging for food or wondering what the GORE-TEX-clad shapes were doing in *their* forest. Rod Saar recalls seeing a whole family of wild boars passing through their campsite – he stayed very still as they could be quite aggressive, especially if they had youngsters with them. The other irritation was the East German mosquito population, which would feast on any exposed flesh during the summer months. It was critical, however, to leave the site as they found it with no evidence that a tour had camped there, which ensured it could be used again.

Deception: Fortune Favours the Brave …

Although using actual camouflage was frowned upon by both BRIXMIS command and the Soviets, other forms of deception were permitted or even encouraged. Tour cars were deliberately chosen to resemble Soviet staff cars, and the duffel coats or parkas worn by tourers looked like Soviet officers' greatcoats, so a bold and cunning tour officer would aim to take advantage of both to fool Soviet sentries or traffic regulators. For example, a tour in the late 1940s tagged onto a convoy of Soviet vehicles, being waved on by traffic regulators at junctions. They ended up in a field where a general was haranguing a large group of soldiers after an exercise and the BRIXMIS team quietly joined the group. Once the general finished his tirade, the tour made a swift exit, smartly saluting the sentries and being waved through by the reggies once more. The 'smart salute' and the similar 'royal wave' were surprisingly successful tactics; for the latter, while overtaking a convoy or on a close drive-by of a military installation, a smiling tour NCO would wave out of his window with his right hand while he held his Dictaphone in his left, recording details of what he was seeing. This friendly gesture tended to put drivers, groups of soldiers, or sentries at ease and distracted them from the tour officer, who was photographing furiously over the NCO's shoulder. Tours also learnt that by flashing the headlights when approaching a checkpoint or gate could fool the sentries into thinking the car contained a senior officer and should pass unimpeded.

Evasion

Tours went to great lengths to evade a pursuer and tales of high-speed chases, epic manoeuvres, and escaping by the skin of their teeth form part of any self-respecting tourer's repertoire of war stories. However, in most cases, these tales of adventure inside the GDR are mostly true. To properly do their job, tours needed to be free from surveillance by the Soviets, East German Stasi, or Vopos. This was particularly the case for air tours, who had a limited choice of suitable OPs. On the other side, the

Soviets, Stasi, and Vopos were just as motivated to observe, catch, and preferably disrupt the tour. It was not until the fall of the Wall and opening of the Stasi archives that the true extent of surveillance and inter-agency cooperation was known – tours often had absolutely no idea that they were being watched, with their every move being photographed and laboriously logged.

However, tours were able to evade most of the 'overt' surveillance directed at them using a variety of techniques. BRIXMIS tour cars were typically better than the opponents' vehicles – a sweeping but generally true statement, especially in the early years of the Mission. As discussed in Chapter 5, 'Tools of the Trade', BRIXMIS had a succession of high-performance and highly modified vehicles at their disposal, the best available on the open market – Opels and Mercedes, mainly, some BMWs. They were modified and maintained by army mechanics to the highest standards and ran on high-octane Western fuel, although the strengthening and underbody protection added extra weight. The vehicles used by the opposition were typically variable. Western cars, acquired or stolen to order, were rare in the GDR, instantly identifying the vehicle as belonging to narks, and although they theoretically had similar performance to Mission cars, this was blunted by the poor-quality fuel available in East Germany. Homespun civilian vehicles from the Soviet or East German state-controlled motor industries (Ladas, Trabants, or Wartburg Knights) handled badly and had to run on the low-octane fuel – along normal roads, they would normally struggle to keep up, especially when the advanced driving skills of the Mission drivers is factored in. Off road, the modifications made to tour cars (and later with retro- or factory-fit four-wheel drive) normally allowed them to escape from their pursuers across ploughed fields or through forests, leaving unmodified road cars bogged-in, although some Soviet off-road military vehicles would give tours a run for their money. However, the performance and manoeuvrability of the Western vehicles and skill of the drivers normally won the day.

In September 1987, Captain Stephen Harrison was on tour in the Rheinsberg gap, north-west of Berlin, with Sergeant Eddie Fannon MBE (Tour NCO) and Sergeant Mick Rostron (driver). They found their way blocked by a BRDM-2 wheeled armoured reconnaissance vehicle, which was accelerating towards them with two soldiers sitting on top. They were armed and wearing camo uniform, which suggested they were Spetsnaz special forces; Harrison's instruction to his driver was simply, 'Mick, get us out of this.' The track was too narrow to execute a three-point turn, so he began reversing at high speed, with Harrison photographing the pursuers through the front windscreen. Rostron then executed a perfect 'J-turn', spinning the G-Wagen on its axis within the width of the track and then seamlessly accelerating away, while throwing up a big cloud of dust. However, the BDRM-2 was still in the chase and emerged from the dust, albeit further back now, as one of the soldiers on top raised his weapon and fired three short bursts at the G-Wagen, which thankfully missed. Using the Mercedes' forward speed advantage, they lost the BDRM-2 round a bend and tried to put some miles between them and the hornets' nest they had stirred up. Unfortunately, the excitement was not over for the day and as they drove down a minor road, a GAZ-66 truck pulled out from behind some trees and tucked in behind the tour car. Up ahead they saw a second GAZ-66 approaching fast – the Soviets were trying to execute a 'sandwich' on them. Harrison gave a similar 'get us out of this' command to Rostron, and the G-Wagen began to swerve from side to side across the road. The approaching GAZ-66 tried to match each of the G-Wagen's swerves, but because the Mercedes could handle much better than the lumbering Soviet truck, it soon out-swerved them, and while the GAZ was on the wrong side of the road desperately trying to stay upright, Mick was able to accelerate past it and off to safety – an extraordinary piece of driving.[44]

A similar escape took place in the mid-1960s with Corporal Colin Brierly RCT driving Major John Parry MBE, south of Leipzig. They were being chased by a Soviet one-ton truck (probably a ZIL-157) and were keeping their distance until they were forced to stop at a level crossing with the barrier down. Brierly did a swift three-point turn to head back the way he had come but the ZIL had parked across the road and shuffled back and forth to block every attempt Brierly made to slip past him. In the meantime, the train had passed, and the barrier lifted, but an officer from the truck leapt out, ordered the cars waiting at the crossing to stay where they were and tried (in vain) to get the signalman to lower the barrier again. This gave Brierly a chance to react – the only problem was, he was facing the wrong way. Brierly slammed the car (which was facing the wrong way) into reverse and sped off on the wrong side of the road, overtaking (backwards) the cars waiting at the crossing. Moving as fast as reverse gear would let him, he bumped diagonally over the crossing and then overtook (still going backwards) the cars on the other side of the crossing before reversing into an entrance to a field, slamming a grateful gearbox into first gear and making good his escape. The length of this manoeuvre was more than 100 yards, skipping round the waiting cars, a furious Soviet officer, and a crowd of onlookers without hitting anything. His passengers, who had no idea of what he planned, sensibly kept quiet and let him get on with it. Another

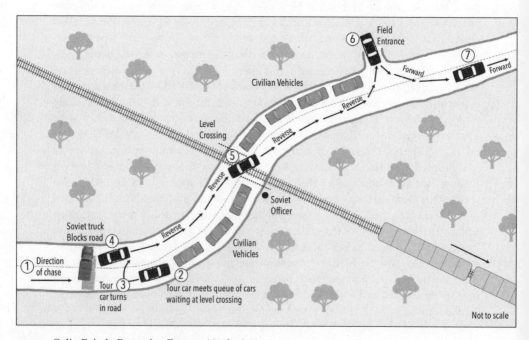

Colin Brierly Reversing Escape. (Author)

Plate 1. The sign outside the original BRIXMIS Mission House at Geschwister-Scholl-Straße 51 in Potsdam. The 'House' was actually a compound of seven buildings which included an officers' mess, soldiers' mess and quarters building, the chief of Mission's house, an office building, and two further residential buildings, each with two flats, and a pond in the middle of it all. There were also stables for three horses, and a motor transport (M/T) area. The site was wrecked in July 1958 in a staged riot, so the Mission moved to a much nicer property on Seestraße. (BRIXMIS Association Archives)

Plate 2. The front of the BRIXMIS Mission House at Seestraße 34-37 in Potsdam. The Mission relocated to Seestraße at the end of 1958 following the riot at the original Mission House, and remained there until the Mission closed in 1990. It was a sizeable villa with plenty of room for entertaining, with gardens leading down to the lake. With the Mission House warrant officer in charge, the domestic staff were all East German and in the pay of the Stasi or KGB, plus there was a Vopo hut opposite the entrance keeping an eye on the comings and goings of Mission personnel and reporting them to the Stasi control room. (BRIXMIS Association Archives)

Above: **Plate 3.** BRIXMIS BMW 501 parked at the back of the BRIXMIS Potsdam Mission House, c.1959. The steps led down to a tiered formal garden sloping down to the Heiliger See lake. As well as being used as the formal liaison HQ for the Mission and a stopping off point for tours, it was also a pleasant weekend retreat for Mission personnel and their families. The BMW 501 (or possibly a 502) was launched in the early 1950s as a completely new vehicle, the first new BMW since the end of the war. The BMW marque had a short association with the Mission, being replaced by a long line of Opels, and latterly, Mercedes. (BRIXMIS Association Archives)

Opposite below: **Plate 5.** The BRIXMIS pass for Senior Aircraftsman Paul F Brown, signed by Colonel Pinchuk, Chief SERB, on 13 December 1965. Brown's position was 'Clerk', but it is likely he was an RAF driver with the Mission. Other ranks and vehicle passes were signed by Chief SERB, a colonel, while officers' passes were signed by Chief-of-Staff, GSFG, a three-star general. This pass gave the bearer the right to cross the Glienicke Bridge into East Germany and (theoretically) gave him the quasi-diplomatic protection of the Commander-in-Chief, GSFG. (BRIXMIS Association Archives)

Above: **Plate 4.** An aerial shot, presumably taken from the BRIXMIS Chipmunk, of London Block at the Olympic Stadium Complex in West Berlin. London Block was home to HQ BRIXMIS, HQ Berlin Sector, the British Military Government, and Allied Staff Berlin. An adjacent wing (Gloucester Block, seen on the bottom left of the picture) contained the HQ Berlin Infantry Brigade. BRIXMIS occupied the top floor of London Block including the distinctive curved corridor on the right-hand side of the shot. (BRIXMIS Association Archives)

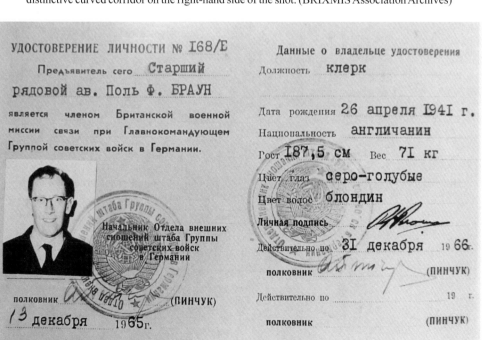

УДОСТОВЕРЕНИЕ ЛИЧНОСТИ № I68/E

Предъявитель сего **Старший**

рядовой ав. Поль Ф. БРАУН

является членом Британской военной миссии связи при Главнокомандующем Группой советских войск в Германии.

Данные о владельце удостоверения

Должность **клерк**

Дата рождения **26 апреля I94I г.**

Национальность **англичанин**

Рост **I87,5 см** Вес **71 кг**

Цвет глаз **серо-голубые**

Цвет волос **блондин**

Личная подпись

Действительно по **31 декабря** 19 **66**г.

полковник (ПИНЧУК)

Действительно по 19 г.

полковник (ПИНЧУК)

Начальник Отдела внешних сношений штаба Группы советских войск в Германии

полковник (ПИНЧУК)

I3 декабря 1965г.

Plate 6. BRIXMIS visit to Plötzensee Prison, Charlottenburg-Nord, Berlin, 1982. Plötzensee was a Nazi prison where almost 3,000 people were executed for their political views or for resisting Hitler's regime. BRIXMIS facilitated the visit for Albert Zalilov, whose father Musa Dzhalil, a renowned Soviet poet and political officer, was executed in 1944. The group included Captain Peter Williams (BRIXMIS interpreter), Major Willie Macnair (BRIXMIS operations officer in the kilt); Colonel Rubanov (Chief SERB); Colonel Roman Zvyagelsky (Senior Correspondent 'Krasnaya Zvezda' ('Red Star' Soviet Army daily newspaper); Lieutenant Colonel Albert Zalilov (Soviet chemical troops and son of Musa Dzhalil); and Group Captain Richard Bates (Deputy Chief BRIXMIS). (BRIXMIS Association Archives)

Plate 7. Brothers in arms – Major Yuri Pliev (SERB), Captain Peter Williams (BRIXMIS), Senior Lieutenant Dmitri Trenin (SERB), and Captain John Apps (BRIXMIS), swapping caps at the Potsdam Soviet Officers' Club, 1982. Socialising with the officers at SERB was part of the job and could be useful during detentions as they would often be consulted or summoned to the scene. (BRIXMIS Association Archives)

Above: **Plate 8.** View of the Glienicke Bridge taken from a BRIXMIS tour vehicle from the West Berlin side, approaching the automatic rolling gates, the first stage of border controls to enter East Germany. The configuration of the checkpoint changed over the years – this photo is from the mid-1980s when the massive concrete chicane had been removed, but there were typically several layers of controls to pass through. Passes would be handed over for inspection at the Soviet office seen on the left, and the Vopos had an office on the right from where they would report the comings and goings of mission personnel to the Stasi control room. (Phil Temminck via BRIXMIS Association Archives)

Below: **Plate 9.** The Glienicke Bridge between West Berlin and Potsdam, as photographed from a US Army bus carrying the 298th Army Band back from an event at the US Mission House in Potsdam. The shot looks towards the West Berlin side of the bridge, showing the automatic roller gates and a BRIXMIS Opel Senator heading in the opposite direction. (Dan Hermann)

Plate 10. BRIXMIS OPEL Kapitän No. 61 and driver, 1963. Judging by the smart uniform and shiny paintwork, this car must have been on official or protocol duties rather than touring. The plate number predates the 1–19 sequence seen in many BRIXMIS images, which was introduced in the 1970s. (BRIXMIS Association Archives)

Plate 11. BRIXMIS Opel Senator No. 6 in the snow. Rather than use snow chains, the Senator was fitted with winter (mud and snow) tyres which were used all year round and worked well with the FF four-wheel-drive system allowing the car to traverse most types of terrain. At the front, there is the high-visibility AMLM number plate, the small infrared headlights (for use with night-vision goggles), and large spotlights. These lights, in conjunction with the main headlights and sidelights, could all be controlled independently from a switch box where the central armrest would normally be. The under-body protection ('panzer-plate') is also visible. (Phil Temminck via BRIXMIS Association Archives)

Right: **Plate 12.** Demonstrating the use of the sunroof as an aid to observation on BRIXMIS Opel Senator No. 2. Although the sunroof was kept closed during transits, it was useful when the team were observing targets, either to give the driver a better view for security, or to give the officer/NCO a raised photographic/observation position. The Mercedes G-Wagen had a proper cupola built into the roof allowing the tour officer to stand up from his centrally mounted rear seat. This vehicle had broken down and the tour party were waiting for a recovery team to arrive from Potsdam – the photograph is taken from the top of a barn just behind the stranded Opel. Mid 1980s. (Phillip Temminck via BRIXMIS Association Archives)

Below: **Plate 13.** With permanent four-wheel-drive, impressive off-road performance, and a bumper mounted winch, the Range Rover had the potential to be the perfect tour car. However, the early models were slow on the road, leaky, draughty, and unreliable – very much a product of the 1970s British motor industry. They were popular, however, with air tours who would use the specially reinforced roof as an elevated photograph platform. (BRIXMIS Association Archives)

Above: **Plate 14.** Mercedes G-Wagen No. 9, the first G-Wagen in BRIXMIS service. Note the roof cuploa, front 'bull bars', the additional headlights, bumper-mounted electric winch, and high-visibility AMLM number plate. The G-Wagen was a very capable tour vehicle – it was reliable, had excellent off- and on-road performance, room for the tour party in relative comfort, space for all the tour equipment; and five doors. Corporal Wayne Fury is grilling a sausage … over a primus stove. 1982. (BRIXMIS Association Archives)

Above: **Plate 16.** Squadron Leader Andrew Pennington in his one-man GORE-TEX tent at a Z-platz. The tour officer and NCO always camped outside the tour car, whatever the weather, while the driver slept inside for security. The GORE-TEX tent was a big improvement over the traditional 'basha' shelter, and every tourer would customise his own set up with inflatable mattresses, space blankets, or foam mats. An experienced tourer could be snugly zipped up in his sleeping bag inside his hooped tent in under two minutes, in total darkness and in all weathers. (Andrew Pennington)

Opposite below: **Plate 15.** A rare photograph of BRIXMIS de Havilland Chipmunk WG486 flying alongside a Soviet MI-8 (NATO reporting name HIP-C) helicopter, presumably photographed from another Soviet helicopter or one of the American or French observation aircraft based in Berlin. WG486 was based at RAF Gatow from 1987 until 1994 so the photo might have been taken after the fall of the Berlin Wall. (Albert Grandolini Collection)

Plate 17. An East German Mission Restricted Sign or MRS. These signs (the horizontal lines are red) were positioned close to sensitive military installations that the East Germans or Soviets did not want the AMLMs to see. However, the validity of the signs was not covered under the 1946 Robertson-Malinin Agreement which governed Mission activity, so they were routinely ignored by tours – in fact, an MRS was an advertisement that there was something worth investigating nearby. These signs were often cited during detention negotiations but as they had no official standing, the tour officer would completely ignore them, something that infuriated the East Germans. (BRIXMIS Association Archives)

Plate 18. Staff Sergeant John Jones and Corporal Robbie Woods contemplate how they are going to extricate Opel Senator No.12 from a deep hole on a TAC route before some Soviet tanks turned up, 1982. Unless there was a tree nearby to winch from, they would have had to have used a ground anchor. The car also carried mats which could be used to give the wheels grip. Failing that, they would have to rely on a passing tracked vehicle or farmer's tractor to pull them out and accept the inevitable detention. (Peter Williams via BRIXMIS Association Archives)

Plate 19. A BRIXMIS Opel Kapitän stranded in deep water, late 1960s. These vehicles did not benefit from the retro-fit four-wheel-drive system fitted to later saloon tour cars and also had limited ground clearance. Although the engines were powerful, the cars were weighed down with tour kit, extra fuel, and the steel 'panzer-plates' welded to the chassis for under-body protection. This recovery would have involved hand winching by a cable attached to one of the nearby trees – a very wet and muddy experience. (BRIXMIS Association Archives)

Plate 20. An air tour looks to the heavens. This may be a Stasi surveillance photograph as the third member of the tour, the driver, always remained in the car for security – there was no time for candid shots of colleagues. The tour officer is using a 1,000 mm mirror lens, an MTO or Nikon, with a pistol grip to help him hold the hefty combination steady. The NCO is observing through binoculars, spotting for the officer, and calling out details to the driver inside the car, who would note them down in his notebook. (BRIXMIS Association Archives)

Left: **Plate 21.** Cartoon from the 1950s by an anonymous BRIXMIS member. The caption says '*Now we'll see what they do with their barrack fences*', poking fun at the Soviets who were erecting tall fences round their barracks and installations in East Germany to stop the AMLMs from peering in. In the early years, some 'Local' tours around the Potsdam area were conducted on horseback, giving the rider a useful elevated position. (BRIXMIS Association Archives)

Below: **Plate 22.** A Soviet traffic regulator (known as a 'reggie'). They were distinctive in their white helmets with red stripes and their black and white striped batons used to direct traffic and were often armed. The reggie in the photo appears to be directing civilian traffic, but most were used to direct military convoys. They were pre-positioned at junctions, often days in advance, and when the convoy arrived, they would send it in the required direction. This approach allowed large military convoys to move in complete radio silence, and without having to rely on map reading skills, which were limited in the Soviet military. Reggies either belonged to the parent unit or to the local Komendatura. (BRIXMIS Association Archives)

Plate 23. Corporal Wayne Fury, Major Peter Williams, and Staff Sergeant Graham Geary with Soviet officers during a 'town tour' at Gardelegen, 1988. A town tour would involve BRIXMIS personnel travelling to a garrison town (Gardelegen was close to the huge Letzlinger-Heide training area) and making low-level contact with Soviet soldiers in bars and beer gardens. They were able to pick up useful low-grade intelligence (ORBAT, for example) as well as project British 'soft power' in a common brotherhood of soldiery. (BRIXMIS Association Archives)

Plate 24. A Soviet BMP-1 tracked infantry fighting vehicle photographed on a TAC (Tactical) route in East Germany. TAC routes were off-road thoroughfares for tracked vehicles that criss-crossed the country and were used to deploy or transit armoured vehicles. They were therefore ideal spots to observe armoured KIT. (Andrew Pennington)

Above: **Plate 25.** Close-up photograph of a MT-12 (Grau index 2A29) 100 mm anti-tank gun in East German NVA service. It is from a sequence of detailed close-up images that show the gun's working parts, controls, and even the data plate with its serial number and year of manufacture (04217, from 1974). These shots involved being right up next to the gun and were very risky for the tour officer. (Andrew Pennington)

Opposite above: **Plate 26.** Running a column: A GAZ-66 BBV (Box-bodied vehicle) photographed from a fast-moving tour car on 24 March 1989. Running a column was a dangerous manoeuvre because an oncoming vehicle could easily pull into the tour car's path. The GAZ-66 was a 4x4 truck used widely by the Soviets in a wide number of variants. BBVs were typically used for command, control, and communications and the tour NCOs compiled an extensive database of the different types. Vehicle registration numbers (VRNs) and unit numbers were recorded during the drive-by, along with vehicle type and quantity. (BRIXMIS Association Archives)

Opposite below: **Plate 27.** Photograph of a well-known escapade from 27 July 1983. During a daytime rail-watch at Prödel, a KIT train loaded with the new Soviet BMP-2 tracked infantry fighting vehicle stopped right in front of the tour OP. Staff Sergeant Ken Wike RA announced that he wanted to take a closer look to see if they could determine the calibre of the gun, which was a pending intelligence requirement. He climbed up on the rail car and onto the nearest BMP-2, holding his Dictaphone against the muzzle for scale so Captain Peter Williams could photograph it. Before jumping off, Wike jammed an apple he was carrying over the muzzle to create an impression that could indicate the calibre. Sergeant Wike received a BEM for his daring exploits. (BRIXMIS Association Archives)

Plate 28. East German armoured personnel carriers, jeeps and trucks line up at the 1986 October Day parade in East Berlin, with the iconic television tower in the background. Although BRIXMIS' remit did not include East Berlin, Mission personnel would be sent over to observe and photograph the East German hardware on display, and tours would be deployed to follow the vehicle convoys, as shown in this image, back to their bases. (Ralph Brooks)

Plate 29. BRIXMIS air tour photograph of a Soviet Mi-8PPA (NATO reporting name `HIP-K`) electronic countermeasures helicopter used to jam enemy electronic signals, 19 March 1989. Helicopters were dangerous because they could spot tours on the ground and radio through to their base to send out soldiers. On occasion, the helicopter would be flown very aggressively at tours, missing the heads of tour personnel by just feet. (BRIXMIS Association Archives)

Plate 30. BRIXMIS air tour photograph of a Soviet MIG-29 (NATO reporting name FULCRUM), 15 March 1989. This sort of image was the life-blood of air tours, who would position themselves at the ends of runways to capture details of the aircraft as they took off or came into land. They would be interested in weapons loads, navigation, surveillance or electronic countermeasure pods, or any unusual lumps, bumps, or antennae. It was a real skill to get clear images of a moving aircraft against the sky using a heavy and manual long-lensed camera. (BRIXMIS Association Archives)

Plate 31. Oblique aerial photograph taken from a BRIXMIS Chipmunk showing the barracks of the 281st Soviet Divisional Artillery Regiment at Schönwalde, with the regiment's self-propelled howitzers and supporting armoured vehicles lined up in the open, and the trucks/fuel bowsers under cover. Note the dilapidated state of the buildings. On the far left of the image there appears to be an assault course. (BRIXMIS Association Archives)

Above: **Plate 34.** Fitting chains to the tyres of a BRIXMIS Opel Kapitän II with a Stasi car observing, mid 1950s. As soon as the BRIXMIS tourer took his camera out, the agent (nark) turned away so his face could not be photographed. The Kapitäns were powerful but heavy and did not benefit from the four-wheel-drive system fitted to later vehicles, so chains were sometimes needed in very muddy conditions or in snow. Tour cars were often tailed by narks, and it was the driver's job to lose them using the superior performance of the Western cars and skilful (and often aggressive) driving. Note the duffel coat being worn by the tour officer. (BRIXMIS Association Archives)

Opposite above: **Plate 32.** Overhead shot taken from a BRIXMIS Chipmunk of a Soviet T-64 Main Battle Tank undergoing a main gun barrel change – the turret is jacked up for access. Considerable intelligence could be obtained from observing vehicles undergoing maintenance when the Soviets were less diligent in hiding their secrets. This included discovering the calibres of weapons, the ammunition loads, or ongoing maintenance issues. (BRIXMIS Association Archives)

Opposite below: **Plate 33.** Detailed overhead photography of the elusive 2S6 'Tunguska' (Grau index 2K22) tracked integrated air defence system taken from a BRIXMIS Chipmunk. This powerful system was designed to counter low-level threats such as the American A-10 Thunderbolt II 'tank-buster' aircraft, and had four 30mm cannons and four SA-19 (NATO Reporting Name GRISON) surface-to-air missiles – a deadly combination. The AMLMs had been searching for this weapons system for some time, so it is believed the Soviets decided to 'show' the vehicle to the missions to confirm their new capability. Note the display boards next to the vehicles, which were used for training – it was sometimes possible to get readable photographs of these boards. The vehicle on the left is the equally interesting SA-13 (NATO Reporting Name GOPHER) fully amphibious tracked surface-to-air missile system. (BRIXMIS Association Archives)

Plate 35. The wreckage of Opel Admiral No. 7 after being rammed by a 4.5-ton NVA URAL-375 truck, which climbed the car's bonnet, smashed the right-hand corner of the passenger compartment, and continued right over the car before it toppled on its side. Sergeant Bob Thomas, the tour NCO, was trapped in the car with a badly broken leg, 1976 (BRIXMIS Association Archives)

Plate 36. Brigadier Learmont, Chief BRIXMIS, and Corporal Boland in shiny black Senator No.1, 12 August 1982. Note the large No.1 plate and one-star general plate to the left of it. This car was written off later that day in a deliberate ramming by an East German NVA truck Athenstedt. After this incident, the car used for the chief's tours would be painted in standard olive drab. (BRIXMIS Association Archives)

Plate 37. Stasi photograph of the aftermath of the incident on 12 August 1982 at Athenstedt, where a 12-ton NVA Tatra-148 truck rammed BRIXMIS Opel Senator No.1 in a deliberate ambush, with the intention of killing one or more of the passengers. The car contained Brigadier John Learmont, Chief BRIXMIS, Captain Peter Williams acting as tour 'NCO', and Corporal John 'Benny' Boland as driver. The truck pushed the car off the road where thankfully a small fruit tree stopped it from rolling – amazingly the occupants only suffered cuts and bruises, a testament to the strength of the highly modified Senator. Brigadier Learmont can be seen leaning against the tree, with a Stasi photographer in the background. The truck can be seen still embedded in the driver's door – Boland remained at the wheel to ensure the security of the car was maintained. The van on the left is blocking the car's escape (there was another truck behind it) and although the car was driven onto the recovery trailer under its own steam, it was a write off. (BRIXMIS Association Archives)

Above: **Plate 38.** Squadron Leader Martin Common climbs over the front seat of his Range Rover to negotiate with the Soviet Komendant during a detention at Athenstedt on 13 September 1984, with Master Engineer 'Chippy' Lee in the background. The tour was detained close to the same NVA radar facility where Brigadier Learmont was ambushed in 1982. Blocked in by vehicles from the base and 'tarped' (which can be seen in the photo), Common elected to 'accept' the detention rather than try to evade – it was only six months after the murder of Adjudant-Chef Philippe Mariotti near Halle. Note the impracticality of the three-door Range Rover – Common is having to climb over the front passenger. (BRIXMIS Association Archives)

Opposite above: **Plate 39.** Captain Stephen Harrison holds court with the local Komendant during a detention, photographed through the rather dirty windscreen of the tour's G-Wagen. For some reason he is gesticulating with a Soviet traffic regulator's (reggie) black and white baton, used for directing vehicles. Detentions could be lengthy affairs, with the tour officer using his wits and language skills to baffle the local Komendant who was responsible for investigating the tour's transgressions. (BRIXMIS Association Archives)

Opposite below: **Plate 40.** A Soviet BRDM-2 wheeled armoured reconnaissance vehicle in hot pursuit of a BRIXMIS tour car, photographed by Captain Stephen Harrison, September 1987. Thanks to Sergeant Mick Rostron's skilful driving, the BRIXMIS Mercedes G-Wagen was able to evade the pursuers even after the soldier on the right (probably GRU Spetsnaz because of his camo uniform) opened fire. (BRIXMIS Association Archives)

Plate 41. A Stasi photograph of the aftermath of the fatal ramming of a MMFL Mercedes at Halle-Lettin, 22 March 1984. An NVA 4.5-ton URAL-375 truck and trailer were deliberately driven at the Mercedes, smashing it off the road and pushing it down a small bank. Adjudant-Chef Philippe Mariotti, the car's driver, was killed instantly, Capitaine Jean-Paul Staub, the tour officer, was seriously injured and taken straight to hospital, while tour NCO Adjudant-Chef Jean-Marie Blancheton elected to stay with Mariotti and the car until help arrived from Berlin, despite being injured himself. This was the first fatality in the history of the AMLMs but unfortunately not the last – Major Arthur D. 'Nick' Nicholson was shot and killed by a Soviet sentry on 24 March 1985 at Ludwigslust-Techentin. (MMFL Association Archives)

example of skilled and fearless driving, and trust from the tour officer and NCO that the driver knew what he was doing.

Lieutenant Colonel John Cormack, tour officer 1964–1965, described a very dramatic manoeuvre to evade a persistent nark car. They drove into an open field that had a ditch running right across it. Cormack asked his driver, Corporal Jackson, whether he fancied having a go at leaping the ditch in their heavily laden two-wheel-drive Opel Kapitän. Jackson was up for it, so after lulling the narks into a false sense of security by driving around the field for a while, Jackson revved the engine, hurtled towards the ditch, up the bank, and did an 'American television'-style leap over the ditch leaving the nark Mercedes stranded on the other side. The key to this sort of tactic was the total trust in the driver and his vehicle, backed by the knowledge that the M/T workshop could repair most damage inflicted by these sorts of manoeuvres.

Evasion could also be 'kinetic', using the power and weight of the armoured tour cars to clip, wing, push, shove, or ram the opposition's vehicle. Although the Soviets routinely used these tactics against mission cars, it was risky to give them a taste of their own medicine, leading to high-level protests or even a PNG for the tour officer – a very one-sided relationship. However, as with every decision on the ground, there had to be a quick risk/reward calculation followed by swift, firm action. Clipping unmarked Stasi cars was much more common and less likely to escalate to a protest. By a quirk of the RMA, any damage to East German civilian property, including vehicles, had to be compensated by the Soviets (just as damage inflicted by SOXMIS had to be compensated by the British occupation authorities). In 1981, a tour commanded by Captain Nigel Shakespear managed to damage ten out of the fourteen Vopo and Stasi vehicles that had been deployed to stop them getting away from Karl-Marx-Stadt, where the tour had been observing Soviet rocket artillery. Despite furious complaints from the East Germans, the Soviets refused to PNG Shakespear, and only issued him with a perfunctory reprimand.

There were a wide range of set-piece evasion manoeuvres that were honed over time. In the early years, the most used technique was simply to outrun the opposition, literally disappear into the sunset thanks to their superior vehicles and better fuel, and there were several variations on that theme. The 'crossroads' was a popular technique in the late 1950s, where a tour car would build up a lead (the 'accelerator' technique) so the pursuer would lose visual contact with them ahead of a known crossroads or road junction. By the time the pursuer reached the intersection, their target could have gone left or right or, in the case of a roundabout, straight on. Tell-tale clouds of dust in the summer, muddy tyre marks or tracks in the snow were the downsides of this technique. A variation on this would be to dive into a farmer's yard in the hope the pursuers would sail right past them, clouds of dust, barking dogs, and angry farmers notwithstanding. The pursuers could not always rely on the locals to help them –in the East German police state, it was wise not to risk getting involved with the 'organs of State Security'. Most people would avoid any interaction, although party members would inform the authorities of the sighting. An advanced variant was the unofficial (or unauthorised) fly-off or UFO. Rest-stops are a common feature of German autobahns – they are more than a lay-by but less than a motorway services – and take the driver off the main carriageway, often into a pleasant, wooded area. They may have picnic tables, and possibly toilets. However, tours did not use these for picnics – some rest areas had a 'back door', a track leading off into the countryside or forest allowing the tour car to escape, often leaving the pursuer on the hard shoulder, waiting for them to emerge after their convenience break, which of course never happened. These UFOs were carefully reconnoitred and committed to memory – nothing tactical would be marked on the maps in case they fell into unfriendly hands. The 'wives' tale' and 'bomb burst' were two ruses developed in the late 1950s; in December 1958 Deputy Chief Group Captain John Boardman and Squadron Leader Hans Neubroch spent the night at the Potsdam Mission House with their wives (probably the original site at Geschwister Schollstraße – the Mission did not fully move to Seestraße until after Christmas 1958). The following morning the wives drove out the compound in a Mission car and headed south towards Leipzig, picking up the narks on the way. Five minutes later, Boardman, Neubroch and their driver left the compound to begin their day's work, without the interference of the narks, who spent their day following Mrs Neubroch and Mrs Boardman as they went shopping. The two 'tours' met up at a hotel in Eisenach and the following morning successfully repeated the subterfuge.[45] This technique was developed into the 'bomb burst', where the tour car and two or more decoy cars burst out of the compound at once, all heading in different directions. The narks had to pick one of the cars to follow, so there was less of a chance that they would choose the right one. After a while, the decoy cars would turn round and return to the compound, hopefully leaving the real tour unmolested.

Sometimes it was all about covering one's tracks … literally. The tyres on the Western cars used by the AMLMs were very distinctive from the locally made East German versions, both in size and tread pattern. The tread marks left in snow, mud or even dust could quickly be identified as coming from a mission vehicle, and this was particularly problematic close to the precious airfield OPs. Squadron Leader Rod Saar describes the technique to disguise the car's tracks, taught to him by his predecessor, Squadron Leader Frank White. The driver would stop just past the desired turn-off and Saar would leap out of the car and lay ground sheets over the road. The tour car would then be slowly reversed over the ground sheets before making the turn, thus leaving no tracks behind them. If any grass was disturbed in the process, Saar would brush the blades back up with a leafy stick – all to protect the security of the OP.[46] During detentions, the Stasi could be seen taking photographs of tyre tracks, and it was later discovered that tyre-track spotting was taught in Stasi training schools. Other evasion techniques were far less dramatic and involved driving around slowly until the nark car ran out of fuel or overheated, allowing the tour car to proceed with their route. In the early years of the Mission, it was sometimes possible to get the local *komendant* to intervene on the tour's behalf by playing the 'fellow wartime ally' card – there was no love lost between the Soviets and East Germans.[47] If the tour needed to get to 'friendly' territory because of a piece of hot intelligence that needed to be delivered quickly, a medical emergency, or it had become unwise to return to Berlin for operational or security reasons, they could make for the checkpoints at the western end of the main road corridor between West Germany and Berlin – Marienborn on the East German side of the Inner German Border, and Helmstedt (Checkpoint ALPHA) in West Germany. Having run the gauntlet of the Soviet guards (who would probably check with SERB or their *komendant* whether there were any outstanding issues with the tour), they could go to the nearby NAAFI Roadhouse (restaurant/shop), which was equipped with an STU-II secure telephone link to Berlin (installed in case the roadhouse was used as part of `LIVE OAK` operations to reinforce West Berlin via the road corridors).

Detentions

Tours would do their very best to avoid or evade the opposition, but sometimes these efforts failed, and the tour was captured, or in Mission terms, 'detained'. Sometimes detentions occurred by chance, where the tour stumbled on some Soviet (or East German) soldiers who took exception to their presence, while other times they were detained as part of a planned counter-mission ambush. Experience would sometimes help tours avoid known danger areas or operate in a way that reduced the risk of being caught, but often it was simply down to luck, or the lack of it. Tours would normally try to get away, but sometimes it was easier and less dangerous to simply accept the detention and de-escalate the situation. Tour cars were sometimes deliberately rammed, which rendered them undriveable, 'tarped' so they could not see out, or boxed in with vehicles (jeeps, trucks, AFVs or even tanks), but when weapons were raised and the safety of the tour personnel was directly threatened, it was normally time to give in. On occasion the deal was sealed by placing landmines in front of and behind the wheels of the tour car.

After that first contact a detention could go in many different directions, from the benign, to the farcical, to the violent. If the captors were East Germans, who the AMLMs refused to have anything to do with, the presence of a Soviet officer and/or local *komendant* was demanded. If the captors were ordinary Soviet troops, then the presence of the *komendant* was requested. If there was not a suitable linguist in the tour party, they carried cards in German and Russian with instructions for the captors to call the *komendant*. If the tour party were still in the car, they would remain inside, with berets on, doors locked, and windows closed (even in hot weather) until he arrived. They would use the time to hide away their tour equipment under blankets and coats, and squirrel away any exposed films in any number of secret nooks and crannies in the car's interior. Sometimes the tour car would be 'tarped' where a heavy tarpaulin was pulled over the vehicle so the occupants could not see out – this could be very unpleasant and even dangerous in hot weather. If they were out of the car, they would try to engage with their captors and try to talk themselves out of the situation – the tour officer would attempt to 'talk the hind legs off' the detaining officer, while the driver and tour NCO could continue the observation, noting passing vehicles and activity. On the arrival of the *komendant*, and not before, the tour officer would surrender the three tourers' and the vehicle's passes, which meant the 'official' detention had begun. After tourers' passes were stolen during detentions leaving the personnel stuck in the GDR, an agreement was reached between BRIXMIS and SERB that tour officers would *only* surrender their passes to a properly identified member of the Komendatura.

The *komendant* would normally investigate the background to the detention, take statements and have photos taken, and then the tour would normally be invited to accompany him to the Komendatura; on other occasions, the whole rigmarole from detention to release would take place at the scene, depending on how serious the alleged infraction was. At the Komendatura, the ritual pantomime would continue, a sometimes-lengthy interrogation and negotiation, with accusation and counteraccusation, and endless debate of the facts. Although the East Germans may have been instrumental in stopping the tour, they would never be invited into the interrogation, which would have irritated them considerably. It was the *komendant's* job to try to prove the 'guilt' of the tour and he would painstakingly prepare an *Akt*, a pseudo-affidavit statement designed to incriminate, written within strict parameters and often after numerous phone calls with higher authority. He would then invite the tour officer to sign it, which the officer would politely refuse to do, as per policy.

Assuming the tour officer was a Russian linguist, he might use this pointless negotiation as a way of practising his Russian. If he was in the mood to make mischief, he could quickly baffle and tie the *komendant* up in knots of confusion with the irrepressible and often bizarre British sense of humour.[48] Bird watching was widely used an excuse to explain away the cameras and binoculars carried by the tours, with a variant on that theme being photographing 'architectural and scenic highlights' – there were some architectural gems scattered around the GDR, but most of the country was very drab and run-down, making this variant of excuse all the more comical. Another tactic was for the tour officer to give the *komendant* his life story, useless 'chicken feed', but the Soviet officer was obliged to take it all down verbatim in the *Akt*. The officer could take some pleasure knowing that some clerk had to type up the notes from the lengthy encounter, some GRU officer would carefully analyse every sentence back at SERB or GSFG HQ at Zossen-Wünsdorf, with it all being translated into German, meticulously analysed again by the Stasi, and then placed in the tourer's personal Stasi file. Although the car and contents were meant to be inviolable, sometimes the only way to satisfy the *komendant* was to hand over cameras so he could open the backs and fog (and therefore ruin) the film. It was against policy, and would be seriously frowned on at HQ, unless the tour NCO or driver had the sense (or opportunity) to surreptitiously swap the exposed film in the camera (which contained hard-won intelligence) for a new unexposed film. The *komendant* would then take great pleasure in fogging it, and the cost to the Mission would only be a few marks for a wasted film.[49] During the detention, however, the driver and sometimes the tour NCO would normally remain in the car with the doors locked to keep the contents secure.

It was also possible to collect useful intelligence *while* being detained from inside the Komendatura, such as names, ranks, units, field post offices, etc. Captain Stuart Money MBE describes a detention in 1964 where the not-very-bright duty orderly took him to a room that was used for conferences by Komendatura and local garrison officers and had all kinds of maps, notices, and military information posted on the walls. He spent the night memorising as much of this valuable ORBAT information as he could![50] The tour report would include descriptions and as much biographical information of the individuals they engaged with, which was all filed and cross-referenced back at HQ.

Eventually, and after much time had been wasted (which might have been the objective of the detention in the first place), the tour would be released and allowed to continue their tour or return to Berlin, although sometimes their infraction was deemed so serious that the tour was escorted all the way back to the SERB offices in Potsdam where the next act of the pantomime would play out, although on several occasions the escorting officer had to ask the tour to show them the way.

Some Soviet officers were belligerent, some taciturn, while others could be quite sociable, and it was here that time invested previously on goodwill visits would pay dividends. If the tour officer and *komendant* had met before, then the formalities might be accompanied with large amounts of Russian vodka, or the whisky tours carried for such occasions. The *komendant* would put on a good show of righteous indignation on the phone or when superiors were in the room but would revert to his former garrulous self as soon as they were on their own again. On other occasions, however, the atmosphere could be much darker, intimidating, or threatening, sometimes accompanied by incidents of extreme violence, as described later in this book. Detentions could be lengthy affairs, sometimes lasting several days. Major N. L. R. 'Bob' Griffiths RM was involved in one in the early 1950s where he was held under guard in a bare room and interrogated frequently. After three or four days, the tour was released, and they returned to Berlin. They discovered that SERB had not informed BRIXMIS HQ of their detention, and their plight had been escalated all the way to the Foreign Office, who threatened SOXMIS with dire consequences, eventually securing their release. It was also extremely worrying for the tourers' families, who had no idea of their whereabouts or even if they were still alive. The tour was of course completely unaware of all the fuss being made on their behalf.[51]

Not all detentions were violent or dramatic and became surreal or even comic. In 1958, Squadron Leader Hans Neubroch was taking Flight Lieutenant Huw Madoc-Jones out on his first tour only to be ambushed outside the tour car by a party of armed Soviet soldiers. Madoc-Jones, a Russian linguist, harangued the Soviet officer in perfect Russian, creating a diversion that allowed Neubroch to sneak round the back of the vehicle and safely stow all their camera equipment. While a major was summoned from the airbase (so he could converse on equal terms with Squadron Leader Neubroch – the Soviets were very conscious of rank), Neubroch suggested to the Soviet soldiers that they might like to do a song and dance routine while they waited. Astonishingly, they did not take offence and agreed, so in a matter of minutes, the tour had gone from being threatened by armed soldiers to watching an impromptu variety show. When the major arrived, he sent the tour on its way with his good wishes. In 1972, a Soviet captain of engineers took exception to the car Group Captain Jim Corbishley OBE AFC (Deputy Chief BRIXMIS 1972–1974) was being driven in, hitched it to his GAZ-69 jeep and proceeded to tow the bemused occupants around East Germany for the next seven hours. His meanderings included transiting a PRA, which yielded unexpected intelligence for the tour crew. The tour was eventually released, and the sapper captain was never seen, or heard of, again. In April 1977 a mapping tour near Ludwigslust not far from the Inner German Border was stopped by the local *komendant*. Rather than begin the usual accusations and admonishments, the Soviet officer got a bucket of water and cleaned the mud off the BRIXMIS vehicle's high-visibility registration plate. Satisfied it was clean (and therefore visible to Soviet and East German forces), he sent the car on its way. The tour stopped at the first convenient puddle to 'muddy-up' the plate again and continued their tour. In 1981, a tour comprising Captain Peter Williams (tour officer), Sergeant Martyn Woods RA BEM (tour NCO), and Corporal Steve Evans RCT (driver) was in a forest OP observing a river crossing exercise at the Elster-Gallin crossing site on the River Elbe when they were jumped by a squad of heavily armed special forces soldiers (probably specialist engineer reconnaissance troops). The local *komendant* arrived and decided the tour and its car needed to be on the other side of the river: Opel Senator No. 2, which weighed more than two tons, was therefore winched onto the loading deck of a PTS-M tracked amphibious vehicle, which then shot off at an alarming speed through the forest with everyone holding on for dear life, hitting the water without skipping a beat, and emerging a few seconds later on the opposite bank – an exciting, unexpected, (and very revealing) close-up demonstration of Soviet amphibious capabilities.[52] In February 1984 a tour was detained at a rail/road OP by Soviet soldiers on foot, who managed to creep up behind the vehicle and chain it to a tree before emerging to laugh themselves silly when the tour car tried, in vain, to escape. In another incident that year, a Soviet officer in a UAZ-469 jeep pursued a tour car down the wrong way of a busy city dual carriageway to finally ram them, only to see his jeep fall apart, allowing the tour car to escape. It could so easily have ended badly for the tour, innocent pedestrians, or other road users but thankfully the only casualties were the UAZ-469 and the officer's injured pride.

End of Tour

At the end of the tour, the party would call in at the Mission House in Potsdam to confirm they were still alive and in fair condition, have a brew or cold drink and (out of earshot of the local staff and away from the bugs that were almost certainly placed around the building) have a chat with the Mission House Warrant Officer or any other tourers there, sharing any new or useful intelligence. The driver would take the opportunity to hose off the worst of the mud and debris and make any cosmetic repairs to the car before running the gauntlet back across the Glienicke Bridge. Searching tour cars on the bridge was forbidden (a courtesy that was not always observed inside the GDR), however, any damage to vehicles would be methodically noted and photographed as evidence of 'illegal' activities while on tour. The tour party would then finally cross back into West Berlin.

The first stop would be at the USMLM HQ on Föhrenweg in Dahlem, where the tour officer would complete a 'tour highlights' form, detailing all important findings, intelligence or learning points, with copies going to the USMLM and MMFL. They would then head back to London Block having dropped off their personal kit at their homes/quarters on the way. The tour officer and NCO would drag their holdalls and hessian sacks of malodorous booty up to the top floor, book the tour back in with the duty officer, hand over the BRIXMIS copy of the tour highlights form, and deposit their films with the Special Section for processing. They would normally then head home for a much-needed bath and some sleep; however, it was the convention at the Mission that regular duties and social responsibilities had to be honoured even if the officer had just returned from a long and arduous tour, so it was not uncommon to see tour officers nodding off to sleep at the dinner table! The driver, on the other hand, was not finished until he had cleaned the car inside and out and prepared it for servicing the next day. The officer and NCO would reassemble the following morning to sort out their kit, and hopefully see their photos that had been processed and printed (or mounted as slides) overnight. The first task was to debrief the ops officer and then the tour officer and NCO would start the reporting process before the whole cycle began again, planning for their next adventure in the GDR.

Airborne Operations[53]

The aerial reconnaissance sorties flown by BRIXMIS personnel from 1956 to the close of the Mission were known variously over the years as Operation SCHOONER, NYLON, FARNBOROUGH, PHILARIA, and lastly OBERON, and owed their existence not to the 1946 Robertson–Malinin Agreement that created BRIXMIS but to the earlier Four-Power Agreement on Rules of Flight signed on 12 December 1945. All four allied powers were now firmly ensconced in their respective sectors, so it made sense to attempt to regulate the airspace over the city. The Soviets had already agreed to three twenty-mile-wide air corridors permitting traffic up to 10,000 feet, connecting the British and American zones of occupation to West Berlin (the French had to overfly the British or American zones to reach the air corridors), but with all the military, commercial and short-hop patrol or 'communication' trips by the allied powers the airspace quickly became congested and very dangerous. The solution was to create an area of controlled airspace big enough to allow navigation and a reasonable margin of safety around Berlin's main airports (Gatow, Tempelhof, Schönefeld, and later Tegel) and its numerous military or auxiliary airstrips. The Berlin Control Zone (BCZ) was in the form of a circle with a twenty-statute-mile- (seventeen-nautical-mile-, thirty-two-kilometre-) wide radius and a 10,000 feet (3,048 metre) ceiling, centred on the old Kammergericht (Supreme Court) building in the West Berlin district of Schöneberg.* Critically, this meant that allied aircraft had the right to fly anywhere they wanted within this 1,257-square-mile (3,255-square-kilometre) zone, although throughout the Cold War the Soviets continued to claim the right of movement was only over the Western sectors and lodged all sorts of complaints, which the Western Allies duly ignored. RAF Gatow maintained a Percival Prentice trainer aircraft for the purpose of exerting the right of access over Berlin and to allow pilots stationed at the airfield to go flying; the Soviets were very sensitive to having Western combat aircraft based in the city, so only very benign trainer aircraft were deployed. The BCZ airspace was controlled by the four-power Berlin Air Safety Centre (BASC), based in the Kammergericht building.†

---

* There was never a formally agreed *minimum* height for flying within the BCZ, although the Soviets tried to argue that a minimum height of 1,000 ft had been agreed back in 1946 – the allies rejected their claims.

† The Berlin Air Safety Centre (BASC) was the only four-power organisation to last the course, with the ACC and *Komendatura* both collapsing in 1948 and Spandau prison being demolished in 1987 after its sole occupant, Rudolf Hess, committed suicide.

The need for an aerial reconnaissance capability within the Mission became evident during the June 1953 riots in East Berlin (and other cities in the GDR). Chief BRIXMIS, Brigadier Meadmore, who had also served as deputy chief between 1949 and 1950, complained bitterly that he was unable to send his expert observers up in an aircraft to use that extra perspective to see how the East Germans and Soviets were handling the disturbances.[54] The station flight at RAF Gatow, on the other hand, had been sent a two-seater de Havilland Canada Chipmunk T.10 trainer aircraft and, citing the right of transit around the BCZ, a Gatow-based pilot flew one (or possibly two) sorties over East Berlin successfully observing the withdrawal of the Soviet tanks to their barracks at Neuruppin, north-west of Berlin. While this limited surveillance was useful, it was not under the auspices of BRIXMIS so did not meet Meadmore's requirements, but the seed had been sown. BRIXMIS did not have permission to operate *inside* East Berlin; but a small observation aircraft such as the Chipmunk could overfly all of it with impunity, albeit avoiding the civilian airfields by the prescribed margins. There was also the anomaly that the 1,257 square miles of the BCZ included some PRAs and regular TRAs. The December 1945 Rules of Flight agreement covered allied aircraft *arriving in* or *leaving* the BCZ via the three air corridors but there were no rules in place to cover air movements *within* the BCZ; therefore, a routine communication flight or a familiarisation flight for a new commander, for example, had to be logged with the four-power BASC where the Soviet representative would stamp the flight card 'Safety of Flight Not Guaranteed'. Therefore, there was considerable official reluctance to allow formal aerial 'reconnaissance' sorties as any transgression, perceived or actual, or a crash, could spark an international incident. To send the Chipmunks up (the original was joined by a second in 1954) Meadmore had to accept an unusually high degree of oversight from London. The Joint Intelligence Committee (London) submitted flight requests to a mini-Cabinet comprising the prime minister, the foreign secretary, the secretary of state for war, and the secretary of state for air (combined in 1964 into the secretary of state for defence) for approval. The Foreign Office became increasingly involved as the approval process for Chipmunk flights was combined with the Pembroke air corridor flights (Operation HALLMARK) and at times of increased tension, the prime minister personally authorised individual or limited multiple (single figures) flights after consulting his mini-Cabinet.* Operations were also scaled back when there were changes of government in Whitehall, to reduce the risk of an incident for the fledgling administration. The value of aerial reconnaissance (and the quirks of the BCZ) became apparent when the Berlin Wall went up in August 1961; Wing Commander J. H. 'Dickie' Dyer and the deputy chief, Group Captain Gordon Young, were the first allied personnel to see the extent of the barbed-wire barrier, albeit from

---

* RAF Germany ran photographic reconnaissance missions along the three Berlin air corridors throughout the Cold War. Known as Operation HALLMARK, 60 Squadron (and predecessors) operated predominantly Percival/Hunting Pembrokes out of RAF Wildenrath in West Germany. In a similar quirk of East–West relations to the Chipmunk flights in the Berlin Control Zone, the Pembrokes were able to fly over areas excluded from BRIXMIS ground tours by PRAs, filling in important gaps in the intelligence picture. Their imagery could identify targets for BRIXMIS ground tours to investigate and vice versa.

500 feet. They were able to confirm that the large numbers of additional Soviet troops that had been brought in at short notice from the Soviet Union were being kept well back, and the fragile four-power arrangement appeared to still be intact – critical and timely intelligence at a very tense moment. By the end of the year, the situation in Berlin had stabilised sufficiently for the Cabinet Office to authorise a series of flights that were to be executed at the discretion of the GOC Berlin, and this pattern continued right through until the Mission closed in 1990. The GOC consulted with the British Military Government in Berlin for any political considerations before giving his approval. From the late 1960s, the pattern settled onto five flying days per fortnight, in coordination with MMFL aerial reconnaissance missions (the US operated independently until the mid-1970s).

Security surrounding the operation was tight – the missions themselves were TOP SECRET, the intelligence product (Chipmunk recce photographs and reports) was always classified SECRET (sometimes even TOP SECRET) and omitted from the BRIXMIS annual reports, and the link between BRIXMIS and the Chipmunk operation remained classified throughout its life. While the actual flights could not be disguised, great lengths were taken to obscure their true purpose. With all air movements having to go through the BASC, the myth was established that RAF pilots stationed in Berlin had to undergo regular 'continuance training', practise flying to maintain their 'flying pay', and this, along with other excuses, were submitted on the flight plans, to which the Soviet BASC representative would always add his 'Safety of Flight Not Guaranteed' stamp. The pilot's logbook would always say something vague like 'local flying'. Legitimate 'continuance' sorties were also undertaken that took in the whole of the BCZ (rather than just circuits and bumps at Gatow) to help 'camouflage' the reconnaissance trips, and recce flights followed exactly the same air traffic control procedures as the 'legitimate' sorties. Steps were also taken to hide the identity of the aircrew as much as possible.

a) At London Block, Chipmunk aircrew wore army greens with BRIXMIS patches on their sleeves like their ground-based colleagues.
b) On flying days, they would wear normal RAF uniforms (no BRIXMIS insignia) and would be driven to RAF Gatow in normal military cars rather than the distinctive BRIXMIS vehicles.
c) For flying they would wear normal flight suits, again without any BRIXMIS insignia.
d) The pilot's name, however, had to be entered on Form 700, the official paperwork he signed on accepting the aircraft from the ground crew, but the observer's name was not recorded.

RAF Gatow was right next to the outer Berlin Wall and the East German border guards in their observation towers close to the airfield perimeter used powerful binoculars, telephoto lenses, and long-distance microphones to spy on Gatow operations.

a) The aircrew would, therefore, get in the cockpit inside the hangar with the doors closed and were pushed out onto the apron with helmets and goggles on (or visors down), and a similar procedure was followed on landing.

b) Apart from the necessary commands and calls for the push out, engine start, taxying and take-off, there was no conversation while on the ground.*

The de Havilland Canada DHC-1 Chipmunk T.10 was a single-engine, fixed-undercarriage, two-seat trainer aircraft that entered service with the RAF in 1950. The RAF maintained two airframes at RAF Gatow from 1956 to 1990, and while they were never part of the Mission's ORBAT, they were used almost exclusively in the aerial reconnaissance role. The Chipmunk was well suited to the role – it was relatively quiet (rather important for a so-called covert operation), very manoeuvrable (in fact it was fully aerobatic), a relatively stable photographic platform, very reliable, and because it was commonly used as a training aircraft by the RAF (and Army Air Corps), it was familiar to many at BRIXMIS. A full specification for the Chipmunk and details of the airframes used by BRIXMIS are included in the appendices.

Flying in the Chipmunk, however, was not for the faint-hearted. The aircraft could be flown from either of the tandem seats, and initially the observer sat in the back, but they soon found that having the observer in the front seat produced better results. In the confined space of the BCZ, they flew to Visual Flight Rules (VFR, where the pilot was responsible for avoiding any other aircraft) and pilots were constantly looking out for somewhere to put the aircraft down in an emergency. Although the instruments on the Chipmunk were basic, it was possible to fly on instruments if the weather closed in, and it was not unheard of that an aircraft was talked down to land by radio on a ground-controlled-approach (GCA). BRIXMIS coordinated flying days with MMFL, who flew similar reconnaissance sorties, but until the 1970s, the equivalent American flights were controlled by United States Command Berlin (USCOB), who flew wherever and whenever they liked, risking target conflicts and mid-air collisions – as with ground tours, it was important that targets were not 'over-toured' from the air. There were normally two to three Chipmunk sorties a week, generally flown in a clockwise direction around the BCZ (unless the observer was left handed or the targets required it) with flights lasting around two hours, but as they were flown at low level (notionally 1,000 feet, but often at 500 or even 300 feet), ground turbulence and buffeting was severe, and the high g-forces of tight manoeuvring made the experience mentally and physically gruelling.† Having reached the target or spotted something of interest, the pilot would attempt to line up his left wingtip with the target and commence a tight circuit round it.[55] The front-seat passenger needed to be a contortionist to swivel round in his seat

---

* Similar security measures were taken at RAF Gatow with the 60 Sqn Pembroke photo-reconnaissance flights that flew along the Berlin air corridors. Aircraft for Operation LARKSPUR, the American BCZ operation, were not hangared at Tempelhof, so the pilots had to walk out to the aircraft with their helmets on, and their camera equipment in their helmet bags.

† To ensure the Chipmunk did not get in the way of larger military or commercial air traffic, it had to seek permission from air traffic control to climb above 1,500 ft, except in an emergency.

to get the necessary camera angle and brace himself to minimise camera shake, while the pilot maintained a constant bank (as much as 60°) using large amounts of rudder to allow photography over the low wing – a very strong stomach was a prerequisite.*
Turbulence and violent manoeuvres aside, the aircrew also had to cope with freezing temperatures – they would normally fly with the canopy pulled back by about eighteen inches so the observer in the front seat had a clear view, but even when closed, the rain would still get in. All the photography was handheld (as opposed to the fixed cameras on the 60 Squadron Pembrokes and a short-lived experiment on the Chipmunks in the late 1950s), so the photographer had to make notes on his knee notepad, swap cameras, change lenses, empty and reload films, and mark the exposed film cannister with the roll number and the ASA it was shot at, all with wet or frozen fingers (they normally wore thin chamois flying gloves), and avoid, at all costs, dropping the equipment through the open canopy; although it soon became obvious that these Chipmunk sorties were not the 'continuance' or 'familiarisation' flights they claimed to be, it would not have been politic to drop a camera with a partially exposed film with photos of military bases and equipment into the laps of the Soviets or East Germans. The simple solution was to have small chains attached to both camera and lens and to always use the camera neck strap.

Up until 1980, pilots for the Chipmunk sorties came from either within the Mission or from RAF Gatow, both using the 'continuance training' excuse for being in the air. It was advantageous for a pilot to have spent some time doing ground-based tours so he could better appreciate the different perspective of viewing the same targets (vehicles, tanks, aircraft, airfields, installations, etc.) from above. Therefore, prospective new pilots would spend several months on-pass earning their BRIXMIS stripes as normal tour officers. They would then go off-pass (transferring their BRIXMIS pass to another RAF officer) and begin Chipmunk tours for a period. Training for the flights was limited to one 'standard tour' flight around the BCZ with the outgoing pilot, and as with ground tours, new pilots were crewed with experienced observers until they knew the ropes. After a Chipmunk was hit by Soviet rifle fire in April 1975, the non-pilot observers were given crash courses in how to fly and land the aircraft, in case the pilot was incapacitated by enemy fire. It was also common for the deputy chief to fly Chipmunk sorties, as well as the station commander and operations officer (who was also the Chipmunk instructor) from RAF Gatow, all typically experienced pilots. Most pilots were commissioned officers, but up to the mid-1970s, there were still non-commissioned sergeant pilots or master pilots flying in the RAF and they served with BRIXMIS and regularly flew the Chipmunk.†

---

* The RAF had no high-wing aircraft in its inventory, although the army had the Auster AOP.6. The Bird Dog, Beaver, Chiricahua, and Broussard aircraft used by the Americans and French had a high wing, so they had less of a problem.

† Sergeant pilots became common after the First and during the Second World War, and they continued to fly afterwards as pilots IV, III or II, with flight sergeant pilots as pilot I. Warrant officer pilots were redesignated as master pilots. Non-commissioned pilots were gradually phased out by the late 1970s, with the RAF pilot cadre becoming all-officer.

For pass-holding BRIXMIS aircrew, it was not uncommon to go up in the Chipmunk immediately after a ground-based tour or go out on the road straight after a Chipmunk sortie. There were clearly benefits to tour officers having this dual perspective, but by the late 1970s, it was recognised that this dual role (ground *and* air) could quite reasonably lead to fatigue and compromise flight safety. This acceptance coincided with a servicewide shortage of qualified pilots after many took early retirement mid-career following the 1974 Defence Review. In April 1981, Group Captain Peter Botterill CBE, AFC (Deputy Chief BRIXMIS 1979–1981) decided to add an additional post as a full-time Chipmunk pilot to solve both issues, the first being Flight Lieutenant R. B. G. 'Brian' Milton. He would fly the Chipmunk, contribute to the reporting, and would sometimes go 'on-pass' and do some ground tours – the 'continuance training' excuse therefore became increasingly hard to justify. Observers were almost always BRIXMIS pass-holding RAF tour officers, mostly aircrew (pilots and observers who were familiar with aircraft operations and had learnt to cope with the nausea-inducing manoeuvring and turbulence). Although it was not formalised in the same way as for the pilot, certain officers (perhaps those with the strongest stomachs) specialised as Chipmunk observers and could therefore concentrate on the different skillset required for aerial photography; however, both pilots and observers were not exempt from the mandatory Saturday morning vehicle/ aircraft recognition training.

Occasionally a non-aircrew RAF or a brave army tour officer would be taken up, but early representations to have regular army observers were rejected on safety grounds – it was explained that in the case of an emergency, with only around two minutes of dead-stick flying time from 1,000 feet, a high level of teamwork would be required to ensure a successful outcome, and this could only be found in well-trained and experienced RAF aircrew (or so they claimed). However, Major General Peter Williams, an army tour and ops officer in the 1980s, made one trip and did not enjoy the experience: 'I did so only once and emerged feeling battered, bilious and amazed that anyone could work effectively in such primitive and demanding conditions, let alone produce photographs in focus.' Group Captain Andrew Pennington, who served as a flight lieutenant tour officer (August 1985–February 1987) and squadron leader operations (February 1987–October 1988), was not aircrew, so found the experience as a Chipmunk observer just as challenging:

> For someone not used to flying, the change from level flight to turning while looking through what was effectively a narrow tube [the lens] while banking, before ending up straight and level again, generated a feeling of illness which manifested itself in the copious number of sickbags that I had taken the precaution of bringing with me. This, however, was not allowed to disrupt the operation, and the next target was treated in exactly the same way.

Observers initially used Leica M3 or M2 cameras with 130- or 200-mm lenses getting excellent high-definition images from around 500 feet, and then, as the Mission transitioned to Nikon, the Chipmunk flights moved with them. With the introduction of compact mirror lenses with long focal lengths, such as the Nikon 500-mm and 1,000-mm lenses, the Chipmunk could fly a bit higher, reducing some of the drama (and risk) while still getting excellent images. Air photography techniques and equipment are discussed further in Chapter 5, 'Tools of the Trade'. Although spy satellite technology improved dramatically throughout the Cold War, it could never hope to get the angles or the level of detail that could be achieved from the front seat of the Chipmunk – famously, the serial number of a tank engine undergoing maintenance could be read from a photograph taken at around 500 feet. The vagaries of pre-GPS navigation and the airspace required to manoeuvre the aircraft meant that the twenty-mile limit was sometimes exceeded, but the aircrew would normally not mention these minor course deviations in their reports, unless it had been unofficially sanctioned by command. Some targets were right on the twenty-mile outer rim of the BCZ, such as the airfield at Werneuchen (where half of the runway was *inside* the BCZ and the other half *outside*), the SAM site at Glau, and the SCUD unit at Alt Rüdersdorf. By the 1980s, the political risks of straying too far outweighed the potential rewards, and so adventures outside the BCZ were banned, although the Chipmunk could still get good-quality oblique photos outside the zone by skirting the rim and using a long lens. The AMLM aerial sorties could sometimes make life difficult for ground tours with their low flying stirring up the opposition and compromising otherwise secure ground OPs; sometimes two mission aircraft would find themselves in the same bit of sky – flying days were alternated with the French, but the Americans tended to go up as and when they wanted to.

Tasking for the Chipmunk came from the same sources as ground-based tours, although it inevitably had more of a Berlin emphasis with the extra level of GOC approval and higher security, but sorties were briefed by Squadron Leader Ops in the same way. It was estimated that there was never less than 10 per cent of the *whole* GSFG ORBAT within the BCZ at any point in time, and virtually all the different types of equipment used by the Warsaw Pact were on view at some point – a very target-rich environment, especially in the 1980s when GSFG and the NVA were re-equipping with more up-to-date equipment. The area was packed with hundreds of Soviet and East German military installations: headquarters, barracks, fighter bases, helicopter bases, missile units, maintenance depots, training areas, and live-firing ranges, all protected by an elaborate network of anti-aircraft batteries with their associated radar installations and command-and-control set-ups. Observers reported seeing rows and rows of tanks, APCs, artillery pieces, aeroplanes, and helicopters – seemingly more than the whole British Army or RAF possessed. In addition, much of Eastern Europe's transport infrastructure was routed through the city – all visible from above. By the late 1970s/ early 1980s, as army/RAF and intra-mission touring became more integrated, so did the Chipmunk flights – it was not uncommon for the Chipmunk (or MMFL/USMLM equivalent) to fly in the morning, returning to base to brief a ground-based tour who were departing that afternoon; tours could then head straight for these activities to hoover up more intelligence.

On returning to Gatow, the pilot would hand the aircraft back to the ground crew who would undertake the necessary servicing and maintenance. On returning to London Block, the observer would hand the films to the Special Section for processing,

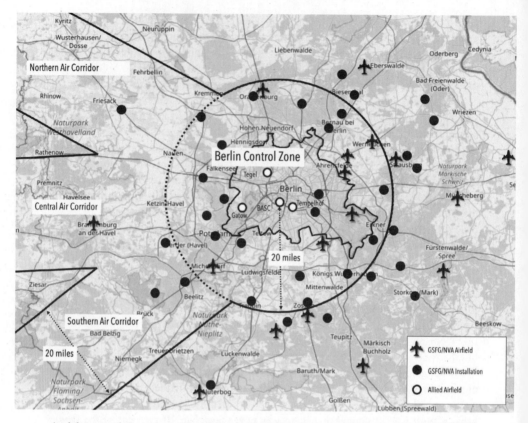

Aerial reconnaissance targets within or near to the Berlin Control Zone. GSFG/NVA airfields included conventional airbases, but also motorway landing strips and 'agricultural' airstrips. GSFG/NVA installations included barracks, bunkers, training sites, and logistics sites/ammo dumps. 60 Squadron RAF Pembroke aircraft would also photograph targets along the three Berlin air corridors. (Author using OpenStreetMap base mapping)

and the crew would then match the roll and frame numbers to the target locations. Unlike ground-based tours, Chipmunk aircrew did not fill out a tour highlights form, but the Weapons/Research teams made initial assessments of the imagery and an IMMEDIATE signal would be sent to JHQ, Bonn, and/or London with any critical or time-sensitive intelligence. The aircrew would typically write up their full reports within a few days, and the prints or slides with their accompanying narratives (graded SECRET or higher) would then be sent to JHQ Rheindahlen for further analysis by the photographic interpreters of 6 Intelligence Company (PI) and then on to the relevant desks at the MoD. Chipmunk sortie reporting was kept out of the normal BRIXMIS reporting process for security reasons.

Over time, through their penetration agents or by simple deduction, the Soviets and East Germans became fully aware of what these small aircraft were up to, although there was little they could do about it, short of causing a major incident.* It was an open secret among many of the Potsdam garrison and local East Germans. However, it did mean that the AMLM aircraft were often tracked by anti-aircraft defences such as the ZSU-23-4 tracked anti-aircraft gun system, and occasionally they were buzzed by fast jets or helicopters or targeted by signal flares fired from the ground. They regularly overflew exercise areas where soldiers were firing their weapons and tossing hand grenades. There was only one occasion, on 20 April 1975, when a BRIXMIS Chipmunk, piloted by Master Pilot Graham Forrester with Squadron Leader Brian Speed in the observer seat, was hit by a Soviet rifle bullet. After returning from an otherwise uneventful Sunday morning sortie, the ground crew pointed out a large bullet hole in the propeller spinner, and when the photos were developed, they could see a Soviet soldier standing next to a BMP-1KSh taking aim – an inch or so back and the bullet could have disabled the engine causing a crash; a foot or two back and it could have hit one of the aircrew. The spinner was duly replaced and the holed one resided in the BRIXMIS Ops office for many years after.

The aircraft were remarkably reliable, and only one incident of engine trouble is recorded in thirty-four years of Chipmunk operations, when Squadron Leader Hans Neubroch had engine trouble on a sortie in 1957 and had to divert to Tempelhof in the US sector for an emergency landing. However, if the aircraft did suffer engine failure or was forced down by gunfire or hostile aircraft, the options for the aircrew were limited. From 1,000 feet (and they mostly operated well below that) there was only about two minutes of dead-stick flying time before they hit the ground. In those two minutes, the pilot had to search for somewhere safe to put the aircraft down; as most of their flying was done over the Soviet sector or the GDR, they would be landing (or crashing) in hostile territory. It was the observer's job to destroy any incriminating material in the cockpit that would suggest to the opposition that the flight was engaged in covert or elicit photography. His first task would be to fog the exposed films. These were stored in a long, slotted tube inside the cockpit with the tail end of each film protruding through the slot. The observer was meant to grab all these tails and pull the five-feet-long film strips out of the cannisters, exposing them to light, fogging the emulsion and therefore destroying the evidence. Crews also carried pen knives or tin openers so the end of the film canister could be popped off, allowing the film to unravel and fog, but this was not practical if there were lots of films to destroy. The observer was then meant to put the cameras, films, and any documents (target maps, etc.) into a green fabric bag specially provided for the purpose and dump them overboard into one of Berlin's many lakes. The reality would have been very different, of course. If the aircraft was going down, the aircrew would have had seconds to react – the observer may have had the chance to fog the films, but searching for a suitable lake in which to jettison the equipment was pure fantasy. Assuming the crew survived the crash landing uninjured and remained conscious, their orders were to stow all the cameras inside the aircraft, open the fuel

---

* Following the fall of the Wall and the opening of some of the Stasi archives, it became apparent that RAF Gatow officers' mess manager, the affable Herr Muths, had been a Stasi agent for many years. He was subsequently reassigned to the station headquarters in an administrative post, where he was able to continue with his espionage (Saar, *BRIXMIS*).

cocks to release the highly inflammable aviation fuel and ignite it all with a signal flare, destroying all the evidence. If they landed inside the GDR, it would be their BRIXMIS colleagues who would come looking for them; if inside East Berlin, it would have been a team from the Berlin Infantry Brigade. Thankfully none of this ever happened.

The Soviets had just as much right to conduct photo-reconnaissance sorties over West Berlin, but they seldom did, as their spies in the community reported everything they needed to know. However, they occasionally made their presence known with high-speed, low-level passes over West Berlin, sometimes breaking the sound barrier with the resulting sonic boom shattering windows.

The quality of the photography and therefore the intelligence extracted was exceptional, and these sorties provided invaluable ORBAT intelligence on local units and significant technical intelligence on Soviet equipment. In 2000, Group Captain Richard Bates AFC, Deputy Chief BRIXMIS 1981–1983 and later head of the Intelligence Branch at HQ Strike Command, commented that 'a very high proportion of the British Army's technical intelligence "take" has rightly been attributed to this single operation'.[56] Airborne operations in the Chipmunk would occasionally produce some real scoops, simply by being able to view from above.

a) In July 1959, there was an early scoop with the first sighting outside of the Soviet Union of the V-75 'Dvina' (NATO reporting name SA-2 GUIDELINE) surface-to-air (SAM) missile.[57] It was previously spotted at the 1959 May Day parade on Red Square in Moscow, but had never been seen close-up, or with its accompanying radar. A battery had been spotted from the ground at a former Luftwaffe air defence site at Glau, south-west of Berlin, on the outer rim of the BCZ, but ground tours had not been able to get close to it. On 16 July, Squadron Leader Hans Neubroch took the Mission's electronics expert, Squadron Leader Harry Nunwick, up on a normal clockwise circuit around the BCZ, but at Glau, dropped down to about 300 ft and made some very tight turns allowing Nunwick to get lots of photos of the missiles and their FAN SONG radar vehicles. Neubroch quickly returned to Gatow, and the pair rushed to London Block to get the films developed – the results were tremendous. The following morning Neubroch and Nunwick flew the prints to JHQ Rheindahlen and personally briefed C-in-C RAFG. The pictures were then sent on to London, where the Tech Int boffins were ecstatic. C-in-C RAFG later informed them that the pictures were on US President Eisenhower's desk the following Monday.*

b) During 1972, photography mainly taken by Flight Lieutenant Alan White from the front seat of a Chipmunk enabled BRIXMIS to determine the

---

* The SA-2 GUIDELINE system was used to great effect during the 1960s – a missile shot down the U-2 spy plane piloted by Francis Gary Powers over Sverdlovsk, Soviet Union on 1 May 1960, shot down a Taiwanese-flown U-2 over Nanking, China, in September 1962, a USAF U-2 over Cuba in October 1962 during the Cuban Missile Crisis, and was used to devastating effect during the Vietnam War.

complete ORBAT of the Soviet 10 Guards Tank Division, photographed as they were being cleaned or serviced at their barracks or during training – each piece of armour having a unique side number.

c) The Soviet T-64 tank entered production in 1966 and was first seen in public in 1970, but was kept away from Western eyes, only being issued to GSFG some six years after entering service. Even then, tank units went to great lengths to keep it out of sight from ground and aerial tours, and it was unclear what the calibre of the main gun was. The same troops, however, did not take the same care with their ammunition boxes and a BRIXMIS Chipmunk flight photographed a neat row of containers whose markings confirmed the GSFG T-64s had a 125-mm main gun, as opposed to the 115-mm gun it was originally specified with. In 1976, Squadron Leader Roy Marsden was the first to get an aerial photograph of the tank itself when it was spotted out on the wash-stand and captured it with a 1,000-mm lens. Useful detail could normally be obtained when guns, ammo loads, hatches, and turrets were removed for maintenance.

d) Another sortie managed to photograph a dry-run for an entire divisional headquarters command-and-control centre, with all the communications cable carefully laid out on the ground. The detail from 300 ft and a 1,000-mm lens was extraordinary – there was no comparable intelligence from any other source for more than a decade.[58]

e) The Soviet airfield at Werneuchen, north-east of Berlin, was in a PRA so was out of bounds to ground-based tours but was right on the outer rim of the BCZ – one end of the runway was *inside*, the other *outside*. The Chipmunk could therefore fly there, but the imperfect art of aerial navigation meant that they would easily stray outside their legal limit and be susceptible to hostile enemy action. In 1974/75 it became a high-priority target for the Chipmunk crews after the new Soviet supersonic MiG-25 (NATO reporting name FOXBAT) jet interceptor was stationed there. Pushing their luck, the Chipmunk was able to fly at around 200 ft right over the flightline, obtaining excellent detailed photography of the upper surfaces of the MiG-25, including areas exposed for servicing.[59]

f) In the mid-1970s, Squadron Leader Roy Marsden spotted some unusual earthworks at Kagel, just to the east of Alt Rüdersdorf, and took some photographs. He had inadvertently discovered the construction of a huge, buried radio antenna, which operated at very low frequencies and permitted long-distance communications with submarines. Intelligence reports had hinted of such a development, but no one knew what to look for. Although it was just outside the BCZ, the Chipmunk would overfly the area every five to six weeks to see how the project was progressing, capturing every stage of its construction. Within two years, nature had reclaimed the site and there was no sign that anything had been there.

g) Aerial photographs taken by the BRIXMIS Chipmunk over Krüpelsee, a lake used by the Soviet Army for amphibious training (river crossings, pontoon bridges, small ferries/rafts to transport tanks and heavy vehicles), improved the understanding of Soviet amphibious tactics and techniques, which helped ground tours when observing other river crossing exercises around the GDR.

h) In the 1980s, a coordinated campaign involving BRIXMIS and MMFL aerial reconnaissance assets was tasked with getting detailed close-up imagery of the Soviet SPN-30 (NATO reporting name PAINT BOX) radar jammer, which reportedly could jam the terrain-following radar used by NATO bombers, interfere with NATO's airborne early-warning capability, and send cruise missiles off course, thus putting NATO's strike capability at risk – clearly a very high-priority intelligence target for NATO. Ground tours and ELINT operations had failed to find them, but aerial photography of the radar vehicles taken over the Schönwalde and Kremmener forests *within* the BCZ answered all of Tech Int's questions and allowed suitable countermeasures to be developed.[60]

i) A sortie in the mid-1970s with Squadron Leader Vince Robertson as observer chanced upon a P-40 'Bronja' (Grau index 1S12, NATO reporting name LONG TRACK) air defence radar tracked vehicle. He managed to get shots of it with its hatches open, before the Soviet crew closed them, but only when they got back and analysed the photos did they realise that they had clear photographs of the cables connecting the main dish to the vehicle, which had been an outstanding request for some time. The boffins could then estimate the thickness of the cables, which gave them an idea of the power required, and thus the strength of the radar – an important technical scoop.

There was always a risk that intelligence taken from aerial photography could be misinterpreted or subject to a 'wish-fulfilment' filter. In 1979, the Americans were paranoid that the Soviet OTR-21A 'Tochka' nuclear-capable tactical ballistic missile (NATO reporting name SS-21 SCARAB) had been forward deployed to East Germany. With its relatively short range (43 miles, 70 kilometres), it would have been a key component of any Soviet invasion of West Germany. A BRIXMIS Chipmunk sortie photographed a large cylindrical object on a railway flatbed truck, which analysts believed to be proof that the SS-21 had indeed been deployed. The find was of such magnitude that it found its way in the CIA's daily presidential briefing. Subsequent photography, however, proved that the cylindrical object was *not* an SS-21 but a new Soviet unmanned aerial vehicle (UAV, drone), probably the Tu-141 VR-2 'Strizh' (Swift) that was equipped with an airborne data relay (ADR), which beamed live television pictures to a beyond-line-of-sight ground station. This was still quite a scoop, but not the SS-21 scoop that the CIA were hoping for.[61]

Reporting, Classification, Customers, and the Intelligence Machine

The BRIXMIS intelligence product was just one component of a very complicated machine that worked 24/7, 365 days a year throughout the Cold War to ensure that NATO, and in particular British Forces, Germany (BFG), were ready to meet the threat they faced across the Iron Curtain. The reporting process began as soon as the tour arrived back in West Berlin. Their first stop was at HQ USMLM at Föhrenweg 19/21 where a 'tour highlights' form was completed in triplicate. This was quickly circulated to all three AMLMs that ensured that any time-sensitive or urgent intelligence was swiftly passed up the chain of command. If the situation demanded it, another tour or other intelligence assets could be despatched to take up the chase. The following morning, the tour crew would get into the office for about 0800 hours, ready for the morning briefing at 0830. The tour officer and NCO would then start to sort through all the photographs, which had been processed overnight by the Special Section, matching the film and frame numbers to the notes (notebooks or Dictaphone recordings) taken at the time, and any identifying marks – *Bort* or vehicle registration numbers, etc. – would be checked against the card index database (and later the Project ELECTRIC LIGHT computer system). The Weapons Office and Research team would be brought in to look at any significant equipment sightings, scoops or ORBAT updates, which would prompt further analysis and detailed reports (typically graded SECRET or above) to their 'customers'.

The significance of a sighting was often not realised until the photos were closely examined the following day, and a 'fluke' turned into a 'scoop'. Perhaps one of the best examples of this was from September 1989 at the Storkow NVA training area. Captain Steve Gibson MBE RE was on tour with Warrant Officer Paul Seager RE (Tour NCO, also in charge of the Geo section) and Corporal Stan Matthews RAF (driver) observing NVA training. Coming to a fire break in the forest, they spotted a huge but unfamiliar vehicle through a gap between the trees. It was about three times the size of a British Army 4-ton truck and appeared to be carrying four large cylinders or cannisters on its back, and their (quite reasonable) assumption was that it was some kind of bridging system with flotation devices, especially as the NVA were known to practise amphibious operations in this area. Unusually, there were both NVA and Soviet soldiers all around it who quickly spotted the tour car – it was not clear whether they were armed. The only option was a 'smash-and-grab', so Matthews accelerated quickly towards the target, swinging the G-Wagen round so Gibson could get a shot out of the side window – they were only 100 metres away and the soldiers were approaching quickly. Gibson grabbed the Nikon F3 with the 85-mm lens and quickly fired off two shots capturing the rear three-quarters of the still-unidentified target. Wanting to get closer to the action, he did an ultra-quick lens change and got one more shot with the vehicle filling the frame, before Matthews beat a very hasty and dramatic retreat into the forest. The tour made it safely back to Berlin, noted their sighting of a 'U/I (Unidentified) engineer amphibious vehicle' on the tour highlights form and handed the films over to the Special Section. Early the next morning, the tour crew was summoned from their quarters to a meeting with the Weapons officer, who had already seen the photos – he revealed that it was not an engineer amphibious vehicle (although that was a good guess given the location) but an SA-10B GRUMBLE Surface-to-Air Missile (SAM) system that had never been seen in Germany before – a major scoop for the mission, and of strategic significance to NATO. Within days the photos had reached the Pentagon and it was even included in the US president's daily intelligence brief, all down to a chance sighting, a hunch, a misidentification, some skilful driving, rapid photography, and nerves of steel.[62]

Good intelligence was of no use unless it was disseminated promptly to the Mission's customers, either through the 'tour report' or a 'Technical Intelligence' report on a specific piece of KIT that would be fast-tracked to JHQ Rheindahlen, NATO HQ, or to the MoD in London. In the early years, the tour officer was responsible for producing the tour report, but over time the task was split, with the officer writing up any significant findings, unusual or serious incidents, and detentions. He would also summarise any surveys they had made, such as a training or deployment area. The NCO, on the other hand, would write up all the KIT spotted, with supporting photos. The driver would be consulted to add his recollections or perspective as needed. Although it was important to capture the key findings of a tour swiftly while the intelligence was still fresh and before the tour crew got distracted by their next outing, routine tour reports would normally follow within a month of their return, written up to the prescribed format and appended with all relevant sketches and photographs, classified CONFIDENTIAL or higher. Individual tour reports would be circulated within the Mission, copied to the other AMLMs, and sent to the key customers in Berlin, at JHQ Rheindahlen and the MoD in London.

From the 1970s onwards, the Mission began to suffer from 'information overload' – the rearming and modernisation of the GSFG and NVA meant that the volume of raw intelligence material coming out of the Mission threatened to swamp their customers. Brigadier Crookenden (Chief BRIXMIS 1971–1972) introduced more analysis and interpretation of the material, rather than just pumping raw intelligence up the chain. By the early 1980s, it had become policy for the Weapons and Research teams to undertake the first-line analysis of the material at London Block on behalf of their clients, therefore passing on a more polished and refined product; BRIXMIS was becoming an integrated, end-to-end intelligence operation, and even began to generate its own tasking, reflecting their customer's overall objectives.

Every quarter, BRIXMIS command would produce a digest of the intelligence collected, and note other key points, such as detentions or other incidents. Before 1966, the reports within were non-attributable, but after they carried the officer's name. However, after the killing of Major Nicholson in 1985 the Mission began anonymising the tour reports, with tour personnel being given a codename: officers had Red prefixes, NCOs Green, and drivers Blue; for example, Major Peter Williams, SO2 Ops, was Red 47. The first reports were classified TOP SECRET, reflecting the wartime obsession with secrecy, but they were progressively downgraded to SECRET (March 1955) and then CONFIDENTIAL, and the frequency of reporting was reduced to biannual, and then by the early 1970s, annual, reflecting the workload involved in compiling the reports, remembering that the key findings were always reported directly to customer departments under SECRET or TOP SECRET cover.* BRIXMIS

---

* There were five levels of classification in the Government Protective Marking Scheme for British military and government secrets: TOP SECRET, SECRET, CONFIDENTIAL, RESTRICTED, PROTECT, and UNCLASSIFIED. The effects of releasing information marked as CONFIDENTIAL include considerable infringement on personal liberties, material damage to diplomatic relations, or to seriously disrupt day-to-day life in the country. In 2014, they were consolidated to just three levels: TOP SECRET, SECRET, and OFFICIAL.

reports would be circulated to a controlled list of recipients in London, West Berlin, and West Germany including:

Ministry of Defence
MoD DI 3 (Army and Air) – the various Defence Intelligence Staff (DIS) desks at the MoD in London, and through them the secretary of state for defence.

MoD Tech Int (Army and Air) – the Technical Intelligence desks at the MoD in London, and through them the secretary of defence. The DI 3 and Tech Int desks produced the majority of BRIXMIS tasking requests.

School of Service Intelligence – based in Ashford, Kent ran the Intelligence (Special Duties) courses to prepare AMLM personnel for their postings. Directing staff were constantly in touch with the Mission.

Foreign Office
British Embassy, Bonn, and through them the Foreign Office in London.

British Embassy, East Berlin – opened on 16 April 1973, and through them the Foreign Office in London.[63] Before that, the Foreign Office was represented by the British minister, who was also deputy commandant.

JHQ Rheindahlen
CICC Germany – the Commanders'-in-Chief Committee (Germany) or CICC(G), top-level command for British Forces, Germany at JHQ Rheindahlen, including C-in-C BAOR and C-in-C RAFG. The intelligence team at JHQ was also responsible for BRIXMIS tasking.

HQ BAOR – Headquarters of the British Army in Germany, originally based at Bad Oeynhausen, and then consolidated with HQ RAFG at JHQ Rheindahlen.*

HQ RAFG (CIO) – Chief Intelligence Officer, Headquarters of RAF Germany, originally based at Bad Eilsen, and then consolidated with HQ BAOR at JHQ Rheindahlen.

BLO to SOXMIS – the British Liaison Office (BLO) was responsible for SOXMIS (based at Bünde, near Herford and Bad Oeynhausen), the equivalent to the Soviet SERB in Potsdam. Learning about BRIXMIS experiences allowed the BLO and RMP to better monitor and/or intercept SOXMIS operations.

---

* BAOR was a theatre-level (akin to 'Front-level' in GSFG) command with its own 4-star C-in-C. I (BR) Corps was a 3-star corps-level command (akin to an 'Army' in GSFG).

Berlin

HQ Berlin (British Sector) – British commandant and GOC Berlin Infantry Brigade.

BMG Berlin – British Military Government, commandant, and minister (latter absorbed by the British Embassy in East Berlin when it opened in 1973).

FMLM – (MMFL), and through them, HQ Forces Françaises en Allemagne (FFA, in Baden Baden), and the Ministère de la Défense in Paris, with their reports shared (theoretically) reciprocally back.

USMLM – and through them HQ USAREUR (originally in Frankfurt and then Heidelberg), and the Pentagon in Washington D.C., with their reports shared (also theoretically) reciprocally back.

TAREX – Target Exploitation, a branch of US Military Intelligence tasked with gathering intelligence from refugees and defectors (including the flood of Republikflüchtlinge before the Wall went up), especially concerning enemy equipment, dovetailing with the collection efforts of USMLM.

HQ BAOR and HQ Berlin (British Sector) were members of the Intelligence & Security Group, abbreviated to 'G Int & Sy' or 'Int & Sy Gp' who coordinated the various army intelligence activities across West Germany and in Berlin. The group included front-line Intelligence Corps units in West Germany but also 6 Int Coy (PI), the photographic interpretation specialists at Rheindahlen, and 3 Int & Sy Coy who were based in the same building as BRIXMIS in West Berlin (Coy is the British Army abbreviation for Company). RAFG maintained its own parallel intelligence organisation, and relevant teams at NATO's Supreme Headquarters Allied Powers Europe (SHAPE, in Mons, Belgium) would be kept in the loop by their counterparts in the above organisations.

The intelligence chiefs at JHQ Rheindahlen had the daunting task of compiling a coherent intelligence picture and threat assessment from a broad range of sources, much of which could be contradictory or even misinformation planted by the opposition. These sources included:

BRIXMIS – ground tours.

BRIXMIS – aerial reconnaissance sorties.

Various Intelligence Corps units in West Germany and other NATO countries.

SIGINT operations: 26 Signals Unit (26SU) at RAF Gatow and Field Station Berlin (FSB, Teufelsberg), US Army Security Agency and NSA at FSB, and the 6912 Electronic Security Group, USAF, at Marienfelde.

14 Signals Regiment (Electronic Warfare), Royal Corps of Signals – providing electronic warfare support to 1 (British) Corps.[64]

51 Squadron, RAF – Special Duties squadron operating SIGINT (ELINT and COMINT) flights.

60 Squadron, RAF – Berlin air corridor photo-reconnaissance flights (Operation HALLMARK).

GCHQ – SIGINT from Government Communications Headquarters and their Five Eyes partners, including the NSA.

MoD – 'processed' intelligence from the DIS and Tech Int desks.

SIS – HUMINT from the Secret Intelligence Service (SIS) and Five Eyes partners, including the American CIA.

Coordinating all the material was a challenge and there was a real danger that vital or time-sensitive tactical intelligence would fall through the cracks or be held up in this multi-agency and multinational bureaucracy. Therefore, in the mid-1980s, the then Chairman of the CICC(G) at JHQ Rheindahlen (and thus effectively C-in-C British Forces Germany), Air Marshal Sir Patrick Hine, created the Berlin Tactical Analysis Cell (BTAC) to rapidly review intelligence material and disseminate it to the relevant front-line units.

A good example showing how the pieces of the intelligence jigsaw came together was the case of the mystery wing pods on the MiG-27M FLOGGER-J strike/attack aircraft from Altenburg airfield in the late 1980s. Altenburg, between Leipzig and Dresden, was popular with tours because it tended to receive a lot of new KIT direct from the Soviet Union. A BRIXMIS tour established an OP at the end of the runway and observed a large group of FLOGGER-Js taking off, noticing an unusual pod on one of the wing pylons that had not been seen before, and the new feature was captured on film and the times and *Bort* (side) numbers were recorded as per standard operating procedures. Around forty minutes later the aircraft landed and were duly photographed/ logged again. Later in the day, the tour was treated to a repeat performance, except that when the aircraft landed, the mysterious pods were now open, revealing empty interiors. On returning to Berlin, they filed the tour highlights as normal, but when they arrived in the office the following morning, news of their sighting had spread, and the mission/intelligence community were clamouring for more information. It transpired that the first FLOGGER sortie went down to the air-to-ground range at Gadow Rossow as a rehearsal for a coordinated live-firing demonstration that afternoon using the new pods, which turned out to be KMGU cluster bomb dispensers – all of which was observed by a USMLM tour, who matched the number of aircraft, their *Bort* numbers and the timings observed by the BRIXMIS tour at Altenburg. The demonstration had also been monitored by SIGINT and radar operations (FSB Berlin, USAF Marienfelde, RAF Gatow), who could also match the *Bort* numbers and landing timings from the aircrafts' radio traffic and call signs. When all these component parts were assembled by analysts at JHQ Rheindahlen and other NATO HQs, it gave a really accurate account of a large-scale Soviet Air Force ground-attack operation.

The CONFIDENTIAL classification of BRIXMIS reporting was a double-edged sword – it potentially downplayed the real value of the intelligence (and the risks taken to acquire it), and often was considered 'inferior' to 'higher-grade' intelligence from high-tech (and therefore high-cost) sources such as SIGINT, ELINT or satellite reconnaissance. The immense cost of these 'higher-grade' intelligence sources created an inherent bias in their favour – it cost so much that it must be good – as opposed to the much lower-cost BRIXMIS 'ground truth', a sort of intelligence snobbery that the Mission had to fight against for most of its existence.

It did, however, permit distribution to (and use by) a wider audience, even down to front-line units such as 1 (BR) Corps based in West Germany. Another benefit was that intelligence analysts could usefully attribute material from other more sensitive sources to BRIXMIS, allowing it to be more widely circulated (and used) without risking the source. The 'Annual Report', therefore, became increasingly 'sanitised' of anything too revelatory and ended up being more of a PR tool, with the real business being transacted directly with their customers in separate 'Technical Reports', graded SECRET or above. Although it was not confirmed until the Stasi archives opened after the fall of the Wall, the main reason for the gradual 'sanitisation' of BRIXMIS reports was the belief that the Stasi had placed long-term penetration agents among the clerical or janitorial staff at JHQ Rheindahlen and even HQ Berlin, and some recipients were known to be lax on document security.

BRIXMIS also liaised with the wider intelligence community in Germany such as the BSSO(G) and BSIU(G). The British Services Security Organisation (Germany), or BSSO(G), was an offshoot of MI5 and had offices at Cologne, Bonn, West Berlin and at JHQ Rheindahlen.* Their job was counterintelligence, helping protect British military installations from espionage and later from terrorist action. They liaised with the West German security agencies at federal level (Federal Office for the Protection of the Constitution, Bundesamt für Verfassungsschutz or BfV) and at state level (State Office for the Protection of the Constitution, Landesbehörde für Verfassungsschutz or LfV), and other national security services. In 1968 the intelligence side of BSSO(G) was detached to become the British Services Intelligence Unit (Germany) or BSIU(G), which was affiliated with SIS – the SIS Berlin Station was on the floor below BRIXMIS in London Block.[65]

BRIXMIS was also in contact with the 18th Military Intelligence Battalion of the US Army (the American equivalent of the BSSO(G)) and the US National Ground Intelligence Center (NGIC) in Charlottesville, Virginia (the equivalent to the British Tech Int (Army)), which was the main source of tasking for USMLM. Analysts from DIS, Tech Int and NGIC would meet their NATO opposite numbers annually at conferences, such as the Allied Land Technical Weapons Intelligence Conference (ALTWIC), to share intelligence trends, and this cooperation, combined with the intra-mission (army and RAF) and inter-mission (BRIXMIS, MMFL, and USMLM) coordination, described above, proved to be very successful.

---

* The British Services Security organisation (Germany), BSSO(G), was established in 1954 and was the successor to the post-war British Forces Security Unit (BFSU).

BRIXMIS and the other AMLMs tried to stay out of the public eye, but occasionally there was some unwelcome attention. In the 1970s, some classified AMLM photography found its way into the Western aviation media but despite extensive investigations, the culprits were never discovered. The Mariotti (1984) and Nicholson (1985) murders (see Chapter 6, 'The Opposition') inevitably reached the international news media, and there were occasional critical articles in the Soviet press, enthusiastically reprinted in the East German state-controlled press. However, it was not until the publication of Tony Geraghty's book *Beyond the Frontline* in 1996 (later published as *Brixmis: The Untold Exploits of Britain's Most Daring Cold War Spy Mission*) that the Mission entered the British public's consciousness. *Beyond the Frontline* was produced with the cooperation of the MoD and BRIXMIS Association, and Tony's original notes are available to researchers at the BRIXMIS Association archive held at Liddell Hart Centre for Military Archives at King's College London. Steve Gibson, a former tour officer who is mentioned in this narrative, followed Geraghty with his book, *BRIXMIS, The Last Cold War Mission*, in 1997.

Mapping[66]

Military operations rely on up-to-date mapping, never more so when operating behind 'enemy' lines, so the pre-war maps of East Germany used by the Mission for pre-tour planning, navigation on tour and post-tour analysis were less than ideal – bridges destroyed in the Second World War were not replaced or were rebuilt in different places, tracks had become busy roads and vice versa. The quartermaster could not go out and buy some new ones because all maps in the GDR apart from large scale road atlases were classified. Improving the Mission's maps therefore became an ongoing task. There were five key maps used by the Mission:

> M641 series – 1:100,000 scale used for operational planning (including the vertical louvre blind system in the ops room) and, before the M745 being available, for tour maps, patched together in sets of four sheets.

> M745 and later M536 series – 1:50,000 scale used in the main corridor 'wall' map and for tourers' 'strip' maps.

> M841 series – 1:25,000 scale used for recording detailed information used in tour planning, and for marking up answers to questions posed by the Geo team on 'Mapping' tours.

> M444 series – 1:500,000-scale 'road' map used to plot PRA and TRA boundaries.

> 1501 series – 1:250,000-scale 'road' map used to plot PRA and TRA boundaries.

The most obvious mapping resource at the Mission was the thirty-metre-long 'wall' map, which ran the whole length of the curved corridor at the Mission offices at London

Block. Made from M745 (and later M536) 1:50,000 sheets, it was mounted in five sections progressing from north to south and contained every single Soviet and East German military installation and point of interest including every MRS, all marked by colour-coded pins. The tour officer/NCO would identify targets and their grid reference in any given area from the pins, and from that, access the relevant target files from Research. When it was not being pored over by tour officers and NCOs preparing for their next tour, it was covered by heavy curtains. Each tour officer and SNCO prepared their own set of M745/M536 1:50,000 'strip' maps by sticking together west–east adjacent maps to form a strip. Adjacent pairs of strips were then taped back-to-back and unclassified information such as PRAs, lay-bys, MRS locations or cartographic/topological corrections were marked by hand. The resulting map was then laminated with Fablon (transparent sticky-backed plastic), concertina folded, and carried in an aircrew navigator's map case. These carefully patched map sets were passed on to their successors and periodically replaced when they wore out, or where there was a major change, such as a PRA.

Mapping is taken very seriously by command for obvious reasons, and common NATO standards ensured units from different nations could easily operate alongside each other. The somewhat 'homemade' nature of BRIXMIS maps was therefore an issue, but they muddled through for the first twenty years or so, with limited resources at HQ, and with BAOR and UK map depots rapidly being depleted of the meagre stocks of GDR maps held there. In the early 1970s, a professional cartographer (Survey Technician Staff Sergeant, and later Major, Alan Gordon) was seconded from BAOR with a brief to shake up the Mission's mapping. The solitary member of the team, Corporal Ian Walker, finally received some basic training in cartography, and Gordon could also call on the resources from BAOR, including a huge map library and large format dye-line printers that could produce on-demand, one-off copies of any map held.* Being integrated with the BAOR survey function also ensured any updates found their way to the Mission, who reciprocated with mapping intelligence gleaned from tours.

The PRA/TRA boundaries issued by SERB were annotated by hand onto large-scale Soviet maps, and contained many inconsistencies, so a PRA map given to BRIXMIS could differ slightly from one given to USMLM, etc. To avoid confusion and potentially risky mistakes, whenever new PRA or TRA maps were issued, the AMLMs reviewed them and agreed a definitive version (normally with the *least* amount of excluded territory), which was then sent to 14 Field Survey Squadron Royal Engineers (becoming 14 Topographical Squadron in 1977) in Düsseldorf, who overprinted 1:500,000 (M444 series) and 1:250,000 (L501 series) sheets of the GDR showing the agreed exclusion areas in yellow. With systems in place to update maps when PRA changes were made, or when TRAs were imposed, it considerably reduced the workload of the operations teams and reduced the risk of dangerous mistakes in the field.

Tour planning was made much easier for the ops team with the introduction of the vertical louvre map in the ops room. The JHQ library had managed to compile a full set of 1:100,000 M641 series maps for the GDR and supplied dye-line copies to the team.

---

* Dye-line, diazo, or whiteprint copying uses a photographic process and replaced the blueprint process commonly associated with engineering or architectural plans.

The Geo team split them into long thin vertical strips, which were then laminated in transparent plastic and fitted to a set of top-lit floor-to-ceiling louvres in the operations office that worked on the same principle as vertical venetian blinds. On one side of the louvres was the top half of the GDR, and by pulling on a cord, the louvres would rotate to reveal the bottom half. These strips were annotated with the current disposition of Soviet and East German forces in East Germany and were used to monitor exercises, large-scale troop movements, force concentrations, etc. The map remained hidden behind heavy curtains in the high-security ops room (a secure room, in a secure part of the BRIXMIS offices, which were in themselves a secure wing of London Block) and showed a strategic snapshot of the GDR that was used to brief the chief, senior officers, and individual tour officers.

Another important innovation was the update to the M745 1:50,000 used in the map corridor and carried in the field by tours, which had become seriously out of date. A trial was arranged in 1975 to collect mapping updates to a single map sheet, L1938, covering the Rostock area, including the new autobahn linking the port to Berlin. Tours were tasked with driving down *every* road and usable track, checking the mapping and correcting it as needed. All these amends were collated, and a standardised set of corrections (symbols, colours, and abbreviations) was devised allowing a single colour overprint to be made onto the existing NATO-compliant M745 map. Amends included:

- New roads (especially the new autobahns) were added using the accurate rally-spec tripmeter and compass fitted to the dashboard to capture the relevant information.
- Existing roads were driven and had their drive-ability or 'going' classified:
  - Solid overprint lines – all-weather main roads.
  - 'Pecked' lines – 'all-weather loose-surface' tracks or forest fire breaks.
  - Dotted lines – 'fair-weather loose-surface' tracks.
- 'K' stones, numbered kilometre 'milestones' used to pinpoint the location of a sighting along an otherwise featureless road.
- Route numbers were added in bold to aid navigation.
- Lay-bys and *parkplätze* rest stops on autobahns were marked, and unofficial fly-offs (UFOs) noted but not printed on the maps.
- Numerous variations of railway crossings were logged.
- Railway cuttings and bridges were also marked as these were a rare opportunity to photograph KIT from above.
- The huge *Kombinats* (collective farms) were shaded and marked with a 'K' for *Kombinat*.
- The UTM grid and map sheet number were added *inside* the grid square, as the borders of the maps (known as marginalia) were normally cut off when creating the strip maps. The map's legend, also part of the trimmed-off marginalia, was printed on a separate A4 sheet as OR163.
- Area 'deletions', features that no longer existed (including towns and villages razed to make way for huge open-cast 'brown' coal mines), were shaded over.
- New urban building projects were noted.
- New dams and reservoirs and resulting new road layouts were recorded.

The cartographers were limited to a single overprint colour and chose purple because it stood out better against the base mapping. They therefore had to be creative with the notations, not having multiple colours to work with. Target information was *not* added, nor were PRAs, which were subject to change.

The trial was deemed a great success and it was agreed that the Mission would collect revision data for the *whole* of the Soviet Zone (excluding, obviously, PRAs). This amounted to 214 of the 245 sheets covering the country (thirty-one sheets were wholly contained within PRAs so remained a mapping 'black hole') – a huge task in anyone's estimation. 'Mapper' tours became a high priority for the Mission, fitted in and around normal tasking, and because this was a BAOR/BRIXMIS initiative, BRIXMIS handled most of the workload.

Tours would be sent to specific locations with a list of questions to answer, such as: What sort of rail crossing is there?, Is there an exit into the forest from this rest area?, Can the entrance to this facility be seen from that copse?, Does this track go left or right at this junction?, Is there a passable gap in these trees?, and so on. Mappers were not universally loved by tourers, used as they were to the cut and thrust of KIT-orientated tours, but they were strategically important, and therefore had the buy-in from command. After each mapper tour, the Geo team were formally debriefed, and the revision data was added to a master overlay sheet, using the agreed new notation; this saturation coverage of the GDR did highlight numerous new targets, which were fed back to the ops team for further investigation. When the team was satisfied the area covered by the sheet was sufficiently 'mapped', often after several iterations, the master overlay was sent to 14 Field Survey/Topological Squadron to be overprinted on the old base maps, 300–400 copies at a time. 3 BAOR Map Depot would then distribute the finished maps to the three AMLMs and other users in the intelligence community. This monumental task was finished by 1979 when all 214 sheets (expanding to 222 sheets as PRAs were opened up) of the first edition of the newly christened M536 1:50,000 series of maps of the GDR were completed. Around this time, the US Defense Mapping Agency Topographic Center (DMATC) finally got round to issuing an updated set of M745 base maps, which picked up some of the big changes, such as autobahns and open-cast mine workings. They still did not fully meet the need for BRIXMIS tourers, so were used as base maps for subsequent M536 overprints, albeit with a bit less purple ink used.

The updated tour mapping was the first ever bespoke mapping project undertaken by the Royal Engineers Survey team, which reflected the value JHQ placed on BRIXMIS intelligence, and was notable in that most of the data collection was undertaken by amateurs on the ground, as opposed to being based on detailed aerial photography. As with many Cold War innovations, the whole exercise became largely irrelevant with the fall of the Wall, the close of the Mission, and German Reunification.

Chapter 5

Tools of the Trade

'BRIXMIS played a unique and central part in the
winning of the Cold War over the 45 years of its existence.
The number of personnel involved was small, but the value of their
work was out of all proportion to those numbers.'

Air Chief Marshal Sir Roger Palin
KCB OBE MA (2017)[1]

The success of BRIXMIS touring was dependent on the skills of the tour personnel and the quality of the equipment they were issued with, and the Mission was lucky to be equipped with the best that was available. Its vehicles needed to transport three men and a lot of equipment in relative comfort and across very challenging terrain and have the performance to outrun the opposition. Photography was central to their intelligence-collection task, which required the best cameras, lenses, and film available on the market and a professional photographic laboratory to produce prints and slides to distribute to their 'customers'. They also needed a huge variety of specialist equipment to complete their mission. With funding from the Occupation Budget (see below), BRIXMIS was able to bypass normal MoD procurement and deal directly with manufacturers to source equipment to their very exacting specifications. This often meant trialling new products before they were launched, and if they survived the rigours of touring, then they would probably survive use by professional users or the public. This unorthodox arrangement also meant that they could source items from rather unorthodox places. BRIXMIS also benefitted by having a highly skilled team of in-house technicians backed by experts from the Berlin garrison allowing them to fine tune, modify, and (frequently) repair equipment as needed.

Uniforms

Inside West Berlin, Mission personnel wore their normal military uniforms, although some Special Forces or Intelligence Corps personnel were 'badged' as other regiments: for example, SAS as Parachute Regiment and Intelligence Corps as Royal Corps of Transport, Royal Signals, or the regiment they were in before joining the Intelligence Corps. In the field, however, they adopted a far more practical uniform, but always stopped short of wearing camouflage clothing – this would imply that they were dressed for operational activities, which would be against the *spirit* of the agreements. Initially, tourers wore the normal battle dress associated with their parent service (for example, army No. 5 Uniform – blouse, trousers, puttees, and boots with a red BRIXMIS shoulder flash) but this evolved into a more practical and unique combination that was common across both army and RAF tours and was much better suited to touring. It comprised plain green '60 pattern 'olive' green fatigue trousers (long after the British Army had transitioned to Disruptive Pattern Material, DPM, camouflage), plain green shirt (no tie), the famous green 'woolly pully' army jumper, and RAF flying boots for warmth. Individuals sometimes customised certain elements, for example some wore East German NVA boots to disguise any footprints they inadvertently left, and odd bits of obsolete kit, such as a favourite (non-camo) combat smock, found their way into tour holdalls.[2] Formal headgear, normally a beret (or regimental equivalents, such as the Scottish 'Balmoral' bonnet), was only worn for crossing into the GDR, for visits to the *Komendatura*, or when being detained. For outer wear, the tourers favoured Canadian-style parkas with fur-trimmed hoods, which were warm and great for stashing supplies in.

The other AMLMs took distinctly different approaches to uniforms when out in the field. The French (MMFL) wore V-neck jumpers and barrack-style trousers with shoes, which was smart, and very much in the spirit of the Noiret–Malinin Agreement, but impractical in the field. In the 1980s, the Americans (USMLM) began wearing camouflage combat uniforms and combat boots, which was extremely practical, and excellent for concealment, but might have been construed as contrary to the spirit of the Huebner–Malinin Agreement and tended to elicit a more aggressive response from the opposition, especially from the Soviets, as only Special Forces wore camouflage in the Soviet Army. After US tour officer Major Arthur Nicholson was shot dead by a Soviet sentry in 1985, one of the excuses given by the Soviet authorities was that the sentry assumed he was US Special Forces as he was wearing camouflage clothing and was therefore up to no good. In contrast, the SOXMIS and SMLM tours in West Germany were subject to the same agreements, but frequently contravened them, with tour personnel donning 'civvy' leather jackets to blend in with the public (although if challenged, SOXMIS personnel would have pointed out that those sorts of jackets were routinely worn by Soviet aircrew). However, as per the agreements, all AMLMs wore bold insignia on their sleeves to identify who they were.

Touring Equipment

Tours never had to beg, borrow, or steal their equipment – they were able to afford the best kit available because it was all funded by the West German Federal Government via the West Berlin Senat as part of the Occupation Budget, reflecting the allies' unique status as occupying powers. Tour cars would be crammed with equipment, stowed for quick access and rapid concealment – the rear windows were fitted with curtains that could be drawn to hide all the kit on display. Saloon (sedan) cars typically had a large secure boot (trunk), which would be carefully packed with occasionally used equipment (camping kit, recovery kit, spare wheels, etc.), while the intelligence-collection kit (cameras, films, binoculars, etc.) would be packed around the tour officer on the back seat and in the footwells, for easy and quick access. The recovery equipment is discussed below. When the Mission moved to four-wheel-drive SUV-type vehicles (Range Rovers, Mercedes G-Wagens), the boot was accessible from inside, allowing the tour officer in the back seat to reach back to access equipment. Special stowage bins were fabricated in the REME workshops to fit into the luggage compartment, making packing the vehicle and retrieving equipment much easier. When the rear bench seat of the G-Wagen was replaced with a centrally mounted rally-style seat for the tour officer, this freed up even more space for equipment.

From the late 1950s, tours became preoccupied with photography; so much of their kit consisted of camera bodies and a variety of lenses, some of which were quite bulky. They are described in some detail below. Similarly, maps were core tools for the tour, carefully prepared back at base and carried in RAF navigator bags, as already discussed. Special tools were developed for certain jobs, such as a borehole drill to determine the different layers of airfield runways, a micrometer to gauge the thickness of tank armour, or a special tungsten-tipped chisel to collect samples of the metal used on the outer armour of Soviet tanks. On occasions, keys were copied, or special devices fabricated to gain access to buildings or vehicles. Because the inviolability of tour vehicles could not be guaranteed, with the contents occasionally being searched or even stolen during detentions, the various gadgets and gizmos had to be hidden in plain sight, in the vehicle toolkit, for example. Occasionally very specific and secret equipment was carried for specific tasks, developed by DIS1e, from the Defence Intelligence Staff's Directorate of Scientific and Technical Intelligence, their very own 'Q' Branch. This specialist equipment needed to be protected at all costs as the Soviets were past masters at reverse engineering (copying) Western technology. One such device was a huge long-range directional microphone christened the BLACK BANANA, which could pick up sounds several kilometres away. At about five feet long, it was tricky to handle and conceal. The microphone could be used to record the exhaust note of a tank or the firing of a new anti-aircraft gun to establish the rate of fire (known as ACOUSTINT). Another was a thermal imaging (TI) camera, introduced in the late 1980s. This recorded the thermal signature of the subject, illuminating specific 'hot spots' that would be unique to that vehicle type, such as exhausts, brakes, engines, doors, and windows, and could 'see' through camouflage. These 'signatures' helped troops identify the enemy when they were using their own thermal imaging devices such as tank sights or thermal imaging cameras. However, the cameras were prototypes requiring their own cooling system, that took up the space normally used by a spare wheel in the back of a G-Wagen. The Mission had two TI sets, kept under lock and key by the Weapons Office because they belonged to the Tech (Int) boffins back in London – allegedly each set cost about £30,000 (1980s prices) and the chief at the time, Brigadier Foley, ordered that they must not, under any circumstances, fall into enemy hands, but should, instead, be smashed up.[3]

Camera equipment aside, tours would always carry several pairs of binoculars, and monocular spotting scopes – it was rather convenient that some of the world's best optics were produced right on the Mission's doorstep at the Carl Zeiss factory in Jena, and excellent-quality binoculars could be obtained inside the GDR for relatively little money (in Western terms). The Mission favoured the Carl Zeiss 10x40 and 15x50 Deltrintem models. The 1970s saw the introduction of two key pieces of technology, which were to transform touring. First, the pocket-sized Dictaphone tape recorder was introduced for the tour officer and NCO, which allowed them to record a running commentary with the recorder in his top pocket, keeping his hands free to hold the maps or grab the dashboard during lively manoeuvres. It could also record the sound of weapons firing (ACOUSTINT) or be used to record the time from weapons release to detonation. The second item was far more sophisticated and initially very secret – American AN/PVS-5 Night-Vision Goggles (NVG). These second-generation goggles could work in two modes: 'active' where the subject or road was illuminated by an infrared light source, such as the 'yellow' lights fitted to the front of the tour car; or 'passive', which amplified the available light (stars or moonlight). While 'active' produced a better image for the wearer, it could be picked up if the subject had infrared sensors on their vehicle. 'Passive' mode, at the time, was undetectable. Using infrared headlights and active mode on the driver's goggles, it was possible to drive at night in complete darkness, which must have been a frightening experience for the other passengers.

Tours carried no two-way radios so operated in complete radio silence, in effect war conditions. To head deep into enemy territory without a radio may have seemed foolish, but that was one of the unique characteristics of touring. To operate over the long distances travelled in the GDR, reliable radio equipment would have been bulky which would have reduced space for mission-critical equipment. East German public telephones were rare, invariably vandalised, and probably bugged, but in emergencies, the tour could visit the nearest *Komendatura* and ask them to contact SERB, who would relay a message to the Potsdam Mission House to come to their rescue. However, it suited the Mission to be incommunicado so Chief BRIXMIS could remain detached from any shenanigans that took place on tour and could reliably tell his opposite number in SERB that he knew nothing about it but would vigorously investigate it – plausible deniability. This obvious charade suited all parties, and the tour personnel enjoyed the freedom it gave them. The only exception was the TALON SNATCH pager device introduced in the 1970s, as discussed above. The vehicles kept their car radios, allowing the crew to listen in to East German radio and to tune in (where possible) to BFBS, AFN, Radio Free Europe, RIAS, or the BBC World Service. Tour personnel would also bring along a selection of cassette tapes so they could argue about what to listen to. Apart from pocket or bushcraft knives, they carried no weapons.

Food

Tours needed to be self-sufficient for the duration of the tour, with rations and camping stoves to boil water for the obligatory brew stops and to heat up food. Tour members living in the mess would get their rations from the kitchen there (sandwiches, cooked sausages, cheese, crackers, snack bars, fruit, and so on), personnel in married quarters would prepare their own, and it was the custom to cook a communal curry (sometimes *inside* the car) during a long rail-watch or similar activity, where each member would contribute a tin or two of a suitable ingredient – a vegetarian in the crew caused endless problems. Recipes were developed by trial and error, improved by curry pastes from the Indian shops in West Berlin and other exotic ingredients, and passed on as part of BRIXMIS folklore. They even had self-heating tins of soup supplied by the Americans, although these had to be used with discretion as to a trigger-happy Soviet guard, they resembled a hand grenade! All rubbish was crushed, bagged up, and taken back to Berlin. In the early years, tours would sometimes eat at restaurants or cafés in East Germany, but this practice declined in line with the increased narking (as it did with staying in hotels). However, bakers or ice cream shops were everywhere, and their produce was of excellent quality (brötchen, windbeutel cream cakes, and the famous 'Berliner' doughnuts), although following the Chernobyl disaster in 1986, dairy products had to be avoided for fear of radioactive contamination. A stash of cigarettes, whisky, and other Western goodies was often carried, not for the tour crew, but as leverage/reward/inducement/bribes in emergencies.

Photography and the Special Section

Photography would turn out to be core to the Mission's output, but it was not always like that. In the early years of the Mission, tourers relied on their own notes, sketches, and memory to brief a sketch artist back at HQ, who would produce identikit-style drawings to go in their reports; the Foreign Office, which exerted a degree of control over the Mission at that point, was against tours using cameras, because they could (quite reasonably) be construed to be espionage tools. The results were nothing more than visualisations (childlike in some cases) and could not in any way be described as technical intelligence. In 1949, they experimented with using a Robot II camera to photograph some coastal installations at Rostock. The Robot II, launched in 1938 by German manufacturer Otto Berning & Co, was an innovative design using a clockwork mechanism to advance the film (the original designer was a watchmaker). The spring was wound up by turning the large knob on the top of the camera, and with practice, it was possible to shoot up to four frames a second, ideal for a quick burst of images and predating the motor drive by several decades. It was, however, fiendishly difficult to use, which was hardly suitable for the complete novices tasked with taking the photos. Rather than use the familiar 35-mm film cassette introduced by Kodak in 1934, the Robot II used a bespoke loading system that involved winding a length of unexposed 35-mm film onto a special spool before loading it in the camera. The photographer composed the image through an offset viewfinder, rather than by looking through the lens itself, so there was always the risk of a novice photographer obscuring the lens with his hand or camera strap, misaligning the camera with the subject, or even leaving the lens cap on and bringing home a blank film. After taking the pictures, and hopefully not stripping the sprocket holes from the film in the process, the photographer then had to carefully remove the take-up spool with the exposed film wound round it and replace it with an empty one as well as a new spool of unexposed film. Hardly suitable for covert photography in the field by complete novices, and the early results were unsurprisingly poor, but this experience highlighted the importance of developing a proper photographic capability.

Around 1950, Corporal Joe Jones, the RAF sketch artist who interpreted the tourer's observations into drawings, was tasked with introducing a proper photographic capability for the Mission despite having no experience in this field. He purchased (on the Occupation Budget) several East German Praktica single-lens-reflex (SLR) cameras, which were cutting-edge technology at the time, and all the necessary equipment to develop, print and enlarge the images.

Compared to modern cameras, the Prakticas were still difficult to use, and required training and lots of practice. Rather than the eye-level viewfinder used in modern cameras, the user had to look down into the camera, not easy when tracking a moving vehicle or airfield. There was an adaptor that could be clipped to the viewfinder to allow the user to look in the same direction as the subject, but the resolution was poor and did not permit detailed focusing, so was risky in the tour setting. The lenses were interchangeable, but were screw mounted, which was slow and fiddly in the field, and of course, all the settings (focus, exposure, aperture, etc.) were manual. Corporal Jones's drawing skills were still occasionally required if a subject was deemed too sensitive or dangerous to photograph. Recognising the need to improve the photographic capability further, two RAF photographic technicians (Pattison and Taylor) were seconded from RAFG, and the Special Section was born. These specialists also provided much-needed photographic training for touring personnel, as in the late 1950s, photography was still a niche (and expensive) hobby, and most people would not have used such a complex piece of equipment before.[4]

As the Special Section became more established, they replaced the Prakticas with Leica M3s and later the cheaper M2s. The M3 and M2 were *rangefinder* cameras, a technology that Leica pushed while Japanese manufacturers were perfecting SLR technology. With a rangefinder camera, the subject is not viewed through the lens but through an offset rangefinder using a complex mechanism to focus the image. On a single-lens-reflex camera, the user looks through the lens and therefore whatever the photographer sees, is what ends up on the film (WYSIWYG). However, the picture quality using the M3 or M2 was excellent, and the format had other advantages too: the cameras were smaller and lighter, and the shutter was very quiet with no momentary blackout of the viewfinder or discernible shutter lag, all important characteristics when shooting covertly. Another benefit was that the lenses had a bayonet, as opposed to a screw fitting, which made lens changes much quicker and more reliable, although this advantage was somewhat negated by having to use the bulky Visoflex lens housing (effectively turning the *rangefinder* camera into an *SLR* camera) for the longer 200-mm and 400-mm Telyt lenses that were popular with ground tours or the 130-mm and later 200-mm lenses popular with the Chipmunk observers. The viewfinder was offset to the left of the camera, so assuming the photographer used their right eye to compose the picture, they could shoot with both eyes open, again useful when shooting moving targets, although good results could also be obtained by shooting 'over open sights' (not looking through the viewfinder) when scanning or panning a subject.

This format of camera did, however, have some drawbacks. As the photographer was not looking through the lens, they could not see exactly what was being captured on the film until it was processed, with the risk of missing the intended subject (parallax error), and it was possible to shoot a whole film without removing the lens cap or ruin the picture with a hand, camera strap or branch in front of the lens – rookie errors, but quite possible in the stressful environment of a tour. A separate light meter had to be used to get the right exposure settings, or basing it on experience, especially important when photographing aircraft against the sky.

The RAF photo specialists introduced the technique of 'pushing' the film to capture detail in low-light conditions. The cameraman would use a relatively fast film, 400 or even 800 ASA (ASA defines the film's sensitivity to light) and set the exposure as if the ASA was much higher. Back at HQ, the photo technicians would then 'over develop' the film by several 'stops' during processing, treating the film as if it had a higher ASA than the film was categorised at. The results could be dramatic, capturing important details that were not visible to the naked eye. On later cameras, it was possible to set the ASA on the camera, and it was possible to push a 400 ASA film up to 6,400 ASA when shooting in poor light conditions, further enhanced at the processing stage.

As technology moved on in the 1960s, so did the Mission's photographic capability with the Leicaflex SL, Leica's first foray into the SLR market. An SLR uses a reflex mirror to bounce light up from the lens onto a flat ground-glass screen, which is viewed through the eyepiece. The photographer sees what the lens sees, so he can be certain of the picture's composition, the exact framing, the exact point-of-view, the exact perspective, and sometimes the exact depth-of-field. Compared to rangefinder cameras, SLRs were bigger, heavier, noisier, suffering sometimes with shutter lag (including the viewfinder going black during the exposure) and arguably had inferior optics, but as the technology developed, the benefits outweighed these shortcomings. The Leicaflex was a big step forward from the excellent but quirky M2 and M3, with through-the-lens (TTL) metering and an ASA setting, giving the photographer much more control over exposure without having to use an external light meter or rely on guesswork. When photographing objects silhouetted against the sky, such as an aircraft, antennas, or radar equipment, it was common to *overexpose* the shot by one or two aperture stops to ensure detail was captured on the subject, because the exposure meter in the camera would take a reading of the brighter sky (being the largest area in the viewfinder) and therefore *underexpose* the target. Equally, if possible, it was wise to 'bracket' exposures when dealing with static sites. The Leicaflex also had a bayonet lens fitment, speeding up lens changes, and as the user looked through the lens, it overcame the shortcomings of the rangefinder cameras. Another new feature was the ability to attach a motor drive unit, automatically advancing to the next frame by keeping the finger on the button and allowing burst shooting of up to four images a second (similar performance to the clockwork Robot II from the 1940s but without the quirkiness). The motor also allowed fast rewinding of the film back into the cannister, which was noisy but quick. The bulky motor unit, however, was even larger than the camera itself, making the combination unwieldy, especially with a big lens, and had a tendency to jam, mangling the film in the process.

During the 1970s, the lens of choice for both long-distance ground and aircraft targets was the Russian-made 1,000-mm MTO telephoto lens. Dmitri Maksutov designed the Maksutov Tele-Objectiv (MTO) 1,000-mm catadioptric lens in 1941 using a combination of mirrors to condense a long focal length into a relatively small package. BRIXMIS arranged for the lenses to be purchased by the British Embassy in Moscow, shipped to the UK in the diplomatic bag and then sent out to BRIXMIS HQ in Berlin; the irony of covertly photographing Soviet military equipment using a Soviet-made lens was not lost on the tour personnel. The lens was big and heavy and when combined with a Leicaflex SL MOT motor-driven camera body, it was a hefty piece of kit, but the weight helped stabilise the camera and gave the tour photographer a unique capacity to shoot good images a long way from the subject. Also available was the Leitz 560-mm f/5.6 Telyt-R lens, which could achieve amazing detail at a distance. It was not a mirror lens, so was long and unwieldy (530 mm long and 2.33 kg) but could apparently capture the rivets on an overflying MiG-21.[5] A pistol grip made the handling of long lenses easier and careful panning while tracking fast-moving aircraft could produce excellent images, and use of automatic exposure settings, as they became available, reduced the workload a little, allowing the photographer to concentrate more on composition. Another useful technique was to shoot two shots in quick succession, which potentially allowed the photographic interpreters to create faux-3D images by viewing offset pairs of images through a stereoscope, a technique pioneered by the photo-reconnaissance experts at RAF Medmenham during the Second World War. This was quite hit and miss as normal stereoscopic photography used two cameras set at specific angles, but in the right circumstances, a skilled photographer could achieve an approximation of a stereo image, revealing more details for interpretation.

Unsurprisingly, tours burnt through a lot of film, and they carried dozens of unexposed rolls in the tour car. After spotting some KIT and getting some shots, a partially exposed film would be wound back into the cannister, wasting the remaining exposures but ensuring that a fresh film was in the camera for the next opportunity and speed-changing of films became a useful skill. It was not unheard of that in the scrabble to get the appropriate camera/film/lens combination, an empty camera was picked up, with the tour officer busily firing off what he thought to be a thirty-six exposure film only to open the camera back and find it empty – with a manual wind camera, an experienced photographer could tell if there was a film in it because of the tension on the winder, but not so with a motor drive. Apart from the shame of all the missed intelligence, much ribbing by the other tour crew members would ensue.

The films used at the Mission varied over time as new products came onto the market. Tour officers and Special Section were encouraged to experiment with new films or processing/developing, but never on an operational mission – only when the film/technique had been 'approved' by the ops team would it be deployed on tour. The films used included Ilford FP3, HP3, and HP5, Agfa ISOPAN ISS, and Kodak Tri-X black and white negative and Ektachrome colour slide. In the early days of the Special Section, they also used West German Adox black and white film.

Transparency or slide film became increasingly popular in the 1980s because of its fine grain, the ability to view the image on a lightbox or project onto a screen for instant analysis, or to make colour prints using Kodak Type R or Ektachrome, or Ilford Cibachrome (positive-to-positive) colour reversal paper. There were also various specialist films available, such as Kodak high-speed infrared film, which captures a different section of the light spectrum, and is useful when photographing terrain, revealing people and objects in the open, changes in the landscape caused by human activity; for example, disturbed ground from armoured vehicle movements, camouflaged equipment or dug-in troops, all of which may be invisible to the naked eye. It's also very good at distinguishing hard edges of manmade structures (vehicles, buildings) from the soft appearance of undergrowth, foliage, tree cover, or manmade camouflage.* Exposed films, especially of particularly sensitive subjects, were hidden inside the vehicle in case the tour was detained, and the car searched – safe from all but a full strip-down search.

In 1971, Squadron Leader Rod Saar MBE, Squadron Leader Operations, visited the World Photographic Fair in Düsseldorf to select the next generation of cameras for the Mission. He chose the Nikon F2, the successor to the hugely successful Nikon F, and the favourite of professional photographers around the world. It was robust, packed with features and combined with the reliable new Nikon motor drive (frame advance *and* film rewind), was the perfect tool for the touring photographer. Apart from a small battery for the TTL light meter, the camera body was totally mechanical and with interchangeable viewfinders and lenses, it catered for all eventualities. It became the standard camera for both RAF and army tours and began a relationship with the Nikon F series that continued until the end of the Mission, beginning with the F2, then the F3 in 1980, and the F4 in 1988.†

By the mid-1970s, paired with the F2 and its successors, the Mission had a wide range of lenses to suit all kinds of different scenarios, with the older lenses being converted to use the Nikon 'M' bayonet fitting – each officer had their particular favourites.‡ In 1973 they replaced the Soviet 1,000-mm MTO lens with the higher-quality Nikon Reflex-NIKKOR 1,000-mm f11 mirror lens, which was soon followed by the Reflex-NIKKOR 500-mm f8 lens (both of which could be used with a doubler adaptor) and even the huge Reflex-NIKKOR 2,000-mm f11 lens, which because of its size was only suitable for ultra-long-distance covert photography of static ground targets.

It was possible to shoot the 1,000-mm MTO/Nikon lens out of the opened window of the tour car, supported on a sleeping bag or similar improvised support to achieve good results when photographing fixed installations such as SAM or radar sites or handheld for air shots, assisted by a pistol grip for stability – tri- or mono-pods were not practical because they would hamper a quick escape. The aperture on the big lenses was fixed, so the only controls available were ASA (setting the camera at a different ASA to the nominal rating of the film) and shutter speed, which was a challenge for aircraft photography. The shutter speed was set according to the light conditions, but to capture detail on the underside of aircraft, additional exposure was required, adjusting the shutter speed between shots. Such photography improved with practice and the tour officer would work out his own minimum shutter speeds to ensure clear images – this could be as slow as 1/250th with a 1,000-mm lens.

A camera body with motor drive and a medium-length (85-mm) lens was always in the tour officer's lap ready for a snatched KIT shot at a moment's notice. Another body/ drive with a 180-mm lens was stowed in a box or bag next to the tour officer, next to a

---

* As a countermeasure, military vehicles are sometimes painted in IR absorbing paint. Alternatively, items can be painted in IR reflective material, so they stand out.

† The F4 was designed for autofocus lenses but was backwards compatible for all manual focus Nikon lenses, so presumably BRIXMIS used the more advanced camera body with the tried-and-tested manual-focus Reflex-NIKKOR lenses.

‡ Photos from the 1980s show Tamron lenses being used as well as Nikon.

500- or 1,000-mm set-up – all the lenses were interchangeable; the tour officer might be running colour slide film in one of the cameras and black and white print film in another. The tour NCO kept a 35-mm autofocus point-and-shoot camera to hand, which he could use should the opportunity arise. When operating on foot away from the tour car, often dangerously near the subject, the photographer would use an 85-mm or 135-mm and a 500-mm mirror (MTO or Reflex) set-up, both of which could reasonably be carried by one person, allowing for a quick getaway if necessary. Additional flexibility was obtained by using a two-times doubling adaptor, which for example turned a 135-mm lens into a 270-mm lens, or a 500-mm lens into a 1,000-mm lens, albeit with a small drop in resolution.

During the 1980s, tour photography benefitted from a specialised piece of military kit, the Davin Modulux 130 'Starlight' Image Intensifier (II), like the Individual Weapon Sight (IWS) that could be fitted to the British SLR Rifle (self-loading rifle, not single lens reflex!). The Modulux was a bulky device that was fitted onto the camera lens, concentrating the available light to allow low-light photography. Any light source from the subject would appear as a white 'flare out' in the picture, and if the subject's headlights were turned on, the whole image would be wiped out. Although a limited amount of 16-mm cine footage was shot in the 1970s, when video cameras became available in the early 1980s, they were introduced to supplement still photography. The Mission trialled the Olympus VX-301 before settling with the improved VX-303 in 1985. Despite being low resolution compared to modern equipment (it was impossible to make out VRNs, for example) they were particularly effective in capturing activity in training areas, 'running columns', photographing long KIT trains, recording flying patterns and tactics, and for terrain analysis. When mounted on a metal pole mounted just behind the passenger seat, the video camera could be turned on to record everything through the windscreen, leaving the tour officer to take still photos with the Nikon. The video camera could also take the Nikon camera lenses, boosting the range to the equivalent of a 5,500-mm long lens, and could record sound, picking up the tour NCO's commentary as they went or record audio of what was going on outside, such as the sound of vehicle engines or guns firing. Video tapes (VHS) also picked up radar emission blips and could be used, when slowed down many times, to reveal certain characteristics of helicopter or tank engines (allegedly).

As the tour officer sat on a centred and slightly raised rally-style seat in the back of the G-Wagen, he was also perfectly placed to shoot with these cameras through the windscreen, bracing against the video pole if necessary. Although the list of photographic equipment was common to all tours, individual tour officers may have taken additional kit to suit their individual style or technique.[6] A full photographic kit list is included in the appendices. Tours got through a lot of film, and back at HQ, the Special Section were kept very busy with film processing and print making: the peak year for films processed was 1988 (10,558), while the peak year for prints made was 1983 (498,000). In 1988, 36,183 colour slides were produced.[7] The move to longer tours and the gradual switch to slide film in the 1980s led to significant increases in workload for the small team in the section. Although digital cameras were on the horizon as the Cold War drew to a close, they were never used by the AMLMs, despite being 'early adopters' of other technologies. This was because the quality and resolution of the early cameras was poor, digital storage at the time was unreliable and there was a risk that it could be retrieved from the disk even when deleted. A camera film offered amazing resolution when paired with decent equipment and in the hands of an expert, plus it could be fogged (and therefore ruined) in seconds.

From the early days of sketch artists to the highly skilled technical professionals of the 1970s and 1980s, the Mission improved its photographic capabilities as technology developed, in some cases field testing new equipment for manufacturers. With a professional lab set-up back at HQ, top-quality equipment, solid on-the-job training, much practice, and a lot of experience in the field, BRIXMIS was able to consistently support their observations with high-quality imaging. One can only imagine how the introduction of quality digital SLR (DSLR) cameras in the late 1990s and the advent of good-quality mobile phone cameras and dashcams would have transformed tour photography.

Airborne Tour Equipment

Like ground tourers, the Chipmunk observer used 35-mm cameras with a variety of lenses. Early operations used a hand-wound Leica M3 or M2 camera body with a 130-, 200-, or 400-mm Teylt (Leica) lens. During the late 1950s/early 1960s the Mission experimented with an oblique 70-mm Vinten F95 photo-reconnaissance camera with a four-inch lens in a fixed frame (in a similar set-up to the cameras fitted to bombers and specialist photoreconnaissance or PR aircraft). This had the advantage of being a 'stand-off' camera, operated discreetly as the aircraft was simply going about its business, and the large-format 70-mm film could yield excellent results. The F95 could also produce carefully calibrated stereo pairs of images that could be viewed through a stereoscope to produce a faux-3D image. However, there were three fundamental issues with the F95, which led to its discontinuation in 1962: first, the aircraft's basic electrical system struggled to produce enough power to operate the camera; second, to obtain decent results the aircraft needed to be flown straight and level at precisely 1,000 feet, which was tough in the confined space of the BCZ; and third, a large fixed camera was hard to disguise if the aircraft was forced down over hostile territory, and the 250 feet of film in the camera's magazine was hard to fog quickly in an emergency; handheld cameras were much easier to disguise or dispose of. The idea owed more to senior officers' rose-tinted experience with PR Spitfires during the Second World War than the practical realities of the BCZ and the idea was quietly dropped.

In the mid-1970s, the Chipmunk observers followed the ground-based tours and moved on to Nikon F2 and then F3 camera bodies with motor drives and a variety of lenses: a 180- or 200-mm lens for standard work, 500-mm and 1,000-mm mirror lenses for close-ups, although the 1,000-mm mirror lens was still heavy and unwieldy in the confines of the cockpit and required level flight to get good results. Other lenses, such as a 35-mm, 55-mm, or 135-mm, were used for wider views. All the equipment was tethered to the observer by various means, partly to stop them flying around the cockpit during violent manoeuvres but mostly to stop them falling out through the open cockpit, thus presenting the Soviets with *prima facie* evidence that the aircraft was operating as a reconnaissance platform.

Kodak 32 ASA Panatomic-X (Pan-X) black and white film was the chosen medium for aerial photography for much of the Mission's existence – the panchromatic negative film had a very fine grain that picked out a lot of detail and gave a realistic rendering of different tones, but also could be pushed by exposure (it was typically shot at 64 ASA) and processing to much higher ASA ratings (up to 6400 ASA) to improve contrast and detail. They also used Ilford HP4 or Kodak 400 ASA Tri-X black and white film when a faster film was necessary. By the 1980s, they had transitioned to 100 and 400 ASA Kodak Ektachrome colour transparency (slide) film. A typical sortie would get through fifteen to twenty rolls of film, although the observer could stash a further twenty or so rolls in the capacious lower pockets of his flying suit. When a film was finished (which could be very quickly with the motor drive fitted), the observer removed it from the camera leaving the film tail protruding, would write the roll number and the ASA rating used on the film cannister, and slide it into a long slotted cannister tube inside the cockpit.

Tour Vehicles

The most important tool for touring was the tour vehicle. It had an unusual significance within the Mission, providing transport, shelter, protection from the opposition (and the means to escape and evade), storage for all the touring equipment, kitchen facilities, and an office. To be a successful tour vehicle, it had to:

- Have room for three personnel in reasonable comfort.
- Have high-performance, on- and off-road and the durability to withstand some very robust driving – nowhere else in the British military would they permit the sort of driving experienced day in, day out with the Mission.
- Have space for all the touring and camera equipment.
- Have space for all the food and camping equipment (three people for up to a week).
- Be a stable platform for photography and observation, with the tour officer sometimes standing on the roof for a better view.
- Be as unobtrusive as possible.

Consequently, the quest for the perfect touring car was ongoing through the life of the Mission and the fleet developed in line with the automotive industry, constantly improving as technology and performance developed. From the outset, vehicle mechanics from REME attached to Berlin Infantry Brigade and the Mission's own M/T workshops made modifications that would enhance the performance of the vehicles. However, the Mission started with more modest transport, Second World War-vintage Humber Box cars. These were designed at the start of the war and produced right through to 1945. The Box variant of the Humber Heavy Utility was designed as a command vehicle and had a downward-opening tailgate and upward-opening rear window panel, much like the Range Rover would have some thirty years later. It was powered by the same 85 bhp in-line six-cylinder side-valve 4,086-cc petrol engine as the civilian Super Snipe, driving all four wheels (four-wheel drive, 4x4, or 4WD). The frame for the bodywork of the Heavy Utility was made of ash wood, with steel or aluminium alloy 'Birmabright' body panels. While the two-wheel-drive Snipe or Super Snipe was quite nippy for a car of that era (with a top speed of more than 75 mph), the extra weight of the body panels and four-wheel-drive system (more than three-quarters of a ton) made the Humber Box's performance rather pedestrian.[8] It was slow, uncomfortable, and had a poor cross-country performance, in fact, everything a good tour car should not be.

The first tour cars for the Mission were painted dark red (maroon) with the Union Flag on the roof, sides, and rear, plus a Soviet Army numberplate issued by HQ GSFG. Unlike the later car numbers, the plate had a six-character registration number, such as C8-64-78, where 'C' is the Cyrillic alphabet 'S'.[9] The Humber Boxes were soon replaced by khaki-coloured Humber Snipes for touring and Super Snipe staff cars for the chief and deputy chief, which were a marked improvement in performance, albeit with the retrograde step of being two-wheel drive so not particularly suited to off-road use. At the time, officers had personal use of war-surplus American Jeeps, painted black with the name of the Mission stencilled in white Cyrillic lettering on the panel under the windshield. They attracted a lot of attention from the Soviets but were only used in and around Potsdam or for going back to West Berlin, and not for touring.

In the mid-1950s, SERB transitioned from the subdued six-character numberplates to new larger high-visibility yellow plates. They were approximately 37 x 18 centimetres featuring a large national flag denoting the nationality of the touring party, a large number identifying the actual vehicle, and the name of the mission (in Russian for the allied Missions, in English or French for the SMLMs). The car number ranges were allocated to specific AMLMs; for example, by the 1970s BRIXMIS had numbers 1–19, USMLM 20–29, MMFL 30–9, SOXMIS in the British Zone 40–49, SMLM in the US Zone 50–59 and SMLM in the French Zone 60–69, meaning that each car was easily identified and, in theory, tracked by the opposition.[10] The AMLMs objected to the introduction of the new plates, but SERB refused to budge. It therefore became common touring practice to 'muddy-up' these bright yellow plates in a convenient puddle as soon as possible after leaving the Mission House. After the tour, which probably had added quite a bit more mud, the vehicle would stop off at the Mission House where the worst of it could be hosed off before crossing back over the bridge. Excessive wear and tear to the vehicle or damage to the body work would be carefully noted, photographed, and held up as evidence of possible illegal activity. Each car had its own touring pass, just like the tourers themselves, which was handed over for inspection at the Glienicke Bridge along with the touring party's passes.

By 1955, the fleet had been replaced by West German-made Opel saloon (or sedan) cars, beginning a relationship with the American-owned German car manufacturer that would last until the mid-1980s: first Kapitäns, then Admirals, and finally Senators. The Mission did experiment with a Mercedes and BMW saloon in the late 1950s, but these soon gave way to an all-Opel line-up. A saloon had a lower profile, which helped concealment, and looked much like a civilian car or even a military staff car. Over the years as the technology developed, the Opels became more and more capable. The early

Kapitäns (second, third, and fourth generations) were underpowered, cramped, and had limited range, but the Kapitän A model, launched in 1964, overcame some of these problems. The Kapitän B, launched in the late 1960s with a three-speed automatic gearbox, became a very capable car, albeit with limited ground clearance and only rear-wheel drive. It had a 2.8 engine delivering a top speed of 180 kph (112 mph) before modifications. The 2.8 Kapitän B was phased out in 1970, but the design lived on until 1977 as the 2.8 Admiral B, with the same engine. In 1974, the Admiral FF (Ferguson Formula) conversion was introduced to the Mission, giving the vehicle four-wheel drive, solving at least one of the model's drawbacks (the development of the 4WD Admiral FF is discussed in detail below). The 2.8 Admiral B was replaced in 1978 by the 2.8 Senator A1, giving the Mission a more modern design to work with, albeit with similar performance. In 1982 the BRIXMIS saloon tour car development reached its zenith with the launch of the Opel Senator A2; its 3.0-litre engine and four-speed automatic transmission gave a blistering top speed of 191 kph (119 mph), and 0–60 mph in 10.4 seconds (0–00 km in 11 seconds). This performance would be dented by the FF 4WD and BRIXMIS modifications to transform the base model into a tour car, but it was still a very fast car for the time.[11] BRIXMIS opted to remain with the older-style carburettor-based fuel system (despite it being badged 3.0i) because problems were easier to diagnose and fix in the field. Although Chief BRIXMIS (car No. 1) normally used Opel Senators for his official car, there was a period in the 1980s when he had a Mercedes S-Class saloon as a staff car *in addition* to his Senator touring car (all courtesy of the Occupation Budget).

In the late 1960s, before the arrival of the FF 4WD conversion for the Opel saloon cars, the Mission trialled a 'Safari' LWB (long-wheel-base) Land Rover. This pioneering 4x4 vehicle had remarkable off-road performance and was loved by air tours, who could use the roof as a convenient raised photographic platform. SERB raised objections because of its military pedigree, but these soon became immaterial when the vehicle was written off in a road-traffic accident. The Tour NCO, Senior Aircraftsman Geoff Goulding, suffered a broken knee in the accident, and to add insult to injury, the tour was detained for fourteen hours by the Soviets. The Land Rover may have been amazing at slow-speed off-roading but was frustratingly slow on the road and was therefore not replaced.

1974 brought a potential solution to the 4WD problem with the arrival of the Range Rover, combining the extraordinary off-road capability of the original Land Rover with a more 'elegant' design and (theoretically) better on-road performance.[12] Launched in 1970, it was the first vehicle to deliver permanent 4WD; it also had a split tailgate, reminiscent of the Humber Box. It had no power steering, no inertia reel seatbelts (lap belts only fitted to the seats), had shiny vinyl seats, and only three doors, which was not ideal (the tour officer would have to climb over or round the front seats to get out in an emergency), but it had plenty of storage space and its permanent 4WD and impressive ground clearance made up for the shortcomings. The drivetrain, chassis, and suspension were superb allowing massive axle articulation, allowing all four wheels to stay in contact with the ground over difficult terrain where they were needed, rather than spinning in thin air. The incredible approach and departure angles (the degree of slope the vehicle can handle), and an amazing 45° tilt angle (how far the vehicle could be tipped before it toppled over) all made it a fantastic off-road vehicle. A vehicle was successfully tested on-pass, and in 1975 the first new Range Rovers arrived at the Mission. As with the Safari Land Rover, air tours used its height as a photographic platform, either through the non-standard Webasto electric sunroof, standing on the lowered tailgate (which is what it was designed for) or even climbing up on the roof. If the 4WD was defeated and the vehicle got bogged-in, tours could use the factory-fitted Fairey power-take-off capstan winch (later replaced by the powerful Warn 8000 electric winch) that had been fitted in the front bumper to get them out of trouble. Despite all its promises, the Range Rover was a divisive choice. There can be no denying that it was a product of the 1970s British motor industry (the less said about that, the better), had numerous reliability issues (drivetrain and carburation), and tours complained about them being draughty and leaky (1970s panel fit); however, when it came to capability, in the hands of a skilled driver, the Range Rover could not be equalled.*

The introduction of the Mercedes Geländewagen or G-Wagen in 1979 had the potential to offer a more reliable 4x4 vehicle.[13] Launched to the press in February 1979, BRIXMIS organised a test in Berlin between one of their Range Rovers and the new SWB Mercedes Geländewagen 230GD. While traversing a slope that the British vehicle coped with easily (the Range Rover had a 45° tilt angle), the G-Wagen toppled onto its side and was therefore discounted as a potential tour vehicle. However, in December 1979, the LWB 280GE G-Wagen was being heavily promoted in the motoring press and when BRIXMIS adjutant Lieutenant Colonel Smith received an invitation to a demonstration of the new 280GE at Heiligensee in the French sector, he passed it on to the newly arrived lead tour driver, Staff Sergeant Dave Picton, back for his second posting at the Mission. Accompanied with one of the drivers from the 230GD fiasco, Picton attempted to recreate the conditions in which the SWB vehicle failed, and soon demonstrated the LWB could perform as well if not better than its British counterpart, without the quirks and reliability concerns. Despite scaring the Mercedes Benz salesman witless with his 'robust' driving style, Staff Sergeant Picton managed to blag a four-week loan of a new 280GE. Lieutenant Colonel Smith sent over the glossy Mercedes brochure to SERB and managed to get the 280GE accepted on-pass where it was put through its paces as the Potsdam duty vehicle and on all British 'local' tours for that month, getting everyone used to seeing it, and ticking all the boxes for the very demanding BRIXMIS tour drivers. Key factors in the decision were the capable 4WD system, the individual lockable axle differentials and its four doors, something the Range Rover did not have at the time, plus it did not leak or break down so much. The car was returned (relatively) in one piece to the dealership (who were blissfully unaware that it had been over in the East) and a new Mercedes 280GE was ordered from the Daimler Steyer Puch factory in Graz, Austria, for long-term evaluation; the Berlin Senat (who distributed federal funds to the occupation forces) were more than happy to 'buy German' and a vehicle that had been intended for the

---

* In a piece of BRIXMIS folklore, Dave Picton describes a particular Mission Range Rover being overtaken by a Trabant on the Berlin ring road and couldn't even get to 100 kph on the flat.

Bundesgrenzschutz, the West German federal border guard (BGS), was delivered to Berlin in autumn 1980, entering service as car No. 9. The first tour in No. 9 was to the Dora-Nordhausen area on an RAF (air) tour with Flight Lieutenant Dave Downes (tour officer), Staff Sergeant Dave Picton (tour NCO), and Master Air Loadmaster (MALM) Max Colton (driver).

Around the same time, BRIXMIS trialled one of the new Audi Quattros, the car that changed Audi's fortunes and took them to success in the World Rally Championship. It may have been a successful road and rally car but it was not up to the rigours of touring. A demonstrator was 'borrowed' from the West Berlin Audi dealership in Spandau and taken for a 'gentle' drive around the Grunewald training area. Unfortunately, it broke after about twenty minutes and had to be trailered back to the dealership. Despite this setback, in 1988 the Mission acquired an Audi 200 Quattro on trial, but that broke too, ending their short relationship with the Ingolstadt marque.

Early versions of the G-Wagen were underpowered and had part-time 4WD, a manual gearbox and transfer box with manually operated front- and rear-axle diff locks, but in 1981 these were superseded by more powerful four-speed automatics, with electronically operated diff locks and the ability to change through the transfer box while on the move, turning it into a very sophisticated off-road machine. There were, however, teething problems: early models had the annoying habit of conking out in hot weather and refusing to restart until they had cooled down, a less-than-ideal occurrence in a tactical situation. The problem was diagnosed by an East German village Trabant mechanic, who discovered that an additional fuel filter (probably to cope with the poor-quality East German fuel) fitted above the rear axle and next to the exhaust was overheating. Mercedes and the M/T workshop reluctantly agreed that the Trabant mechanic was right, the filter was removed, and the problem disappeared. The Mercedes had a built-in roll cage (for safety), flat sides (making it easier to pass through narrow gaps), optically flat all-round glass (for better photography), and individually lockable doors (for greater security). The G-Wagen may not have had the blistering on-road performance of the Opel Senator, but its off-road and cross-country capability made it a winning choice, and by 1986 the whole touring fleet had been replaced by G-Wagens and the model adopted by the other AMLMs. Several Senators were retained as staff cars and as Chief BRIXMIS's shiny black official car, and there was also a minibus for administrative work, for cultural tours, and shopping trips to the East.

Among tourers, everyone had their favourite vehicle, and would argue passionately that *their* choice was better than *yours*, but they all had their pros and cons. The Opel saloons, especially when fitted with 4WD, had great on- and off-road performance, and benefitted from a lower profile that was easier to hide. When painted in military green, they could easily be mistaken for a Soviet staff car, allowing tours to bluff their way out of trouble. However, they were more cramped, and the limited ground clearance meant that their off-road capability (wading, climbing angle, over heavily rutted tracks, or tank TAC routes) was limited. The Mercedes top speed of 96 mph (155 kph) was respectable but short of the Senator's blistering on-road performance, but their ability to smoothly transition from autobahn to a ploughed field or farm track made up for that. The bumper-mounted electric winch made extricating the vehicle from thick mud and ditches far easier and the roomy cab had more space, and therefore comfort, for the tourers. On the other hand, the G-Wagen was more conspicuous, had large reflective windows, and its pseudo-military styling tended to elicit more of an aggressive response from the opposition. There was a cost consideration too – parts were easier to obtain and cheaper, and it was estimated that a G-Wagen would have the on-pass life (damage apart) of two Senators.

Taking everything into account, and risking the wrath of the die-hard saloon fans, the Mercedes G-Wagen was (probably ...) the ultimate touring vehicle – it had the on-road speed, amazing off-road capability, and the means to get itself out of trouble. To quote Steve Gibson, a former tour officer, 'Alongside the Nikon F-3 camera and the GORE-TEX hooped bivvie tent, the "G-Wagon" [*sic*] ... probably commanded the heights of aids to touring by the late 1980s. It was a near perfect a piece of military equipment as had been experienced by many experienced soldiers.'[14]

Modifications

To the uninitiated, the Kapitäns, Admirals, and Senators of the 1970s and 1980s looked like standard road cars; however, when they disappeared into the distance on the open road (especially East Germany's autobahns) or across a field, it quickly became clear they were anything but standard. To handle the extreme conditions of touring, from the very outset, BRIXMIS adapted and modified their vehicles to suit the mission. Anything to make life easier for the tour crew was considered, and if successful, was adopted. Over the years, the specifications evolved with experience, such as lighting configurations, switch positioning, tyres, and so on.

The first modifications were modest – changing the vehicle colour and adding longer-range fuel tanks – but as experience was gained in the field and technology developed, the vehicles became highly modified. Vehicle colour developed with experience and as the British Army experimented with different approaches. The maroon of the first Humber Box cars gave way to War Department khaki, but the first Opels were glossy black, in the hope they would be mistaken for Soviet staff cars. By 1957, the nark activity had increased to such a level that it became prudent to repaint the cars in matt olive drab, which was easier to conceal. SERB objected to this new colour scheme until it was pointed out that USMLM vehicles had been olive drab from day one. In the mid-1960s, there was a short-lived experiment painting them in the glossier deep bronze green that was the standard colour across the British Army, and in the 1970s, an experiment to paint them in civilian colours (red, blue, white) to make them look like civilian cars, but it was soon realised that the gloss or coloured paint made them very easy to spot in woods and undergrowth, so the vehicles were repainted in a matt olive drab finish, a practice that continued until the end of the Mission.* The first Range Rovers, however, were delivered from the factory in shiny grass-green paint, with a black vinyl-covered roof; they were left that

---

* The British Army did not fully transition to matt olive drab (often combined with matt black in a camo pattern) until the early 1970s, in line with the rest of NATO.

way for a while to see how it looked in the field, the logic being that from a distance it looked a bit like a military truck with a canvas tilt, but after a while they were resprayed in olive drab like the rest. Chief BRIXMIS's Admiral or Senator (Plate No. 1) was maintained in a shiny gloss black finish with a Union Jack pennant and one-star general's plate on the front bumper, suitable for high-level liaison or protocol use and occasionally touring – it was felt that the No. 1 plate and pennant gave it sufficient 'protection' from the opposition. However, after Brigadier Learmont's car was ambushed and deliberately rammed in 1982, Chief BRIXMIS ran a glossy black Senator for protocol use, and toured using a standard olive drab Senator, albeit still sporting the No. 1 and one-star plates. In the 1970s, the deputy chief used a white Admiral/Senator for a while, which was sometimes used on-pass in the GDR primarily because it looked very much like a civilian vehicle and that deception could be useful in certain circumstances.

Cars were driven hard and would typically be returned to Ordnance Services, the Berlin Infantry Brigade's main logistics hub, after 60,000 kilometres to be replaced on a 'new-for-old' basis. If the vehicle was beyond economic repair because of an accident or aggressive intervention by the opposition, it was written off and replaced. All the BRIXMIS modifications were stripped out to be fitted to the replacement, and the vehicle was refurbished and used in non-touring roles at BRIXMIS, or disposed of, often as a staff car to other units in the Berlin Infantry Brigade, where performance was less of an issue.* For example, former BRIXMIS vehicles went to 247 (Berlin) Provost Company, Royal Military Police, 3 Intelligence & Security Company, or to 62 Squadron, Royal Corps of Transport for the Brigade infantry battalions to use for Flag Tours in East Berlin. One former Mission Range Rover was converted as a VIP parade vehicle with the roof cut off, painted glossy black, with the open top trimmed in leather, folding seats (also in leather) and plush red carpet. It was used at the Allied Forces Day parade in Tiergarten and at the Queen's birthday parade on Maifeld next to the Olympic Stadium. Failing that, the 'used' vehicles would be passed to *VEBEG*, *Verwertungsgesellschaft für besatzungseigene Güter*, the West German Federal Disposal Sales and Marketing Agency tasked with disposing of surplus civilian or military equipment funded by the Federal Government. New cars would arrive from the dealership (for example, the British Leyland dealer in Düsseldorf supplied the Range Rovers, while the Berlin Mercedes dealership supplied the G-Wagens) at the Ordnance Services vehicle park, and from there, they would be issued to BRIXMIS and begin their conversion into highly modified, high-performance touring cars.

The Mission's M/T section was housed in garages on the north side of London Block. This small 'first-line' workshop, run by an RCT or REME staff sergeant, was responsible for the regular servicing and maintenance of the fleet, but could also handle minor modifications and repairs. The M/T section worked closely with Shop 4, 14 Field

---

* Former tour cars (stripped of their tour conversions) were used as Berlin duty vehicle, the Potsdam duty vehicle and as a training vehicle for new arrivals to the Mission.

Workshops, REME, in Alexander Barracks, Spandau, for major modifications and repairs. The list of BRIXMIS modifications was extensive:

- A new paint finish, as above.
- Strengthened suspension – new springs and body stiffening kits were fitted to a vehicle straight from the factory.
- Armoured underbody protection, the so-called 'panzer' plates, were fitted underneath all tour vehicles, originally to provide protection to the front and rear drivetrain, and to allow the vehicle underside to 'slide' when required over mud, sand, snow, and even rocks, without 'bogging in'. Before 4WD became available, cross-country driving involved using speed and kinetic energy to get across the terrain. The panzer plates then evolved into protection for the front and rear differentials and for the petrol tank on the Admiral and Senator, adding as much as half a ton to the weight of the vehicle.
- After a bad accident in a USMLM Range Rover, a substantial internal roll cage was retrofitted to the Range Rover fleet *inside* the crew compartment, running behind the front seats (taking up a lot of space), and going back through the rear wheel arches and onto the rear of the chassis. The G-Wagens had built-in roll cages that took up less space.
- All-terrain tyres on reinforced wheel rims (winter tyres in winter, with snow chains as needed).
- Long-range fuel tanks – fuel availability was patchy inside the GDR, and was of poor quality, making the engines 'pink' and cough. If the tour was forced to fill up at one of the Minol petrol stations (where pump attendants would routinely report the location of tours to the Vopos), the remaining fuel was drained when the tour returned to Berlin and used to clean parts. In the early days, West Berlin fuel was carried in jerry cans, but later, extra fuel tanks were fitted. The 3.0i Senator, for example, had a 180-litre (100+80) tank. The Range Rover had to have a second electric fuel pump fitted to eliminate the problem of fuel evaporation because of the excessive heat in the engine bay.
- Roof hatch fitted – more than a sunroof, it allowed the tour crew to stand up through the aperture to get a better view (when stationary!). The G-Wagen had a more secure factory-fit 'cupola', as specified by the BGS, that allowed the tour officer to stand up through it.
- The Range Rovers were fitted with a reinforced false roof because the original British Leyland roof buckled when tour officers used it as an observation platform. The G-Wagens also got a new flat roof to make it a more stable photographic platform.
- The G-Wagens were fitted with tubular steel bull-bars to protect the front wings.
- Various extra lights were fitted to the front of the car with a custom lighting panel inside the car – more details below.
- Winches – recovery points (towing eyes) were fitted to the front and rear for use with winches. Tours carried manual winches and ground anchors to use when recovering the vehicle if it got bogged-in. The Range Rovers and G-Wagens had power winches fitted to their front bumpers – see 'Recovery' below.

- The Range Rovers had an electrical cutout switch fitted under the driver's seat because of short-circuiting issues with the towing hitch connections that caused all the lights to come on even though the ignition was turned off – thankfully, no tour was ever detained because of this fault.
- Seats – for most of its history, BRIXMIS tour cars used the standard seats fitted in the car, but with the Mercedes G-Wagen, the normal seats were replaced with RECARO rally-style seats in the front and a centrally mounted RECARO seat in the back for the tour officer.
- A Halda Tripmaster rally-spec mileometer was fitted to give precise distances for navigation and map reading.
- All interior surfaces were blacked out with tape to stop them reflecting in the windscreen and spoiling the photographs.
- Custom storage crates were designed and built in the workshops to fit in the back of the 4x4s to hold all the tour equipment that would normally be stored in the boot of the saloon cars. Kit could be easily accessed over the back seat or via the split tailgate/rear door and could quickly be covered to hide the contents from prying eyes. The crate was designed to fit snugly between the two spare wheels stored vertically on either side of the rear storage compartment. The crates also made checking, loading, and unloading the tour equipment easier.
- Curtains were fitted to the back and rear side windows to hide the tour equipment and the photographic activities of the tour officer.
- Extra map lights were fitted in the front and rear.
- If electric windows and door locks were fitted, they were converted to manual – tours preferred manually operated windows and locks because they were silent in operation.

Four-Wheel Drive

The biggest modification, however, was not undertaken by 14 Field Workshops REME, but by a specialist company based in Coventry, England. In 1966, the Ferguson Formula 4WD system (FF, after its inventor Harry Ferguson, as in Massey Ferguson), based on the 4WD drivetrain used in tractors, was pioneered in the 140-mph Jensen FF sports car, however, despite trying to sell the technology to other car manufacturers, there were few takers. In 1971, the technology was picked up by a new company, FF Developments, and was fitted to two Triumph Stag sports cars as proof of concept. In 1974, BRIXMIS organised a trial on the new 2.8 Opel Admiral B model – the engineering involved in converting a rear-wheel-drive executive saloon into a 4WD monster was extensive, and cost around £5,000 at 1974 prices. A front differential had to be fitted, with a new custom oil sump. From there, front drive shafts needed to be attached to new front hubs, and a prop shaft to the rear of the car. The prop shaft was then fitted to a chain box on the rear of the torque converter housing (which acted like the transfer box on a Land Rover) allowing drive from the torque converter to be transmitted (via the prop shaft) to the front axle; all this engineering had to work reliably in the most extreme of conditions. Performance was also enhanced with a Mullard anti-lock braking system, one of the first of its kind.*

The converted vehicle was put through its paces at the Military Vehicles and Engineering Establishment (MVEE) and Fighting Vehicles Research and Development Establishment (FVRDE) in Chertsey, Surrey, which had various test tracks to (theoretically) simulate the conditions that the car would face in the GDR. Having successfully passed all their tests, the test car and a second converted vehicle were collected from FF Developments and driven back to Berlin, where they went to 14 Field Workshops REME for their final transformation into tour cars (electronics, panzer plates, fuel tank, and so on). Despite its limited ground clearance, the executive saloon had become a very competent high-performance military vehicle. However, it quickly became apparent that the tests at MVEE/FVDRE were nowhere near as tough as the typical driving environment in the GDR, and so key components (drive shafts, front wheel bearings) were failing. An FF engineer was invited to Berlin and treated to a driving display around the ranges in Grunewald and returned to Coventry with his nerves in tatters and a brief to substantially strengthen the drivetrain. A kit of strengthened parts quickly arrived in Berlin and the first two Admirals were modified and let loose on tour in the GDR.

A total of six Opel Admirals were converted at FF Developments with three on-pass at any one time, two held in the Ordnance Services vehicle park as replacements, and one at 14 Field Workshop. Future FF conversions were undertaken at 14 Field Workshop using FF-supplied kits, and when a vehicle came to the end of its 60,000-kilometre tour of duty, the FF parts were removed, tested, and recycled onto new cars as the cycle of new-for-old continued. Feedback from the drivers and mechanics was passed back to the FF engineers, who modified the kits as needed. The Opel Admiral was replaced in 1978 by an all-new model, the Opel Senator A1 – it had a similar performance to the Admiral B, but with a new modern monocoque design, rather than the chassis construction of its predecessor. In the rush to get the vehicle introduced, no one considered how the monocoque would cope with the heavy loads and robust driving style associated with touring. The passenger compartment was rock solid with crumple zones at the front and rear, but after a few tours the body shell began creasing and cracking just in front of the front windscreen and behind the rear screen, and the front McPherson suspension struts began popping up through the front wings.

14 Field Workshop REME called their contacts at Opel HQ in Rüsselsheim in West Germany to ask for their help – Opel ran a World Rally Championship team at the time (winning the driver's championship in 1982) so had experience with the sort of conditions a tour car would experience. The Rüsselsheim engineers requested various measurements – weights and body height, with and without conversions (FF 4WD, panzer plates, fuel tank, etc.), and with and without a typical touring boot load; the data was sent across to the factory, followed by a newly FF-converted but unissued Senator for them to work on. The solution involved more engineering work but was well within the capabilities of 14 Field Workshop – two steel channel U sections were welded

---

* The anti-lock braking system made by Mullard/Girling was cutting edge in the early 1970s.

from the back of the boot to the front firewall bulkhead, which prevented the front and rear of the vehicle flapping around. In addition, Opel's Motorsport division reinforced the front suspension turrets with special steel cups, provided new springs, and a self-levelling suspension system was installed, all of which could be supplied to 14 Field Workshop in kit form. Soon, the A1 Senators were being issued with three conversions: the FF, the Opel, *and* the BRIXMIS conversion. Because of the unique circumstances in West Berlin, the 'Berlin budget', and the strong relationships built between the REME mechanics and their counterparts at Opel, BRIXMIS, a small and largely unknown Berlin-based unit, was able to circumvent the normal British Army bureaucracy (and further inadequate testing at MVEE/FVDRE) and call on one of the world's top rally sport teams to deliver a solution to their problem.

Custom Lighting

One of the most cunning tools used by all the AMLMs was the modified lighting circuits and custom lighting controls fitted to tour cars, sometimes referred to as the 'James Bond switch'. Positioned on the transmission tunnel between the front seats, they gave the driver and Tour NCO complete control over all the lights on the vehicle, which could be individually controlled, and the left and right side operated independently. This was particularly useful in car chases at night, where they could 'go dark' at the flick of some switches (with the driver using night-vision goggles and infrared front spotlights) or replicate the lights of a motorcycle or small civilian car (for example, a Trabant), thus confusing the pursuer. They could control the following:

- Master control – turn off *everything* in an emergency.
- Side lights – could be operated separately, with individual lights mimicking low-intensity East German motorcycle lights.
- Front 'yellow' spotlights – these were infrared lights for use in the dark in conjunction with night-vision goggles.
- Headlamps – could be operated separately, with individual lights mimicking brighter motorcycle lights.
- Headlamp and spotlight dimmer – a rheostat control to adjust the brightness of the front lights on the vehicle.
- 'Trabbie' lights – toggle switches with pre-set combinations to mimic the lighting (front and rear) of the ubiquitous East German Trabant car.
- Brake lights – to turn the brake lights on or off.
- Rear lights – controlled independently.
- Numberplate light – turned on or off.
- Internal lights – on/off switch to control all internal lights: compass, tripmeter, dash, map lights and lighting panel.
- Switches were back-lit to help identification and to indicate their status (on or off).

The indicators and the horn could be isolated to stop accidental use. BRIXMIS folklore has a Stasi car going off the road during a high-speed pursuit after missing a sharp

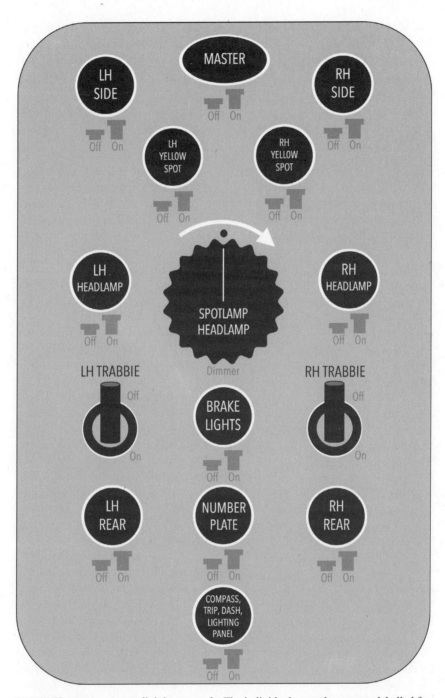

BRIXMIS tour car custom lighting controls. The individual controls were not labelled for security reasons and the configuration varied over time. (Author, representative sketch based on original brief to 14 Field Workshops REME, G-Wagen Lighting Control Panel BRV639, 22 October 1984)

bend because the tour car had switched off its brake lights to disguise its hard braking. Although tour cars were meant to be inviolable (like an embassy or diplomatic bag), the East Germans violated this protocol on many occasions and will therefore have seen the custom lighting panels up close, but not the wiring loom behind them. This knowledge probably would have had little impact on Stasi tactics.

Recovery

Tours operated in very challenging conditions inside the GDR, and while their vehicles were highly modified, incidents that required some form of recovery were not uncommon, preferably without attracting the attention of the opposition. Even with 4WD and all-terrain tyres or chains, cars would frequently get stuck or bogged-in, especially in muddy conditions, over deep ruts, in soft sand, deep snow, or when fording a stream or flooded area. Tyres and wheels were also vulnerable to damage in high-speed or violent manoeuvres. Tours were also not immune to ordinary road-traffic accidents, especially in icy conditions or over the treacherous cobble stones that were still found in many East German towns, and it was not good news to have an accident involving East German civilian vehicles, especially if East German citizens were injured in any way. Tour personnel did not normally use seatbelts when touring – they needed the freedom of movement, although they were worn in West Berlin, during long transits across the GDR, and when chasing trains or other high-speed runs – so the risk of injury in an accident was high. Equally, despite excellent maintenance, vehicles sometimes simply broke down. To add insult to injury, while stranded because of these sorts of incidents, tours were very vulnerable to being detained by the ever-present narks. It should also be noted that tour cars were also subjected to deliberate and violent intervention by Soviet or East German vehicles, ramming or forcing them off the road and resulting in serious damage and injuries to tour personnel. Because of these scenarios, vehicle recovery was a major preoccupation for tour personnel, who were issued with specialist recovery equipment and given extensive training in recovery techniques during the BRIXMIS Intelligence (Special Duties) Course at Ashford and in continuance training on the test routes in Grunewald. Tour drivers were normally competent mechanics, who could diagnose and sort out many mechanical problems in the field, and therefore mechanical components (such as carburettors) were favoured over more modern electronics (fuel injection).

The saloon cars relied on the time-honoured practice of hand winching – BRIXMIS used a Trifor hand winch (jokingly known as 'handraulic') with an extra-long steel cable (strop) made by a local Berlin firm. The cable was fed through the winch, attached to the vehicle at one end, and to something solid (a tree, rock, or another vehicle) at the other. A long collapsible handle was then attached to the winch, which was manually operated, ratcheting the cable through various gears, pulling the vehicle along. The introduction of powered winches with the Land Rover and then the Range Rover cut down on the physical effort. The Safari LWB Land Rover and Mk.1 Range Rover were fitted with a power-take-off capstan winch made by Fairey Engineering, which harnessed the power of the engine to turn the winch. This was replaced in the mid-1970s with the Warn 8000 electric winch, which was turned by its own electric motor, although it required a double battery charging system to provide

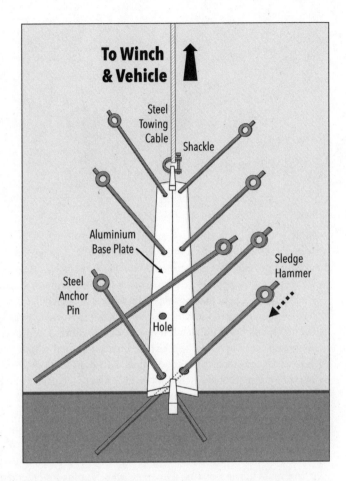

To Winch & Vehicle

Steel Towing Cable

Shackle

Aluminium Base Plate

Steel Anchor Pin

Hole

Sledge Hammer

Ground anchor for vehicle recovery. (Author)

enough electrical power.* The 8000 proved so reliable that when the Mercedes G-Wagen came along, the Warn 8000 was also specified, although 14 Field Workshop REME had to modify a front bumper from a British Army Bedford MK truck to accommodate it until a factory solution could be found.

Recovery in the field was rarely straightforward and so a wide variety of techniques were taught to tour personnel. In absence of a tree or solid fixing point, the tourers had to use a ground anchor – a three-feet-long aluminium plate with fixing eyes at both ends, perforated to take eight three-feet-long steel spikes or pins, that would be bashed into the ground with a sledgehammer.† The winch would be shackled to the anchor plate, providing the solid base from which to winch from. This of course assumed that

---

* The Warn 8000 winch was designed to pull 8,000 lb (3,629 kg, 3.6 metric tonnes, 3.57 imperial tons). The 'kerb' weight of the G-Wagen, *before* any modifications, was 2,065 kg or 4,553 lb, but this increased to about 3,500 kg when loaded and modified.

† The standard MoD ground anchor plate was made from steel, but BRIXMIS had them manufactured out of aluminium to save weight without compromising on strength.

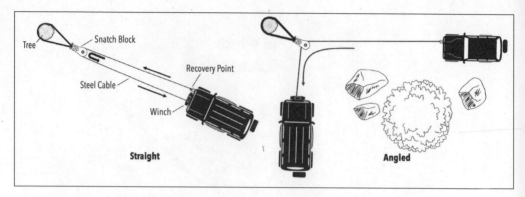

Vehicle recovery using snatch block. (Author)

the ground was sufficiently soft to penetrate with the spikes, and sufficiently hard that they would not pop out under load. Once the vehicle was recovered, the tourers then faced the job of trying to remove the spikes from the ground; not an easy task, although the spikes had holes in the ends that a line could be attached to.

If the ground was too soft for a ground anchor to work, tourers could use a technique called the 'baulk holdfast' as a last resort. This traditional approach involved digging a big hole and burying a pile of logs (the 'baulk') around which the recovery cable had been passed, thus creating the solid base to winch off. BRIXMIS adapted this technique by burying the spare wheel – the softer the ground, the deeper the hole![15] The tour also carried a device called a snatch block that made the winch more versatile. By doubling the cable back through the snatch block, the power of the winch was doubled, which helped with difficult recoveries. The snatch block also allowed indirect winching round an obstacle.

Wheel changes were handled using a four-ton bottle jack or the manufacturer's side jack and tours carried one or two spare wheels, plus an emergency instant puncture repair aerosol can. The jacks could also be used to help recover a bogged-in vehicle. By placing the jack on the board that was carried for this purpose, the car could be lifted to allow the rut to be filled in with stones. Alternatively, the car could be pushed forwards or backwards off the jack onto more solid ground. The BRIXMIS M/T section investigated using inflatable air bags to help with recovery, using the same compressor that was used with the self-levelling suspension. Unfortunately, this was one innovation too far and they could not get buy-in from the powers that be.[16]

It is worth noting that occasionally a friendly local farmer would help a tour by pulling them out of trouble using his tractor or even his horse (much of East German agriculture was still horse drawn for years after the West mechanised). It was always a toss-up when encountering a local – many did not like the Soviets and were happy to help allied personnel in distress, while others were loyal to the regime and would immediately report the tour to the Vopos or were ordinary citizens afraid that if they helped the 'enemy' they would get into trouble with the authorities. It should also be noted that all these techniques took time and generated quite a bit of noise – both an issue when trying to evade the narks. They were also hazardous, in the days when health and safety was less of a concern. It should also be noted that it was the tour officer's and tour NCO's job to handle recovery, while the driver remained behind the wheel.

If a vehicle was beyond repair in the field, the recovery process was somewhat convoluted. The tour officer would always insist on seeing the local *komendant*, refusing to deal with any East Germans officials on the scene. Tours had no way of directly contacting their base in Potsdam, let alone BRIXMIS HQ in West Berlin, and public telephones in the GDR were few and far between (and seldom worked), so they would have to rely on the *komendant* to contact SERB in Potsdam, who would then contact the Potsdam Mission House, who would then contact BRIXMIS HQ in West Berlin who could despatch a recovery vehicle and the double-axle trailer to bring the damaged vehicle back to HQ. Chief BRIXMIS would always make a point of passing on his gratitude to the SERB officers who assisted in the recovery. Following a tour in 1985 where the engine on a G-Wagen died because of poor-quality East German fuel, the recovery team was despatched from Potsdam, the first recovery they had done for the new 4x4. When they arrived, it quickly became clear that the Mission needed to reassess its approach to vehicle recovery now the Mercedes were on the fleet. First, they discovered that when the G-Wagen was loaded onto the trailer, the Range Rover was not powerful enough to pull the combination from the un-made forest track where the engine had expired. They had to take the car off the trailer, drive the trailer to the nearest metalled road, and then tow the G-Wagen to the waiting trailer. However, once the G-Wagen was winched back onto the trailer, it became clear that the trailer was not strong enough to take its weight. It had coped with (frequently) recovering Range Rovers, but the additional weight of all that German engineering made the wheels on the trailer splay out. The forlorn party had to crawl the 430 kilometres back to Berlin at an average of 40 kph (25 mph), which took them thirteen hours. A trip to the weighbridge the next morning revealed that an operational Mercedes G-Wagen (base vehicle, plus modifications, fuel, tour kit and three crew) weighed in at almost 3½ tonnes – little wonder that the 2-tonne recovery trailer could not cope. An upgraded trailer was quickly ordered on the Berlin Budget, and the Range Rover recovery vehicle was exchanged for a more powerful G-Wagen.[17] New BRIXMIS drivers understood that they were not considered 'proper' drivers until they had taken the trailer both ways through the concrete chicane on the Glienicke Bridge without 'shunting' it. It was so difficult that when a driver managed to pass through the chicane *without* hitting the barriers, there was often a nod of acknowledgement from the Soviet guards on duty. However, in the mid-1980s they took the concrete walls out and tours could drive through the checkpoint in a straight line from the Potsdam side.[18]

Vehicle recovery did have its lighter moments. A BRIXMIS Range Rover had just been recovered after breaking down and was being towed on a trailer by another Range Rover. They happened to bump into a BBC film crew in Eisenach, west of Erfurt, who were making a documentary film on Johann Sebastian Bach (who was born there in 1685). Stopping for a chat with their fellow countrymen, one of the film crew was seen pointing to the trailered Range Rover and asking the tour officer, Major Chris Hughes, 'Tell me, do you always carry a spare car?'[19]

Chapter 6

The Opposition

'Treat the buggers like gentlemen but behind the scenes,
take them to the f**king cleaners.'

General Sir John Learmont
KCB CBE on the Philosophy of Liaison
Chief BRIXMIS 1982–1984[1]

The primary objective of the three AMLMs was to collect intelligence on the Group of Soviet Forces Germany (GSFG). The GSFG was around 380,000 strong, spread over 777 mostly ex-Wehrmacht barracks in 276 different locations across the GDR, with 47 airfields and 116 training grounds or ranges, all of which were of interest to tours. This was the Soviet Union's front line against NATO in Europe, and although the quality of the troops varied enormously, it included many crack units armed with the most modern equipment. Tour personnel had to contend with armed sentries, random interventions from soldiers acting on their own initiative or under the direction of their officers, and specific anti-mission patrols or ambushes by Spetsnaz special forces or the specialist 'blocking' units that were set up in the 1980s. These teams would attempt to detain tours, and then hand them over to the local Komendatura to investigate the AMLMs' alleged illegal activities. Although the average Soviet conscript cared little about these foreigners driving around the countryside, specialist troops such as rocket artillery, radar and communications units, and special forces were well trained, highly motivated, and aggressive.

The AMLMs also had to report on the activities of the 175,000-strong East German Nationale Volksarmee (NVA), the National People's Army, with their land, air, and naval forces at bases and airfields around the country. They had primarily a second echelon role (like many of their non-Soviet Warsaw Pact compatriots), working with mostly second-hand equipment passed down from the Soviets, but were still a formidable fighting force. Their equipment improved during the 1980s, but despite having a stronger officer corps and NCO cadre, they were still hampered by ideological dogma and a terminally ill economy. In addition, the AMLMs will have encountered the huge East German police state. The uniformed element comprised:

Volkspolizei (c. 80,000 Vopos, People's Police, plus a further 170,000 volunteers),

Grenzpolizei (c. 47,000 GrePos, Border Guards),

TransportPolizei (c. 8,500 TraPos, Transport Police),

Kampfgruppen der Arbeiterklasse (c. 210,000 KdA, paramilitary factory militia).[2]

All these different paramilitary organisations were similarly armed (although the Grenzpolizei possessed heavier weaponry) and uniformed and worked in conjunction with the vast Ministerium für Staatssicherheit, the Ministry of State Security (see below). All these organisations would, to a greater or lesser degree, attempt to disrupt mission operations and detain tours, and although the AMLMs did not officially 'recognise' East German authority, that did not stop the various arms of the East German police state from actively targeting tours, physically detaining them (often violently), before handing them over to the local *komendant*.

The East German civilian population were a mixed bunch, reflecting the contradictions of the state. Most were indifferent to AMLM activity, like the three wise monkeys, cowed by decades of repression or simply wise enough not to put their head above the parapet and engage with the authorities. If unobserved by officialdom, they were normally polite and often helpful – they could help with recovering stranded vehicles, telling the tour about recent military activity, or even suggesting OPs that could not be seen from the road. The party faithful, however, lapped up all the state propaganda and could be nasty and vindictive. The challenge for the tours was to tell them apart.

The Stasi

The Ministerium für Staatssicherheit (MfS) was established in 1950 to be the 'Sword and Shield' of the party, modelled closely on the Soviet NKVD/KGB, although they would give their own 'Prussian' take on the role of secret police, regularly operating outside the rule of law and acceptable practice. They formed a 'state within a state', and penetrated every aspect, every stratum, of East German society and continued to work with the KGB right until the fall of the Wall. They were literally on every street corner, with around 90,000 full-time employees at its peak (one for every 180 of its citizens), and a huge network of Inoffizieller Mitarbeiter (c. 174,000 IMs, informers, one in 95). Kidnapping and murder were among the many tools they deployed in their dual role of internal repression and external subversion, and the infamous Stasi prison at Berlin-Hohenschönhausen was the venue for many horrors, physical and psychological torture. Despite an early reputation as little more than state-employed thugs, the Stasi developed into a very sophisticated counterintelligence operation.

Main Department VIII (Hauptabteilung, HA VIII) of the MfS focused specifically on the surveillance, analysis, and disruption of AMLM activities out on the ground in the GDR and were a constant nuisance to the AMLMs. A debrief of a former Stasi lieutenant in late 1990, therefore after the fall of the Wall, gave a good picture of the MfS infrastructure tasked with countering the AMLMs.[3] The counter-mission unit was part of Abteilung 5 (Department 5) of HA VIII with its headquarters in East Berlin.

Abteilung 5 had a staff of about eighty-five people, and was split into seven *Referaten* or sections as follows:

Referat 1 – ran all unofficial members working against the AMLMs including the Mission House workers.

Referat 2 – worked to develop awareness of AMLM activity among the GDR's population. They also liaised with HQ MfS on matters of army counterintelligence.

Referaten 3 and 5 – deployed the surveillance teams, three in the north of the GDR and five in the south.

Referat 4 – included the analysis cell and eavesdropping section, who also tapped the phone lines in and out of the allied mission houses.

Referat 6 – oversaw all admin matters.

Referat 7 – controlled the surveillance teams on the ground using two-way radio.

The aims of Abteilung 5 were:

a) Prevent espionage against military targets.
b) Prove AMLM espionage activities.
c) Execute deliberate planned detentions.
d) Gather information on individual AMLM personnel and their families.

A 1985 Stasi handbook (*Das Wörterbuch der Staatssicherheit*, Second Edition) gave details of the AMLMs and summarised what the Stasi was doing to counter them:[4]

Under the existing and future conditions of the class struggle, the Ministry of State Security has an increasing number of tasks to implement in conjunction with the GSFG military counterintelligence authorities [GRU, KGB] and other organs of state of the GDR, in particular the People's Police [Volkspolizei, Vopos], to further restrict the intelligence operations of the missions, to reveal, initiate prophylactic measures against, to prevent, and to obtain documentary evidence of the subversive abuse of mission rights and other transgressions of their members. Depending on the nature and severity of the subversive abuse of these rights and authorised activities and on any other transgressions, the relevant organs of the GDR may apply the following measures against mission measures:

The systematic use of uniformed or plain clothes personnel to disrupt possible or implemented intelligence operations by the missions.

'Sandwiching' of their vehicles when it is evidently clear that mission members intend to operate, are operating or have operated illegally.

Prevention of the removal of evidence of illegal activities by the missions, but with due respect to the inviolability of the individual, the mission members and of their vehicles' [lip service, as this was frequently ignored].

When Military Missions have committed illegal activities, organs of the GSFG are authorised to seize any evidence [not according to the RMA], to detain the personnel and to take them to the local garrison commandant's office to clarify the matter.

To facilitate planned detentions or ambushes, the department maintained links with the KGB and GRU with their Spetsnaz (special forces) ambush squads. The GRU relied on the MfS to plan the ambushes, but Spetsnaz soldiers would make the arrests, supported by Stasi officers in Soviet uniforms. Abteilung 5 apparently had no links to GSFG/WGF.

Stasi surveillance vehicles were initially crewed by three narks: a driver, a navigator, and a radio operator, but by the 1970s, radio technology had improved (even for the East Germans) and they dispensed with the separate radio operator. They would drive in unmarked cars, normally Wartburg Knights, but also Ladas, Trabants, and sometimes Western cars that had been stolen to order or confiscated from Western motorists who fell foul of the East German authorities. The move to mostly domestically produced surveillance vehicles in the early 1970s may have reduced the performance of the vehicles but improved their ability to blend in with other road users. Normally, if a tour spotted a car containing two or three adult males, typically with their leather jackets hanging from a hanger in the back, it was most likely a Stasi vehicle, although in the 1970s, the MfS tried to mix things up by sometimes placing a female agent in the passenger seat. Nark cars would regularly swap numberplates, but tours kept lists of suspected plates to refer to. These mobile units would try to catch the tourers in the act and photograph them as they committed their 'crimes'. Just as the tours themselves, the surveillance teams would use long-lensed cameras, but also 16-mm movie cameras, and Minox sub-miniature 'spy' cameras for covert photography, sometimes from their car, but also covertly by walking past tour personnel or hiding in bushes.

The MfS also relied on an extensive network of static observation posts all over the country manned by unofficial collaborators (IM, Inoffizieller Mitarbeiter) who would report sightings to the central Abteilung 5 control room, which would then pass the information to the surveillance teams via radio. Every *Bezirk* (administrative region) had a local Stasi unit subordinate to HA VIII. In the early days of the AMLMs, the narks would try to follow tour vehicles from the moment they crossed the Glienicke Bridge or Potsdam Mission House, but this proved to be a huge drain on resources, so they became more reliant on radio-controlled interceptions and by using geographical chokepoints (such as between PRAs). Even then, there could be as many as a dozen Stasi cars engaged in a surveillance operation against a single tour car, that's around thirty-six agents on the ground, all in radio contact with each other, plus coordination staff at HQ and then the endless reports that would get produced and carefully filed – a huge resource to keep a mobile tour car under surveillance.

The primary objective behind all this effort was to obtain hard evidence of 'illegal' espionage or intelligence-collection activity that could be used to persuade the Soviets to curtail AMLM activity in the GDR. The Soviets, however, were happy to turn a blind eye to the AMLMs, knowing full well that the continued existence of their missions in West Germany depended on the (relatively) unhindered activity of the allied missions in the GDR. This did not stop the MfS from generating masses of paperwork in their ongoing but futile quest.

Nark Baiting

Some tours took great pleasure in having a bit of fun with the opposition, who seldom shared the joke or gave the impression of having a sense of humour at all. This was especially true with the East German Stasi, commonly known as 'narks'. This mainly puerile and unofficial activity often brightened up a long and boring tour and contributed to the unit's folklore and esprit de corps. Nark baiting often involved silly pranks like following a nark car (as opposed to being followed by) all the way back to their base, or choosing a route that was bound to get the nark car bogged-in, and then gallantly offer to winch them out, which was always refused on principle. Pointing a camera at a nark would often scare them off or put them in a fugue state where they refused to engage or even make eye contact, acting like they were not there. This baiting would also be extended to the Vopos, where tours would deliberately sabotage a Vopo speed trap by parking up on the central reservation for a cup of tea, and flashing warnings to oncoming cars to slow down, robbing the Vopos of their fines. Tours took their work very seriously, but such antics went some way to relieving the stress and tension that accompanied touring.

Pass Politics

The pass issued by SERB to named individuals in the Mission was a vitally important document, more precious than an ID card or passport. Without it, a mission member could not enter East Germany or tour, and withdrawal of the pass was effectively a PNG. It also (theoretically) gave pass-holders the 'protection' of their chief's accreditation to the Commander-in-Chief of the GSFG, which would make most Soviet officers think twice before laying a hand on a tour member; however, there were numerous occasions where it made no difference at all. Despite their importance, the Soviets/East

Germans made numerous crude attempts to use the passes to curtail mission operations. These included switching the specimen signatures held by Komendaturas so they no longer matched the signature on the passes, rendering them invalid; changing the small print (which was in Russian) to state the AMLMs were now responsible to the East German government, not GSFG; or even running off with the tour officer's pass, leaving the officer stranded inside East Germany.[5] After several incidents of pass thefts, an agreement was reached with SERB that tour members would *only* surrender their passes to an officer of the Komendatura, who, theoretically, had been briefed on the niceties of the RMA. The Mission was issued fifteen vehicle passes plus one for the recovery trailer, all matched to individual chassis numbers. Like touring passes, they could be exchanged such as when a vehicle had to go into the workshop or was mileage-expired and was being replaced with a new vehicle. If a vehicle was travelling to the UK for FF 4WD conversion or for use on an Ashford training course, the distinctive BRIXMIS plates would be changed for normal Berlin Sector military plates.

Incidents

BRIXMIS history is packed with incidents – some dangerous and life threatening, others with serious political and diplomatic significance, and some verging on the farcical. The best way of highlighting the adventures, the dangers, the violence, and the occasional absurdities of touring is to tell some of the individual stories of incidents through the Mission's forty-four-year history. The specifics surrounding the incidents also help illustrate the many different facets of touring and Mission operations.

Rügen Roundabout

On 17 December 1952, a tour was sent to Rügen, a strategically important island on the Baltic coast, believed to be the site of submarine bases and other military installations.* In the early hours of the morning, Major Mike Reynolds RM, the Royal Navy representative and Major Vincent Harmar RA set off from a snowy Potsdam on what would turn out to be a long and rather dramatic tour. They arrived at the north coast unmolested, crossed over the bridge, which was only manned by a few Vopos, and looped round to the south of the island to check out a former naval mine depot at Tilsow that had reportedly been reactivated (it had not), skirted south of the island capital Bergen auf Rügen and across to Binz without being stopped. This part of the island was highly militarised, with East German units based at Binz and Prora, and the Soviets at Granitz, so was a key target for the AMLMs. The tour noticed several small 'No Entry' signs in German and the coast road up to Prora was blocked by a manned barrier. After a quick

---

* On the east coast of Rügen is Prora, a huge building complex constructed by the Nazis between 1936 and 1939 consisting of eight identical buildings stretching for 4.5 km (2.8 mi) along the beach. Across the bay from Rügen is Peenemünde where the V-1 and V-2 rockets were developed by the Nazis during the Second World War.

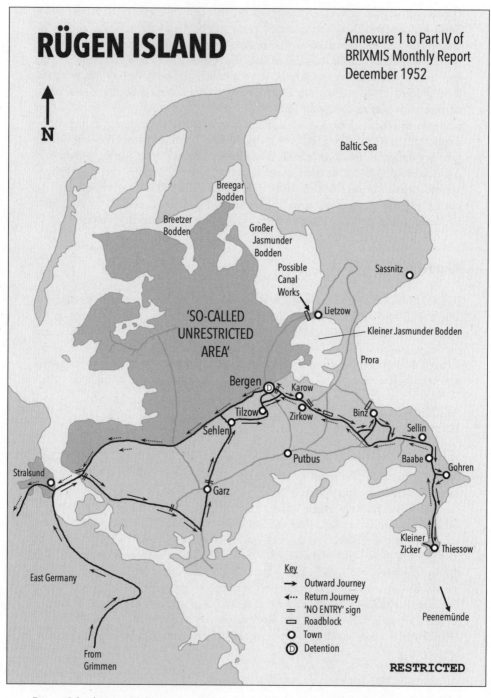

Rügen Island tour, 17 December 1952. (Author, based on BRIXMIS Monthly Report, December 1952)

and non-eventful tour of the southern peninsula, the tour headed for their main objective, which was to investigate reports of canal construction at Lietzow, north of the Kleiner Jasmunder Bodden lake, which could link it to the Großer Jasmunder Bodden lake and thence to the sea, creating a possible ship or submarine haven. With the coast road north blocked at Binz, the tour had no option but to divert via Bergen, where they were detained by a Soviet captain, who was waiting for them in his Jeep, and were escorted to the Komendatura. This was about 1530 hours. A short while later, the *komendant*, a Lieutenant Colonel Lunivov, arrived and asked what they were doing on Rügen. Harmer replied that they were 'looking for an agreeable summer resort and one could never be too early in planning one's holidays'. He had heard that 'Rügen was renowned for its scenery and the courteousness of its inhabitants'. Looking out at the snow building up outside, Lunivov suggested that choosing a holiday at that time of year would be a lot easier by looking at a brochure. They then began a long-winded argument as to whether the island was restricted to AMLMs and the differing opinions about MRSs, with the *komendant* arguing that the whole of the (interesting) southern half of the island was out of bounds, while the (mostly uninteresting) north was open.

An *Akt* was laboriously prepared, with numerous phone calls up the chain of command, but eventually the *komendant* put his signature to it, only to be rebuffed by Reynolds and Harmar, who, as per the policy, refused to sign. After a while and faced with having to spend the night in a grim hotel in Bergen auf Rügen (tours were still staying in hotels at this stage), Reynolds and Harmar suggested a face-saving compromise – they would sign a codicil to the *Akt* stating that they refused to sign and highlighting that 'NOT being in a forbidden zone, we refuse to sign an Akt saying we were.' The circular argument continued for some hours during which the power kept cutting in and out (a common occurrence in the GDR) and a soldier would repeatedly appear with a lit candle. At 2040 hours the British party was eventually released and began the long journey back to Berlin, but the drama was far from over.

The tour was then escorted off the island where a reception party of three armed Soviets and seven armed Vopos was waiting for them. Rather than wave them through, the officer in charge insisted they proceed to the Stralsund Komendatura where their documents were minutely examined for the *second* time that day. Then at Demmin, which was less than an hour into their 200-kilometre (124-mile) return journey, they were stopped by a Vopo at gunpoint, who demanded to see their papers. When told the AMLMs did not recognise the GDR or his authority, he became hysterical, cocked his pistol, and began waving it about. The situation was diffused by the arrival of a Soviet officer in a Jeep, who had been sent from Stralsund to make sure they were heading straight back to Potsdam. He berated the Vopo for drawing and then cocking his sidearm and ordered him to holster it immediately. Escorted by the Soviet officer, they finally made it back to Berlin, but were ambushed again in Treptow by Vopos, requiring the intervention of the officer again. After three more checkpoints, they finally got back to Berlin at 0345 hours, twenty-four hours after setting off. This one tour experienced a serious escalation in anti-mission activity: the imposition of arbitrary and illegal PRAs by a local officer, and repeated armed intervention by the East German Vopos, all of which prompted a strongly worded protest to SERB.[6] This incident, and others, led to the whole of the Baltic coast being placed in a PRA, which remained until the late 1980s.

The 1953 Riots

In June 1953, an increase in work norms (the productivity rate that determined how much workers earned) prompted a walkout by construction workers in East Berlin. The walkout soon led to major demonstrations, prompting the Soviets to send in three divisions (1st Mechanised Division, 14th Guards Mechanised Division, and tanks from the 12th Guards Tank Division) to respond to the demonstrators with overwhelming force. BRIXMIS driver Corporal Len Holman RASC had been sent out to do some chores and was parked up in a side street in Potsdam checking his shopping list when he saw a ragged group of T-34 tanks hurtle round the corner in front of him. He noted that their arrival in the city was clearly rushed and unplanned – the tanks were covered in mud, as if they had just come from the training area, they were not travelling in normal regulated tactical columns, and that they were not accompanied by supporting units – the scale of the riots had clearly caught the Soviets by surprise. As well as the T-34s, the Soviets brought a stunning range of heavy weaponry into the city, including self-propelled tank destroyers, anti-aircraft artillery, mortars, and armoured cars. In addition, they brought pontoon bridging equipment, in case key bridges were blocked or destroyed – all in response to demonstrations by *unarmed* civilians.[7] Holman rushed back to the Potsdam Mission House to report what he had seen to HQ but arriving there, he found the telephone lines had been cut in the main hallway. The only person on site apart from the Royal Signals radio man was Maria, an East German maid, who was clearly the culprit and was instantly dismissed. Holman, therefore, had to get the signaller to radio the news through.

The following day, Holman went out on tour with Wing Commander R. W. Hurst and Captain Sidney Aurich to see how far the riots had extended. They visited Brandenburg, Magdeburg, Halle, and Leipzig, and were detained six times, including experiencing an attempt to break into the tour car. The day after, he did a similar trip, this time with Major Chris Hallett and Flight Lieutenant Ted Bliss, visiting Magdeburg, Wittenberg, Perleberg, Kyritz, and Nauen, getting away with only being detained four times. When confronted by armed East German soldiers, Hallett ordered Holman to 'run the bastards down', and they duly jumped (or were knocked) out of the way. Holman had to then stop to pick up Bliss, who was out of the car, which allowed a Vopo lance corporal to wave his pistol in Holman's face; Holman took offence to this, got out of the car, and gave the lance corporal (who was a good foot shorter than the British driver) a right talking to. After which, Holman got back in the car, and they drove off leaving a rather cowed Vopo JNCO in a cloud of dust. Some weeks later, Holman was introduced to Foreign Secretary Anthony Eden as the driver who had been arrested ten times in two days!

Although BRIXMIS had no official remit *inside* East Berlin (the RMA covered the Soviet Zone, which then became the GDR, but *not* the four-power-controlled city), it appears that BRIXMIS personnel were despatched into the Soviet sector (East Berlin) to see what was going on – their observation and language skills were invaluable, and they had a lot of experience working inside the GDR. Thirteen tours in all were despatched during the month observing the Soviet deployment in the city, but on 25 June and, against all the four-power agreements, the Soviets closed the

Soviet sector (East Berlin) to all Western observers, allowing the clean-up to take place unobserved.[8] After high-level protests, the sector crossings were reopened on 1 July, but the Soviets used roadblocks to keep Mission vehicles away from their troop positions. The lack of aerial reconnaissance capability became a key issue for the Mission following their experiences in June and July of 1953, which prompted the acquisition of two de Havilland Chipmunks for Mission use, beginning in earnest in 1956.

Askwith PNG

BRIXMIS was to get its first PNG in 1956, linked to Soviet sensitivity about their intervention in Hungary. In November 1956, Lieutenant Colonel A. M. (Mark) Askwith was detained twice in quick succession inside the GDR. During the first incident, he told the local *komendant* that he had just seen five GSFG divisions move up to the Polish border ready to intervene if the disturbances in Hungary spread to neighbouring Warsaw Pact countries. The *komendant* denied any knowledge of the troop movements and decided to take him to the main Leipzig Komendatura for further questioning. At Leipzig, a similar argument ensued, with the senior *komendant* calling his headquarters for instructions and vigorously denying that any uprisings, troop movements or interventions had taken place. After a long wait, Askwith was released, but from that moment he was a marked man. A few days later, on 7 November 1956 (October Revolution Day), Askwith was detained outside a Soviet barracks near Bernau. A group of Soviet officers (somewhat worse for drink) began haranguing Askwith about the disastrous British intervention in Suez, which was just coming to an end, to which Askwith responded in kind about their intervention in Hungary. The Soviets knew only what their political officers and army newspapers had told them and had no idea of their country's brutal repression of the Hungarian demonstrators or the earlier problems in Poland; however, they had been informed of Britain's humiliation over Suez. The argument continued until the arrival of the *komendant* and after more phone calls to headquarters, Askwith was released. A few days later, he was PNG'd for 'exceeding his duties as a liaison officer' and 'making false statements about Soviet policy'.[9] This was the Mission's *first* official PNG, and all the more interesting because it was related to wider world events.

The Battle of Rembrandtstraße

Brigadier Charles Wynn-Pope took over as Chief BRIXMIS in March 1955. His hard-charging approach to touring coincided with an increase in harassment of tours by Stasi narks but when he presented Chief SERB, Colonel Sergeyev, with irrefutable evidence of Stasi involvement, Sergeyev denied that they were involved and said that the drivers of the cars were simply 'authorised citizens of the GDR' or 'members of the local agricultural committee who were merely interested in foreign cars'. In August 1957 Wynn-Pope decided to 'deliver' one of these so-called 'authorised citizens' to

Chief SERB to prove his point. He set out in his Opel Kapitän on a local (Potsdam) tour accompanied by Lieutenant Colonel Charles Critchley, his GSO1. As usual, several nark EMW 309 cars began tailing the tour as soon as it left the Mission compound on Geschwister Schollstraße and followed the chief's car around Potsdam, which headed towards the Berliner Vorstadt district, close to the Glienicke Bridge.* Wynn-Pope, who was driving, turned into Rembrandtstraße where the SERB offices were located, which at the time was a one-way street. Right outside Sergeyev's office, Wynn-Pope slammed on the brakes and reversed at speed into the Stasi EMW. The Opel suffered little damage, but the impact broke the EMW's front axle and cracked the radiator, which emitted clouds of steam. Wynn-Pope leapt out of the car and attempted to grab the driver and drag him into SERB. Meanwhile, the second nark set about Critchley with a tyre lever. The Scottish officer's Balmoral cap took most of the lever's blow before the BRIXMIS driver (who was in the passenger seat) shoved Critchley's assailant into the gutter and sat on him. The narks from the second vehicle rescued their comrades and they all made off at speed in the second EMW leaving the wrecked car in the middle of the road. Sergeyev was unimpressed with Wynn-Pope's antics and refused to believe his story, insisting they had had a simple road-traffic accident, as backed up by the Vopo incident report. A few days later, Wynn-Pope received a letter from SERB informing him that if he presented himself again to the guards at the Glienicke Bridge, he would be refused entry into East Germany, effectively giving the chief a PNG. The incident became known as 'The Battle of Rembrandtstraße' and went down in history as the only time a Chief BRIXMIS was PNG'd (although Brigadier Packard's 'safety was not guaranteed' in 1960, an effective PNG – see below).[10]

BRIXMIS and the Spy

In the late 1950s tours were regularly being ambushed by narks deep inside East Germany, believing they had succeeded in losing their tails earlier in the tour. This pattern suggested that the Stasi had prior knowledge of the tour's itinerary, reinforced by comments from the narks that 'we always know where you're going to be'. Chief BRIXMIS, Brigadier Fitzalan-Howard, ordered an enquiry to try to discover the source of the leak, and the investigating officers followed the paper trail. Every Thursday or Friday, the following week's tour programme was typed up onto a stencil and cyclostyled (duplicated) using a mimeograph machine. Copies were circulated to the chief and deputy chief, adjutant, every tour officer, the M/T department, and a copy was posted on the ops room noticeboard. Copies were also sent to the MMFL and USMLM ops teams, JHQ Rheindahlen, and sometimes to the Berlin SIS station, just one floor below BRIXMIS HQ in London Block at the Olympic Stadium complex. Someone on that rather wide distribution list was passing the itinerary to the Stasi, the very people the tours were trying to avoid. The enquiry came up blank, but security protocols around tour itineraries were tightened up and distribution was reduced to just five hand-typed

---

* The EMW, made by Eisenacher Motorenwerk, was the East German rip-off of a pre-war BMW model.

(not duplicated) copies: the chief, the ops officer, the ops room notice board, MMFL and USMLM. This seemed to do the trick, and random ambushes reduced in frequency.[11] In 1961, SIS officer George Blake was arrested for spying for the Soviets since 1951, including during his stint in Berlin (April 1955 to April 1959), shocking the intelligence establishment to the core.* It seems quite probable that while Blake was stationed in Berlin, he had been passing copies of BRIXMIS tour itineraries to his Soviet handlers, who in turn passed them to the Stasi, who then staked out the routes, waiting to ambush the tours. The link between Blake and the Mission was reinforced by the 2018 obituary of Major Peter Chitty MBE, who was a tour officer between 1957 and 1960. The obituary said that Chitty did some work inside East Germany for Blake with the full knowledge of Chief BRIXMIS, so it seems probable that the leak of tour itineraries can be attributed to George Blake, and the fall in random ambushes attributed to Fitzalan-Howard's tighter OPSEC was probably more a result of Blake being posted back to London.

Packard and the Narks

Brigadier John J. Packard succeeded Brigadier Fitzalan-Howard as Chief BRIXMIS in November 1959 and had some big boots to fill. In June 1960, he was involved in an incident that would prematurely end his posting as chief and his career in the army. Packard was due to go on tour with Lieutenant Colonel Critchley but was hassled by narks from the moment he crossed the Glienicke Bridge at around 0800 hours. Squadron Leader Harry Nunwick had just returned from an early tour and offered to show his boss an escape route out of Potsdam that he had successfully used in the past. The plan was to divert down a track near the village of Michendorf, which would bring them out through woods near Ferch, a hamlet at the bottom of Schwielowsee lake; this cross-country detour would normally shake off any tail, but to be sure, Nunwick would follow the chief to act as a rolling roadblock as needed. Just by the turn-off they passed a barracks used by the Volkspolizei-Bereitschaften (VPB, the People's Police Alert Units), the paramilitary and riot police arm of the Volkspolizei (Vopos).

As expected, the two nark cars picked up the tourers as they left the Mission House, and after Packard's car turned down the track, Nunwick slowed down to hold up the narks and allow the chief to escape. However, a little way along the track, Packard's car was stopped by a prone VPB sentry armed with a light machine gun who refused to let them pass 'because there was an exercise in progress'. Packard tried to explain who they were, but the confused sentry blew his whistle to summon assistance. At that moment, the leading nark car overtook both Mission vehicles, crashed through the undergrowth, and came to a halt in front of Packard's car, knocking the sentry flying, while the second nark car blocked the road behind Nunwick's car, cutting off any escape from behind. Summoned by the whistle, a squad of VPB arrived on the scene, removed their injured comrade and their officer consulted with the narks. VPB

---

* George Blake was convicted and sentenced to 42 years in prison in May 1961. He escaped from prison in October 1966, finding his way to the Soviet Union. Blake retired to his dacha outside Moscow and died on 26 December 2020, at the age of 98.

trucks took over roadblock duties and the narks disappeared. Surrounded by armed troops and not allowed out of their vehicles, the tourers realised they were in trouble so fogged all their films and destroyed any notes they had. It was now about 0930. At 1100 several nark cars arrived, dispensing a team of Stasi thugs who attacked the BRIXMIS cars with rocks, clubs, and branches, smashing all the windows. They then forced the doors open, hauled out the tourers (Packard included), and proceeded to beat them up, strip the tour cars clean, and steal all their kit. After half an hour's extreme violence, during which the inviolable tour car and a British general officer were violated, they departed and the VPB guards moved back in, forcing the shaken-up tourers back into their vehicles, which were now full of broken glass and ripped upholstery. Packard demanded that the Soviet *komendant* was informed immediately but it took until 1500 for him to arrive. Because of their proximity to Potsdam, it was the Potsdam *komendant*, Colonel Aktyurin, who was summoned, and he was accompanied by a representative from SERB; they had been told that a Mission vehicle had forced their way into an exercise area and had seriously injured an East German soldier. Packard was quick to correct this piece of fiction, but it was clear they were in serious trouble. After speaking to the VPB officers, the Soviets told the tour party that they were free to leave but they should head to the Komendatura where they could give their side of the story. The Soviets departed but as the British made to leave, they were stopped by a VPB officer who told them they were his prisoners and would remain so until he received orders from his superiors, irrespective of what the Soviets had said. At about 1730, the now furious *komendant* arrived back, demanding to know why the British were still being held and not sitting in his office, as requested. He berated the junior VPB officer, who backed down and the ring of armed VPB soldiers melted away. The party got to the Komendatura at around 1800 hours, made their statements and finally got back to the office at about 2030 hours.[12]

This was an unprecedented attack on Chief BRIXMIS, and a strongly worded protest was delivered by C-in-C BAOR to his opposite number, who appeared genuinely shocked by the incident. Without giving an actual apology, C-in-C GSFG said that all the tour's property would be returned, and they hoped that BAOR would not retaliate against SOXMIS.[13] To rub salt into the wound, several weeks later Walter Ulbricht held a televised press conference where he presented all the tour's 'espionage' kit. Holding a 1:100,000 map up to the camera (which probably should not have been taken into East Germany), he said that the yellow markings by certain cities were targets for NATO germ warfare (they were simply markings to denote towns and cities of a certain population). Other benign cartographic symbols were said to be targets for saboteurs. Following Ulbricht's television appearance, HQ GSFG informed General Sir James Cassels, C-in-C BAOR, that Brigadier Packard's 'safety could not be guaranteed', an effective PNG.

Brigadier Packard retired early from the army in 1961 at the age of 51. For years it was assumed that he resigned after being traumatised by the incident; however, just before he died in 1993 Packard revealed that the reason for his resignation was that his boss, General Cassels, refused to back him against the Soviets and had accepted his PNG without any great argument; a man of principle, Packard kept the real reason for his resignation to himself.[14] Some months after the attack, Lieutenant Colonel Critchley was summoned to SERB to collect the kit taken in the incident. With typical German thoroughness, an inventory listed every item, with serial numbers noted, and all the equipment was carefully wrapped in clean white tissue paper. All personal items had been carefully examined to check for hidden messages or concealed compartments. The collar of Critchley's pyjama jacket had been slit open, the lining of his bag removed, the soles of his slippers stripped back, his toothpaste and shaving cream tubes slit open, his shaving brush cut in half, and every single razor blade had been removed from the packet. They even returned his rations, now mouldy and malodorous but carefully wrapped in paper. No maps or reading matter of any kind were returned. This story was typical of many incidents involving the Mission, with extreme violence followed by political intrigue, followed by procedural courtesy, but the involvement of the chief was a troubling and dangerous development.

The BRIXMIS Wives and the Berlin Wall

In August 1961, just after the Berlin Wall had gone up, Chief BRIXMIS asked two BRIXMIS wives to test the allied right of access into East Berlin for him. Without consulting their husbands, he sent Mrs Dyer (the wife of Wing Commander Dyer, who was busy flying the Chipmunk around the BCZ looking at the barbed-wire barriers) and another Mission wife across the newly constructed Checkpoint CHARLIE in a marked BRIXMIS staff car on the pretext of buying some tickets to the Berliner Oper, The ladies passed through scores of soldiers on both sides, including the commanding officer of the Royal Military Police in Berlin with his revolver at the ready, nonchalantly waved their passes at the East German guards and crossed into East Berlin unmolested. While they drove around, a woman flagged the car down and pleaded for them to take her across to the West in the boot of their car. BRIXMIS personnel were under strict instructions to refuse such requests, however desperate they may be. First, it could be a provocation, and second, although the mission cars supposedly enjoyed the same inviolate status as diplomatic vehicles, experience had shown that the East Germans did not always respect that convention – both scenarios would have resulted in a serious incident.

Corporal Day

On 10 March 1962 Corporal Douglas 'Duggie' Day RAF was driving Nick Browne in a marked BRIXMIS Opel Kapitän to the Stahnsdorf area, south-east of Berlin and outside the new outer Berlin Wall. Browne wore the uniform of a lieutenant colonel but was in fact an SIS officer with the cover of a civilian 'economics expert' at the Mission (at the time, there were still civilians holding 'local' army ranks who toured in uniform). Around midnight, they found themselves at the junction between Schleusenweg and Ernst-Thälmann-Straße in Kleinmachnow, which was about 300 metres south of the outer Berlin Wall. Having missed their turning, they proceeded to turn around in the road at the junction unaware that there was a Grepo station in two requisitioned villas on

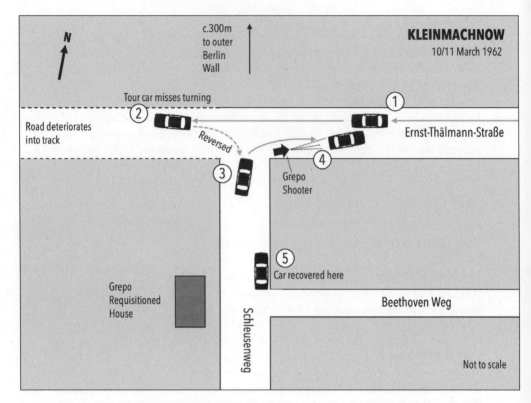

Corporal Day shooting, 10 March 1962. (Author, based on contemporary incident reports)

the west side of Schleusenweg 100 yards or so south of the junction. The Grepos must have been alerted by the sound of the reversing car – this was a residential backwater that would have been deserted at that time of night – and as the car began to move eastward back along Ernst-Thälmann-Straße several bursts of automatic weapon fire were directed at it from the right rear at a distance no further than twenty-five yards – the large high-visibility Mission numberplate was illuminated and as they were on a local 'urban' tour, it would not have been 'muddied up'.

There were no warning shots and Day was hit by the first burst of fire and several times again with subsequent bursts, with the car coming to a halt just a few yards from the junction. Browne, who had been sitting in the right-hand back seat, was miraculously uninjured and jumped out to give first aid to Corporal Day, who was in a bad way with multiple bullet wounds. Browne demanded to see an officer and insisted that an ambulance be sent for immediately; after a forty-minute wait Day was eventually taken to hospital, but Browne was not allowed to go with him. Remaining with the car, he attempted (in vain) to stop Vopo officers photographing every bit of the car, inside and out. One of them furtively stole Browne's map case and was seen running away with it in the direction of the Grepo station. Browne was detained until the following morning when he accepted Chief SERB's offer of a lift back to Potsdam Mission House where he could raise the alarm, some seven and a half hours after the incident. A BRIXMIS recovery team picked up the Opel later that morning, and there was a tense stand-off with a belligerent Grepo lieutenant who was waving his pistol around, objecting to them taking pictures of the scene. There was evidence that the East Germans had tried to get access to the boot of the car, although, unusually for a BRIXMIS mission, there was nothing incriminating inside.[15]

The negotiations began immediately for Day's release and the Soviet attempts to interrogate the very poorly corporal were blocked by a succession of redoubtable BRIXMIS wives who maintained a twenty-four-hour watch at his bedside.[16] Day was moved to the British Military Hospital in West Berlin on 19 March 1962 and underwent a series of operations including the removal of one of his kidneys. Forensic analysis by the West Berlin police revealed that the Grepo emptied the magazine of his 7.62 MPiKM (East German AK-47) at the Mission car from a kneeling position as little as 4 metres away, with at least twenty-one bullet holes and further ricochets seen on the bodywork.[17] A defector report from August 1962 stated that the Grepos had received a 'tip off' that a car with six would-be *Republikflüchtlingen* (defectors) would be in the area that night and should be apprehended using lethal force if necessary.[18] Thankfully, Corporal Day made a full recovery and remained with the RAF, retiring as a warrant officer in 1991.[19]

The Bundestag Episode[20]

In March 1965, the allied commandants of Berlin controversially agreed to a request from the West German Bundestag (their parliament, which normally sat in Bonn) to hold a session at the Kongresshalle in Tiergarten, West Berlin, which, in the eyes of the Soviets, was a severe provocation. The Soviet response was typically heavy handed. Their first act was to close all the land routes to West Berlin to stop any members of the Bundestag from travelling on East German soil, claiming the autobahn was needed for military manoeuvres, the first major disruption of road traffic since 1949. Next, they put virtually all the GDR into a TRA, severely limiting AMLM activity. Supersonic Soviet fast jets were directed over West Berlin delivering sonic booms that smashed windows and terrorised the citizens, and Western civilian aircraft flying down the air corridors to the city were buzzed by Soviet and East German fast jets, including a British European Airways Viscount airliner carrying the West German president Heinrich Lübke. It was not just Berlin that received Brezhnev's wrath; he mobilised his forces across East Germany: the 35th Motorised Rifle Division from Dallgow-Döberitz and the 10th Guards Tank Division from Krampnitz, both crack front-line units, were deployed along the Inner German Border, and an airborne division from the Soviet Union was dropped onto the Letzlinger Heide training area, north of Magdeburg – all very serious developments.

Major David Bird was out on a normal forty-eight-hour tour to the north of the GDR, returning to Potsdam via the east side of the Letzlinger Heide training area when all this kicked off, and joined the Helmstedt autobahn via an UFO (an unofficial fly-*off* could also be an unofficial fly-*on*) to find it completely devoid of traffic.

He promptly left the autobahn and established an OP in a wooded area in time to witness an entire Soviet division moving purposefully west along the autobahn – it did not appear to Major Bird to be an exercise. The tour rejoined the autobahn and headed towards Potsdam in a high-speed and hair-raising chase with Vopos and narks, finally getting back to the Mission House where they were besieged for several days. The intelligence on the troop movements, however, was radioed to BRIXMIS HQ and passed up the chain. Over the next few days, BRIXMIS sent twenty-four tours into the GDR to enforce their right of movement and gather more intelligence and faced unprecedented nark activity – every single tour was detained. The Helmstedt autobahn was not covered by the hastily imposed TRAs, and all the junctions and exits were blocked by Vopos or narks, but tours still managed to reach it across country and via UFOs. Major John Parry did just that, with Major Angus Southwood out on his first tour, and observed another BRIXMIS tour car hemmed in by half a dozen nark vehicles on the opposite side of the carriageway. The tour officer, Major Peter Chitty, was being manhandled by some narks but seemed to be holding his own, so Parry continued, only to be detained a few miles on. A few days later another Parry/Southwood tour was busy being detained at the Ziesar exit of the autobahn and was lucky enough to witness the eastward transit of a whole Soviet airborne division, signalling the end of the crisis.

There is no doubt that the allied powers' decision to invite the Bundestag to West Berlin was provocative and some reaction should have been expected from the Soviets. However, the scale of the mobilisation and nark activity was unprecedented and very worrying – all BAOR's Indicators of Hostility had been met, suggesting the Soviet activity was the prelude to war.[21] Thankfully, sensible heads prevailed, and NATO did not respond in kind, which could have easily escalated into much more than just sabre rattling. Thankfully, the Bundestag did not repeat their visit (a planned sitting in 1968 was railroaded by the Soviet invasion of Czechoslovakia) and prompt another heavy-handed response from Moscow.

BRIXMIS and the FIREBAR Crash

The FIREBAR Incident is celebrated as one of BRIXMIS's finest hours – not for its tales of derring-do and adventure, but for the far less glamourous but equally important job of 'liaison'. In this case, BRIXMIS 'liaison' made possible one of the biggest intelligence coups of the 1960s.[22]

On 6 April 1966, a brand-new Yak-28P (NATO reporting name FIREBAR) jet interceptor suffered a double flameout and, having been refused permission to make an emergency landing at nearby RAF Gatow by Soviet air traffic controllers, was forced to ditch in the Stößensee, a narrow body of water at the very top of Havel Lake in the British sector, killing both aircrew instantly. BRIXMIS personnel were at the heart of the four-week operation, fulfilling their liaison brief as the official (and only) interface between the British occupying force and GSFG. BRIXMIS interpreters were at the scene throughout to manage the Soviets who had encamped in force on the shore and ensure that the tensions did not explode into a major diplomatic incident.

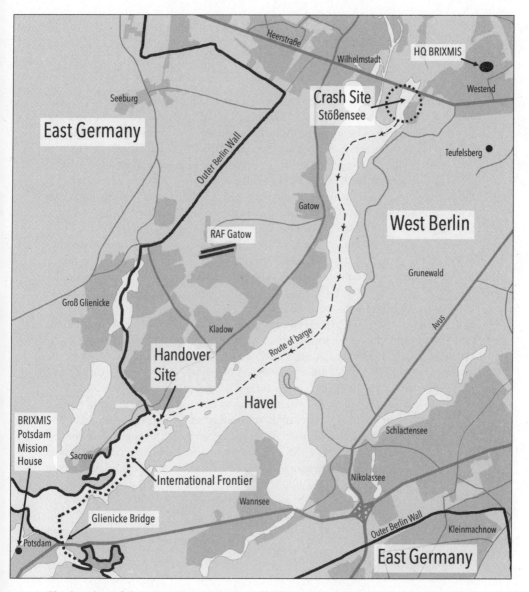

The location of the FIREBAR crash, 6 April 1966, and subsequent recovery operation. (Author, based on contemporary reports)

The tail of the aircraft could be seen sticking out of the water, but at this stage the British did not know exactly what they were dealing with. BRIXMIS Squadron Leader Operations Maurice Taylor went out on a small boat to take some flash photographs of the tailplane, activity that enraged the Soviets even more. Returning to London Block to get the film processed, Taylor and RAF Junior Technician Eddie Batchelor compared the prints to some photos of the Yak-28P taken by the USMLM at Finow airfield the previous month – from the distinctive antennas on the tail, they could positively identify the crashed aircraft as the brand-new Soviet supersonic interceptor. It was now essential to give the boffins as much time as possible to investigate the wreckage and acquire as many of its secrets as possible before having to hand it back to the Soviets.

The Mission's role as middlemen allowed the intelligence collection to proceed covertly, while the overt recovery of the aircraft and crew distracted the Soviets. By shuffling official notes back and forth from the lakeside (representing HQ SERB and HQ GSFG) to the nearby Olympic Stadium (HQ BRIXMIS, HQ British Sector, and the British minister), they made space for urgent discussions to take place between JHQ Rheindahlen, the MoD in London (and through them the boffins and scientists), the Foreign Office, and lastly the Americans, who were also keen to learn about this brand-new aircraft. What followed was an exercise in classic British diplomacy – soothing the enraged Soviets with the liberal application of officers' mess whisky while obfuscating for Queen and Country. BRIXMIS painstakingly negotiated the return of the bodies of the pilot and weapons operator, and eventually the return of the wreckage, which they managed to delay for several weeks. This allowed the top-secret covert recovery of the aircraft's radar, avionics and one of the engines, which were raised from the water and shipped back to the UK for investigation right under the noses of the Soviets. Metallurgical samples were taken from the engine and then it was surreptitiously returned to the lakebed, only to be 'discovered' a second time. The radar and avionics mysteriously 'disappeared', much to the dismay of the air force general who paced up and down on the shore, fuming at his inability to influence events. The intelligence coup for the West was enormous – the FIREBAR was at the cutting edge of Soviet military aviation and was a major threat to NATO, and the boffins at the Royal Aircraft Establishment at Farnborough, England and their colleagues in the USA learnt all about the latest Soviet jet engine technology, the aircraft's attack radar, and the IFF interrogator/transponder, which allowed them to develop electronic countermeasures (ECM) for NATO bombers such as the British Vulcan. BRIXMIS's role in this was critical – 'managing' the Soviets at the scene while buying time for the boffins to comprehensively exploit this sad but very welcome gift from the Soviet Air Force.

The Myagkov Distraction

On 2 February 1974 KGB Captain Aleksei Myagkov chose to defect while on a cultural trip to the Charlottenburg Palace in the British Sector.* Finding his way to the police station opposite the palace, he told the desk officer that he wanted to defect to the West – the desk officer sensibly called RMP duty officer, who duly alerted Major David Webb-Carter, GSO2 (Int) at Sector HQ at the Olympic Stadium. Webb-Carter

---

* Brigadier Baines described Myagkov as GRU, while David Webb-Carter (GSO2 Intelligence at HQ Berlin) and Tony Geraghty have him as KGB. Geraghty also has him as a long-term SIS asset.

immediately despatched a Russian-speaking NCO to the police station to take Myagkov into protective custody, alerted his chain of command to seek permission for an exfiltration – the only safe way out of West Berlin was by air – and arranged to have Myagkov moved to a British Services Security Organisation (BSSO) safe flat inside the Olympic Stadium complex.* Logistics notwithstanding, approval for such an operation would have to come from Rheindahlen and probably London – all this would take time to arrange. He also called his opposite number at BRIXMIS, Major Roy Giles, GSO2 (Operations), to warn him that the Mission's 'liaison' skills might be needed at some point. Meanwhile, Colonel Skurikhin, the deputy chief at SERB, had requested 'an urgent meeting' with Chief BRIXMIS, Brigadier Baines, at the SERB offices in Potsdam – no reason for the meeting was given. Skurikhin was told that Baines was en route back to Berlin from West Germany, but the request would be passed on as soon as he arrived. When Brigadier Baines arrived back in Berlin, he asked Roy Giles to join him at the chief's official residence, Stuhmer Allee 10, for a 'council of war'.

The BRIXMIS team kicked into action, as this was exactly the sort of 'liaison' that they excelled at. Skurikhin was told that as Baines had just returned from holiday, 'would he be so kind as' to come to Stuhmer Allee for the meeting, an unusual (and unprecedented) but not unreasonable request, and Giles, a Russian speaker, could interpret. Baines decided that it would be better that he was 'not in' when the SERB party arrived, allowing him to 'make his entrance' at an appropriate time, so left for a briefing at HQ BRIXMIS. For the time being, Colonel Skurikhin would be left in the capable hands of Honor Baines, the brigadier's wife, and Major Giles. The two of them began a marathon session of polite chit chat (dutifully translated into Russian and back to English), accompanied by light refreshments, increasing amounts of alcohol, and more substantial meals of eggs and bacon as required. Giles offered Skurikhin the use of the house telephone to report his progress, although he insisted on 'standing by' (listening in) 'in case of any queries'. While Honor entertained the Soviets, Giles arranged for the SERB car to be 'boxed in' by the BRIXMIS Berlin duty car, and the Potsdam duty car – the Soviets were going nowhere without BRIXMIS's permission.

Baines arrived from Sector HQ and listened to Skurikhin's request for an interview with Myagkov, replying that he would be glad to personally pass it on to GOC Berlin. On the way out, he showed Roy Giles a teleprinter message from Douglas-Home, the British foreign secretary in London, saying, 'I understand you have the Soviet delegation in your official house: you are instructed to retain them there, and under no circumstances release them until instructed', later clarified as until Myagkov had cleared East German airspace. Baines then departed again to Sector HQ, while Mrs Baines and Major Giles continued the polite conversation (schools, housing, comparative salaries – Skurikhin found it difficult to believe that 10 Stuhmer Allee was a house for just one family). The brigadier returned a while later and told Skurikhin that he would *not* be permitted access to Myagkov but that he was being well looked after, and GOC Berlin would keep SERB

---

* Geraghty has Myagkov being accommodated at BRIXMIS HQ, not a BSSO(G) safe flat.

informed via Chief BRIXMIS. Much of this business could have been transacted over the phone, but the elaborate pantomime (indeed a 'Whitehall farce') suited the British, who were feverishly trying to organise Myagkov's exfiltration. The Berlin Infantry Brigade Alert Platoon was also deployed to the Olympic Stadium because of reports that a pair of Soviet Volga staff cars – presumably a GRU (or KGB) snatch squad – was in the area.

As darkness fell, London confirmed that Myagkov could be exfiltrated by air, but an aircraft had to be sent from West Germany. It was also decided to use a helicopter to make the short hop from the Olympic Stadium to RAF Gatow, for fear that a road convoy would be intercepted by the Soviets. At about 0100 hours, Myagkov, now in plain clothes, was driven the short way to the waiting aircraft that had landed on the Maifeld, surrounded by heavily armed soldiers – Myagkov was bundled in and the helicopter took off.

Back at Stuhmer Allee, Skurikhin was getting a running commentary on the phone from the agents observing the scene at Sector HQ ... a British Army helicopter had just landed on Maifeld ... a group of men had run to it ... all the floodlights had gone out ... the helicopter had taken off. As these words were spoken, a helicopter flew low over the residence to Skurikhin's dismay.

Arriving at RAF Gatow a few minutes later, Myagkov was put straight into the waiting Pembroke, which was escorted down the air corridor to West Germany by two RAF fighters. Having received confirmation that Myagkov had crossed the border, Baines informed Skurikhin that Myagkov was now in the hands of the British civilian authorities, who would be responsible for his welfare, and that Skurikhin was free to return to Potsdam.[23] This example, like the FIREBAR story above, demonstrates the contradiction that was at the heart of the Mission's role. BRIXMIS was able to maintain a sense of decorum and professionalism when 'liaising' and facilitating with the Soviets, their sworn enemies, while furthering the objectives of their own side at the same time.

Laser Danger

During 1979 a new threat emerged for tourers. A BRIXMIS team at Krampnitz had a lucky escape having been lasered by a dismounted tripod-mounted laser rangefinder, probably a DAK-1 (NATO reporting name SAGE GLOSS). This equipment was used for artillery or tank gunnery range finding and was so powerful that it would blind anyone looking directly into the beam, obviously not a concern during hostile action, but to use them aggressively in peacetime was a worrying development. On this occasion, no one was injured, but the beam burnt a hole in the shutter mirror of a Nikon F3 camera that was being used, demonstrating just how dangerous it was. In 1981 a BRIXMIS tour on the Haufeld training area became the second team to be deliberately targeted by an artillery laser, this time from a device mounted on an ACRV-2 (IV-14 series artillery command and recce vehicle) one kilometre away away. The tour, comprising Captain Peter Williams, Sergeant Tony Haw QGM BEM (Green Howards), and Lance Corporal Tony Parkinson, were aware of the potential threat and when the interior of the car started to glow red, dropped their cameras and binoculars, and quickly moved away. A team from Tech Int (Army) at the MoD's Defence Intelligence Staff flew to Berlin soon after to ask the team about the incident, especially the colour of the laser – the original laser rangefinders from the early 1960s used ruby lasers with a bright red beam, but most applications transitioned in the late 1960s to the equally dangerous Nd:YAG (neodymium-doped yttrium aluminium garnet) lasers, which were invisible. The laser that illuminated Williams's tour car in 1981 was clearly of the older ruby type, which suggests the Soviets were still using the old technology for range finding or retained the devices for use against personnel. The Soviets had once again demonstrated that they were willing to act in a dangerous fashion against AMLM members, with little or no concern about the consequences.

Athenstedt

Even Chief BRIXMIS was not immune from the violent actions of the opposition. Back in 1960, Brigadier Packard had been held at gunpoint, but in August 1982 the NVA, as directed by the Stasi, came closest to killing the chief of the British mission in a planned ambush outside a small village called Athenstedt, 10 kilometres north-west of Halberstadt and 50 kilometres south-west of Magdeburg. Athenstedt was a nondescript village but was home to an NVA early-warning radar station belonging to the 613rd Radar Company (FPN 74055) of the 61st Radar Battalion and therefore of interest to the AMLMs – it became an incident 'hot spot' with four serious incidents between 1978 and 1984.[24]

The first incident happened on 25 September 1978 to a USMLM tour. As it was passing the radar site, an East German sentry suddenly dropped a red and white striped cantilever gate (a *schlagbaum*, a wooden or metal barrier) across the road directly on top of the tour vehicle. The gate glanced off the bonnet and up onto the roof causing minor damage, but the vehicle was able to continue with the tour.[25]

On 13 March 1979, another USMLM tour came to grief at the same spot, albeit in a more spectacular fashion. Lieutenant Colonel Ed Hamilton and Staff Sergeant Hans Tiffany were heading out of Athenstedt at about 1300 hours in Dodge Ramcharger No. 29 when a 14-tonne Tatra 813 truck stormed out of the radar site into the side of the tour vehicle, pushing it off the road where it rolled twice and ended up on its side. Hamilton was taken to the nearby civilian hospital and the tour car was ransacked, photographed from every angle, and all the equipment confiscated. Hamilton remembered seeing a house at the very edge of the village that could have been a Stasi/NVA lookout post, warning the radar site so the driver of the Tatra 813 could get his timing right – it is likely that the East Germans would have practised the manoeuvre in advance.

The third Athenstedt incident was on 12 August 1982 involving Brigadier Learmont, the new chief, who was on tour with Captain Peter Williams acting as tour NCO and Corporal John 'Benny' Boland as driver. The army operations officer, Major Willie MacNair, had carefully designed a tour route that would give the chief a good feel for the ground and for the variety of targets on offer, such as army barracks, training areas, communication and radar sites, rail and road intersections, and even a small number of mapping tasks, while keeping him away from particularly sensitive (restricted) or otherwise dangerous areas. It was also decided that they would not use one of the olive drab Opel Senator or Range Rover tour vehicles, but would use his shiny black Senator No. 1, displaying a one-star general's plate alongside the distinctive yellow BRIXMIS numberplate, sending the message that the chief was not on an intelligence-gathering patrol, but was on a liaison or protocol visit. The tour was heading south through a 22-kilometre corridor between the IGB PRA boundary at Osterwieck and the Quedlinburg PRA boundary at Halberstadt, a bottleneck designed to funnel AMLM traffic so the East Germans and Soviets could monitor and, if possible, ambush them. Williams, who was navigating, took them south on the L84 (a minor B road) from the village of Badersleben to Danstedt via Athenstedt. He was aware there was an NVA radar site in the vicinity, but being an 'army' tour officer, was not particularly interested in a 'typically dull' RAF target. The tour left the village, presumably passing Hamilton's Stasi OP, and passed and duly ignored an MRS sign, only to realise the 'typically dull'

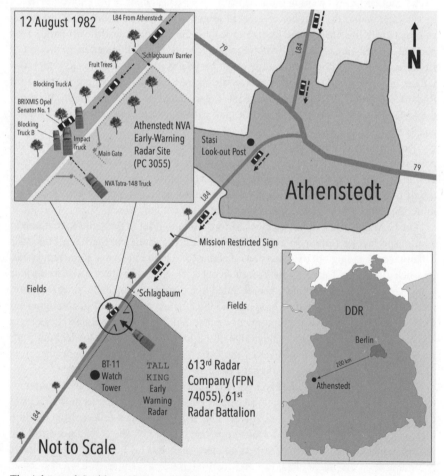

The Athenstedt Incident, 12 August 1982. (Author)

RAF target was a huge radar installation with its own BT-11 watchtower, set just back from the road. Williams asked the chief in the back seat to cover up all his camera equipment and ordered Boland to floor it and get past the site as quickly as possible. As they passed the start of the site, Williams saw a man leap out of the ditch and lower a *schlagbaum* across the road, blocking any escape route to the rear. As the tour car passed the site entrance, now travelling at about 60 kph, a huge 11-tonne Tatra-148 truck came speeding out, hitting the Opel Senator amidships and forcing it off the road – the car would have almost certainly rolled (like Hamilton's Ramcharger did) had it not been stopped by a fruit tree by the roadside. The windscreen and the driver's side window were smashed, and the Tatra's bumper ended up through the driver's window, but the car's chassis and underbody armour stopped it being crushed by the impact and miraculously no one was seriously hurt.

With Boland severely dazed and all the doors jammed by the impact, Williams asked the chief to hold the fort inside the vehicle, while he climbed out of his window to remonstrate with the large numbers of jubilant NVA airmen and Stasi who were flocking to the scene. In no uncertain terms, Williams told the nearest NVA officer that this was no way to treat a general (his actual words were '*Mein general ist nicht amusiert!*') and that the Soviet *komendant* must be summoned immediately. In the meantime, narks were crawling all around the car taking photographs to use as 'evidence' of the tour's 'illegal' activities. Having made it clear that no one was going to be allowed to break into the car, the initial tension subsided and Williams – now joined outside by Brigadier Learmont, who uttered the immortal words in his appalling German, '*Mein bloody auto ist kaput*' – made a brew to help settle their nerves. When one of the narks poked his camera a little too close to Captain Williams, he was rewarded by half a cup of hot coffee in his face. Fearing that he had gone too far in 'assaulting' a Stasi official, Williams immediately apologised to Brigadier Learmont, who replied along the lines of, 'It's a good thing you did it because I was just about to do the same!'*

The Halberstadt *komendant* eventually arrived, and the incident settled into a normal, more leisurely detention, with the Soviet officer taking statements from the East German personnel involved so he could prepare his *Akt*, and the recovery vehicle and trailer was summoned from Potsdam. Six hours after the ambush, Major MacNair and the recovery crew arrived on site and the Senator was winched away from the Tatra – amazingly it could be driven under its own steam onto the recovery trailer, and the party headed home, reaching Berlin in the early hours. The REME workshops at Alexander Barracks estimated the rebuild of the DM40,000 car at DM64,000, so it was beyond economical repair and written off; understandably, Chiefs BRIXMIS never toured again in their shiny black official cars – they used normal tour vehicles. It also became clear that local knowledge from RAF tours (who all knew the area as 'Suicide Alley' and avoided it at all costs) was not being routinely shared with army tours, and vice versa, so the incident acted as a catalyst for improved army/RAF integration. The importance of thorough

---

* The Stasi report from Athenstedt specifically described the 'Kaffee in das Gesicht', or coffee in the face incident. It also described the ramming as a 'road traffic accident'!

tour preparation had also been demonstrated.* In 2011, Williams, who retired as a major general, visited the site of the incident and met with Hartmut Lüderitz, the driver of the Tatra-148. Former Unteroffizier (Sergeant) Lüderitz confirmed that the ambush had been explicitly at the instructions of the Stasi (sanctioned by no less than its chief, Erich Mielke) and the base had received a thirty-minute warning of the tour's arrival from the Stasi office in Halberstadt, which explains the large number of Stasi agents on site. Lüderitz received an extra two weeks' leave for his part, but he understood that if he had succeeded in killing an AMLM member, he would have received six weeks' leave and a bonus of 1,000 marks. Williams believes that the Stasi planned to attack and preferably kill a member of the AMLMs, *irrespective* of which mission and who was in the car – Brigadier Learmont would simply have been a bigger prize. Unfortunately, the AMLMs would not have to wait too long before the Stasi achieved their objective.[26]

Brigadier Learmont's narrow escape would not be the last incident at Athenstedt. On 13 September 1984 Squadron Leader Martin Common, with Master Engineer 'Chippy' Lee and Corporal Alan Hanson in Range Rover No. 3, were detained outside the gates of the radar site. Blocked in by NVA vehicles from the base, Common elected to accept the detention rather than attempt a risky escape (it was only six months after the Mariotti killing – see below), and the Range Rover was duly 'tarped'. Thankfully the rest of the incident proceeded without any escalation and the tour was sent on its way.

The Mariotti and Nicholson Murders

Despite some very near misses, the three missions survived thirty-seven years (thirty-eight in the case of BRIXMIS) of touring in the GDR without a fatality, but in 1984, and again in 1985, that was to change. Despite receiving vague intelligence that the Soviets or East Germans were planning an attack on an AMLM tour, operations continued unabated, with every tourer crossing the Glienicke Bridge knowing that they were potential targets.[27]

On 22 March 1984, Capitaine Jean-Paul Staub was leading an MMFL tour in the Halle-Lettin area, north-west of Leipzig, in Mercedes saloon No. 32 with tour NCO

---

* Brigadier Learmont was getting frustrated with how long it was taking for the recovery team to arrive so sent Captain Williams and the *komendant's* assistant, a young senior lieutenant, to the village to phone Potsdam for an update because there was, 'apparently', no phone at the NVA site. All the public telephones in the village had been vandalised, so they called at the local Vopo station to use their phone – it appeared to be unoccupied, but there was a large button next to the door, so the senior lieutenant pushed it. Rather than summon the Vopos, it triggered the air raid siren on the roof, waking up the whole village. The Russian thought this was hilarious and urged Captain Williams to push it again before the pair of them jumped back in the UAZ jeep and made a swift exit, giggling like naughty schoolchildren. The following day, Brigadier Learmont was summoned to SERB to receive a dressing down on behalf of C-in-C GSFG, being told that 'My Commander-in-Chief considers you are a hooligan!' This may have got lost in translation a bit, because 'hooliganism' was viewed as a very serious crime in the Soviet Union.

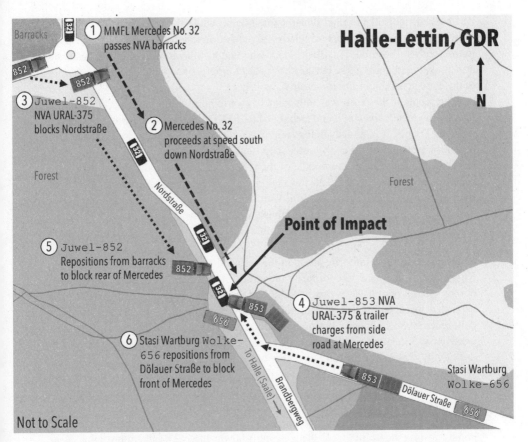

① MMFL Mercedes No. 32 passes NVA barracks

Halle-Lettin, GDR

N

Barracks

③ `Juwel-852` NVA URAL-375 blocks Nordstraße

② Mercedes No. 32 proceeds at speed south down Nordstraße

Forest

Forest

Point of Impact

⑤ `Juwel-852` Repositions from barracks to block rear of Mercedes

④ `Juwel-853` NVA URAL-375 & trailer charges from side road at Mercedes

⑥ Stasi Wartburg `Wolke-656` repositions from Dölauer Straße to block front of Mercedes

Stasi Wartburg `Wolke-656`

Dölauer Straße

Not to Scale

Nordstraße

To Halle (Saale)

Brandbergweg

The Mariotti fatal collision, 22 March 1984. (Author, based on contemporary Stasi and MMFL reports. Mapping c/o Openstreetmap)

Adjudant-Chef Jean-Marie Blancheton and driver Adjudant-Chef Philippe Mariotti.* Their objective was to see whether the NVA 11th Motorised Rifle Division (MRD) had deployed as part of a major NVA exercise (YUG-84). The tour did a planned drive-by of their barracks but seeing a lot of NVA activity, did not hang around to take pictures. As they were driving south on Nordstraße an NVA 4.5-ton URAL-375 truck and trailer (weighing more than 10 tons on the road) appeared out of a side road, veered across the central reservation into the path of the Mercedes and smashed into the front left corner, killing Mariotti instantly.† The impact was so great that the heavy Mercedes

---

* The French Army rank adjudant-chef is equivalent to a British Army warrant officer.

† The plaque mounted on a large boulder marking the spot on Nordstraße running between Halle and Lettin where Mariotti was killed reads in French and German: '22 March 1984, To the memory of Adjudant-chef Philippe Mariotti, member of the French Military Liaison Mission to the Group of Soviet Forces in Germany, he was the victim of a ramming by a vehicle from the security services of the DDR.'

was pushed right off the road down a small bank, while the truck mounted the tour vehicle and came to rest on its mangled roof. Staub was seriously injured and evacuated immediately to hospital, but Blancheton, who had also been injured in the head and arm, bravely remained at the crash site to guard Mariotti's body and ensure the security of the damaged vehicle and its sensitive contents.*

The scene of the crash was immediately swarming with Stasi agents, joined a bit later by the local *komendant* and Deputy Chief SERB, such was the seriousness of the incident. Despite it obviously being an ambush, the 'official' version was that Mariotti had been weaving all over the road supposedly 'under the influence' and the NVA driver had to drive along the middle of the road to avoid hitting the Frenchman, who subsequently skidded and crashed at high speed into the front right-hand side of the truck! Following the fall of the Berlin Wall, the Stasi archives revealed the full extent of the planning and execution of the ambush, which involved a team of nineteen agents working on a round-the-clock shift basis, nine vehicles, and the local KGB office. In the ambush they used two huge NVA URAL-375 trucks (driven by NVA soldiers but with a Stasi agent in NVA uniform sitting in the cab) and several unmarked Stasi Wartburg Knight radio cars, used to coordinate the attack. It transpired that the Stasi officer in charge, Oberst (Colonel) Gerhardt Wolff, had not obtained permission from Berlin to use lethal force, and was duly reprimanded; however, the driver of the truck and his colleagues involved in the actual ambush all received a bonus of 1,000 marks. The Stasi were not specifically targeting an MMFL tour, but any AMLM vehicle that arrived in the vicinity – such was the random nature of the game.

A year later, the tight-knit AMLM community had to face another tragedy, this time involving a USMLM officer. On 24 March 1985, Major Arthur D. 'Nick' Nicholson and his driver Staff Sergeant Jessie Schatz headed out on tour in Mercedes G-Wagen No. 23, tasked with gathering intelligence on the new Soviet T-80 main battle tank, hoping to investigate the tank sheds at the Ludwigslust 475 sub-calibre range near Ludwigslust-Techentin in the north-west corner of the GDR, and on the other side of the road from the boundary of the Lübtheen PRA. After carefully observing the shed for some time, they gingerly made their approach, allowing Nicholson to jump out and photograph some open-air training poster boards and a tank mock-up. They then repositioned to the other end of the shed where Nicholson hoped to make entry and photograph whatever was inside.

As Nicholson was trying the door to the shed, a Soviet sentry, Junior Sergeant Rjabtsev, emerged from the treeline some 75 metres away and rapidly approached the Americans with his AK-74 raised. Without a warning (something which the Soviets would deny later), the guard opened fire – the first shot narrowly missed Schatz, but a subsequent shot hit Nicholson in the torso. Rjabtsev held his gun to Schatz's head while his tour officer bled out and died just a few metres behind the Mercedes.†

---

* Blancheton, the tour NCO, refused to let the East Germans take Mariotti's body to a mortuary because he feared they would inject his corpse with alcohol to fake evidence proving that Mariotti was drunk, and it was that which caused the 'accident'.

† A memorial stone to Major Nicholson was unveiled on the twentieth anniversary of his death at the turnoff from the B-191 that led to the Ludwigslust-475 sub-calibre range.

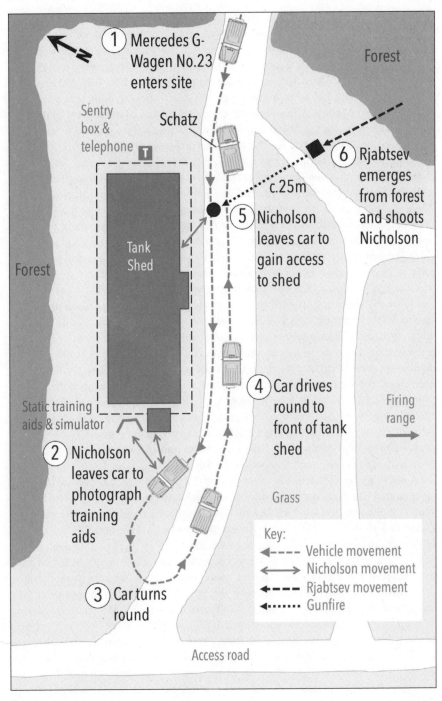

1 Mercedes G-Wagen No.23 enters site

Sentry box & telephone

Schatz

6 Rjabtsev emerges from forest and shoots Nicholson

Forest

c.25m

5 Nicholson leaves car to gain access to shed

Tank Shed

Forest

4 Car drives round to front of tank shed

Firing range

Static training aids & simulator

2 Nicholson leaves car to photograph training aids

Grass

Key:
- - - - Vehicle movement
⟷ Nicholson movement
- - - Rjabtsev movement
••••• Gunfire

3 Car turns round

Access road

The scene of the Nicholson fatal shooting, 24 March 1985. (Author, based on contemporary Stasi and USMLM reports)

While the response to the Mariotti killing had been deliberately kept low key, the Nicholson shooting blew up into a major international incident, which eventually threatened inter-mission solidarity. The recriminations between the Soviets and Americans were bitter, with the situation escalating very quickly and even reaching the White House and Kremlin – the first US–Soviet crisis since Mikhail Gorbachev had taken over in Moscow. A key sticking point was a loophole in the Huebner–Malinin Agreement that classified 'places of disposition of military units' as being *restricted* to the missions – the clause only appeared in the HMA and not in the RMA or NMA. Therefore, according to the Soviets, the USMLM tour had no right to be there and Rjabtsev was entitled to use lethal force, acted properly and within his standing orders. However, as with most confrontations with the Soviets, the facts were confused and obfuscated by political influence. There is every possibility that the Soviet guard acted independently but given the Stasi operation to ambush an AMLM tour at Halle-Lettin the previous year, it is also possible that the guard was fronting a more elaborate operation, especially given the sensitivity of the new T-80 tank. BRIXMIS chose to resume touring as soon as possible after Major Nicholson's funeral, but the American negotiations with the Soviets lasted almost a year, during which USMLM activity was severely restricted.[28] The thrust of the US negotiations was to iron out some of the grey areas associated with touring, thus making the activity safer for their personnel; however, this caused some inter-mission friction, especially with the British, who had been actively exploiting the inherent ambiguities in the practice since 1946 and felt that the creation of rules (especially surrounding MRSs) would *hamper* BRIXMIS operations, not aid them. As a result, BRIXMIS was forced to distance themselves from the changes USMLM were pushing for, falling back on the terms of their own agreement with the Soviets, the RMA. Intelligence continued to be shared, but the solidarity between BRIXMIS and USMLM was tested in the process. It was several years before USMLM regained their momentum and recommenced the full range of activities, including socialising with the Soviets.[29]

A contributing factor to the incident was the probability that the AMLMs had 'over-toured' the tank sheds at Ludwigslust-Techentin, alerting the Soviets to their interest in the site. In October 1984 an MMFL tour was disturbed while examining a tank and shot at. USMLM had visited there twice in 1985, on 25 January and 18 March, the second visit being only six days before Nicholson's death, so it would have been clear to the Soviets that more tours could be expected as they searched for the elusive new Soviet tank, and that an ambush was feasible. A subject brought up several times by the Soviets in the negotiations (and long recognised by BRIXMIS personnel) was the issue of USMLM members wearing *camouflaged* combat uniform (woodland BDU), which was the standard uniform of the US military. In the Soviet military, camo was only worn by special forces at the time, so the average conscript soldier could have assumed the Americans were special forces and therefore up to no good – camo was known to elicit a more aggressive response from ordinary soldiers during a detention. As a result, BRIXMIS continued to wear non-camo olive green uniforms long after the British Army transitioned to DPM camouflage.

Violence

Violence was an ever-present threat to BRIXMIS tours despite the protections supposedly provided by the mission agreement; however, unlike most examples of conflict, it was almost universally one-sided. *Unarmed* tours would be subjected to violent assaults by *armed* opponents but could not retaliate without risking an almost certain PNG, thus ending their posting with the Mission – tourers repeatedly showed their fortitude through self-restraint in the face of extreme provocation. The pages of this book have detailed some examples of this violence, in two notorious cases leading to the death of tour personnel, but it is worth reflecting on the dangers tour personnel faced every time they crossed the Glienicke Bridge.

First, it should be remembered that in most cases the tour had every right to be where they were according to the terms of the RMA. The Soviets and/or East Germans may not have appreciated the presence of the green painted cars lurking in the bushes and had the right to detain the tour if it was deemed acting outside those terms, but the levels of aggression and physical violence far exceeded that right. Second, serious incidents involving the Soviets or East Germans would, of course, be raised with SERB and if necessary, protests were made at C-in-C or even governmental level, although very little would ever come from them – apologies or remedial action were extremely rare. In almost every case, the Soviet (or East German) account of the incident relied very little on the truth. A violent ramming would be classified as a road-traffic accident with the mission vehicle to blame ... a shooting incident would be blamed on the unarmed tour member sufficiently scaring the armed sentry that he discharged his weapon in fear of his life. Third, every incident involving violence, injury, accident, or damage was carefully reviewed, and lessons learnt were shared with current tour personnel, the other missions, and the training school at Ashford, building a huge base knowledge and experience of operating inside East Germany. Finally, it is important to note that much of the violence was meted out by Stasi thugs or NVA troops – because the Western Allies did not diplomatically 'recognise' the GDR, all complaints involving East Germans had to be processed through SERB and GSFG, adding an extra layer of complication and more opportunity for obfuscation. While there is no doubt that the Soviets were in overall charge, they had a complicated and delicate 'parent and child' or 'master and servant' relationship with the East Germans, where privately they may have been shocked and dismayed at the Stasi's tactics, they publicly supported them. That said, after the fall of the Berlin Wall, the true extent of the collusion and collaboration in counter-mission operations between the Soviets and East Germans was discovered, including the existence of special Soviet 'blocking' units, adding an extra layer of nuance and confusion.

Physical assaults were relatively common, and included having the car windows smashed with rocks or rifle butts, occupants being dragged out of the car and beaten up, held at gun point, tied up, or bundled into the back of a truck. In the 1972 incident that led to his PNG, Squadron Leader Rod Saar was knocked to the ground by a member of a Spetsnaz hit squad, given a good kicking and had the muzzle of an AKM rifle shoved into his neck. In 1974 Squadron Leader Brian Speed was tied up and bundled into the back of a ZIL-130 truck at gunpoint, breaking his collarbone. In 1975, Flight

Lieutenant Leslie Davies and his team were bundled into the back of a GAZ-66 4WD light utility truck and the canvas cover was tied tightly down, trapping them inside on a very hot day for several hours. In 1982, Flight Lieutenant Alan Bouchard, Sergeant Tony Haw, and Corporal Anderson were ambushed by a group of Soviet soldiers, who dragged Bouchard and Anderson out of the car, assaulted them and tied them up away from the car. After a struggle, Haw was extracted and tied up with the others and they remained like that for four hours. In most of these incidents, the tour car was ransacked, and the contents stolen, despite the inviolability promised by the RMA.

Rammings could be particularly violent, where the Soviets and East Germans used their vehicles as battering rams to smash into vehicles, pushing them off the road, rendering them undriveable, and in many cases injuring the occupants. The strengthening and armour added to tour cars ('panzer plates', roll cages) protected the occupants to a certain degree, but it was hard to argue with the impact (sometimes high-speed impact) of a massive truck. In 1976, Major Simon Gordon-Duff's tour car was forced off the road by two motorcycles, presumably ridden by Stasi. He was then rammed by a 4.5-ton NVA URAL-375 truck, which climbed the bonnet of the Opel Admiral, smashed the right-hand corner of the passenger compartment, and continued right over the car before it toppled on its side. Sergeant Bob Thomas, the tour NCO, was trapped in the car with a badly broken leg. An East German ambulance and NVA soldiers from the base arrived but only the ambulance crew plus a few civilians were permitted to help Sergeant Thomas – the NVA officer called his troops away. Sergeant Thomas was eventually freed and taken to an East German hospital, but a very shaken and bruised Gordon-Duff and his driver had to wait twelve hours before the BRIXMIS recovery crew arrived from Berlin. In 1981, a tour car was repeatedly rammed by a massive 21-ton MAZ-537 tank transporter tractor unit, but managed to make a miraculous escape. In 1983 a tour was forced to reverse 1.5 kilometres along a track at high speed with a 12-ton KrAZ 255B and a 3.5-ton ZIL-131 truck in hot pursuit, eventually being rammed by both vehicles. In 1985 a tour comprising Captain Guy Potter, Sergeant Nick Rowles, and Corporal Paul Roberts was pursued at high speed by a GAZ-66 truck with Komendatura markings. It drove into the side of the tour car at about 40 kph, lifting the car off the ground and ripping two tyres off the wheel rims. Soviet soldiers then piled out of the GAZ and began attacking the tour car with shovels and bricks. The tour managed to escape and found a garage in the small village of Schorbus to make some basic repairs. With the tour car up on jacks and one wheel off, the GAZ caught up with them again, spilling out the same soldiers who surrounded the vehicle, this time armed with assault rifles. In full view of the tour party, the soldiers were ostentatiously issued with live rounds, which they loaded into their weapons, made them ready and flicked off the safety catches. The officer accompanying the soldiers was heard to give his men permission to shoot, if necessary. While the tourers were talking to the local *komendant*, a Soviet officer leant into the car, stole Rowles's tour bag, and ran off. Tours were also subjected to aggressive ultra-low-level attacks by Soviet and East German helicopters, missing the car or tour personnel in the open by only a matter of feet.

Over the years, tour cars and tourers were shot at on numerous occasions – the Corporal Day and Major Nicholson incidents illustrate just how dangerous these could be. Apart from these high-profile cases, the relatively few injuries because of shootings can be attributed to three key factors. First, although most Soviet sentries carried live ammunition, their marksmanship was poor, and most shots missed their target. Second, the robust construction of tour cars and the large amount of equipment carried provided extra protection for the occupants. Third, experience ensured that most tours avoided these situations in the first place, but if fired on, the skills of the drivers (and quick reactions of the NCOs and officers) normally allowed the tour to escape, albeit with a few more ventilation holes in their vehicle. A good example was from 1976 when the Mission GSO1, Lieutenant Colonel Coe, was on tour with tour NCO Sergeant Ben Campbell and driver Corporal Alan Gough in the Dresden area. Against the advice of his NCO, Coe climbed over a barracks wall in the early hours of the morning to photograph what was inside. As he was climbing back over, he was spotted by a guard in a watchtower, who opened fire, hitting the tour car several times. Coe made it back to the car and Gough left the city at speed, only pulling over so Campbell could have a frank discussion with the lieutenant colonel about his life choices. Some of the injuries inflicted on tour personnel over the life of the AMLMs were life changing (or fatal in two cases), but apart from high-level protests, the AMLMs could do little in response. However, their ultimate weapon against violence or unreasonable behaviour was reciprocity.

Reciprocity

The principle of reciprocity was at the heart of mission operations for both East and West – *whatever you do to us, we can do to you* – and that simple principle allowed the AMLMs to coexist within the complex geopolitical landscape of Cold War Germany. In theory, any breach of the 1946/1947 agreements on one side would lead to an equivalent act by the other, and this was understood by all parties, at least at senior levels. Both sides recognised the value of their missions (perhaps for different reasons), and the valuable intelligence that would be lost should they be stopped, and this was normally enough to self-police the system. The mechanism most associated with reciprocity was making somebody persona non grata (PNG), which banned them from entering or forced them to leave a country. For example, if the Soviets PNG'd a BRIXMIS officer (for crimes real or imaginary), a SOXMIS officer (often an innocent bystander) would automatically be PNG'd, in the same way as reciprocal diplomatic expulsions, and vice versa. Other methods included restricting mission access by increasing PRAs or imposing TRAs (which would normally be countered by an equivalent restriction), or by pointedly excluding (or uninviting) the opposition from high-profile formal functions or events. An invitation to the Queen's birthday parade at the Olympic Stadium and the reception after at the Mission House was much sought after and the Soviets were obsessed with keeping up appearances. However, while the scorecard was meant to be even, in practice, many of the outrages perpetrated by the Soviets and East Germans (shootings, rammings, physical violence, theft of equipment) resulted only in protests that led nowhere as the allied powers would not countenance the sort of anti-mission tactics employed by the Soviets and East Germans. Although the tactics of Western counterintelligence personnel tasked with monitoring the SMLMs may have been robust at times, they certainly lacked the violence and brutality routinely meted out to British, American, and French tours.

HQ BAOR was often slow to recognise the need for swift and proportionate retaliation to incidents involving the Soviets; in the early years, especially under the influence of the Foreign Office, it could often take weeks or months for a decision to be made and by the time a sanction was agreed, the moment had passed. There was also a tendency for every incident to be looked at in isolation, rather than as an evolving pattern of behaviour that could be used to challenge the Soviets. Reciprocity was not tested until 1952 when the AMLMs began to experience a much more hostile touring environment inside the GDR. Detentions increased, as did harassment, overt surveillance, and pass problems, and passive measures included increases in PRA/TRAs, the establishment of excessive numbers of road barriers, roadblocks, and checkpoints across the country, and even the availability of good-quality fuel. The Soviets denied they were clamping down on AMLM tours and they could not be held responsible for the actions of the East Germans (which of course was nonsense). The three AMLMs met on 28 April 1952 to discuss the countermeasures that could be introduced in the three former Western zones of (West) Germany, recognising that collective action would be far more effective than unilateral efforts. Effective 27 June 1952, USAREUR, BAOR, and FFA (Forces Françaises en Allemagne) began a policy of overt surveillance on all SMLM vehicles, thus radically curtailing the effectiveness of their touring (and presumably other espionage activities). The Soviets protested, until it was pointed out that they had ignored similar protests by the AMLMs in the Soviet zone. The Soviets approached BAOR first to ask that in return for stopping the surveillance on SOXMIS, they would reciprocate with BRIXMIS, and this was subsequently rolled out with USMLM, MMFL, and the other SMLMs, returning to a more 'enlightened' touring environment.

A prompt response to an incident was critical. Major Jonathan Backhouse was PNG'd in 1966 after being detained behind an MRS at Oranienbaum, near Dessau. This offence was relatively minor (the AMLMs did not recognise MRSs as they were not covered by the mission agreements) and certainly did not warrant a PNG but despite protests, GSFG refused to reverse their decision.[30] After weeks of discussion between JHQ Rheindahlen, Bonn, and London, the Foreign Office ruled that no action should be taken because Harold Wilson, the prime minister, was about to pay an official visit to Moscow. Three months later the FO changed their mind and authorised a reciprocal PNG, and a random SOXMIS officer, Major Sokolov, was detained for a minor infraction and immediately PNG'd. This late PNG, however, backfired, when the Soviets instantly retaliated (choosing to ignore the original connection between the Backhouse and Sokolov PNGs) and PNG'd a new BRIXMIS officer, Squadron Leader Neil McLean, the very next day.[31] The Soviets clearly knew how to play the game, and were happy to play hardball, while the British could be a bit too 'British' about such things. The Americans, on the other hand, deployed their Counterintelligence Corps energetically, ensuring any incident involving the USMLM was immediately repaid in kind to the SMLM in the American zone (although they would draw the line at shooting).

The job of keeping tabs on the SOXMIS tourers was given to 19 (Support) Platoon, 113 Provost Company, Royal Military Police. They drove high-performance, modified white police cars, which led to their British nickname, the 'White Mice' (SOXMIS called them the 'Crows'). Members of 19 SP Platoon would wait outside the gates of the SOXMIS compound in Bünde and tail the Soviet tour cars to try to limit what they saw, detaining them if they entered a PRA/TRA. The SOXMIS crews would, of course, do their best to evade the White Mice, such was the game. Interventions were robust and could involve boxing-in or 'blanketing' using British Army blankets to cover all the windows, the British equivalent to 'tarping', but incidents of bodily violence against SOXMIS tourers were rare and would prompt instant retaliatory action against BRIXMIS. BAOR soldiers and their families were issued with SOXMIS cards (BAOR Form 674 or BFG Form 66) that gave instructions of what to look for and who to call if they spotted a SOXMIS car. 19 (Support) Platoon operated overtly, working together with their covert colleagues from 28 Intelligence Section based at Herford. Soviet troops in East Germany were issued a similar card following the Nicholson incident but were much less likely to respond – few would want to voluntarily get involved with the organs of state security and would typically ignore any unusual activity, unless they were with a senior or political officer.[32]

The only documented reversal of a PNG was with Major Bob Godfrey and Major Patterson in 1970 where a specific threat of retaliation against SOXMIS prompted a very surprising U-turn from GSFG. The Soviets appeared to be particularly concerned that unilateral East German action would jeopardise their position in West Germany, although after the fall of the Wall in 1989, the Stasi files revealed a high degree of coordination and complicity between the two communist regimes.

Conclusion

'That Gorbachev, he's got a lot to answer for!'
Former tour NCO to
Major General P. G. Williams
CMG OBE (2008)[1]

The End of the Mission

The writing had been on the wall for some time, with Gorbachev's *perestroika* (reconstruction or restructuring) and *glasnost* (openness) reforming policies, although the signals on the ground inside the GDR were mixed. On one hand, there were troop withdrawals from East Germany, and on the other, rearmament continued, with new military technology appearing, while a strong and resolute NATO watched from West Germany, and the AMLMs watched from within. The Group of Soviet Forces Germany (GSFG) was renamed the Western Group of Forces (WGF) on 1 June 1989 under General Snetkov and their stance, allegedly, shifted from offensive to defensive, although the rearmament would suggest otherwise. There was also a dangerous breakdown in discipline, reflecting, perhaps, the death throes of the Soviet Union, which would only survive another eighteen months. Touring became far more unpredictable and therefore dangerous, as Soviet soldiers, from the commanders to the conscripts, began to think for themselves, and detentions became fraught with confusion and continued violence. Meanwhile, across East Germany, the will of the long-suffering East German population began to push back on Honecker's hard-line regime. The fall of the Berlin Wall on Thursday, 9 November 1989 came as a surprise to most, not least the East Germans. Erich Honecker's prediction in January 1989 that the Wall would last a hundred years was overtaken by events, but few predicted the seismic changes that were on the horizon.

Chief BRIXMIS, Brigadier Ian Freer, was out on tour with Captain Ian Cameron-Mowat as his tour NCO and Corporal Kevin Powell as his driver, noting among other things, a new section of East German border fortification, a triple-layered monstrosity bristling with electronic sensors and insulators – presumably electrified. The first they heard that something was amiss was via the BBC on the car radio. They returned to Potsdam immediately to be greeted by zombielike creatures stumbling around the town – worse-for-wear East Germans having returned home after the party of their lives. Some, presumably die-hard communists, looked shell-shocked. Others were positively jubilant, waving, smiling, and congratulating Freer's party, when in reality, their part in this momentous occasion involved sitting in a wood in East Germany, cooking a curry and munching Crunchie bars! 'The opening of the Berlin Wall on 9 November 1989 was totally unexpected. Neither we [BRIXMIS], the people we were coming in contact with, nor the Russians had any inkling that the East German State was about to collapse. It caught us all by surprise.'[2]

From a military viewpoint, the chain of command was desperate to know what was going on, specifically how the Soviets were reacting. SERB were completely in the dark. As for the East Germans, BRIXMIS had no remit to engage with them, so could only report what they saw. The confusion seen by the world on the television was a fair representation of the chaos on the ground. Eventually there was a message from SERB saying that it was a German issue, and their forces would be remaining in barracks, which was at least some relief. The Stasi briefly tried to reassert their authority, but without the support of the Vopos and NVA, who appeared equally baffled, it failed, and people power genuinely triumphed.

The 'back-channel' with the Soviets established through BRIXMIS became very important in the days that followed. General Snetkov, C-in-C WGF, contacted SERB, who contacted BRIXMIS to express his concern about the pace of events in Berlin, specifically the opening of the Wall around Potsdamer Platz (which he wanted stopped for some reason), and his concerns about the security of the Soviet War Memorial in Tiergarten. Freer relayed Snetkov's concerns to GOC Berlin, Major General Robert Corbett, who discussed them with the British Ambassador to West Germany, Sir Christopher Mallaby. In an interesting turn of events, Berlin's unique four-power status had trumped the longstanding BRIXMIS–SERB–GSFG/WGF communications route and Snetkov, normally king of all he surveyed, was usurped by higher powers, being told that his concerns about Berlin were already being discussed at head-of-state (Gorbachev and Thatcher), commandant (Corbett), and ambassadorial (Mallaby) level, and *these were the preferred channels for future discussions* – WGF did not really have a say in the matter. While reassuring him that the West Berlin Police had increased their presence at the war memorial (with the British RMP and Major General Corbett keeping an eye on things), Freer's message was very clear – the balance of power had shifted almost overnight in favour of the West.

One practical implication of the relaxation of travel restrictions for the citizens of East and West Berlin was the incongruous situation where East German Trabants and Wartburgs could cross the Glienicke Bridge freely without any checks, but AMLM vehicles still had to go through the rigmarole of submitting their passes for inspection, often having to queue behind lines of smelly two-strokes after more than three decades of having the bridge to themselves. On New Year's Eve, there was a huge party on the bridge, a surreal experience for all concerned, especially the Soviet guards, who were still on duty and who looked on with bemused curiosity.[3] Another knock-on effect was that the AMLMs could not get away with their habitual lawless behaviour while in the GDR, and people power meant that tours had to become good citizens.[4]

The days for the Mission were clearly numbered, as the strategic threat from the East diminished by the day. The last day of touring was to be Tuesday, 2 October 1990, a day before German Reunification (or Unity) Day. BRIXMIS put out seven tours into

East Germany, on the last day of its existence. They congregated at Klein Behnitz, a tiny hamlet some 40 kilometres west of Berlin, where they were joined by three more crews, and they all enjoyed a barbecue in the shade of some trees and next to a Mission Restricted Sign – a final irony. They all returned to the Potsdam Mission House, joining the Mission staff from West Berlin and members of SERB for a party to celebrate (or commiserate) the termination of the Robertson–Malinin Agreement and the end of the Mission's mission. Brigadier Freer delivered a short speech marking the significance of the day, acknowledging the termination of the RMA that had served them well for forty-four years, but stressing their important liaison work should continue. The party moved outside, and the Union Jack was lowered to the Last Post, played by a bugler from 1st Battalion Royal Welsh Fusiliers, one of the battalions from the Berlin Infantry Brigade. Afterwards, the SERB officers were presented with BRIXMIS plaques and other mementoes, and the party broke up just before 1900 hours. Soon after, all ten BRIXMIS vehicles crossed the Glienicke Bridge in convoy to the sounds of car horns and the waves of Potsdamers who had come out to see them off. Interestingly, the SERB officers seemed 'tired and dispirited' and upset at the rather bombastic and triumphalist USMLM deactivation ceremony the previous day, which was attended by a host of dignitaries, including the Deputy CINCUSAREUR, Lieutenant General John Shalikashvili (a future USCINCEUR, Supreme Allied Commander, Europe for NATO, and Chairman of the Joint Chiefs of Staff), and General Konovalenko, ACOS G2 (Intelligence) WGF, who was humiliated by the spectacle. The British event was much more low key, and Freer and his colleagues did their best to bolster morale and reassure their (former) Soviet counterparts. BRIXMIS also had to make representations to BAOR on behalf of SERB and HQ WGF about the treatment of SOXMIS, which had effectively been gated by new regulations – their liaison mission continued right until the end.

The formal closing ceremony for BRIXMIS took place at the Potsdam Mission House on 10 December 1990 and was attended by Lieutenant General L. V. Kuznetsov, COS WGF, Lieutenant General Tarasenko, C-in-C 16th Soviet Air Army, Air Vice-Marshal P. J. Harding, Deputy C-in-C RAFG, Colonel R. I. Polozov, Chief SERB, with eight other Russian officers, with Brigadier Freer, Chief BRIXMIS, presiding. Among the many guests were two former chiefs: General Sir John Learmont (by now Quartermaster General) and Major General B. W. Davis (Chairman, BRIXMIS Association). The ceremony was closed by a lone piper from the Irish Guards (another battalion of the Berlin Infantry Brigade) playing The Lament.[5]

The Mission House had already been cleared of all furniture that was not needed for the closing ceremony, and the rest was removed in preparation for the formal handover of the site on 3 January 1991. The intrigue was not quite over – the ownership of the mansion at Seestraße 34–37 was passed to the German Federal Property Agency, who were charged with disposing of the legacy assets from the occupation, preferably handing them back to the pre-occupation owners. However, in 1945, the previous occupants had been given just three hours' notice to leave by the victorious Red Army and unfortunately no paper trail survived to identify (or prove) the owners. The former Mission House, probably still containing some of the electronic bugs planted by the East Germans, was eventually sold into private ownership.

The BRIXMIS personnel remaining in Berlin continued their training to stay 'match fit', although they were not sure what game they were in now. Slowly but surely the numbers diminished as regiments and battalions recalled their soldiers from this very unconventional posting. Although the AMLMs were no more, there were still hundreds of thousands of Soviet troops inside the former East Germany, armed to the teeth, and still receiving new KIT from the Soviet Union. With the chaos from home sounding the death knell for the great communist experiment, it became hugely important to know what the Western Group of Forces were up to in the run-up to their agreed departure by the end of August 1994. The threat to NATO was still there, with the centres of power within the rapidly disintegrating Warsaw Pact shifting dangerously with these unprecedented geopolitical changes. The solution was to keep sending tours into the former East Germany, but what authority would they be working under, and what protection would they have? After all, the RMA, NMA, and HMA had all terminated at Reunification. The new player in the mix was the BND, the Bundesnachrichtendienst or German Federal Intelligence Service, whose remit now included the former East Germany. The British made overtures to the Bundeswehr's Liaison Command around the time of Reunification to work with the BND but were rebuffed in favour of the deeper pockets of the Americans. Uncle Sam had created a new unit in Berlin called the Combined Analysis Detachment, Berlin (CAD-B), based in the old USMLM HQ at Föhrenweg 19/21, but following Major Nicholson's death in 1985, they were not going to send their people out without a safety net. A memorandum of understanding (MoU) between USAREUR and the BND was therefore signed on 7 May 1991, which was a watered-down version of the Huebner–Malinin Agreement of 1947, giving CAD-B a pseudo-legal framework in which to operate inside the former East Germany – the intelligence-collection operations would be codenamed BLACKFOOT and GIRAFFE. The deal was that a small unit of the BND (known as 12YA, run by a Bundeswehr lieutenant colonel) would do the actual intelligence collection, and CAD-B would do the targeting and analysis, based on their extensive knowledge of WGF. Unlike the AMLMs, the German tourers, who were mostly Bundeswehr officers, would be using unmarked cars and wearing plain clothes. 12YA would be co-located with CAD-B at Föhrenweg, and the role would extend beyond observing KIT (TECHINT) to recruiting disaffected Soviets (HUMINT) to better understand what WGF was intending. HUMINT sources, their allegiance and obedience probably secured by some compromising material (Kompromat – photos, sound recordings), could then be useful after they returned to the Soviet Union/Russian Federation. All this activity was, of course, contrary to the spirit, if not the letter of the Soviet-German 'Treaty on good-neighbourliness, partnership and cooperation' signed in Bonn by Mikhail Gorbachev and Helmut Kohl on 9 November 1990. These CAD-B/12YA tours were similar to those previously undertaken by USMLM, including the searching of rubbish dumps (a continuation of USMLM's Operation SANDDUNE, the equivalent to BRIXMIS's TAMARISK/TOMAHAWK), which continued to be very fruitful, especially as units prepared for withdrawal, when anything and everything was chucked away.[6] The HUMINT efforts combined covert approaches to Soviet personnel, but also crude overt shopping expeditions where they drove a hire car packed with Western goodies to Zossen-Wünsdorf and let it be known among the soldiers that they were interested in military documents of any kind. Queues of Soviet soldiers would form up at the BND officer's car, with video recorders, toasters, and Sony Walkmans being handed over in exchange for secret documents – a surreal and unique scene.[7]

The BND/Bundeswehr officers, however, lacked the cumulative tactical experience of more than four decades of AMLM touring and soon got into trouble. In April 1991 (a month before the MoU was signed), a Major Weiß of Potsdam-based Verbindungskreiskommando 84 (VBK-84, District Liaison Command 84) was shot and wounded after stumbling onto an ultra-secure enclosure occupied by the Soviet 1648th Mobile Rocket Technical Base where nuclear warheads were reputedly stored. Weiß survived but it could have been so much worse – the relative inexperience of the BND/Bundeswehr tours could have easily got someone killed and damaged the fragile relationship between the newly unified Germany and the disintegrating Soviet Union. After this, the 12YA began to directly involve the hugely experienced operators from CAD-B with intelligence collection on the ground.[8]

Although the British were supposed to see all CAD-B's intelligence, they were not prepared to play second fiddle after leading the AMLM effort for all those years. However, negotiations with the Germans broke down in late spring 1991 – the Germans were already well advanced in negotiations with the Americans by then. The German stipulation that the British Commanders'-in-Chief Liaison Team to the Soviet Western Group of Forces, the CLT, be limited to just two liaison officers plus an interpreter and driver based out of Rheindahlen – 500 kilometres as the crow flies from London Block in West Berlin – was not practical or acceptable. The British therefore decided to launch their own operation, albeit under the radar, and established an Intelligence Corps cell in Berlin called the Joint Intelligence Staff (Berlin) or JIS(B), commanded by Lieutenant Colonel Gordon Kerr, who had transferred from intelligence duties in Northern Ireland.[9] The unit was mostly staffed by former BRIXMIS personnel (who were very happy to remain in Berlin), and they used BRIXMIS's old offices at London Block, adopted the same routines and procedures, and kept most of the back-office infrastructure (wall map, Special Section, ELECTRIC LIGHT). Everything was planned with the same BRIXMIS professionalism, but the biggest differences were the absence of an RMA-style legal framework, and that tours were operating in unmarked cars and in plain clothes. The new unit had a strength of twenty-two (similar mix to BRIXMIS) and four civilians in support.

Over time, the operation took on its own character and became less structured than BRIXMIS, reflecting its more nebulous role. For a start, they dressed casually in civilian clothes, nothing too fancy or trendy, the idea being to blend in with the East Germans – a group photo from 1992 shows an interesting collection of C&A pullovers! Cars were rented from Hertz, usually VW Golfs or similar, and had Berlin numberplates. They were garaged in the former BRIXMIS vehicle yard and every two to three weeks were swapped for shiny new ones. Most tours were crewed by two personnel, and in the early days of JIS(B), experienced former BRIXMIS personnel were paired with newcomers to the unit to pass on the knowledge – occasionally solo tours would be made. This made JIS(B) touring closer to the former USMLM style of touring in terms of risk and split of duties. There were two major geographical differences for JIS(B): first, there were no PRAs or TRAs to restrain them, so the whole of the former GDR was up for grabs; and second, tours only lasted one day – there and back in a day and no overnighting. Therefore, tours going to the far extremes of the former GDR such as the Baltic coast, or down to the Czech border would have fewer objectives than those closer to Berlin. Tours also now had to obey German traffic laws, and while some sections of the German autobahn network had unrestricted speed limits, the quality of road infrastructure in the east meant that longer travel times were expected. The cars were also standard specification, without the BRIXMIS upgrades and added protection, so there were no high-speed, off-road excursions, as experienced with the Mission G-Wagens. However, they carried similar photographic equipment – Nikon F3 35-mm cameras with 500-mm and 1,000-mm lenses, a 35-mm autofocus point-and-shoot camera, stabilised binoculars, and handheld tape recorders. Birdwatching and nature photography were now far more credible excuses if stopped, as was walking around with a dog lead in hand (without a dog on the end), claiming they were looking for their lost dog! Foot recces were far more common. Without the BRIXMIS, USMLM, and MMFL tri-mission coordination, it became more common to bump into fellow post-mission travellers, such as CAD-B operators. Other aspects of the JIS(B) operation, however, were very similar – daily recognition training, daily ops briefings, tasking would come from the same sources, and the post-tour routine was the same (apart from the stop-off at Föhrenweg 19/21). The touring environment changed, of course, as the new unified Germany began to come to terms with itself. The Stasi had dissolved, although the WGF remained in a fluid state as their withdrawal was organised – they were still heavily armed but lacking direction, purpose, and discipline. Security, however, became more relaxed and it was sometimes possible for tourers to pop into guard rooms on bases and have a chat with the soldiers inside. Round the back of bases, a lively trade in Soviet hardware and knick-knacks was being conducted – the going rate for a Soviet assault rifle was DM100. There was also the surreal experience of being welcomed into former closely guarded Soviet installations (still full of formerly closely guarded Soviet KIT) as open days were held, trying to project a benevolent image after four decades of occupation, guided tours included. Sharp-eyed, Russian-speaking, and light-fingered JIS(B) tourers picked up all kinds of useful information, including an operations manual for the T-80 main battle tank, and got to climb inside (and comprehensively photograph) the infamous and highly elusive 2S6 Tunguska anti-aircraft system, previously only seen through a 500- or 1,000-mm lens. JIS(B) also borrowed a Gazelle helicopter belonging to 7 Flight, Army Air Corps to tour from the air, the Chipmunks having been 'returned' to the RAF for their own use, and continued BRIXMIS's TOMAHAWK scavenging, albeit mostly in broad daylight – the Soviets did not seem to care. If questioned, they said they were looking for scrap metal, which in the eyes of the Soviets at the time was a perfectly reasonable explanation. Detentions did occur, which normally involved the local *komendant*, who was still theoretically in charge of his area, and the now unified German police, who now did not answer to the Soviets in any way – tours were normally let off with a 'Don't let us catch you doing this again'. This was still in the days before mobile phones were widely in use, and the former East Germany lagged in cellular infrastructure anyway.

Eventually political pressure curtailed JIS(B)'s unofficial freelancing in the former East Germany, with the British Government valuing their relationship with the new

Germany more than the possible intelligence value from the disintegrating WGF, and JIS(B) was closed in early 1994 – CAD-B lasted until 1996, although they were forced to leave Berlin as the allies departed in 1994. It is believed that the French also had a similar off-the-books operation. Although BRIXMIS was no more, British forces remained in Berlin with their American and French allies until the final Soviet forces left in August 1994 – former BRIXMIS Chipmunks participated in the farewell ceremony flypasts, the last hurrah for this extraordinary unit.

On 17 September 2016, to mark the seventieth anniversary of the signing of the Robertson–Malinin Agreement, a memorial stone was unveiled at the National Memorial Arboretum in Staffordshire dedicated to the men and women who had served with the British Commanders'-in-Chief Mission to the Soviet Forces in Germany 1946–1990. The inscription on the front face is from Major General Miles Fitzalan-Howard, 17th Duke of Norfolk, KG, GCVO, CB, CBE, MC, DL Chief of Mission, 1957–1959, stating:

> *'The Cold War ended with a bloodless victory and the*
> *victory was ours.'*

Afterword

*'BRIXMIS was a unique organisation which operated in
a unique period of history, and its products were
uniquely valuable.'*

John Morrison,
Ministry of Defence (2001)[1]

The afterword of this book has been left to the late John Morrison of the British Ministry of Defence. As deputy chief of Defence Intelligence and head of the Defence Intelligence Analysis Staff (a senior Civil Service position equivalent to a two-star general), Mr Morrison's team at the Defence Intelligence Staff was the chief customer for BRIXMIS's intelligence product and was in an ideal position to comment on their 'uniquely valuable' contribution. The following passage is taken from Mr Morrison's talk at the Royal Air Force Historical Society (RAFHS) Seminar on Cold War Intelligence Gathering, which took place on 18 April 2000.

BRIXMIS was not only unique in its origins but had the following unique attributes.

Access
Despite the vexations of Permanent and Temporary Restricted Areas, BRIXMIS could get up close to Soviet forces and their equipment. It could observe and photograph them from the side, from the air and (in the case of aircraft) from below. In some, by now well-documented cases, it achieved hands-on contact with new pieces of kit or pilfered items.

Legitimacy
BRIXMIS had a right to be what it was and where it was, even if not, strictly speaking, to do the things it did. Unlike a clandestine source, it could not be blown; unlike an attaché, it could not be confined to the capital, although individual members, like attachés, could be declared persona non grata.

Training and Equipment

Because the prime function of BRIXMIS, in reality, was to gather intelligence, it was developed into a highly effective collection machine, kitted out with whatever it needed to do the job, including the special equipment developed by DI51e in the DIS Directorate of Scientific and Technical Intelligence.

Continuity

BRIXMIS provided continuity in two senses. First, continuity of observation. The problem with satellite passes or overflights is that they give you a one-off snapshot; what you get is what you see (although the Chipmunk flights within the Berlin Control Zone were not averse to the odd go-round). In contrast, BRIXMIS could keep a target under observation for lengthy periods and judge the best moment for photography. Secondly, continuity of expertise. Over the years BRIXMIS built up an unequalled understanding of its targets and the best ways of attacking them; by the mid- to late 1970s it was possibly the most professional military intelligence team in the world.

Synergy

In its early years, BRIXMIS was less effective than it could have been because it did not operate as a cohesive team; in later years it did, and in so doing it maximised its potential. Even more important, however, was the synergy between BRIXMIS and other intelligence sources, including, for instance, HUMINT, SIGINT, defectors, and émigrés, which provided tip-offs on the location and timing of potential targets. There was also a very important synergy between BRIXMIS and the DIS desk officers who, together with their US and Canadian counterparts, would meet at the annual Ground Forces Conference. An effective DIS analyst would also make sure of briefing BRIXMIS staff in person, to make sure that they understood exactly what was required and, so far as security allowed, why it was needed.

Timeliness

Many valuable intelligence sources tell you how things were, rather than how they are. A hot item from BRIXMIS could be on the analyst's desk within days.

Releasability

DIS desk officers are driven by two imperatives; to understand everything about their subject of study and to get usable assessments to the people who need them. During the Cold War our own forces, particularly those stationed in Germany, and those of our NATO allies were very important customers. There was nothing more frustrating for the analyst than to prepare an assessment which depended on very highly classified sources which precluded its being disseminated to the front line. BRIXMIS's products were generally CONFIDENTIAL, so a sighting or photograph could provide collateral to unlock key material. Indeed, the customers of DIS must sometimes have wondered how its analysts could derive such a wealth of information from a few fuzzy photographs – little did they know.

In the last resort, BRIXMIS was appreciated by the people who really mattered, the all-source desk analysts who, with their multitude of information streams, understood just how valuable BRIXMIS and its products really were. I would assess it as, quite possibly, the most cost-effective intelligence collection organisation of the past century.

Appendix A

Robertson–Malinin Agreement

REGARDING THE EXCHANGE OF MILITARY LIAISON MISSIONS BETWEEN THE SOVIET AND BRITISH COMMANDERS-IN-CHIEF OF ZONES OF OCCUPATION IN GERMANY

In accordance with Article 2 of the Agreement of "The Control Machinery in Germany" of 14th November 1944, the Soviet and British Commanders-in-Chief of the Zones of Occupation in Germany have decided to exchange Military Liaison Missions to be accredited to their respective Staffs in the Zone and to confirm the following points regarding these Missions:

1. The Missions will consist of 11 officers assisted by not more than 20 technicians, clerks and other personnel including personnel required for W/T.
2. The Mission will be placed under the authority of one member of the Mission who will be nominated and termed the "Chief of the Soviet/British Military Mission". All other Liaison Officers, Missions, or Russian/British personnel operating in the Zone will accept the authority and carry out the instruction of the Chief of the Mission.
3. The Chief of the Mission will be accredited to the Commander-in-Chief of the Forces of Occupation. In the case of the British Zone this means Air Marshal Sir Sholto Douglas. In the case of the Russian Zone this means Marshal of the Soviet Union Sokolovsky.
4. In the case of the British Zone the Soviet Mission is invited to take up residence at or near Zone Headquarters (Bad Salzuflen area).
5. In the case of the Soviet Zone the British Mission is invited to take up residence at or near Karlshorst or Potsdam.

6. In the case of the British Zone the Chief of the Soviet Mission will communicate with the Deputy Chief of Staff (Execution) Major-General Bishop or his staff.

7. In the case of the Soviet Zone the Chief of the British Mission will communicate with the Deputy Chief of Staff Major-General Lavrentiov.

8. Each Mission will have similar travellers' facilities. Passes of an identical nature in Russian and English will be prepared. Generally speaking there will be freedom of travel and circulation for the members of Missions in each Zone with the exception of restricted areas in which respect each Commander-in-Chief will notify the Mission and act on a reciprocal basis.

8. Each Mission will have their own wireless station for communication with its Commander-in-Chief. In each case facilities will be provided for Couriers and Despatch Riders to pass freely from the Mission HQ to the HQ of their own Commander-in-Chief. These Couriers will enjoy the same immunity as diplomatic Couriers.

9. Each Mission will be provided with telephone facilities in the local exchange at their HQ and given facilities for such communications (post, telephone, telegraph) as exist when are touring in the Zone. In the event of a breakdown of the wireless stations the Zone Commander will give every assistance in meeting the emergency by providing temporary facilities on his own signal system.

10. Each Mission will be administered by the Zone in which it resides in respect of accommodation, rations, petrol, and stationery against repayment in Reichsmarks.

   The building will be given full immunity.

11. The object of the Mission is to maintain Liaison between the Staff of the two Commanders-in-Chief and their Military Governments in the Zones.

   The Missions can also in each Zone concern themselves and make representation regarding their Nationals and interests in the Zones in which they are operating. They can afford assistance to authorised visitors of their own country visiting the Zone to which the Mission is accredited.

12. This agreement is written in Russian and English. Both texts are authentic.

13. The Agreement comes into force the moment letters have been exchanged by the Deputies to the British and Soviet Commanders-in-Chief of the Zones of Occupation in Germany.

> (Signed) B H ROBERTSON Lt General,
> Deputy Military Governor, CCG (BE).
>
> M S MALININ Col-General,
> Deputy Commander-in-Chief,
> Chief of Staff of the Soviet Group
> of Forces of Occupation in Germany
>
> Berlin 16th September 1946

Appendix B

List of Chiefs and Deputy Chiefs BRIXMIS, 1946–1990

Chiefs BRIXMIS 1946–1990

Ranks shown as at time of posting.

Major General Geoffrey Evans CB DSO**	1946–1947[i]
Major General Lionel C. Manners-Smith CBE	1947–1948[ii]
Brigadier 'Sammy' Hugh M. Curteis MC	1948–1950
Brigadier Claude H. Dewhurst OBE	1950 –March 1953
Brigadier John E. F. Meadmore OBE	March 1953–March 1955
Brigadier C. D. T. 'Denys' Wynn-Pope OBE	March 1955–September 1957
Brigadier the Hon. Miles F. Fitzalan-Howard MC [iii]	September 1957–November 1959
Brigadier John J. Packard	November 1959–October 1960
Brigadier Thomas C. H. Pearson CBE DSO*	October 1960–October 1961
Brigadier John R. Holden CBE DSO	October 1961–January 1963
Brigadier Douglas L. Darling DSO* MC	January–December 1963
Brig Humphrey 'Bala' E. N. Bredin DSO** MC*	December 1963–July 1965
Brigadier A. D. R. G. 'David' Wilson CBE	July 1965–July 1967
Brigadier David G. House CBE MC	July 1967–March 1969
Brigadier Edward W. Anstey OBE	March 1969–April 1971
Brigadier George W. D. Crookenden	April 1971–October 1972
Brigadier D. A. T. 'David' Baines MBE	October 1972–August 1974
Brigadier Lionel A. D. Harrod OBE	August 1974–October 1976
Brigadier John N. Elderkin	October 1976–January 1979
Brigadier Michael J. Perkins CBE	January 1979–March 1981
Brigadier Brian W. Davis CB CBE	March 1981–July 1982

Brigadier John H. Learmont CBE	July 1982–July 1984
Brigadier Francis 'Frank' G Bevan	July 1984–April 1985[iv]
Brigadier William T 'Bill' Dodd OBE[i]	June 1985–May 1987[iv]
Brigadier John P. Foley OBE MC[i]	June 1987–July 1989
Brigadier Ian L. Freer CBE[i]	July 1989–December 1990

The asterisk (*) next to a decoration denotes that it was awarded twice and is described as 'and bar'. DSC* therefore is described as 'DSC and bar', which means the individual received two Distinguished Service Crosses. Two asterisks mean he was awarded it three times, '… and two bars'.

[i] Most Chiefs BRIXMIS were generalists, with little experience of intelligence collection or working with the Soviets. Dodd, Foley, and Freer, however, all had special forces backgrounds, which were better suited to BRIXMIS operations in the 1980s.
[ii] After Major General Manners-Smith's retirement, the role of Chief BRIXMIS was downgraded to a brigadier's position.
[iii] Later Major General the Duke of Norfolk KG GCVO CB CBE MC DL.
[iv] Lieutenant Colonel Roy Giles was acting chief for three months in 1985 after Brigadier Bevan was posted home for medical reasons (and Deputy Chief Group Captain Burns was also taken ill). Brigadier Dodd took over in June 1985.

Deputy Chiefs BRIXMIS 1946–1990

Colonel/Brigadier Richard Hilton DSO MC DFC*	1946–1947[i]
Brigadier J. E. F. Meadmore	1948–1950
Brigadier D. A. D. Young	1950–1952
Colonel R. P. 'Philip' Mortimer	1952–1955[ii]
Group Captain F. G. 'George' Foot OBE	1955–1957
Group Captain J. 'John' B Boardman	1958–1960
Group Captain Gordon Young CBE	1960–1962
Group Captain Ross Philip Harding CBE	1963–1965
Group Captain William Edward Colahan CB CBE DFC	1965–1967
Group Captain J. F. J. Dewhurst OBE DFC AFC	1967–1969
Group Captain John H. Lewis AFC	1970–1972
Group Captain Jim Corbishley OBE AFC	1972–1974
Group Captain J. C. Forbes DFM	1974–1976
Group Captain Michael John Rayson LVO	1976–1979
Group Captain Peter G. Botterill CBE AFC	1979–1981

Group Captain Richard D. Bates AFC	1981–1983
Group Captain John Burns	1984–1986
Group Captain K. O. Harding OBE	1986–1988
Group Captain G. H. Rolfe CBE	1988–1990
Group Captain M. R. Killick	1990

[i] 1946 to 1952 the Deputy Chief was an army brigadier, and from 1952 to 1955 an army colonel.
[ii] 1955 to 1990 the Deputy Chief was an RAF group captain.

Source: *Story of BRIXMIS*; and Mackie, Colin *Senior Army Appointments 1860-* (gulabin.com).

Appendix C

BRIXMIS Opel Senator 3.0
Specification and Modifications, 1980s

Base Model   Opel Senator A2 sedan/saloon 3.0.

Engine   2,969 cc with four-barrel Rochester Quadrajet carburettor conversion.[i]

Transmission   Aisin-Warner four-speed automatic gearbox incorporating FF (Ferguson Formula) four-wheel-drive system.
Front differential incorporated into custom-made engine oil sump.
New front wheel hubs to take front drive shafts.

Suspension   Uprated front springs and struts from Opel Motorsport Division.
Reinforced McPherson struts.
Pneumatic self-levelling suspension (mechanical sensor fitted to rear differential and pneumatic pump located on right-hand side of engine bay).

Body   Channel section underbody extended underneath boot to take weight of extra fuel tank.
Rear quarter light glass removed and replaced with steel plate, with right-hand side incorporating auxiliary tank fuel filler cap.
100 litres (700 miles) alloy auxiliary fuel tank (on top of the existing 80-litre tank) fitted in the boot behind the rear seats, with a built-in firewall between seat and tank.
Front and rear 'panzer' skid plates to protect the underside of the engine/transfer box and the fuel tank.
Car sprayed Bundeswehr drab brown. (Gelboliv)

Interior   Dark green seat covers on all seats.
Black cloth curtains split in the middle with a Velcro fastening sliding on a top and bottom fixed rail to cover the rear window/rear side windows.
Black non-reflective covering over the top of the dashboard (to eliminate any reflections in the windscreen).
Switch panel to be fitted across the transmission tunnel in front of the gear change lever.
Gearbox oil temperature and gearbox oil pressure gauges to be fitted on the front of the switch panel facing the driver.

Switch panel	Panel lights	Pull switch, on/off.
	Horn	Pull switch, on/off.
	Indicators	Pull switch, on/off.
	Numberplate light	Toggle switch, on/off.
	Brake lights	Toggle switch, on/off.
	Left rectangular light	Toggle switch, on/off.
	Right rectangular light	Toggle switch, on/off.
	Pair of round lights	Toggle switch, on/off.

Fuel tank switch   Toggle switch, on/off.[ii]

Tyres   Pirelli Cinturato mud and snow (all year round).

BRIXMIS Opel Senator 3.0 REME Workshop Requirements

Shop 4, 14 Field Workshops, REME, Spandau, Berlin [iii]
  1. ELECTRICAL MODS (SHOP 4)
    a. Rewire all vehicle lights
    b. Fit fog and spot lamps
    c. Fit map reading lights
    d. Fit oil temp (gearbox) gauge
    e. Fit extra fuel gauge
    f. Fit switch to engine fan
    g. Modify central locking system [iv]

TOTAL TIME 50 HRS = 7 DAYS

  2. MECHANICAL MODS (SHOP 4)
    a. Fit extra fuel tank
    b. Modify all fuel pipes
    c. Fit rear curtains
    d. Fit map pockets
    e. Fit temp sender unit in gearbox
    f. Remove and refit rear suspension

TOTAL TIME 40 HRS = 5 DAYS

  3. TEXTILE/CARPENTER
    a. Manufacture fuel tank spacer
    b. Manufacture curtains
    c. Re-cover front dash (anti-glare) [v]

TOTAL TIME 40 HRS = 5 DAYS

4. BLACKSMITHS
  a. Manufacture extra fuel tank
  b. Modify rear suspension
  c. Manufacture and fit sump guards
  d. Manufacture pipe for fuel lines

TOTAL TIME 95 HRS = 15 DAYS

5. MACHINE SHOP
  a. Manufacture various brackets

TOTAL TIME 7 HRS = 1 DAY
TOTAL TIME FOR COMPLETE CAR = 232 HRS = 33 WORKING DAYS

[i] The Mission specified the replacement of the factory-fitted Bosch Jetronic fuel injection system with carburettors, which were easier to maintain, fault-find and repair in the field.
[ii] The fuel tank switch operated a solenoid to switch from one fuel tank to the other.
[iii] REME – Royal Electrical and Mechanical Engineers.
[iv] Disable the central locking system, allowing each door to be locked/unlocked individually from the interior.
[v] The dash covering was left to the end to avoid damaging it when working on the car. This was the last task in the modification.

To reduce the in-workshop turnaround time, modification packs were manufactured in advance for each model of on-pass vehicle.

Sources: SSgt Dave Picton, *BRIXMIS Tour Car Specifications* (BRIXMIS Association Archives, Box 16 File 24), William Durie via Rod Saar, BRIXMIS Association.

Appendix D

BRIXMIS Tour Equipment Checklist, 1980s

The specifics would vary by individual, preference, and objectives, but this list covers most eventualities – a lot of equipment to fit in a car.

Photographic equipment	
3	Nikon F3 camera bodies with motor drives
3	MN-2 batteries for motor drive units
1	Nikon f2 or f1.4 85-mm AIS lens (f1.4 was introduced in 1981)
1	Nikon 180-mm f2.8 AI or AIS lens (AIS introduced in 1981)
1	Nikon Reflex-NIKKOR 500-mm f8 lens
2	Nikon Reflex-NIKKOR 1,000-mm f11 lens
1	Lens doubler
1	Camera pistol grip with cable
1	Canon autofocus 35-mm camera with built-in flash
Up to 100	Rolls of 35-mm film, 36 exposure, colour and black & white negative, colour transparency in various types & ASAs
1	Modulux night vision device no.14 with canvas case
1	Camera tripod adjustable head no.10
1	Canvas covered camera box
1	Olympus 303 video recorder and case
1	Olympus 303 video camera and case
1	Olympus video supplementary lens
2	Olympus video recorder batteries BP1
1	5-metre video extension cable
1	Olympus power cable
1	Lens cleaning kit
1	Camera bag

Optical	
1	Pair Carl Zeiss binoculars 15 x 60
1	Pair Carl Zeiss binoculars 7 x 35 or 10 x 40
1	Pair small binoculars in soft leather case
1	Pair night-vision goggles no. 739
1	Thermal imager
Tools & spares	
3	Sony tape recorders
6	Spare tapes
2	Plastic earphones for tape recorders
30	Spare AA batteries
2	Prismatic compasses
2	Green plastic torches with red filters and spare batteries
1	Black metal torch with spare batteries
1	Tool roll containing ring/open ended spanners, adjustable spanner (wrench) screwdrivers, hammers, chisel, mole grips, wire
1	Survival knife/tool
1	Micrometer
Maps	
1	Black plastic map bag
2	Set of 1:25,000 target maps
2	Full set of 1:50,000 maps of the GDR
2	Sets of Soviet PRA maps signed by Chief of Staff GSFG
3	British 1:500,000 PRA maps
2	GDR fuel maps
1	Current TRA map
2	Canvas RAF nav bags/briefcases
Misc. & admin	
2	Copies Robertson–Malinin agreement
1	Tourers' aide-memoire – telephone number of the Mission House in Potsdam in case of emergency
1	Copy of Cyrillic alphabet
2	Plastic-covered notebook (loose leaf)
1	List of known Stasi vehicle registration numbers
1	Motorola pager no. 260 (for Operation TALON SNATCH)
2	Pencil cases with contents including grease pencil (Chinagraph), propelling pencil with spare leads, set of coloured mapping pens

1	Large plastic folder
Various	Plastic bags and sacks for storage, keeping equipment dry, refuse and bagging up material gathered on tour (TAMARISK/TOMAHAWK)
Various	East German hessian sacks and paper potato sacks for collecting TAMARISK/TOMAHAWK material (easily jettisoned in emergency)
Various	Rope, paracord, string, duct tape, etc.
1	Large aerosol can of mosquito repellent
2	First aid kits including morphine syringes
Selection	Cassette tapes
Selection	Reading matter
Various	Storage crates for ease of access, loading and unloading*
Recovery	
1 or 2	Spare wheel(s)**
2	Pairs thick winching gloves
1	Aluminium ground anchor plate
9	Ground anchor spikes/pins
1	Sledgehammer
1	Tirfor hand winch with collapsible handle and spare shear pins
1	Steel strop (steel cable)
1	Snatch block and shackles
1	4-tonne bottle jack and handle
1	Manufacturer's side jack
1	Jacking/sand board
2	Sand mats
2	Entrenching tools/folding shovels
1	Pickaxe
1	Instant puncture repair aerosol can
Personal Kit x 3 sets	
1 pair	Sunglasses
1	Electric razor***
1 pack	Chemical heating pads***
1	Charcoal hand-warmer***
1	Swiss Army Knife
1	Personal admin/wash kit/change of clothes
1	Arctic-spec sleeping bag
1	Sleeping mat****
1	Bivouac/basha/GORE-TEX 1-man tent****

Catering	
3 sets	Packed lunches and snacks for the anticipated duration of the tour
3 sets	Communal curry tinned ingredients
1 box	Self-heating tins of soup (for emergencies)
Assorted	Tea bags, instant coffee, sugar, whitener
6 x	Thermos flasks
1 set	Cooking pots
1	Gaz primus stove
1	Petrol stove
1	Plastic wash basin/washing up bowl
4	40 litre water cans

* Custom crates were manufactured in the workshops to fit the Range Rovers and G-Wagens for ease of handling.

** The Opel Admiral carried two spare wheels in the boot, while the Senator could only fit one. The Range Rover carried two spare wheels vertically stowed on either side of the back compartment. The G-Wagen also carried two, but with one inside, and one outside clamped to the rear door. The Stasi sometimes used 'stinger' devices to puncture all four tyres at once, which would have been very dangerous at speed, forcing the tour to stop and be detained, or to drive on flat tyres (run-flat tyres first came on to the market in the mid-1970s, but did not get widespread use until the 1990s).

*** Down to personal preference.

**** Tour officer and NCO would sleep outside the car – sleeping arrangements (bivouac vs. basha vs. one-man tent down to personal choice). The driver would sleep inside the locked car for security so did not require an outdoor shelter.

N.B. A USMLM kit list from the early 1970s also includes Lunasix and Pentax Spotmeter light meters, Hensoldt binoculars, and a pair of PYE two-way radios. The Nikon F2 and F3 used by the AMLMs had through-the-lens (TTL) light metering, so perhaps they were still using separate light meters as back-up. The Hensoldt binoculars were standard issue for the Bundeswehr, and made by the West German Zeiss group in Wetzlow, as opposed to the East German Carl Zeiss (Jena) binoculars used by BRIXMIS. Carrying two-way radios reflects the fact that USMLM tours were typically only manned by two people, so if the tour officer needed to go on a foot recce and out of sight of the tour car, it was advisable to stay in touch with his driver via the two-way radios. BRIXMIS did not use these. Source USMLM annual report 1971 via BRIXMIS Association Archives.

Personal kit varied by individual, and consisted of whatever was needed to make the tourer as comfortable as possible. The following list is what Staff Sergeant Graham Geary BEM wore and took on tour:

Food
 Cheese and ham sandwiches,
 Cooked sausages,

Yoghurt,

3 x tins of sardines (instant protein hit),

2 x tins 'Bully' corned beef and vegetables,

OXO cubes,

Curry powder,

Brew kit (tea, coffee, dried milk, and sugar in plastic pots plus teaspoon and plastic mug),

Knife, fork, 'racing spoon', and tin opener,

Chocolate digestive biscuits,

Tin of Callard & Bowser boiled sweets.

Clothing

Beret (only for crossing the Glienicke Bridge or during detentions),

Roll neck jumper,

Shirt, hairy,

Socks, woollen,

Boots, flying,

Sweater, green,

Denims, lightweight,

Stable belt (wide webbing belt, horizontally striped to represent the wearer's regiment, in Graham's case, dark red with two narrow horizontal blue stripes for the Royal Engineers),

Canadian parka with fur trimmed collar,

Northern Ireland army-issue black leather patrol gloves,

Black woollen US pattern night watch hat,

Quilted winter suit (jacket and trousers),

Geary also wore a 'patch waistcoat' on tour, emblazoned with patches bought from places he had visited.

Personal kit

Book,

Plasters,

Codeine,

Buck 110 folding knife in leather sheath attached to belt,

Soviet pass,

Bivouac/bedroll.

Master Air Loadmaster (MALM, warrant officer) Gary Roberts, tour NCO March 1989–1990, had his own custom bed roll consisting of sleeping bag, space blanket, woollen blanket, GORE-TEX bivvy bag, a 'very deep' air bed and a small pillow, sheltering from the elements in a one-man tent! Squadron Leader Andrew Pennington's used a one-man GORE-TEX hooped tent with built-in groundsheet. He attached an extra groundsheet to the tent for extra insulation and to stop the tent's groundsheet from ripping when opened in the pitch dark on a sharp stone or branch. Inside the tent, the base was made from a foil-backed foam blanket, which in turn was wrapped in a foil 'space blanket' for extra insulation. On top of that was an East German inflatable lilo and then the sleeping bag – tourers were issued with both a summer- and arctic-spec bag, but most just used the winter one. This would all be rolled up into a ready-to-use shelter, with the tent hoops in place, but not secured, and the roll would be held together and compacted with bungees.

Sources: Author via multiple sources including Squadron Leader Andrew Pennington, MALM Gary Roberts, and Staff Sergeant Graham Geary BEM, *The Christmas Local* (Private memoir, undated, BRIXMIS Association Archives).

Appendix E

de Havilland T10 Chipmunk Specification

The RAF operated two de Havilland Canada DHC-1 Chipmunk T.10s based at RAF Gatow. The Chipmunk was a tandem two-seater training aircraft which entered service with the RAF in 1950 and with the Royal Navy in 1965, replacing the venerable DH Tiger Moth. Because it was used so widely in training, most pilots attached to the Mission will have flown it at some stage in their career. The Chipmunk was powered by a single 145 hp (108 kW) de Havilland Gypsy Major 8 engine, which gave a maximum speed of 138 mph (222 km/h), cruising at 103 mph (166 km/h) and with a range of 259 mi (445 km or 225 nmi). It had a Maximum take-off weight of 2,200 lb and a 15,800 ft (5,200 m) ceiling, but generally operated much lower than that.*

The aircraft was fully aerobatic and because of its training origins, it could be flown from either seating position.

Over the life of the operation, nine different Chipmunks were operated:

WG303 from December 1956 until April 1968
WK587 from November 1962 until April 1968
WP850 from April 1968 until November 1975
WP971 from April 1968 until October 1975
WZ862 from December 1974 until June1987
WD289 from May 1975 until June 1987
WG478 from May 1987 until July 1987

---

* Chipmunk sources: < https://www.baesystems.com/en/heritage/de-havilland-canada-dhc-1-chipmunk>, <https://navywings.org.uk/portfolio/chipmunk/> and < http://www.16va.be/vols_brixmis_part1_eng2.html> all accessed 9.8.21, Wright, Kevin and Jefferies, Peter, *Looking Down the Corridors, Aerial Allied Espionage over East Germany and Berlin 1945-1990* (Stroud, The History Press, 2017), and Rod Saar, BRIXMIS Association. BAe Systems, the ultimate successor to de Havilland, have the cruising speed at 119 mph, the max take-off weight at 2,100 lb and range at 280 mi.

WG486 from May 1987 until 1990*
WG466 from 1987 until 1990†

They initially they flew in an all-over silver colour scheme but in the 1970s moved to light aircraft grey, albeit with a black anti-glare panel on the nose. Despite their age, the Chipmunks proved to be very reliable, and between 1956 and 1990, not one aircraft was lost due to mechanical failure.

---

* WG486 remains airworthy and is now with the RAF Battle of Britain Memorial Flight at RAF Coningsby.

† WG466 is currently on loan from the Alliierten Museum in Berlin to Bundeswehr Museum of Military History (MNHM) at Gatow.

Notes

Preface

1. The Parallel History Project on Cooperative Security (PHP) at the Center for Security Studies (CSS), Swiss Federal Institute of Technology (ETH), Zurich <php.isn.ethz.ch>.

Introduction

1. Winston Churchill, 'Sinews of Peace' speech, Westminster College, Fulton, Missouri, 5 March 1946.
2. <winstonchurchill.org/resources/speeches/1946-1963-elder-statesman/the-sinews-of-peace> and <nationalchurchillmuseum.org/sinews-of-peace-history> both accessed 26 August 2022.
3. <rferl.org/a/hungary-1989-east-germany/30156892>, <theguardian.com/world/from-the-archive-blog/2019/jun/12/hungary-austria-open-border-june-1989>, <revolution89.de/en/revolution/more-and-more-east-germans-want-out/escape-via-prague> all accessed 26 August 2022.
4. <bundesregierung.de/breg-de/themen/deutsche-einheit/neues-forum-entsteht-337176> accessed 26 August 2022.
5. <nsarchive2.gwu.edu/NSAEBB/NSAEBB290/index.htm> accessed 26 August 2022.
6. <cvce.eu/en/obj/protocol_between_the_allies_on_the_occupation_zones_in_germany_london_12_september_1944-en-f6ad2306-576d-4705-a772-4e52945aabe9> accessed 28 August 2022.
7. <cvce.eu/en/obj/agreement_between_the_allies_amending_the_protocol_of_12_september_1944_london_14_november_1944-en-76b5c518-9d0c-4d02-9f92-a970c272aa07> accessed 28 August 2022.
8. <cvce.eu/content/publication/1999/1/1/ec18fd66-c681-44ee-baad-97555abffd4f/publishable_en.pdf> accessed 28 August 2022.
9. <history.state.gov/milestones/1937-1945/yalta-conf> accessed 29 August 2022.

10. <avalon.law.yale.edu/wwii/ger01.asp> accessed 29 August 2022.
11. <un.org/en/about-us/history-of-the-un/san-francisco-conference> accessed 29 August 2022.

Chapter 1

1. Robertson–Malinin Agreement, 16 September 1946 (BRIXMIS Association Archives).
2. Robertson–Malinin Agreement.
3. Lieutenant Colonel J. N. Cormack, GSO1 1964–1966, in Lieutenant Colonel N. N. Wylde QGM (Ed), *The Story of BRIXMIS, 1946–1990* (Privately published for the BRIXMIS Association, 1993).
4. Ibid.
5. Major J. M. Symes MC, tour officer 1948–1950, *The Early Years, 1948–1950, The Story of BRIXMIS.*
6. Lieutenant Colonel J. M. Laing MC, RE, senior interpreter and tour officer, 1951–1952, *The Story of BRIXMIS.*
7. As per Lt Col Tony Le Tissier, the last British Protocol Officer (and former Governor of Spandau Prison), *The Story of BRIXMIS.*
8. Cormack, *The Story of BRIXMIS*; and Lieutenant Colonel C. B. Critchley MBE, GSO1 BRIXMIS 1955–1960, letter to Lieutenant Colonel P. D. Dryland MBE MC, 30 August 1967 (BRIXMIS Association Archives).
9. Major N. L. R. Griffiths RM, tour officer 1951–1953, *The Story of BRIXMIS.*
10. Squadron Leader Rod Saar MBE, RAF (retd.), *BRIXMIS: A Secret Journey behind the Iron Curtain, Edition 5a* (Sandhurst: private unpublished monograph, 2021), used with permission.
11. Wing Commander J. H. Dyer MA MBIM RAF, tour officer and Chipmunk pilot 1959–1961, *The Story of BRIXMIS.*
12. Report by Mrs D. F. A. T. Baines on her visit to Soviet Army Shops in Potsdam on Thursday 29 November 1973, BRIXMIS Annual Report 1973 (National Archives via BRIXMIS Association Archives).
13. Group Captain Hans Neubroch, *An Airman behind the Iron Curtain* (Private monograph. 2010, BRIXMIS Association Archives).

Chapter 2

1. Royal Air Force Historical Society (RAFHS), Seminar on Cold War Intelligence Gathering held on 18 April 2000 at the RAF Museum, Hendon, RAFHS *Journal 23, 2001*, used with permission.
2. The Concise Oxford Dictionary of Current English, 8th edition, Oxford University Press, 1992.
3. Cormack, *The Story of BRIXMIS.*
4. Lieutenant Colonel David O'Connor, RA, tour officer 1969–1971, *Behind the Iron Curtain: The Trial of Ekehard Weil* (BRIXMIS Association Archives).

Chapter 3

1. RAFHS *Journal 23.*
2. TOP SECRET signal from War Office to HQ BAOR, 21 November 1951 (BRIXMIS Association Archives).
3. Letter from Sir Ivone Kirkpatrick to General Sir Richard N. Gale GCB, KBE, DSO, MC, CINC BAOR, 10 October 1952, and Brief for Commander in Chief 2nd Tactical Air Force for Commanders-in-Chief Committee 11th March 1955 (National Archives via BRIXMIS Association Archives).
4. TOP SECRET letter from C. H. Johnson, UK High Commission, Bonn to P. Hancock, Foreign Office, 8 December 1953 (National Archives via BRIXMIS Association Archives).
5. Joint Services Intelligence Group (Germany), Comparison of Values of BRIXMIS and SOXMIS, 13 August 1954, TOP SECRET, U.K. EYES ONLY (National Archives via the BRIXMIS Association Archives).
6. Letter on BRIXMIS from R. A. Hibbert, British Embassy, Bonn to C. M. James, Foreign & Commonwealth Office, 10 April 1973 (National Archives via the BRIXMIS Association Archives).
7. Potsdam Riot sources: Neubroch, *RAF Element Brixmis: Further Recollections of Operational Experiences, 1957–59* (RAFHS, *Journal 23)*; Neubroch, *An Airman behind the Iron Curtain*; Neubroch, *Anti-Western Demonstrations in Potsdam, The story of BRIXMIS*; Lt Col C. B. Critchley MBE, *In Contact: Reminiscences of BRIXMIS, 1946–1949 and 1955–1960, The story of BRIXMIS*; and *Transcript of conversation between Tony Geraghty, Lieutenant Colonel Nigel Wylde QGM, and Major General The Duke of Norfolk, Miles F. Fitzalan-Howard MC, Chief BRIXMIS 1957–1959, House of Lords, Tuesday 5 July 1994* (BRIXMIS Association Archives).
8. Memo to Chief from Captain, 'Mission House Staff', 16 January 1991 (National Archives via BRIXMIS Association Archives).
9. Jefferies, Captain I. D., SO3 RES, Declassified SECRET 'Debrief of a Stasi Officer', undated, assume late 1990 (National Archives via BRIXMIS Association Archives).
10. Critchley, *The Story of BRIXMIS.*
11. Captain (later Major *and* Squadron Leader) J. W. L. S. Avery MBE TD AE, *A Few Reflections of a Part-Time Tourer 25 Years On* (BRIXMIS Association Archives).
12. Tony Geraghty interview with Sergeant Mike Seale, SAS, Hereford, 13 June 1995 (BRIXMIS Association Archives).
13. Major David Duncan, BEM, Army Intelligence Support to BRIXMIS; and email correspondence between Warrant Officer Bob Thomas, Intelligence Corps, Research 1976–1978 and Lieutenant Colonel Angus Southwood MBE, 13 October 2004 (both BRIXMIS Association Archives).
14. Tony Geraghty interview with General Sir John Learmont, 23 August 1996 (BRIXMIS Association Archives).
15. Captain Peter Williams, tour officer 1981–1983, Major Peter Williams, army operations officer 1987–1989, later Major General Peter Williams CMG OBE. Correspondence, May 2011 (BRIXMIS Association Archives).

16. Bacon, Corporal Francis, RAF, Special Section 1958–1960, *Reminiscences* (BRIXMIS Association Archives).
17. Warrant Officer Kevin Hawkins, RAOC, Chief Clerk 1987–1990, *The Role of Chief Clerk BRIXMIS* (BRIXMIS Association Archives).
18. Bill Emery, SERCO Systems Engineer 1985–1994, *Projects ELECTRIC LIGHT and GARDEN GATE – a brief overview of computers at BRIXMIS* (Saar, BRIXMIS).
19. Major General (retd.) P. G. Williams CMG OBE, *BRIXMIS in the 1980s: The Cold War's "Great Game" – Memories of Liaising with the Soviet Army in East Germany* (Highworth: Private expanded monograph, July 2008), originally published April 2007 by the Parallel History Project on Cooperative Security (PHP), Center for Security Studies at ETH Zurich and the National Security Archive at the George Washington University on behalf of the PHP network <www.php.isn.ethz.ch>.

Chapter 4

1. Williams, *BRIXMIS in the 1980s*.
2. Williams, *BRIXMIS in the 1980s*.
3. Colonel Angus Southwood, *The Story of BRIXMIS*; and *BRIXMIS Training* (both BRIXMIS Association Archives).
4. Williams, *BRIXMIS in the 1980s*.
5. Critchley, *The Story of BRIXMIS*.
6. Lieutenant Colonel J. M. Laing MC, RE, senior interpreter and tour officer, 1951–1952, *The Story of BRIXMIS*.
7. Critchley, *The Story of BRIXMIS*.
8. BRIXMIS report, July to December 1972 (National Archives via BRIXMIS Association Archives).
9. Gibson, *BRIXMIS*.
10. Morrison, John, *BRIXMIS: The View from Whitehall* (RAFHS, *Journal 23*).
11. Wing Commander Dickie Dyer, *Notes and Comments on BRIXMIS*, undated (BRIXMIS Association Archives).
12. Correspondence between Lieutenant Colonel Roy Giles, Squadron Leader Rod Saar and Tony Geraghty, 2 September 2011 (BRIXMIS Association Archives).
13. Five Eyes Intelligence Community – UK, USA, Canada, Australia, and New Zealand. Critchley, *The Story of BRIXMIS*.
14. Squadron Leader Peter Copland, SLOps 1975–1978, *The Ramblings of an RAF Engineering Officer*, undated (BRIXMIS Association Archives).
15. Cormack, *The Story of BRIXMIS*.
16. Captain David Duncan (BRIXMIS Association Archives).
17. *SSgt Buchan's memoires,* undated (BRIXMIS Association Archives).
18. Interview between Tony Geraghty and Lieutenant Colonel John Cormack, 19 August 1994 (BRIXMIS Association Archives).

19. Thanks to Staff Sergeant Graham Geary's (BEM) detailed description of the Glienicke Bridge process in his monograph *The Berlin Local* (BRIXMIS Association Archives).
20. Corporal Ted Scott, RE, BRIXMIS 1963–1964, *Personal Highlights/Memories* (BRIXMIS Association Archives).
21. Captain Nicholas Boggis-Rolfe, Grenadier Guards, tour officer April 1967–April 1971, *Reminiscences* (BRIXMIS Association Archives).
22. Geraghty–Seale interview (BRIXMIS Association Archives).
23. Huw Dylan, *Defence Intelligence and the Cold War: Britain's Joint Intelligence Bureau 1945–1964* (Oxford: Oxford University Press, 2014).
24. Squadron Leader Frank White MBE, *Memories of a BRIXMIS RAF Touring Officer* (BRIXMIS Association Archives).
25. Flight Sergeant Colin Birnie, *Reminiscences* and *Attempted Detention by a HIND-E* (BRIXMIS Association Archives).
26. Flight Sergeant Colin Birnie, *Oh, How I Love Merseburg* (BRIXMIS Association Archives).
27. Neubroch, *An Airman behind the Iron Curtain*.
28. <mil-airfields.de> accessed 25 February 2023.
29. White, *Memories of a BRIXMIS RAF Touring Officer*.
30. Letter from Squadron Leader Blackford to Tony Geraghty, 18 August 1995 (BRIXMIS Association Archives).
31. Pennington, *BRIXMIS Air Touring*; and Blackford–Geraghty letter (BRIXMIS Association Archives).
32. Sergeant William Roberts, Intelligence Corps, *BRIXMIS Spandau Office 1985–1987* (BRIXMIS Association Archives).
33. Pennington, *BRIXMIS Air Touring*.
34. BRIXMIS Report No. 4022/87, 31 July 1987 (National Archives via BRIXMIS Association Archives).
35. Email correspondence between Larry Kelly USMC, former USMLM member, and Peter Williams (BRIXMIS Association Archives).
36. Captain Stephen Harrison MBE, Royal Tank Regiment, SO3 tour officer, 1986–1988, *Lieberose T-64-B Round and BRDM-2 Rheinsberg Chase* (BRIXMIS Association Archives).
37. Sergeant Edward Roberts, Intelligence Corps and Major General Peter Williams (BRIXMIS Association Archives).
38. Correspondence between Lieutenant Colonel Roy Giles and Squadron Leader Rod Saar (BRIXMIS Association Archives).
39. Ibid.
40. Colonel W. T. Sedgwick, tour officer 1949–1951, *The Story of BRIXMIS*.
41. Neubroch, *An Airman Behind the Iron Curtain*.
42. Critchley, *The Story of BRIXMIS*.
43. Williams, *BRIXMIS in the 1980s*; Pennington, *BRIXMIS Air Touring*.
44. Captain Stephen Harrison, MBE, Royal Tank Regiment, SO3 tour officer, 1986–1988, *Lieberose T-64-B Round and BRDM-2 Rheinsberg Chase* (BRIXMIS Association Archives).

45. Neubroch, *An Airman behind the Iron Curtain*.
46. Saar, *BRIXMIS*.
47. Major N. L. R. Griffiths, RM, tour officer 1951–1953 and Captain S. W. Money, tour officer 1961–1964, *The Story of BRIXMIS*.
48. Major General Peter Williams, *Being detained by the Soviets could be fun: a BRIXMIS detention near Wittenberg, 27–28 August 1981* (Parallel History Project on Cooperative Society, PHP, Zurich, April 2007).
49. Corporal Ted Scott, RE, and Captain Money, 1960s (BRIXMIS Association Archives).
50. Captain Money (BRIXMIS Association Archives).
51. Griffiths, *The Story of BRIXMIS*.
52. Williams, *Being detained by the Soviets could be fun*.
53. Chipmunk sources: RAFHS, *Journal 23*; Williams, *BRIXMIS in the 1980s*; BRIXMIS Association, 'Second updated GSM clasp submission'; Saar, *BRIXMIS*; Sqn Ldr Vince Robertson, *NYLON & FARNBOROUGH* (BRXIMIS Association Archives, 2011); Medmenham Collection, *BRIXMIS Chipmunk Flights, Operations PHILARIA, SCHOONER, NYLON, and OBERON* (BRIXMIS Association Archives, 2010); Kevin Wright & Peter Jefferies, *Looking Down the Corridors, Aerial Allied Espionage over East Germany and Berlin 1945–1990* (Stroud: The History Press, 2017); *Memoir from Sqn Ldr Roy Marsden* via <16va.be>, <keymilitary.com/article/across-wall> both accessed 15 February 2023.
54. *Notes of the use of Soviet troops in aid of the Civil Power 16 June–10 July 1953*, 16 July 1953, prepared for C-in-C NORTHAG by Brigadier Meadmore, Chief BRIXMIS 1953–1955, and subsequent notes by an S2 major from the War Office M.I.3., 21 July 1953 (National Archives via BRIXMIS Association Archives).
55. Pennington, *BRIXMIS Air Touring*.
56. RAFHS, *Journal 23*.
57. Neubroch, *Airman behind the Iron Curtain*.
58. Morrison, *BRIXMIS*.
59. Squadron Leader Brian Speed, air tour officer and squadron leader operations 1972–1975 (Saar, *BRIXMIS*).
60. PAINT BOX sources: BRIXMIS Association, 'Second updated GSM clasp submission'; Saar, *BRIXMIS*; Wright & Jefferies, *Looking Down the Corridors*.
61. Morrison, *BRIXMIS*.
62. Gibson, *BRIXMIS*.
63. 'British Embassy Opens In an office In East Berlin' (New York: *The New York Times*, 17 April 1973).
64. <royalsignalsmuseum.co.uk/14-signal-regiment> accessed 31 January 2023.
65. <powerbase.info/index.php/British_Services_Security_Organisation_(Germany)> accessed 31 January 2023.
66. Major Alan A. Gordon, RE, 'Survey Support to BRIXMIS' (BRIXMIS Association, *The Story of BRIXMIS*) and 'Mapping with a Mission, Series BAOR Misc 536' (BRIXMIS Association Archives).

Chapter 5

1. RAFHS, *Journal 23*.
2. Ian Sanders interview with Captain Stephen Harrison (Cold War Conversations Podcast episodes 250 and 251); and correspondence with Major General Peter Williams.
3. Correspondence with Peter Williams, May 2023, and recollections from Dave Butler (Saar, *BRIXMIS*).
4. 'Joe Jones conversation with Rod Saar, November 2014' (Saar, *BRIXMIS*).
5. Squadron Leader Rod Saar referring to Squadron Leader Frank White's pictures of a Soviet MiG-21 (FISHBED) J fighter at Finow airbase (Saar, *BRIXMIS*).
6. Colin Ward via Dave Butler (Saar, *BRIXMIS*).
7. BRIXMIS Annual Report 1985 and 1990.
8. Humber Heavy Utility <revivaler.com/humber-heavy-utility/> accessed 13 September 2022.
9. Critchley, *The Story of BRIXMIS*.
10. Williams, *BRIXMIS in the 1980s*.
11. Colonel Angus Southwood, *BRIXMIS Vehicles*; and Staff Sergeant Dave Picton, *Four-wheel-drive cars in BRIXMIS 1974–1976 and 1979–1982* (both BRIXMIS Association Archives).
12. Thanks to Dave Picton, BRIXMIS M/T section Staff Sergeant (tour driver 1974–1976 and lead tour driver 1979–1982) for his information on tour vehicles, in particular the introduction of the Admiral FFs, Senator FFs, Range Rovers and Mercedes G-Wagens.
13. Mercedes G-Wagen introduction background c/o SSgt Dave Picton and Col Angus Southwood.
14. Captain Steve Gibson, MBE RE, *The Story of BRIXMIS*.
15. Correspondence with Dave Picton.
16. Ibid.
17. Pennington, *BRIXMIS Air Touring*.
18. Southwood, *BRIXMIS Vehicles*; and correspondence with Dave Picton.
19. Williams, *BRIXMIS in the 1980s*.

Chapter 6

1. Interview between Tony Geraghty and Lieutenant Colonel Roy Giles, 26 May 1995 (BRIXMIS Association Archives).
2. Some estimates have the KdA peak strength at c. 500,000.
3. Jefferies, Captain I. D., SO3 Research, Declassified SECRET *Debrief of a Stasi Officer*, undated, assume late 1990 (National Archives via BRIXMIS Association Archives).
4. Extract from *Das Wörterbuch der Staatssicherheit*, the Stasi Dictionary, 2nd Edition, 1985, translated by Mike Barton (BRIXMIS Association Archives).

5. Critchley, *The Story of BRIXMIS*.
6. Reynolds, *The Story of BRIXMIS;* and *BRIXMIS Monthly Report December 1952*.
7. Meadmore, *Notes of the use of Soviet troops in aid of the Civil Power.*
8. *TOP SECRET BRIXMIS Monthly Report for July 1953* (National Archives via BRIXMIS Association Archives).
9. Critchley, *The Story of BRIXMIS*; and Critchley–Dryland letter.
10. Critchley, *The Story of BRIXMIS*; and Critchley–Dryland letter.
11. Critchley, *The Story of BRIXMIS*; and Geraghty, Wylde, and Duke of Norfolk conversation transcript.
12. Critchley, *The Story of BRIXMIS*.
13. 'British Military Mission Potsdam (Incident)' (Hansard, 18 July 1960 via BRIXMIS Association Archives).
14. Geraghty, Wylde, and Duke of Norfolk conversation transcript; and Cormack/Geraghty interview (both BRIXMIS Association Archives).
15. SECRET BRIXMIS Incident Report, April 1962, Appendix B, Report on Recovery of Car, and Foreign Office memorandum, D. R. Drummond, 28 August 1962 (National Archives via BRIXMIS Association Archives).
16. SECRET Minutes of Meeting at Soviet Liaison Office on 11 March, 18 March and 24 March 1962, and at HQ GSFG on 13 March 1962 and 14 March 1962 (National Archives via BRIXMIS Association Archives); and SECRET Report on action in Potsdam Area covering protests and arrangements for evacuation of Cpl Day: Diary of events for 11 March, 12 March, 13 March, 15–17 March, and 24 March 1962 (National Archives via BRIXMIS Association Archives).
17. 'Ballistics report, Der Polizeipräsident in Berlin, Abteilung K, 5 April 1962' (National Archives via BRIXMIS Association Archives).
18. 'Corporal Day Incident', Annex 'A' to BRX/475/A, 31 August 1962 (National Archives via BRIXMIS Association Archives).
19. Letter from Captain M. K. McNally AGC (RMP) to Lieutenant Colonel N. N. Wilde QGM (misspelt – should be Wylde), BRIXMIS Association, 5 January 1994 (BRIXMIS Association Archives).
20. Gibson, *The Story of BRIXMIS*.
21. Colonel Angus Southwood, *Personal Reminiscences of BRIXMIS, 1965–1968;* and *The Highlight of my Career* (BRIXMIS Association Archives, 2010).
22. Firebar sources: Gibson, *The Story of BRIXMIS*; Saar, *BRIXMIS*; Michael Smith, 'Britain's secret jet crash Cold War coup' (London: *The Telegraph*, 26 December 2003); 'How the West stole the secret in the lake' (London: *The Telegraph*, 24 January 2004); *The FIREBAR Incident in West Berlin, 6 April 1966 – explanatory notes on the files in the BRIXMIS Archives and Personal reminiscences of Colonel (Retd.) A.H. Southwood MBE* (BRIXMIS Association Archives); Tony Geraghty interview and correspondence with Colonel Geoffrey Stephenson, GSO2 (Econ) BRIXMIS, 20 May 1995 and 29 June 1995 (BRIXMIS Association Archives); Correspondence between Colonel Southwood and Tony Geraghty, 21 May 1995 (BRIXMIS Association Archives); and <telegraph.co.uk/obituaries/2022/08/07/lt-col-angus-southwood-officer-involved-covert-cold-war-reconnaissance> accessed 10 November 2022.

23. Baines, *The Story of BRIXMIS*; Correspondence with Lieutenant Colonel Roy Giles (BRIXMIS Association Archives); Tony Geraghty, *BRIXMIS*; and David Webb-Carter, 'A Cold War Incident' <aspectsofhistory.com/a-cold-war-incident> accessed 2 November 2022.

24. Funktechnische Kompanie 613 des Funktechnischen Bataillons 61.

25. USMLM Unit History 1979.

26. Peter Williams, *BRIXMIS in the 1980s*.

27. Thanks to Rod Saar, BRIXMIS Association archivist, for his work in the BStU Stasi archives unearthing the Stasi's reports on the Mariotti and Nicholson murders. Also, a commentary by the late Mike Barton (Int Corps) from the BRIXMIS Association Archives was very useful in clarifying various aspects of the incidents.

28. William E. Stacy, *The Nicholson Incident, A Case Study of US–Soviet Negotiations* (Heidelberg: Headquarters US Army, Europe and 7th Army Military History Office, June 1988).

29. Sources on the Nicholson story: Edward Atkeson, 'Ease tensions in Europe: Allow both side's Generals to know each other' (Washington DC: *The Washington Post*, 19 May 1985); Lt Gen Roland Lajoie, *The last casualty of the Cold War: Lt Col Arthur D. Nicholson US Army, and the USMLM* (Private monograph, March 2004); John J. Miller, 'Our Last Cold War Casualty' (New York: *National Review*, 5 April 2004 and 22 March 2005 (BRIXMIS Association Archives); Lawrence G. Kelley, 'Annex F', *1985 USMLM Annual History* (BRIXMIS Association Archives); Ronald Reagan, Letter to Mikhail Gorbachev, 30 April 1985 (Simi Valley, California: Ronald Reagan Library, 1985); Saar, *BRIXMIS*; Michael R. Shebelskie, 'Incident, The Major Nicholson and the Norms of Peacetime Espionage' (New Haven, Connecticut: *Yale Journal of International Law*, 1986) Vol. 11:521, pp. 521–544; 'Stasi report on fatal shooting of Major Nicholson USMLM to Lieutenant General Neiber, division chief HA VIII, 26 March 1985' (Translated by Bernd Schäfer for PHP, BRIXMIS Association Archives).

30. SECRET minutes of meeting with SERB, 13 May 1966 (National Archives via BRIXMIS Association Archives).

31. Critchley, *The Story of BRIXMIS*; and minutes of meeting with SERB at Potsdam Komendatura, 22 July 1966 (National Archives via BRIXMIS Association Archives).

32. Stacy, *The Nicholson Incident*.

Conclusion

1. Williams, *BRIXMIS in the 1980s*.

2. Captain I. Cameron-Mowat, Royal Signals, *BRIXMIS November 1989, The Story of BRIXMIS*; and letter from Captain Cameron-Mowat to Lieutenant Colonel John Cormack MBE MC, 8 August 1991 (BRIXMIS Association Archives).

3. Warrant Officer (Staff Sergeant Major) Kevin Hawkins, BRIXMIS Chief Clerk 1987–1990, *Nearing the End* (BRIXMIS Association Archives).

4. Brigadier I. L. Freer, CBE, Chief BRIXMIS 1989–1990, 'The Closure of BRIXMIS', letter to members of the BRIXMIS Association, 15 April 1991 (BRIXMIS Association Archives).
5. Ibid.
6. Major Dr Sascha Gunold, '"Withdrawal Under Observation" – How German Military and Foreign Intelligence Contributed to the Withdrawal of Soviet/ Russian Forces from Germany, 1990–1994' in Christoph Meißner, & Jörg Morré (Eds.), *The Withdrawal of Soviet Troops from Central Europe: National Perspectives in Comparison* (Gottingen: Vandenhoeck & Ruprecht, 2021) pp.161–181; and Ian Sanders, 'US Army Intelligence Gathering in the Unified Germany' (Cold War Conversations Podcast, Episode 160, January 2021); and *Treaty on good-neighbourliness, partnership and cooperation, United Nations Office of Legal Affairs, No. 29524* (New York: United Nations Treaty Series 1707, December 1999) pp. 387–421.
7. Holger Stark, 'Operation Geheimnisverrat [Operation Betrayal]' (Hamburg: *Der Spiegel*, No. 37, 5 September 2004).
8. Major Dr Sascha Gunold, 'Schüsse in Altengrabow 1991: Sowjetische Wachposten beschießen Bundeswehrsoldaten' (Shots in Altengrabow 1991: Soviet guards shoot at Bundeswehr soldiers), *Militärgeschichte – Zeitschrift für historische Bildung*, Ausgabe 2/2017 (*Military History Journal of Historical Education*, issue 2/2017) (Potsdam: Zentrum für Militärgeschichte und Sozialwissenschaften der Bundeswehr (ZMSBw) 2017); and Major S. Popov Markushin, 'Incident at Altengrabow' (*Krasnaya Zvezda*, 23 April 1991).
9. Warrant Officer REDACTED, *Joint Intelligence Staff (BERLIN): Life After BRIXMIS* (Private monograph, 2014).

Afterword

1. RAFHS, *Journal 23*, used with permission.

Selected Bibliography

Books

Connor, Ken, *Ghost Force, The Secret History of the SAS* (London: Weidenfeld & Nicolson, 1998).

Cullen, Tony & Foss, Christopher F. (Eds.), *Jane's Land-Based Air Defence 1992–93, Fifth Edition* (Coulsdon: Jane's Information Group, 1992).

Dewhurst, Brigadier C. H., OBE, *Close Contact – with the Soviets in Eastern Germany* (London: George Allen & Unwin, 1954).

Geraghty, Tony, *Beyond the Frontline, The Untold Exploits of Britain's Most Daring Cold War Spy Mission* (London: Harper Collins, 1996).

Gibson, Steve, *BRIXMIS: The Last Cold War Mission* (Stroud: The History Press, 1997).

Gieseke, Jens, *The GDR State Security, Shield and Sword of the Party* (Berlin: The Federal Commissioner for the Records of the State Security Service of the former German Democratic Republic, 2006).

Gunold, Major Dr Sascha, *'Withdrawal Under Observation': – How German Military and Foreign Intelligence Contributed to the Withdrawal of Soviet/Russian Forces from Germany, 1990–1994* in Meißner, Christoph and Morré, Jörg (Eds.), *The Withdrawal of Soviet Troops from Central Europe: – National Perspectives in Comparison*, (Gottingen: Vandenhoeck & Ruprecht, 2021).

Holbrook, James R. *Potsdam Mission: Memoir of a U.S. Army Intelligence Officer in Communist East Germany* (Bloomington, IN: Authorhouse, 2013)

Le Tissier, Tony, *Farewell to Spandau* (Leatherhead: Ashford, Buchan & Enright, 1994).

Long, Andrew, *Cold War Berlin: An Island City, Volume 1: The Birth of the Cold War and the Berlin Airlift, 1945–1950* (Warwick: Helion & Company, 2021).

Long, Andrew, *Cold War Berlin: An Island City, Volume 2: The Berlin Wall, 1950–1961* (Warwick: Helion & Company, 2021).

Long, Andrew, *Cold War Berlin: An Island City, Volume 3: US Forces in Berlin: – Keeping the Peace, 1945–1994* (Warwick: Helion & Company, 2023).

Long, Andrew, *Cold War Berlin: An Island City, Volume 4: US Forces in Berlin: – Preparing for War, 1945–1994* (Warwick: Helion & Company, 2024).

Long, Andrew, *Secrets of the Cold War: – Espionage and Intelligence Operations from Both Sides of the Iron Curtain* (Barnsley: Pen & Sword History, 2022).

Magee, Aden, *The Cold War Wilderness of Mirrors: Counterintelligence and the U.S. and Soviet Military Liaison Missions 1947–1990* (Havertown PA: Casemate USA, 2021).

Mastney, Vojtech &and Byrne, Malcolm (Eds.), *A Cardboard Castle:, An Inside History of the Warsaw Pact, 1955–1991* (Budapest, Central European University Press, 2005).

Münkel, Daniela (Ed.), *State Security:, A Reader on the GDR Secret Police* (Berlin: The Federal Commissioner for the Records of the State Security Service of the former German Democratic Republic, 2016).

Stejskal, James, *Special Forces Berlin: Clandestine Cold War Operations of the US Army's Elite, 1956–1990* (Havertown PA: Casemate USA, 2017).

Wright, Kevin and & Jefferies, Peter, *Looking Down the Corridors: Allied Aerial Espionage Over East Germany and Berlin, 1945–1990* (Stroud: The History Press, 2015).

Wyckoff, Thomas, *Mission: A Cold War Remembrance* (Pittsburg: Dorrance Publishing Co, 2018)

Wylde, Lieutenant Lt Colonel N. N., QGM (Ed.), *The Story of BRIXMIS 1946–1990* (Privately published in 1993 for members of the BRIXMIS Association).

Articles

Atkeson, Edward, *Ease tensions in Europe: Allow both side's Generals to know each other* (Washington DC: *The Washington Post*, 19 May 1985).

Miller, John J., *Our Last Cold War Casualty* (New York, NY: *National Review*, 5 April 2004 & 22 March 2005).

Lectures, Letters Papers, Reports, and Theses

Lajoie, Lt Gen Roland, *The last casualty of the Cold War: Lt Col Arthur D. Nicholson US Army, and the USMLM* (Private monograph, March 2004).

Royal Air Force Historical Society, *Journal 23, Cold War Intelligence Gathering* (RAFHS, 2001).

Williams, Maj Gen (retd.) P. G., CMG OBE, *BRIXMIS in the 1980s: The Cold War's "Great Game" – Memories of Liaising with the Soviet Army in East Germany* (Highworth: Private expanded monograph, July 2008), originally published April 2007 by the Parallel History Project on Cooperative Security (PHP), Center for Security Studies at ETH Zurich and the National Security Archive at the George Washington University on behalf of the PHP network (www.php.isn.ethz.ch).

Williams, Maj Gen (retd.) P. G., CMG OBE, *Being detained by the Soviets could be fun, a BRIXMIS detention near Wittenberg, 27–28 August 1981* (Parallel History Project on Cooperative Society, PHP, Zurich, April 2007).

Talks

Williams, Maj Gen (retd.) P. G., CMG OBE, *Athenstedt: A Cold War Cold Case – The Stasi versus BRIXMIS* (Chelsea: National Army Museum, September 2021).

Williams, Maj Gen (retd.) P. G., CMG OBE, *Athenstedt, A Cold War 'Cold Case'* (St Breward: St Breward Village Hall, March 2022).

Yelamos, Charlotte, *The Archaeology of Cold War Intelligence* (Chelsea: National Army Museum, December 2022).

Websites

16va.be – Hugo Mambour's excellent website on the Soviet air force in East Germany

archives.gov – US National Archives.

avalon.law.yale.edu – the Avalon project at the Lillian Goldman Law Library at Yale Law School is a great source of agreements, treaties, and legislation from the Cold War.

brixmis.co.uk – website of the BRIXMIS Association.

cvce.eu – the University of Luxembourg's digital research infrastructure on European integration, an excellent source of key Cold War-related documents.

coldwarconversations.com – Ian Sanders' excellent podcast Cold War Conversations.

gulabin.com – Colin Mackie's useful resource on British armed forces senior appointments.

history.state.gov – Office of the Historian, US Department of State, Washington D.C.

mil-airfields.de – useful reference site for Cold War East German military airfields.

nam.ac.uk – National Army Museum.

nato.int – the website of the North Atlantic Treaty Organization.

nsarchive2.gwu.edu – National Security Archive, The George Washington University, Washington D.C.

un.org – the website of the United Nations in New York City.

Podcasts

Cold War Conversations (www.coldwarconversations.com), Ian Sanders, episodes 21, 160, 203, 250, 251, 268, 270, and 313.

News & Media Websites

theguardian.com – *The Guardian* newspaper, London.

nytimes.com – *The New York Times* newspaper, New York, N.Y.

telegraph.co.uk – *The Telegraph* newspaper, London.

thetimes.co.uk – *The Times* newspaper, London.

washingtonpost.com – *The Washington Post* newspaper, Washington, D.C.

Acknowledgements

To former BRIXMIS personnel: Keith Bailey MBE, Ralph Brooks, Dave Butler BEM, Nigel Dunkley MBE, Roy Giles CBE, Stephen Harrison MBE, Mick Mansfield, Peter Martin, Kevin Monery, Andrew Pennington, Dave Picton, Nigel 'Nick' Rowles, Bob Thomas, Colin Ward, and Mervyn Watson. Particular thanks to Major General (retd.) Peter Williams CMG OBE, Chairman of the BRIXMIS Association, and Squadron Leader (retd.) Rod Saar MBE, BRIXMIS Association archivist, who have freely given their time and insight throughout this project, answering many questions, and putting me in touch with many former BRIXMIS members, who have also provided much assistance. Thanks to Peter also for checking the manuscript for me and for writing the foreword to the book.

Also to Alliierten Museum, Berlin; BRIXMIS Association Committee; Major General Sir Robert Corbett KCVO, CB, for his unique insight into Cold War Berlin; Robert Freeman, who kindly 'marked' the manuscript for me; Tony Geraghty, who kindly made his research notes available through the BRIXMIS Association Archive; Albert Grandolini, for his help with sourcing images; Imperial War Museums; BRIXMIS Association Archive at the Liddell Hart Centre for Military Archives – King's College London; Hugo Mambour, owner of www.16va.be, an excellent resource on the Soviet air force in East Germany and on allied air operations; Military Intelligence Museum; National Archives, Kew, nationalarchives.gov.uk; National Army Museum; National Cold War Exhibition, RAF Museum Midlands, Cosford; Royal Air Force Historical Society; Todd Shugart for his sage advice; Stasi Unterlagen Archiv (formerly BStU), German State Archives, Berlin; Louis DeVirgilio, for his help with ORBAT information; and Charlotte Yelamos, for her combat archaeologist perspective.

Finally, to my family for their enduring tolerance and moral support!

Index

Main entries are shown in **bold**. Plate numbers shown in *italics*. Certain words or phrases, such as 'army', 'Berlin', 'Potsdam', 'GSFG', 'SERB', or 'GDR', appear throughout the text are therefore not included in the index for space reasons. Generic mentions of 'BRIXMIS', 'intelligence', 'tour' or 'touring' are also not listed, but specific aspects are, with BRIXMIS departments covered under 'BRIXMIS'. Codenames and NATO reporting names are shown in TYPEWRITER font.

BRIXMIS Personnel Index

† Chiefs BRIXMIS
‡ Deputy Chiefs BRIXMIS
§ Acting Chief BRIXMIS, 1985
* 'and bar', a second award of the same decoration; ** 'and two bars', a third.

Ranks are shown as they were whilst serving with the Mission and **at the time of their mention(s)** in the main text – later promotions are for other historians. However, decorations and awards, shown in TYPEWRITER font, relate to the individual, not the rank they hold, and are included in full, as much as the historical record allows. Parent unit, where known, is show in brackets: RA – Royal Artillery; RE – Royal Engineers; RM – Royal Marines; RCT – Royal Corps of Transport; RASC – Royal Army Service Corps; RAOC – Royal Army Ordnance Corps; RTR – Royal Tank Regiment; AAC – Army Air Corps, RN – Royal Navy; SAS – Special Air Service; WRAC – Women's Royal Army Corps.

Alderson, Warrant Officer Harry, 29
Anderson, Corporal, 186
Apps, Captain John, *Plate 7*
Askwith, Lieutenant Colonel Mark, 15, **165**
Aurich, Captain Sidney, 164
Avery, Captain J. W. L. S. 'Jerry', MBE, 34

Backhouse, Major Johnathan, 15, 80, 188
Bacon, Corporal Francis, BEM (RAF), 40
Baines, Brigadier David, MBE (RA) & Honor Baines †, 13, 24, 33, 56, 174–76
Barbour, Staff Sergeant Andy (14 Signal Regt (EW)), 39
Batchelor, Junior Technician Eddie (RAF), 173
Bates, Group Captain, Richard D., AFC (RAF) ‡, 14, 22, 116, *Plate 6*
Bell, Corporal Colin 'Dinger' (RCT), 70
Bevan, Brigadier Francis 'Frank' G. (RE) †, 204
Bird, Major David (14/20 King's Hussars), 171–72
Birnie, Flight Sergeant Colin, MBE, BEM (RAF), 83
Blackford, Captain Brook (RAF), 85
Bliss, Flight Lieutenant Ted (RAF), 164
Boardman, Group Captain John B. (RAF) ‡, 102

General Index